The
Pauline
Writings

The Biblical Seminar
34

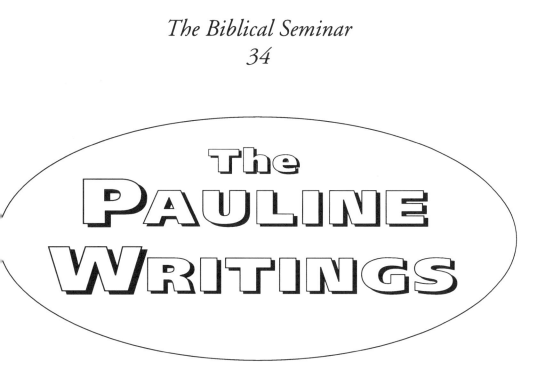

The PAULINE WRITINGS

edited by
**Stanley E. Porter &
Craig A. Evans**

Sheffield
Academic Press

Published by
Sheffield Academic Press Ltd
Mansion House
19 Kingfield Road
Sheffield, S11 9AS
England

Typeset by Sheffield Academic Press
and
Printed on acid-free paper in Great Britain
by The Cromwell Press
Melksham, Wiltshire

British Library Cataloguing in Publication Data

A catalogue record for this book is available
from the British Library

ISBN 1-85075-730-5

CONTENTS

Preface to the Series

This Series, of which *The Pauline Writings* is one, collects what the Series editors believe to be the best articles on the topic published in the first 50 issues (1978–1993) of *Journal for the Study of the New Testament*. Founded in 1978, with one issue in its inaugural year, *JSNT* was produced from 1979 to 1990 in three issues a year, and then, from 1991 to the present, in four issues a year. The continuing success of the journal can be seen in several ways: by its increasing circulation, by its increased publication schedule, by its fostering of a significant supplement series, which has now reached its one-hundredth volume (JSNT Supplement Series), by its public exposure and influence within the scholarly community, and, most of all, by the quality of the essays it publishes. This volume contains a representative group of such articles on a specific area of New Testament studies.

Once it was decided that such a Series of volumes should be issued, the question became that of how the numerous important articles were going to be selected and presented. The problem was not filling the volumes but making the many difficult choices that would inevitably exclude worthy articles. In the end, the editors have used various criteria for determining which articles should be reprinted here. They have gathered together articles that, they believe, make significant contributions in several different ways. Some of the articles are truly ground-breaking, pushing their respective enquiry into new paths and introducing new critical questions into the debate. Others are assessments of the critical terrain of a particular topic, providing useful and insightful analyses that others can and have built upon. Others still are included because they are major contributions to an on-going discussion.

Even though back issues of *JSNT* are still in print and these essays are available in individual issues of the journal, it is thought that this kind of compilation could serve several purposes. One is to assist scholars who wish to keep up on developments outside their areas of specialist research or who have been away from a topic for a period of time and wish to re-enter the discussion. These volumes are designed to be representatively selective, so that scholars can gain if not a thorough grasp of all of the developments in an area at least significant insights into major topics of debate in a field of interest. Another use of these volumes is as textbooks for undergraduates, seminarians and even graduate students. For undergraduates, these volumes could serve as useful readers, possibly as supplementary texts to a critical introduction, to provide a first exposure to and a sample of critical debate. For seminary students, the same purpose as for undergraduates could apply, especially when the seminarian is beginning critical study of the New Testament. There is the added use, however, that such material could provide guidance through the argumentation and footnotes for significant research into a New Testament author or topic. For graduate students, these volumes could not only provide necessary background to a topic, allowing a student to achieve a basic level of knowledge before exploration of a particular area of interest, but also serve as good guides to the detailed critical work being done in an area. There is the further advantage that many of the articles in these volumes are models of how to make and defend a critical argument, thereby providing useful examples for those entering the lists of critical scholarly debate.

Many more articles could and probably should be re-printed in further volumes, but this one and those published along with it must for now serve as an introduction to these topics, at least as they were discussed in *JSNT*.

Craig A. Evans   Stanley E. Porter
Trinity Western University   Roehampton Institute London
Langley, B.C. Canada   England

ABBREVIATIONS

AB	Anchor Bible
ABR	*Australian Biblical Review*
AGJU	Arbeiten zur Geschichte des antiken Judentums und des Urchristentums
ALGHJ	Arbeiten zur Literatur und Geschichte des hellenistischen Judentums
APOT	R.H. Charles (ed.), *Apocrypha and Pseudepigrapha of the Old Testament*
BFCT	Beiträge zur Förderung christlicher Theologie
BR	*Biblical Research*
BWANT	Beiträge zur Wissenschaft vom Alten und Neuen Testament
BZ	*Biblische Zeitschrift*
BZAW	Beihefte zur *ZAW*
CBQ	*Catholic Biblical Quarterly*
CNT	Commentaire du Nouveau Testament
DJD	Discoveries in the Judaean Desert
ETL	*Ephemerides theologicae lovanienses*
EvQ	*Evangelical Quarterly*
EvT	*Evangelische Theologie*
ExpTim	*Expository Times*
FRLANT	Forschungen zur Religion und Literatur des Alten und Neuen Testaments
HTKNT	Herders theologischer Kommentar zum Neuen Testament
HTR	*Harvard Theological Review*
ICC	International Critical Commentary
JAAR	*Journal of the American Academy of Religion*
JBL	*Journal of Biblical Literature*
JJS	*Journal of Jewish Studies*
JR	*Journal of Religion*
JSJ	*Journal for the Study of Judaism in the Persian, Hellenistic and Roman Period*
JSNT	*Journal for the Study of the New Testament*
JSNTSup	*Journal for the Study of the New Testament* Supplement Series
JTS	*Journal of Theological Studies*
KD	*Kerygma und Dogma*
LCL	Loeb Classical Library
LD	Lectio divina
LSJ	Liddell–Scott–Jones, *Greek–English Lexicon*
MTZ	*Münchener theologische Zeitschrift*

NCB	New Century Bible
NICNT	New International Commentary on the New Testament
NovT	*Novum Testamentum*
NovTSup	*Novum Testamentum* Supplements
NTS	*New Testament Studies*
OTS	*Oudtestamentische Studiën*
RevQ	*Revue de Qumran*
RHPR	*Revue d'historie et de philosophie religieuses*
RSR	*Recherches de science religieuse*
SBLSP	SBL Seminar Papers
SJT	*Scottish Journal of Theology*
SNTSMS	Society of New Testament Studies Monograph Series
SR	*Studies in Religion/Sciences religieuses*
ST	*Studia theologica*
TDNT	G. Kittel and G. Friedrich (eds.), *Theological Dictionary of the New Testament*
THKNT	Theologischer Handkommentar zum Neuen Testament
ThWAT	*Theologisches Wörterbuch zum Alten Testament*
TLZ	*Theologischer Literaturzeitung*
TOTC	Tyndale Old Testament Commentaries
TP	*Theologie und Philosophie*
TRE	*Theologische Realenzyklopädie*
TWNT	G. Kittel and G. Friedrich (eds.), *Theologisches Wörterbuch zum Neuen Testament*
TZ	*Theologische Zeitschrift*
WMANT	Wissenschaftliche Monographien zum Alten und Neuen Testament
WTJ	*Westminster Theological Journal*
WUNT	Wissenschaftliche Untersuchungen zum Neuen Testament
ZKT	*Zeitschrift für katholische Theologie*
ZNW	*Zeitschrift für die neutestamentliche Wissenschaft*
ZTK	*Zeitschrift für Theologie und Kirche*

PAUL THE APOSTLE

JSNT 27 (1986), pp. 3-25

PAUL'S APOSTOLIC AUTHORITY—?

Ernest Best

In recent writing on Paul there has been an increasing tendency to speak of and emphasize his apostolic authority. There is no doubt that he claimed to be an apostle; there is equally no doubt that he exercised authority. But when he exercised authority did he do so as an apostle? Almost without exception we answer 'Yes' but would Paul himself have so answered? Did he look on the source of his authority as deriving from his apostolic appointment? I ask this question because it has become almost axiomatic to treat certain actions of Paul as the exercise of his apostolic authority.[1]

A brief imaginary anecdote may open up the issue. Charles, now Prince of Wales, when five years old was at lunch with his parents. He is tardy in clearing up his plate. His mother says to him, 'If you don't finish up your greens you won't get any dessert'. Does she speak to him as his queen or as his mother? From which aspect of her being does she draw her authority?[2] When Paul exercises authority does he do so as apostle, teacher, prophet, pastor, missionary founder? Or, possibly, does he do so because he was a bossy kind of person by nature? In a family one sibling may order the others about though having no recognized position of authority. I do not intend to enter into this last area. That is why I framed my question in the form, 'When Paul exercises authority does he envisage himself as doing so as apostle?' We do not have time to discuss the question of Paul's character, interesting as it may be, and whether the way in which he thought of himself as behaving

1. J.H. Schütz has even entitled his book *Paul and the Anatomy of Apostolic Authority* (SNTSMS, 26; Cambridge: Cambridge University Press, 1975).

2. It is hardly necessary to say that this is an imaginary incident. I have no inside information as to what goes on in the palace.

corresponded completely with his real motivation.

There are a number of questions which must be treated, some more rapidly than others:

1. What is an apostle?
2. When did Paul become aware he was an apostle?
3. What led him to this awareness?
4. In what situations does he assert his apostolic position?
5. When Paul exercises authority under what picture of himself does he do so?
6. How has the stress on apostolic authority arisen?

I

The term 'apostle' is used in a number of different ways in the New Testament.[3] Though in the common mind the twelve apostles are the real apostles since they were chosen by the historical Jesus this is only one way, and that a relatively late way in the primitive church, of defining apostle. Clearly it is not a definition which would have appealed to Paul himself since it would automatically have excluded him. If we examine his own use of the word we see that he terms Epaphroditus who brought him money from Philippi an apostle (Phil. 2.25; cf. 2 Cor. 8.23), also Andronicus and Junia of whom we know nothing as to what they did (Rom. 16.7). At one point he appears to place Silvanus and Timothy as apostles alongside himself (1 Thess. 2.7) and he probably also regards Apollos and Barnabas as among the apostles.[4] When he lists the resurrection appearances of Jesus he apparently views the appearance to the Twelve as different from that to the apostles and as taking place at a different time. The twelve are not then in his mind the same as the apostles.[5] As he continues the list he classes himself with this group

3.   See C.K. Barrett, *The Signs of an Apostle* (London: Epworth Press, 1970), pp. 71-73.

4.   The context of 1 Cor. 4.9 includes Apollos; 9.6 seems to imply that Barnabas has the same right as Paul of apostolic maintenance; cf. A.T. Hanson, *The Pioneer Ministry* (London: SCM Press, 1961), p. 95; W. Schmithals, *The Office of Apostle in the Early Church* (London: SCM Press, 1969), p. 63.

5.   Whether they actually were or not is irrelevant; we are only concerned with the way in which Paul conceived apostleship. J.A. Kirk, 'Apostleship since Rengstorf: Towards a Synthesis', *NTS* 21 (1974–75), pp. 249-65, wrongly concludes that the

of apostles (1 Cor. 15.5ff.), though without defining what determined its membership; the nature of the list proves that it cannot simply have been that its members had seen the risen Lord since others have done this but are not in the group. In particular the Twelve and the apostle group may have had some common members without being identical or one wholly including the other.

If then the use of the term leads to no clear definition as to its meaning its origin is similarly shrouded in mystery. Traditionally it was assumed that when Jesus chose his twelve disciples he himself called them 'apostles'. This is highly unlikely. Mark and Matthew only use the word once each;[6] it is Luke in his Gospel and then in Acts who uses it regularly, in most cases apparently of the twelve. Luke's understanding of the twelve as the apostles may then be taken as a later formulation.[7] Thus the term does not go back to Jesus in any sense of defining a group, though we cannot exclude his use of it in a functional manner. As the name for a defined group of people it may have originated either in the primitive community in Jerusalem or among the first Christians in Antioch. Those who see its origin in the Jewish term *shaliach*[8] favour Jerusalem. Those who reject this origin probably favour Antioch. The evidence is difficult to assess.[9]

There is no need for us to explore these issues. It is sufficient to note that when terms appear in organizations they often come more or less simultaneously from diverse areas. The same term may be used but those who use it because they derive it from different areas may not intend it to signify the same thing. The problem is intensified when the organization uses more than one language and draws on more than one culture. In our case the term probably always retains some sense of being sent, whether by an individual, a group such as a church,[10] or by Christ or God. It would not however be true to say that everyone who

apostles include the Twelve. All we can say is that they may have shared some common members.

6.   Mt. 10.2; Mk 6.30. The word should probably not be read at Mk 3.14.

7.   Cf. R. Schnackenburg, 'Apostles before and during Paul's Time', in *Apostolic History and the Gospel* (Festschrift F.F. Bruce; ed. W.W. Gasque and R.P. Martin; Exeter: Paternoster, 1970), pp. 287-303.

8.   For a review of theories about *shaliach*, cf. J.A. Kirk, 'Apostleship'.

9.   For a recent assessment see C.K. Barrett, 'Shaliah and Apostle', in *Donum Gentilicium* (Festschrift David Daube; ed. E. Bammel, C.K. Barrett and W.D. Davies; Oxford: Clarendon Press, 1978), pp. 93-98.

10.   See 2 Cor. 8.23; Phil. 2.25.

carried out missionary work would have been called an apostle (cf. Phil. 1.14-18). We can also be reasonably certain that Paul was not the first to coin the term or to apply it within the church. The way it appears in his letters implies that there were those who had used it before he did. There was a pre-existing group of apostles of which some would have denied him membership. If he had introduced it no one would have had any grounds for denying its application to him. If he had introduced it we would probably also have been able to discover a unitary conception of its meaning in his writings, and as we have seen this is not the case.

II

There is no doubt that Paul traced his apostleship to his encounter with the risen Lord on the way to Damascus but it is very unlikely that he began to call himself an apostle immediately after that experience. When did he first become aware that he was an apostle? We cannot suppose that Ananias burst into the house of Jonas in the street called Straight in Damascus, raised his hands in greeting and cried, 'Hail, Apostle'. Nor can we suppose that at the moment his sight was restored and he rose from his knees he thumped his chest and proclaimed 'I'm an apostle!'. It was at some later point that he came to realize he was an apostle or, and we cannot exclude this possibility, that for good theological and political reasons he decided to claim to be an apostle.

It is not easy to determine when this happened for it is inextricably bound up with the question of what constitutes an apostle. In his earliest letter (1 Thess. 2.6) Paul describes himself, Silvanus and Timothy[11] as apostles but while Peter and James later recognized his claim as an apostle they would certainly not have accepted Silvanus and Timothy as apostles in the same way. If then there is doubt whether Paul claimed to be an apostle on a level with Peter at this stage, there is no doubt that he was making this claim by the time he came to write Galatians and the

11. A few have denied that Paul intended to include Timothy as an apostle because there is no sense in which he could have seen the risen Lord; cf. A.M. Farrer in *The Apostolic Ministry* (ed. K.E. Kirk; London: Hodder & Stoughton, 1946), p. 128 n. 1; A. Lemaire, *Les ministères aux origines de l'église* (LD, 68; Paris: Cerf, 1971), p. 71. For a more recent and thorough discussion refuting such views see R.F. Collins, *Studies on the First Letter to the Thessalonians* (Leuven: Leuven University Press, 1984), p. 183.

Corinthian correspondence. That the definition has changed is confirmed by Paul's failure to term Timothy an apostle in the address of 2 Corinthians. What was it then that triggered off the change in definition and the claim to parity with Peter?

III

It is highly unlikely that when Paul arrived in a new mission area he began by announcing that he was an apostle. He would not have done this even in a synagogue for the term *shaliach* did not have for Jews any missionary significance.[12] He may of course have said that he had been 'sent' by God to bring the gospel but the use of a verbal form is not the same as the use of the noun. As we have seen the first occurrence of the term is in 1 Thess. 2.6 where Paul includes Silvanus and Timothy with himself as apostles. Before Paul eventually left Thessalonica he must have told the church that he and his fellow-workers had been sent to them by God, or Christ.[13] It is interesting that when he recalls to the Galatian Christians how they first received him he does not say 'You received me as an apostle of God' though he has been emphasizing his position as an apostle. Instead he says 'You received me as an angel of God' (4.14). An angel is of course a messenger as in some sense an apostle is also. I do not suggest that Paul deliberately avoided the word 'apostle' here. He did not use it because it would not have reflected how the Galatians received him; in the beginning of his mission they did not think of him as an apostle.

But in the first two chapters of Galatians and in the letters to Corinth he makes a great deal of being an apostle. What led him to do so? He asserts his apostleship in Galatians because some have argued that he was not an apostle and therefore inferior to those who were apostles. It is unlikely that these critics of his position would have been worried in the slightest by his statement in 1 Thess. 2.6 where he set Silvanus and Timothy on a par with himself; no one would have classed them as on a par with Peter. It is equality with Peter, and some others who cannot be

12. Cf. H. Mosbeck, 'Apostolos in the New Testament', *ST* 2 (1948), pp. 165-200 (169).

13. It is just possible that he said they had been sent by the church in Antioch. This may have been Luke's opinion for it is only in Acts 14.4, 14 that he terms Paul an apostle; see Lemaire, *Les ministères*, pp. 58-61.

identified with any certainty,[14] that is at the heart of the argument over apostleship. Someone may have said to him, 'Certainly, Paul, you are an apostle, but not one like Peter'. Paul, however, claimed to be on a par with him and different only in so far as his field lay with the Gentiles whereas that of Peter lay with the Jews. While Paul uses the phrase 'apostle to the Gentiles' (Rom. 11.12) it would be wrong to assume that he arrived simultaneously at the two conclusions that his mission was to the Gentiles and that he was an apostle on a par with Peter. His mission to the Gentiles will have begun long before he ever thought of himself as an apostle of the Peter-type. There will have been others who would have been classed as apostles alongside Peter. James may have been one but the ambiguity of Gal. 1.19 does not allow us to draw any certain conclusion. In 1 Cor. 9.5-6 when discussing the right of apostles to maintenance Paul speaks of 'the other apostles and the brothers of the Lord and Cephas' which implies a recognized group of apostles even if we do not know who were its members and its precise extent. Since Paul discusses the right of Barnabas as well as himself to upkeep it may be that at least in his eyes Barnabas would have been a member of that group. No matter in what way the group came to be acknowledged as a group it was one in which Paul felt he ought to be included. Since we do not know the exact extent of this group and the names of all those in it we are at a loss to define the qualifications for inclusion in it. We know the claims Paul put forward at various times for his own inclusion. He had seen the risen Lord (1 Cor. 9.1; 15.8-11). His mission work testified to his position; the Corinthians are the seal of his apostleship (1 Cor. 9.2). He had displayed the signs, presumably miracles of healing etc., which were expected of an apostle (2 Cor. 12.12). There was however one qualification which he did not meet: he did not accept financial help from the churches in which he worked. We do not know if there were other qualifications. If there were and Paul met them they need never have been mentioned. The definition of the qualifications may also have changed from time to time. When his opponents found that Paul met a particular set of conditions they had proposed they may simply have changed the conditions in their attempt to eliminate him. Different groups of opponents may also have had different definitions. Finally no one of the conditions by itself would have been sufficient. The apostles were not the only ones who had seen the risen Lord or been successful

14. The names of the group are never listed; John, the son of Zebedee, probably was one (cf. Gal. 2.9).

missionaries or healed the sick. It is simplest to call the group over which there was dispute the Peter-group because he is the only person of whose membership we can be certain.[15]

IV

We must now examine the actual situations in which Paul claims to be an apostle. I detect a curious hangover from the days in which all the letters in the Pauline corpus were attributed to his personal authorship. It could then be said that he normally claimed to be an apostle of the Peter-group in each of them. Today scholars who accept only seven letters (Romans, 1 and 2 Corinthians, Galatians, Philippians, 1 Thessalonians, Philemon) continue to say the same. It is no longer true. Paul only claims to be an apostle in Romans, 1 and 2 Corinthians and Galatians, four out of seven. This is not 'normally'. It is simply indeterminate.[16]

Turning to the letters it is easy to see why Paul makes the claim in the addresses of these four letters. In both Corinth and Galatia there have been those who denied he was an apostle and in the letters themselves he intends to advance reasons why he is. He therefore sets himself up as apostle from the outset. He uses the title in Romans because there he writes to a church which he has never visited and where he wishes to defend the gospel which he has himself linked to his apostleship. He can reasonably surmise after what has happened in other areas that suspicions about his apostleship may have been whispered in Rome. He mentions it therefore but does not make a major point of it as in the letters to Corinth and Galatia. He refers to it again only at 11.14 where in the course of the discussion of the position of Gentiles in the church he

15. Perhaps this group was known as 'the super-apostles'; these are mentioned in 2 Cor. 11.5; 12.11; cf. Barrett, *Signs of an Apostle*, p. 38. This of course implies that 2 Cor. 11.13 refers to yet another group.

16. 'Normally' could well apply to ten instances out of thirteen. Two quotations taken at random from those who accept only seven letters show how easily the wrong conclusion can be drawn. Collins, *Studies*, writes 'Paul normally identifies himself by name and title', i.e. in the addresses of his letters (p. 176). V.P. Furnish in his *II Corinthians* (AB, 32A; New York: Doubleday, 1984), puts the same point slightly differently when he writes, 'The *only* [italics mine] Pauline salutations in which the designation "apostle" is lacking are 1 Thess. 1.1; Phil. 1.1; Phlm. 1'. We might with equal justification say that the term *only* appears in the addresses of four letters, those of Romans, 1 and 2 Corinthians and Galatians.

reminds his readers that he is the apostle to the Gentiles. Strictly speaking he only says here that he is *an* apostle to the Gentiles but all he writes suggests he believes that he has a special relationship to them and consequently most commentators and writers on Paul speak of him as '*the* apostle to the Gentiles'.[17]

Apart from terming himself 'apostle' in the address to Romans he also speaks there of his apostleship: 'Jesus Christ our Lord, through whom we have received grace and apostleship: (vv. 4-5). Because Paul links χάρις and ἀποστολή together here many writers when they see another reference to Paul as given a χάρις of ministry assume that he is then also automatically referring to himself as an apostle.[18] In none of the other passages however does he make that linking. In 1 Cor. 3.10 he is by God's grace a skilled master builder who lays the foundations of the church. There is no need to equate apostle and master builder. To do so only begs the question. Paul is an apostle and did lay foundations but that does not mean that when he laid foundations he thought of himself as an apostle. In 1 Cor. 15.10 he has just affirmed that he is an apostle when he says, 'By the grace of God I am what I am'. If he had stopped there we might well assume that he was referring to the grace of God in appointing him as an apostle but he does not stop there. He continues by saying that it was the grace of God which enabled him to work harder than the other apostles, i.e. he relates God's grace to his activity and not to his apostolic position. In Gal. 1.6 the emphasis again lies on Paul as active in missionary work through the grace given to him and not on his position as apostle. In Gal. 1.15 where he says God had called him through his grace he stresses that he is what he is by God's grace without specifying what that is; the nearest reference indeed is to Paul as 'slave' of Christ. In Gal. 2.9 Peter, John and James perceive the grace that is in Paul; the immediate reference is to the valid mission he has to the Gentiles. In Rom. 15.15-16 Paul relates the grace given to him to his being a λειτουργός in the offering of the Gentiles. Again we do not find the word apostle. Paul thus attaches the idea of God's grace more generally to ministry than to apostolic ministry alone. So in Rom. 12.6 he writes of using the different gifts (χαρίσματα) we have according to the χάρις given to us. This leaves only 12.3 to be considered. Here Paul

17. I have discussed this in 'The Revelation to Evangelize the Gentiles', *JTS* 35 (1984), pp. 1-31 (19ff.).

18. This assumption underlies the otherwise very thorough study of A. Satake, 'Apostolat und Gnade bei Paulus', *NTS* 15 (1968–69), pp. 96-107.

exhorts others by the grace given to him not to think more highly of themselves than they ought to. Many commentators write here of Paul speaking with apostolic authority.[19] But he does not introduce the word. As we have seen there is no necessary connection between grace and apostleship and if so there is no need to envision him speaking as apostle. It is sufficient that he holds a position of leadership. It is however perfectly correct that we should trace back both Paul's belief that he acts under God's grace and his claim to be an apostle to his experience on the Damascus road. But as we have seen there is no reason to think he left Damascus with the title 'apostle' ringing in his ears, though from that time onwards he will have seen himself a special recipient of God's grace.

We now turn from places where Paul does not use the term 'apostle' to those he does in order to determine in what situations he employs it. We have dealt with all the occurrences in Romans and 1 Thessalonians. In 1 Corinthians the word appears in the address. In 9.1ff. we find it used three times. Here Paul asserts that he is an apostle of the Peter group because he saw the risen Lord. Clearly he uses it here because there have been suggestions that he is not an apostle of this group since he did not accept maintenance from the church in Corinth. No positive suggestions are made as to the activity of apostles other than that they preach. The word is used more generally without explicit reference to Paul himself at the conclusion of the discussion of the church as the body of Christ. A number of functions are listed, first apostles, second prophets, third teachers, then workers of miracles, etc., and it is said that not all are apostles, prophets, teachers etc. (1 Cor. 12.27-28). Paul does not say that he is an apostle but his readers would certainly draw this conclusion. But what type of apostle has he in mind? An answer to this depends in part on how Paul conceives the body of Christ here. Does he compare the individual congregation to the body of Christ, in which case it would be the Silvanus-type apostle of whom he would be thinking, or does he compare the whole church, in which case he might be thinking of either the Peter-type or the Silvanus-type? Most commentators believe he has the individual congregation in mind.[20] We should also

19. I shall not list names since I myself have been guilty of this very error; see my Cambridge Bible Commentary on Romans.

20. It is just possible that Paul is thinking of the sum-total of all congregations each of which taken by itself is a body of Christ. The plural 'apostles' could then denote the Peter group.

note that since every other 'title' in the list is oriented functionally
apostle is probably also to be so taken; the emphasis then lies on function[21] rather than on position. Paul again uses the term in the plural and
with a general reference in 4.9 where, after sarcastically referring to the
claims of some Corinthians that they have already attained to all that
salvation has to offer, he goes on, 'I think God has exhibited us apostles
as lowest of all, like men sentenced to death; because we have been
made a spectacle to the world of angels and men'. Here Paul stresses the
difference between what happens to those whom the Corinthians would
presumably acknowledge as important, viz. apostles, with their own
claims to be spiritually rich and spiritually kings. The sign of a true
believer, of an apostle, is not strength but weakness. The final place
where Paul uses the term 'apostle' is in 1 Cor. 15.8-9 where he applies it
to himself as a witness of the resurrection. Here he certainly has in mind
the Peter-type of apostle because of the resurrection allusion (cf. 9.1ff.; at
15.7 he had mentioned apostles as a group). It is natural for him to
include himself as a witness to the resurrection for some have linked this
to apostleship and have doubted his apostleship. When we turn to
2 Corinthians it is again natural that Paul should use the term of himself
in the address since there further questions have been raised about his
apostleship. (That he uses it in 8.23 of those who take the collection to
Jerusalem is irrelevant.) The word appears four times in the final four
polemical chapters (10–13). On three occasions it is used of some who
claim to be apostles, implying again that there is a recognizable group of
apostles,[22] and Paul asserts that he is one no less than any of them, provided they are true apostles (11.5, 13; 12.11). The only evidence he
offers for his own apostleship is his ability to perform signs (12.12).
When he contrasts himself with these others it is in relation to missionary
activity and Christ-like weakness. At one point the question of authority
is raised; these false apostles have ill-treated the Corinthians even to the
extent of striking them. Paul does not assert his authority in return but
says he was too weak to do such a thing.

Paul opens the letter to the Galatians with a reference to himself as an

21. There is a difference here between 'apostle' and the others in the list. In each
of the others the function may be described as active, i.e. the prophet prophesies, but
the apostle does not 'apostle'; he has been sent, i.e. the function is described in a
passive manner; only at Rom. 11.13 where Paul calls himself the apostle to the
Gentiles could the function be described as active.

22. Cf. Barrett, *Signs of an Apostle*, p. 36.

apostle, not one appointed by men but by God. The ensuing discussion centres on the truth of the gospel he preaches rather than on his or others' authority. His gospel has been at stake but he leaves Jerusalem with this accepted and his own area of mission activity, his apostolate, among the Gentiles granted to him by those who claimed a position of importance among the Jerusalem Christians. Paul does not use the term in Philippians other than in relation to Epaphroditus as a conveyer of money and not at all in Philemon or in 2 Thessalonians, if it is by him.

We may sum up: when Paul uses the term of himself it is in contexts where there have been those who have said that he was not an apostle or contexts in which he stresses the weakness of those who are leading Christians or contexts in which there is some connection with either the truth or the proclamation of the gospel. At no point do we find him issuing instructions to others on the basis of his apostleship. But of course this may be implicit in his exercise of authority. He does not need to say that he is an apostle when he instructs others because everyone knows he is. It is appropriate then that we should turn now to examine his actual exercise of authority.

Before we turn to this it is important to note that it is not only apostles who exercise authority. In 1 Cor. 5.1ff. and 6.1ff. Paul expects others to do so. In 1 Cor. 16.15-16 he urges his converts to be subject to Stephanas (cf. 1 Thess. 5.12-13). His envoys, Timothy and Titus, are expected to take action in their missions. Authority and apostleship do not then necessarily go together.

V

Paul did not come to a position of authority by inheritance or election as many do. He himself would have said that God gave him whatever authority he exercised and would have traced this back to his Damascus road experience. While Paul himself may have thought this others might have said that it was granted to him by Peter and the Jerusalem leaders, or at least was not valid until they recognized it. Some may even have said that he exercised it because of his tremendous activity (very active people often grab authority) or his dominating character. We do not need to weigh the relative merits of these possible views. It is however important to say a little about the areas in which authority may be exercised. Jesus exercised authority in exorcism and teaching. In discussing Paul we shall not be concerned with the first of these and only in part with the second. More importantly authority is exercised when rules are set down and where those who break these or other generally recognized rules are punished. We must now examine Paul's writings to see how he does exercise authority in these areas.[23]

We begin by noting that he expected obedience to himself. In such a simple and friendly letter as that to Philemon he can write that he is confident of Philemon's obedience (v. 21). To the Philippians he says, 'Therefore, my beloved, as you have always obeyed, so now, not only as in my presence but much more in my absence, work out your own salvation with fear and trembling' (2.12),[24] and the context shows that the obedience is to himself.[25] It is not then surprising that he should say to the contentious Corinthians that he is ready to punish their every dis obedience, whenever they complete their obedience (2 Cor. 10.6).[26] If we regard the obedience as to Christ it is still offered to Paul as Christ's representative. If Paul expects obedience he is also not slow to issue commands to his converts. Again he writes in the friendly letter to Philemon that though in Christ he could have commanded him he will now only appeal to him (vv. 8-9). That on this occasion he does not issue a command is beside the point; we learn that issuing commands was his normal practice. We learn the same when in respect of the collection he writes to the Corinthians, 'I do not say this as a command...' (2 Cor. 8.8). He would not need to stress that he was not commanding them if they were not accustomed to him doing so. We find the same authoritative note in 1 Thess. 4.2, 'you know what instructions we gave you through the Lord Jesus', or in 1 Cor. 11.17 when introducing the way in which the Eucharist should be celebrated he commences, 'In the following instructions'. Paul commands and expects that he will be obeyed. If we accept 2 Thessalonians as Pauline this emphatic tone is very explicit in 3.6ff. where within a few verses Paul has several times to recall the Thessalonians to the instructions he gave them on his original

23. I have treated the manner in which Paul exercises authority in much greater detail in my 1985 Sprunt Lectures at Union Theological Seminary, Richmond, Virginia, *Paul and his Converts* (Edinburgh: T. & T. Clark, 1988).

24. Cf. 2 Cor. 2.9; 7.15. 7.12 should probably also be classed here.

25. Cf. J. Hainz, *Ekklesia: Strukturen paulinischer Gemeinde-Theologie und Gemeinde-Ordnung* (Regensburg: Pustet, 1972), pp. 221-22.

26. If it is said here that the obedience is to Christ, this is true, but Paul sees obedience to Christ as offered through himself, and therefore as obedience to himself. It is only because he so envisages it that he can think of himself as punishing those who disobey.

visit about the need to work. At 1 Cor. 7.17 he says of the instructions he gives on marriage 'this is my rule in all the churches'—note the '*my* rule'. He has rules for his churches. The Corinthians asked him a number of questions about behaviour and having answered some of these about marriage, food sacrificed to idols, etc., he ends, 'about the other things [presumably things about which they had asked] I will give direction when I come' (1 Cor. 11.34). In respect of the collection for Jerusalem he directs (ἐπιτάσσειν) them as he had directed the churches of Galatia (16.1). Sometimes the authoritarian tone emerges when he only uses the simple word λέγω as in Gal. 5.2.

I have drawn attention to these authoritarian passages in Paul not to prove that he was an authoritarian person but in order to inquire from where he thought he derived his authority. You will have noted that in not one of them did he refer to himself as an apostle; indeed in two of them, Philemon and Philippians, he never described himself as apostle. Surely if he had been concerned about his apostolic authority we might have expected him to have commenced at least once, 'As your apostle I direct you'. In 2 Cor. 1.24 Paul denies that he lords it over the Corinthians and we may take this to mean that he does not regard himself as an authoritarian kind of person. To what then, if not to his apostolic status or to his personality, does he trace his authority?

We require now to examine a little more closely some of the phrases he uses when advising and instructing his churches. We begin with 1 Cor. 7.25 where he says that he has no command of the Lord for the unmarried, but gives his own opinion (γνώμη) as one 'who by the Lord's mercy is trustworthy'. It is clear from this that one source of his authority might be a saying of the earthly or exalted Lord. Occasionally he does use such sayings, in relation to divorce (1 Cor. 7.10), to the right of those who work for the Lord to support (1 Cor. 9.14) and to set out the proper way in which the Eucharist should be celebrated (1 Cor. 11.23, 'I received from the Lord what I also delivered to you...'). By and large however he does not use sayings of Jesus as the basis of his authority.[27] The alternative is to give an opinion as one whom he believes the Lord trusts. His authority comes from the Lord but in some way other than through the teaching of the earthly Jesus. In very similar fashion in a later letter to the same Corinthians who by now are no longer seeking his advice but doubting his right to control them he

27. Even when he does use such sayings he adds his own interpretation as in 1 Cor. 7.11; cf. Hainz, *Ekklesia*, pp. 59-60.

warns them that when he comes he will not spare them so that they may 'have proof that Christ is speaking in' him (2 Cor. 13.2-3). A few verses later he says he writes in this way before he comes so that when he arrives he may not have to be severe in the use of the authority given him by the Lord 'for building up and not for tearing down' (13.10; cf. 10.8). Earlier he had possibly been accused of lining his own pocket out of his missionary work and had retorted, 'we are not, like so many, peddlars of God's word; but as men of sincerity, as commissioned by God, in the sight of God we speak in Christ' (2 Cor. 2.17). He exhorts those with charismatic gifts to acknowledge that what he writes is a command (ἐντολή)[28] of the Lord (1 Cor. 14.37). He reminds the Thessalonians of the instructions (παραγγελίαι) he had given them through the Lord Jesus (1 Thess. 4.2).[29]

Just as in those statements in which Paul demanded obedience to himself, in none of these has there been any reference to himself as an apostle. Instead Paul regards himself as in close touch in some way with the exalted Christ and sees his authority deriving directly from Christ.[30] There are occasions when he appears to leave out the christological reference but probably he always expected it to be understood as present. Or possibly he was just an authoritarian kind of person whose authority found its basis in his own character. In either case his authority was 'charismatic' in the sense of Weber[31] and did not derive from human appointment.

There are a number of places where Paul exercises or threatens to exercise it. The most interesting is 2 Cor. 13.10 where as we have seen he says he wishes to find things in order at his coming, for God has given him the authority both to build up and to tear down. He draws this phrase about building up and tearing down (he uses it also at 10.8) from Jer. 1.10 and 24.6 so that incidentally if he has any picture in mind as giving him authority it is that of the prophet[32] and not of the apostle.

---

28. The variant reading which omits ἐντολή does not affect the sense in which Christ is the origin of Paul's authority.

29. See also 2 Cor. 12.19; 1 Thess. 2.13; 4.2.

30. Cf. Schütz, *Paul*, p. 278, 'He bases his authority on his experience'.

31. See Schütz, *Paul*, and B. Holmberg, *Paul and Power: The Structure of Authority in the Primitive Church as Reflected in the Pauline Epistles* (Lund: Gleerup, 1980), for the application of the insights of Weber to Paul. K. Kertelge, 'Das Apostelamt des Paulus, sein Ursprung und seine Bedeutung', *BZ* 14 (1970), pp. 161-81, regards Paul's apostolate as 'charismatic' in the New Testament sense.

32. For the view that Paul may have regarded himself as a prophet see

There is the same absence of a reference to 'apostle' in the way he treats the case of the incestuous man (1 Cor. 5.1ff.). Paul calls on the church when it is assembled and his spirit is with it to make a decision (he even tells it what decision to take—to deliver the sinner to Satan). Note that he does not say 'when my apostolic spirit is with you'. On one occasion he had to confront Peter face to face. Peter had been getting along happily with Gentiles in Antioch until certain men came from James; he then separated from full fellowship with the Gentiles. Paul says that he rebuked Peter and those siding with him. He does not say that he uttered his rebuke because he was the apostle to the Gentiles but because he spoke for the truth of the gospel. Pushed to the limit Paul does not fall back on apostolic authority but on his understanding of the gospel.[33]

But if Paul does not envisage himself acting as 'apostle' when he instructs, advises and disciplines is there some other role which he sees himself as playing? We turn now to a passage about discipline previously omitted. It is the final section of his discussion of the different groups in Corinth and their failure to hold together recognizably as one church (1 Cor. 4.14ff.). Paul says that some in the church are arrogant and threatens that he will come to them soon when they will find out the kind of person he really is. This is how the passage begins:

> I am not writing this to put you to shame, but to admonish you as my beloved children. Even if you have thousands of guides in Christ, you do not have many fathers. For I brought you to birth in Christ Jesus through the gospel.

and this is how it ends:

> What do you wish? Shall I come to you with a rod, or with love in a spirit of gentleness?

A.-M. Denis, 'L'Apôtre Paul, prophète "messianique" des Gentils: Étude thématique de 1 Thess., II, 1-6', *ETL* 33 (1957), pp. 245-318; T. Holtz, 'Zum Selbstverständnis des Apostels Paulus', *TLZ* 91 (1966), pp. 322-30; J. Murphy-O'Connor, *Paul on Preaching* (London and New York: Sheed and Ward, 1964), pp. 104ff.; J.M. Myers and J.D. Freed, 'Is Paul Also among the Prophets?', *Int* 20 (1966), pp. 40-53; D. Hill, *New Testament Prophecy* (London: Marshall, Morgan and Scott, 1979), pp. 111ff.

33. Cf. Schütz, *Paul*, pp. 123, 145, 157-58, 278, 284; Schmithals, *Office of Apostle*, pp. 39-40; H. von Campenhausen, *Ecclesiastical Authority and Spiritual Power in the Church of the First Three Centuries* (London: A. & C. Black, 1969), p. 35.

A rod is the way to keep children in order, or at least it was in the ancient world (e.g. Prov. 23.13-14).

It is perfectly logical therefore for Paul to move from the image of himself as father and his converts as his children to that of the exercise of discipline.[34] His care for them in advising and directing them is indeed often set in terms of the parent-child relation. They are babes whom he has been forced to feed with milk and not solid food (1 Cor. 3.1-3). When he is worried about the Galatians and fears they may fall away into heresy he writes of them as his little children for whom he may have to suffer birth pangs a second time until Christ is formed in them (4.19). Note here that it is the female aspect of the parent role which is to the fore. Paul indeed employs both aspects. Thus he writes to the Thessalonians that he and his colleagues were gentle among them like a 'nurse taking care of her children' (1 Thess. 2.7; 'nurse' means 'mother' and is so rendered in some English versions for in those days mothers nursed their own children). A few verses later in the same letter he reverts to the male image, 'You know how, like a father with his children, we exhorted each one of you' (2.11). The image is found also in 2 Cor. 6.13, 12.14 and in 1 Cor. 4.17, Phil. 2.22, Phlm 10 of individual Christians who have been converted by Paul. When Paul then looks for the role which he fulfils towards his churches he does not use that of the apostle but that of the parent with his converts as his children. There is one other image he uses which is again associated with him as the one who has converted his readers. He is the master builder; his converts are what he has built (1 Cor. 3.9ff.). It may indeed be because he views himself as builder that he uses the contrast of building up and destroying with which he threatens the Corinthians (2 Cor. 10.8; 13.10). It is however possible that he envisages himself here as playing the role of prophet. There is some other evidence that he may have so seen himself, for example in the language with which he describes his Damascus Road experience.[35] However he never explicitly claims to be a prophet.

It looks then as if the images which Paul acknowledges as motivating him when he comes to advise, instruct and discipline his churches are those that derive from his relation to them as the one through whom God brought them into being. The image of parent was of course widely used in the ancient world. In particular it was used in the Wisdom

34. On this whole area see P. Gutierrez, *La paternité spirituelle selon saint Paul* (Paris: Gabalda, 1968).
35. See note 32.

literature of the wise man, by Cynic philosophers of their relation to those whom they taught, of rulers towards their subjects and of colonists towards their founding cities. Confirmation that Paul's use of the image is no chance or haphazard affair can be seen in its absence from Romans.[36] Unlike his other letters Romans is not written to his own converts and it would therefore be inappropriate to employ it.

There is one other point which brings out some of the significance of this image in contrast to that of the apostolic. It has always been difficult to see why Paul refused financial help from his churches when apostles were entitled to it. Paul himself acknowledges their entitlement in 1 Cor. 9.3ff. His refusal to avail himself of this right landed him in repeated difficulties with his Corinthian Christians who because of it began to wonder whether he was a genuine apostle. Forced for the second time to defend his rejection he answered that it was not the duty of children to lay up money for their parents but of parents for their children (2 Cor. 12.14). In other words even to defend his apostolic position he goes to the parent image. It may well be that long before he came to claim a position as an apostle of the Peter-type he had already formed the practice of refusing financial aid from those to whom he ministered. Claiming the position he was later confronted with the right of apostles to maintenance; since he had already formed his own attitude and was unwilling to go back on it he justifies his position from the major image of parenthood which motivates his conduct.

It is time to recall the initial picture of the Queen, Prince Charles and his vegetables. Its appropriateness to the present discussion may now, perhaps, be more easily seen. The official title is not necessarily the motivating factor. Paul claimed to be an apostle of the Peter-type because it was necessary in order to maintain the truth of the gospel. But he only used the title when others disputed it or might dispute it. Basically he considered himself the parent of those to whom he wrote. The parent of those days had much more authority than the parent of today; he retained control over his children for a much longer period. In the extended family if a son brought home a wife they both came under the authority of the father. So Paul could expect continued obedience from his converts long after he had left them.

Perhaps parent is not quite the correct term. I would prefer to use that

---

36. Even if we accept Ephesians and Colossians as genuine Pauline letters this is confirmed for neither of them was written to those he had converted.

of 'founding father'.[37] It is a well-known sociological phenomenon that those who found organizations tend to control them as long as possible. Though we may speak theologically of Christ as the founder of *the* church, if we were to use sociological terms we would speak of Paul as the founder of the churches in Corinth, Galatia, Philippi, etc. It is then only natural that he should exercise authority in those churches. Now it may be said that founder and apostle are the same. Looking back from our vantage point in history we may equate them but would Paul have equated them? And if he would have done so we have to ask further why he chose to use the idea of parent and not apostle in his actual control of his congregations? There seems no reason other than that was the way he thought. It might be suggested that he chose 'father' because 'apostle' would not have been easily understood by his Gentile converts. That that cannot be true can be seen in his use of the term for those who took the collection to Jerusalem (2 Cor. 8.23; cf. Phil. 2.25) and of Silvanus, Titus and himself as apostles of the non-Petrine type in his very earliest letter (1 Thess. 2.6). Moreover in the letters in which he argues strongly for his own Peter-type apostleship the readers apparently know what the term means. Yet it is in these very letters that he uses the parental image when exercising authority.

There is perhaps one further point which should be made before we leave Paul. If there is any way in which Paul regarded himself as unique then it might be from this sense of uniqueness that he derived his authority. If, say, he looked on himself as an 'eschatological' person whose task was to offer up the fulness of the Gentiles to Jerusalem and so consummate God's plans then he could be seen as giving himself a unique place. Even however if he only thought of himself as an exception among those who had seen the risen Lord ('one born out of due time'), as the last indeed to have done so, and as called to serve Christ in a most singular manner, he might have considered he had a special position before God and therefore possessed an authority different from that of the other apostles. In this way he would be an apostle, and would have to maintain that position if challenged, but would also have been more than an apostle and from that 'more' have derived his authority.[38]

37. The Greeks regularly used the term μητρόπολις of the city which founded a colony (our English transliteration no longer retains this meaning); occasionally the 'father' image is used. On cities and their colonies, see A.J. Graham, *Colony and Mother City in Ancient Greece* (Manchester: Manchester University Press, 1964).

38. We have made no use of Gal. 2.6 since this is a very difficult verse to under-

VI

As we conclude it is not inappropriate to inquire how the emphasis on Paul's apostolic authority should have arisen. As is usual in such cases a number of factors will have contributed.

1. We begin by asking how far the exercise of authority is associated with apostleship in the parts of the New Testament not written by Paul.

Luke is the writer who gives the apostles their clearest position in the New Testament church. He depicts the apostles,[39] or some of them, initiating action, e.g. setting hands on the 'Seven' (Acts 6.6), imparting the Holy Spirit to Samaritan converts (8.14ff.). It is the apostles and *brethren* who approve Peter's action in baptizing Cornelius. When the council meets in Jerusalem to consider Paul's mission to the Gentiles it is the apostles and elders who come together to discuss the matter and it is James, a non-apostle in Luke's eyes, who presides and issues the verdict (15.1ff.). This itself is a decision of the apostles and elders (15.22; 16.4). Later when Paul came for the last time to Jerusalem it is again James who occupies the seat of authority (21.17ff.). Luke does not therefore associate authority necessarily with apostleship but leaves it open for such an association to appear.

In Matthew and Mark the apostles are given authority to exorcise and preach (Mt. 10.2; cf. Mk 6.7-13, 30).[40] Exorcism and preaching have not been areas of activity with which we have been concerned in discussing Paul but the idea of authority is there clearly related to apostleship. The exercise of authority in general also is envisaged for when James and John ask for the best seats in the Kingdom Jesus speaks of the way it is to be used (10.35ff.); however the twelve in this pericope probably represent in Mark's eyes disciples in general including those of Mark's own day and are not to be restricted to the apostles.[41] In Mt. 16.19

stand. It has been used at times to suggest that being an apostle was an *adiaphoron* for Paul. For discussions of the verse, see D.M. Hay, 'Paul's Indifference to Authority', *JBL* 88 (1969), pp. 36-44; H.D. Betz, *Galatians* (Hermeneia; Philadelphia: Fortress Press, 1979), *ad loc*.

39. The apostles appear in Acts primarily as witnesses and missionaries; cf. H. von Campenhausen, 'Der urchristliche Apostelbegriff', *ST* 1 (1948), pp. 96-130.

40. The authority that goes with the twelve thrones (Mt. 19.28; Lk. 22.30) belongs not to this world but to the next.

41. See the discussion in my *Following Jesus: Discipleship in the Gospel of Mark* (JSNTSup, 4; Sheffield: JSOT Press, 1981), pp. 123ff.

Peter is given the authority of the keys but in 18.18 this is given to all disciples. Whatever then that authority is it is not given to the apostles as apostles though it may have been given to one among them and it is not something which is necessarily associated with apostleship.

There is a strange development of the apostolic concept in Ephesians where they become the foundation of the church and recipients of the mystery of Christ (2.20; 3.5); this should not lead us to make a special claim for them for on each occasion prophets are associated with them and these are prophets of the New Testament and not of the Old. Whatever authority belongs to apostles will also belong to prophets.[42]

In the Pastorals Paul is set out as an apostle[43] and instructs and directs Timothy and Titus and through them various churches. Apart from the addresses of the three letters and two references which parallel apostleship with preaching and teaching his apostleship is not stressed in these any more than in the genuine letters. Interestingly when Timothy and Titus are themselves being instructed they are described as Paul's children (1 Tim. 1.2, 18; 2 Tim. 1.2; 2.1; Tit. 1.4). Thus these letters remain faithful to one strand in Paul's pastoral approach.

There are no references to apostles in the Johannine literature apart from Revelation where as in Luke they are equated with the Twelve (21.14). When however we examine the letters we find that the parent/child relationship appears repeatedly as the writer (supposed to be the apostle John?) addresses his readers (1 Jn 2.1, 18; 3.7, 18; 4.4; 5.21; 3 John 4).[44] There is then no play on the writer as apostle.[45]

Thus there are few references to the apostles as possessing a special apostolic authority in the non-Pauline parts of the New Testament and a surprising amount of material that still leaves authority in the area of fatherhood. We require to move on outside the New Testament if we are to discover the source of the stress on apostolic authority.

2. By the third century bishops were tracing their ancestry back to the apostles. By this time bishops were people who exercised authority; it

42. Apostles and prophets may also be interchangeable terms in the Didache; cf. Lemaire, *Le ministères*, pp. 139-40.

43. Some scholars claim that the Pastorals only recognize one apostle, viz. Paul; cf. e.g. Mosbeck, 'Apostolos', p. 199.

44. This may not be the usage in 1 Jn 2.12, 14 where children are set alongside young men and fathers. The use in 2 Jn 1, 4, 13 where we read of the children of the 'elect lady' is difficult.

45. In 2 and 3 John the writer claims only to be a *presbuteros* and not an apostle.

was then natural that they should see in the apostles figures of authority. If they had not their own base would have been rendered insecure.[46]

3. One area in which the authority of the apostles became important in the second century lay in the upholding of orthodoxy over against gnostic heresy. The orthodox traced back their position to the authoritative teaching of the apostles.[47]

4. The process of viewing the apostles as figures of authority had however already begun by the end of the first century. Clement of Rome says that because the apostles realized that there would be strife after they died they appointed others to continue their work (1 Clem. 44.1-2): only those who are regarded as possessing authority can make such appointments. Ignatius says twice that since he is a condemned prisoner he ought not to give orders like an apostle (*Trall.* 3.3; *Rom.* 4.3). He writes also of Christians being subject to the presbytery as to the apostles (*Trall.* 2.2; cf. *Smyrn.* 8.1) and of the instructions or commands given by the apostles (*Trall.* 7.1; *Mag.* 13.1). The apostles are thus beginning to be seen as figures of authority.

5. The modern ecumenical debate which has often centred on the question of the authority of the ministry has kept this aspect to the fore when discussing the ministry's New Testament origin. It is not however proper to force our views of the nature of ministry back on the first century. We can see how erroneous this can become if we look at another area of ministry. For us it is difficult to conceive of a ministry one of whose important functions is not the administration of the sacraments. Yet Paul minimizes his role in baptism, having baptized only a few of the Corinthians (1 Cor. 1.14ff.). He gives instructions about the conduct of the Eucharist but says nothing about who should preside and gives us no clue whether he himself did so in his own churches whenever he was present. Because we are interested in ministerial authority we should be wary of reading this back into the ministry of the original apostles.

6. There are also non-theological factors of which account must be taken. We are much happier dealing with 'offices' than with 'functions'. If 'apostle' was originally descriptive of a function it was natural as time went by that it should be transformed into an office. Officials always exercise authority. So we connect authority with the apostolic office and then with those who exercise the function. From this it is only a short step to speak of Paul's apostolic authority. I find it an enlightening

46. Cf. Farrer, *Apostolic Ministry*, pp. 197ff.
47. Cf. von Campenhausen, *Ecclesiastical Authority*, pp. 158ff.

exercise when I am reading books about Paul and encounter the adjective 'apostolic' before some noun, say apostolic ministry, to omit it. Almost invariably the argument is not affected in any way. It is perhaps more habit then than anything else that leads us to speak of his apostolic authority. There is possibly also a more subtle factor. Paul, I am sure, was not an easy person to get on with. He dominated others; his language was over-vehement. It is so much easier to attribute such behaviour to the 'office' with its title than to a named person who is supposed to be of almost perfect character.

7. There is a sociological need to have some kind of authority. If one authority is rejected, as the Protestant reformers rejected that of the church in the sixteenth century, another must be found, and Scripture took the place of the church. In the first few generations an authority was equally necessary. 'As what was once shared becomes less and less common, the apostle becomes more and more differentiated from others. His status comes to look unique. His relationship to power is not one of interpretation, but one of application. A new sense of authority replaces the original one.'[48] I take it that the original authority was that of the gospel itself. But the gospel is a fluid concept and difficult to formalize. It is easier to see authority as residing in a few easily identifiable people. Hence the development of apostolic authority.

VII

We finish by returning to our starting point. There is no doubt Paul claimed to be an apostle, and that of the type of Peter. There is no doubt that he exercised authority. There must be doubt that these two ideas are necessarily related. Perhaps this can be put in another way. When Paul is concerned with his relations with his converts he does not employ the term apostle; he does so only when he is concerned with his relations with other church leaders. He may then only have used the term when it was politically advisable.[49]

48. Schütz, *Paul*, p. 280; cf. pp. 279, 283.
49. My own awareness of the relative unimportance of the apostolic title for Paul came in the course of the preparation of my Sprunt Lectures (see n. 23). These treat Paul's pastoral relations with the churches he founded. When I looked back on them after I had finished I was surprised to discover that the term 'apostle' never featured.

JSNT 36 (1989), pp. 75-94

PAUL AND THE PHARISAIC TRADITION

Dieter Lührmann

I

Writing to the Philippians Paul tells his readers who he was before he got to know Christ: he was circumcised on the eighth day, he was of the people of Israel, of the tribe of Benjamin, a Hebrew born of Hebrews. He continues: 'as to the Law, a Pharisee, as to zeal, a persecutor of the Church, as to righteousness which is in the Law, blameless' (Phil. 3.5-6). The three terms Law, zeal, and righteousness obviously belong together. Since the times of the Maccabees zeal meant to fight for the Law; righteousness was to live according to the Law. Such had been his confidence, and not a false confidence by any means.

It is only in this passage that Paul says he had been a Pharisee. Nowhere else, where he speaks about his origins,[1] does he mention this. In Acts, however, Luke too has Paul call himself a Pharisee (23.6; 26.5), brought up in Jerusalem at the feet of the Pharisee Gamaliel (22.3; cf. 5.34), as a Pharisee believing in the resurrection of the dead, in contrast to the Sadducees who do not (23.8). This question, Josephus also tells us,[2] marked one of the differences between the Pharisees and the Sadducees.

In the past, the fact that Paul calls himself a former Pharisee led to the question to which wing of this party he may have belonged, to the liberal followers of Hillel[3] or to the more conservative school of Shammai,[4]

---

1.   Cf. Gal. 1.13-14; 1 Cor. 15.9.

2.   See *Ant.* 18.16 referred to soon after.

3.   J. Jeremias, 'Paulus als Hillelit', in *Neotestamentica et Semitica* (Festschrift Matthew Black; Edinburgh: T. & T. Clark, 1969), pp. 88-94.

4.   H. Hübner, 'Gal 3.10 und die Herkunft des Paulus', *KD* 19 (1973), pp. 215-31.

a difference constantly mentioned in the Talmud. But the question also arose whether Paul, coming from the diaspora, had been a Pharisee at all. Were his origins in a more syncretistic, gnosticizing Judaism,[5] or had he belonged to Jewish apocalypticism, converted to its Christian branch?[6]

Recent debates on Paul's understanding of the Law may give the impression that Paul became aware of the Law as a problem only when he encountered Jewish-Christian missionaries, e.g. in Galatia, or when he met James, the head of the Jerusalem church. Only in reaction against them is Paul described as helpless, having no consistent understanding of what the Law meant for Judaism.[7] But if Paul had been a Pharisee before he got to know Christ, the Law must have been fundamental for him, the Law in the specific Pharisaic sense of the 'traditions of the fathers' (Gal. 1.14), including the oral Law as well as the written Torah. But how can we discover what Pharisaism actually was at the time of Paul?

This question has normally been answered by a picture of the Pharisees based mostly on the very polemical view of them given in the New Testament writings, and selected materials from the rabbinic literature were used to verify historically their 'hypocrisy'.[8] It may not only be in Germany that one gets one's basic information about the Pharisees at Sunday School and never gets rid of this picture of 'hypocrites'.[9]

During recent years, however, we have begun to learn that the rabbinic literature does not show what Pharisaism had been before the destruction of the temple, and it has been shown at the same time that neither rabbinic literature nor Pharisaism can be characterized as

---

5.   See e.g. R. Bultmann, *Theology of the New Testament*, I (trans. K. Grobel; New York: Charles Scribner's Sons, 1951), p. 187: 'Paul originated in Hellenistic Judaism...It remains uncertain, however, to what extent he had already appropriated in his pre-Christian period theological ideas of this syncretism (those of the mystery-religions and of Gnosticism) which come out in his Christian theology'.

6.   See e.g. U. Wilckens, 'Die Bekehrung des Paulus als religions-geschichtliches Problem', *ZTK* 56 (1959), pp. 273-93.

7.   This is a very short, and therefore unsatisfactory, remark about e.g. H. Hübner, *Das Gesetz bei Paulus* (Göttingen: Vandenhoeck & Ruprecht, 3rd edn, 1982), ET *Law in Paul's Thought* (Edinburgh: T. & T. Clark, 1984); H. Räisänen, *Paul and the Law* (Tübingen: Mohr [Siebeck], 2nd edn, 1987); G. Klein, 'Gesetz III', *TRE* XIII (1984), pp. 58-75.

8.   See the quotation from Sanders at n. 38.

9.   In Northern Germany coffee with cream on top, but rum inside, is called a 'Pharisee'.

'hypocritical'. Jacob Neusner especially,[10] but also Rudolf Meyer on the German side,[11] have stressed, perhaps over-emphasized, this distinction between rabbinic Judaism emerging after 70 CE, and Pharisaism before 70.

What then can we know about Pharisaism? Our major source is Josephus. He, also a former Pharisee, describes the Jewish parties for his readers in terms of the models of Greek philosophical schools. So the Pharisees look similar to the Stoics:

> Though they postulate that everything is brought about by fate (εἱμαρμένη) still they do not deprive the human will of the pursuit of what is in man's power, since it was God's good pleasure that there should be a fusion (κρᾶσις, or: a judgment, κρίσις?) and that the will of man with his virtue and vice should be admitted to the council-chamber of fate. They believe that souls have power to survive death and that there are rewards and punishments under the earth for those who have led lives of virtue or vice: eternal imprisonment is the lot of evil souls, while the good souls receive an easy passage to a new life (*Ant.* 18.13-14).[12]

When translated into Jewish terminology, the passage shows that the resurrection of the dead and the eternal judgment were fundamental concepts for the Pharisees in contrast to the Sadducees.[13]

> According to another passage of Josephus, the Pharisees had passed on to the people certain regulations handed down by the fathers and not recorded in the Laws of Moses, for which reason they are rejected by the Sadducaean group, who hold that only those regulations should be considered valid which were written down, and that those which had been handed down by the fathers need not be observed (*Ant.* 13.297).

That this conception of the twofold Law, written and oral, goes back to Pharisaism and is not a creation of the Rabbis after 70 CE, cannot be doubted.[14] Paul, when speaking about his time as a Pharisee in Gal. 1.14,

10. Bibliographical references would be numerous; a short survey can be found in his 'The Use of the Later Rabbinic Evidence for the Study of First-Century Pharisaism', in W.S. Green (ed.), *Approaches to Ancient Judaism* (Missoula MT: Scholars Press, 1968), pp. 215-28.

11. φαρισαῖος, *TDNT*, IX, pp. 11-35; cf. his book *Tradition und Neuschöpfung im antiken Judentum* (Berlin: de Gruyter, 1965).

12. This quotation and all following are taken from the LCL-edition of Josephus by H.St.J. Thackeray, R. Marcus, A. Wikgren, L.H. Feldman.

13. Cf. Josephus, *Ant.* 18.16.

14. Cf. P. Schäfer, 'Das "Dogma" von der mündlichen Torah im rabbinischen Judentum', in *idem, Studien zur Geschichte und Theologie des rabbinischen*

stresses his zeal for 'the traditions of the fathers', and in Mk 7.4-5 the conflict with the Pharisees and the scribes is about the 'traditions of the elders'.

The latter passage comes from our second source for Pharisaism, the Gospel of Mark.[15] Mark, writing about 70 CE, takes up stories of conflicts between Jesus and the Pharisees, transmitted in the Jesus-tradition. They deal with questions of eating (2.15-17: with whom to eat; 7.1-5: washing the hands before eating), with the observance of Sabbath (2.23-28; 3.1-5), with regulations concerning vows of *Corban* (7.9-13), with the practice of divorce (10.2-9), and with the question of whether to pay tribute to the Caesar or not (12.13-17)—to sum up, questions not regulated or questions even unforeseen in the written Law, questions of everyday life, however, which needed answers given in the 'tradition of the fathers', the oral Law. These stories show discussions between early Christian and Pharisaic communities, not only discussions, but conflicts leading to persecution of the Church as testified by Paul, who, zealous for the traditions of his fathers, persecuted the Church of God (Gal. 1.13, 23; Phil. 3.6; 1 Cor. 15.9).

A similarly polemical tone is found in the Woes against the Pharisees in the Synoptic Sayings Source Q (Lk. 11.39-52/Mt. 23.1-35).[16] Here additional information about the Pharisees is given with regard to tithing (Lk. 11.42/Mt. 23.23; cf. Lk. 18.12), with regard to the prestige they enjoyed (Lk. 11.43/Mt. 23.6), and with regard to their concern for the tradition (Lk. 11.47-48/Mt. 23.29-30). Again these Woes show a sharp difference between Jesus and his followers on the one side and the Pharisees on the other, and again this difference derives from the Pharisees' concept of a Law alongside the written Torah.

A polemical view of the Pharisees can also be found in some writings of the Qumran library.[17] It is the Pharisees who are attacked when, in

Judentums (AGJU, 15; Leiden: Brill, 1978), pp. 153-97, who, however, does not take into account Gal. 1.14 and Mk 7.4-5.

15. Cf. my article 'Die Pharisäer und die Schriftgelehrten im Markus-evangelium', *ZNW* 78 (1987), pp. 169-85, where I tried to show that for Mark the Pharisees are the opponents of the past in questions of the oral Law, while the scribes are partners in conflicts about Christology. In general cf. my commentary *Das Markusevangelium* (Tübingen: Mohr, 1987).

16. Cf. J. Freudenberg, 'Die synoptische Weherede' (dissertation Münster, 1972); J.S. Kloppenborg, *The Formation of Q* (Philadelphia: Fortress Press, 1987), pp. 139-47.

17. Cf. Meyer, *TDNT*, IX, pp. 28-31.

the Damascus Document, teachers are mentioned who 'sought after smooth things, chose deceits, kept watch with a view to lawless deeds', who 'justified the wicked and condemned the righteous', 'their deeds were uncleanness before God' (CD 1.13-17).[18] Josephus calls the Pharisees 'the most accurate interpreters of the Laws' (*War* 2.162); for the Zadokite Essenes of Qumran, however, they are only men-pleasers. Again it seems to be the conception of the oral Law, the Pharisees' application of the Law to everyday life, that made the difference. The Essenes had their own interpretation of the Law; Pharisees and Essenes were rivals.

Even if we add some materials from the rabbinic literature,[19] we do not have much similar to Paul. Almost nothing of what we find in all these sources is of interest for Pauline theology except what Josephus says about resurrection and eternal judgment. All of these sources for our knowledge about Pharisaism provide information from the outside: former Pharisees like Josephus and Paul, opponents of the Pharisees like the early Christian Jesus-tradition or the Qumran-Essenes, the Rabbis as the Pharisees' heirs are our informants.[20] So, again, what evidence do we have to build a picture of what it meant to Paul to be a Pharisee before he got to know Christ?

II

At least since Julius Wellhausen's epoch-making book on the Pharisees and the Sadducees of 1874,[21] the *Psalms of Solomon* have been understood as a document of Pharisaism. This view has been held by German scholars such as Herbert Braun in his influential article of 1951,[22] to which I shall return, Gerhard Maier,[23] Joachim Schüpphaus,[24] but also the Dane Svend Holm-Nielsen in his German edition of the *Psalms of*

18. Translation according to R.H. Charles in *APOT*, II, p. 802.

19. Cf. Neusner, 'Use of Later Rabbinic Evidence'.

20. The picture would not be changed by the Gospels of Matthew, Luke, John or apocryphal gospels, by Acts or by *Assumption of Moses* 5.5-6.

21. *Die Pharisäer und die Sadducäer* (Göttingen: Vandenhoeck & Ruprecht, 3rd edn, 1967).

22. 'Vom Erbarmen Gottes über den Gerechten', *ZNW* 42 (1950–51), pp. 1-54 = *idem, Gesammelte Studien zum Neuen Testament und seiner Umwelt* (Tübingen: Mohr [Siebeck], 2nd edn, 1967), pp. 8-69.

23. *Mensch und freier Wille* (Tübingen: Mohr [Siebeck], 1971), p. 300.

24. *Die Psalmen Salomos* (ALGHJ, 7; Leiden: Brill, 1977), pp. 130-37.

Solomon[25] and George Nickelsburg in his introduction to the intertestamental literature[26] see the *Psalms of Solomon* as a typically Pharisaic
document; and H.E. Ryle and M.R. James gave their edition of 1891 the
subtitle: 'Psalms of the Pharisees, commonly called the Psalms of
Solomon'.[27]

This view, however, has been questioned following the discovery of
the Qumran library. In his article on 'The Religious Background of the
Psalms of Solomon (Re-evaluated in the Light of the Qumran Texts)'
Jerry O'Dell[28] comes to the conclusion:

> It is not necessary, indeed it is misleading, to dissect all the Jewry of the
> inter-testamental period into distinct religious and political groups. There
> were without a doubt a number of deeply spiritual and eschatologically
> orientated men who belonged neither to the Pharisees, Sadducees nor to
> the priestly minded Qumran Essenes, but were nonetheless religious Jews.
> Such a man, or group of men, was the author of the Psalms of Solomon.[29]

At the same time Herbert Braun in his article for the third edition of
Die Religion in Geschichte und Gegenwart[30] saw the *Psalms of
Solomon* as only 'near to the Pharisees, but typical also of broader
Jewish circles'. Already in 1957 in his two volumes on Jewish-heretical
and early Christian radicalism, he did not treat the *Psalms of Solomon*
but instead took *Pirqe Aboth* 1–4 to characterize Pharisaism, though he
did not use this term.[31] Referring to O'Dell's article, E.P. Sanders sees
'the Psalms of Solomon as coming from a broad religious movement
which cannot be precisely identified with Pharisaism'.[32] R.B. Wright
in his edition of the *Psalms of Solomon* for 'The Old Testament
Pseudepigrapha' calls them either Pharisaic or Essene in origin,[33] but the
general editor, James H. Charlesworth, rebukes him by an insertion:

---

25. *Die Psalmen Salomos, Jüdische Schriften aus hellenistisch-römischer Zeit*,
IV/2 (Gütersloh: Gerd Mohn, 1977), p. 59.
26. *Jewish Literature between the Bible and the Mishna* (Philadelphia: Fortress
Press, 1971), p. 212.
27. Cambridge: Cambridge University Press, 1891.
28. *RevQ* 3 (1961), pp. 241-57.
29. O'Dell, 'Religious Background', p. 257.
30. Vol. V (1961), pp. 1342-43.
31. *Spätjüdisch-häretischer und frühchristlicher Radikalismus* (2 vols.;
(Tübingen: Mohr [Siebeck], 1957), see I, pp. 2-14.
32. *Paul and Palestinian Judaism* (London: SCM Press, 1977), p. 388.
33. (Garden City: Doubleday, 1985), II, p. 642.

'It is unwise to label these psalms as either Pharisaic or Essene.'[34] P.N. Franklyn in the most recent study of the *Psalms of Solomon*[35] decides: 'There is more evidence, supplied by Jerry O'Dell and Robert Wright, for linking these psalms with Qumran' than for linking them with Pharisaism.[36] The latter's article was not available to me, but Wright does not say this in his introduction to his edition.[37] Jerry O'Dell, however, cannot be named in favour of this view. He only assembled a list of possible Qumran parallels.

If I, following the traditions of some fathers, take the *Psalms of Solomon* as a Pharisaic document, showing to some degree Paul's Pharisaic traditions, I am aware of the difficulties, even dangers, of such an attempt. E.P. Sanders comments on Herbert Braun's interpretation as follows: He 'has conformed the Psalms of Solomon to the picture of Pharisaic Judaism which is usual in Christian, and especially Lutheran scholarship, and which is usually supported by quotations from rabbinic literature'.[38]

I hope that what I am going to say does not stand and fall with the question of the Pharisaic origin of the *Psalms of Solomon*. I hope that those in doubt may take them as *a* possible tradition behind Pauline theology if not as his *Pharisaic* tradition. But what I am going to say is mostly to discuss Herbert Braun's important and (at least in Germany) influential interpretation of the *Psalms of Solomon* and of Pharisaism in general. Braun throughout his article of 1951 wanted to show the 'ambiguity' of these psalms, the oscillating character of their theology, and he looked for what was *really* meant in the wordings to unmask 'Pharisaic hypocrisy' behind the actual text.

The *Psalms of Solomon* were edited for the first time in 1626. They are preserved in Greek and Syriac only,[39] but the original language must have been Hebrew. Allusions to Pompey's invasion of Palestine in 63

34. *The Old Testament Pseudepigrapha*, II, p. 642.

35. 'The Cultic and Pious Climax of Eschatology in the Psalms of Solomon', *JSJ* 18 (1987), pp. 1-17.

36. Franklyn, 'Cultic and Pious Climax', p. 17.

37. If, as I think, R.B. Wright is the Robert Wright of the quotation.

38. *Paul and Palestinian Judaism*, p. 395.

39. For the Greek text, see A. Rahlfs, *Septuaginta*, II (Stuttgart: Deutsche Bibelgesellschaft, 1979), pp. 471-89; for the Syriac, see *The Old Testament in Syriac according to the Peshitta Version edited by the Peshitta Institute Leiden*, IV.6 (Leiden: Brill, 1972); the English translations are from the edition of R.B. Wright (see n. 34).

BCE and to his death in 48 BCE in Egypt indicate a date in the first century BCE though the individual psalms of this collection may come from different periods.[40] Concerning their form, they follow the patterns of biblical and apocryphal psalms. I doubt if anyone would identify them as non-canonical if they were read in a service.

In the following I shall concentrate mostly on the third of these psalms and I shall try to interpret it in its own right as a document of Jewish, probably Pharisaic, theology.

1	Why do you sleep, soul, and do not praise the Lord?
	Sing a new song to God, who is worthy to be praised.
2	Sing and be aware of how he is aware of you,
	for a good psalm to God is from a glad heart.
3	The righteous remember the Lord all the time,
	by acknowledging and proving the Lord's judgments right.
4	The righteous does not lightly esteem discipline from the Lord;
	his desire is (to be) always in the Lord's presence.
5	The righteous stumbles and proves the Lord right;
	he falls and watches for what God will do about him;
	he looks to where his salvation comes from.
6	The confidence of the righteous (comes) from God their saviour;
	sin after sin does not visit the house of the righteous.
7	The righteous constantly searches his house,
	to remove his unintentional sins.
8	He atones for (sins of) ignorance by fasting and humbling his soul,
	and the Lord will cleanse every devout person and his house.
9	The sinner stumbles and curses his life,
	the day of his birth and his mother's pains.
10	He adds sin upon sin in his life;
	he falls—his fall is serious—and he will not get up.
11	The destruction of the sinner is forever,
	and he will not be remembered when (God) looks after the righteous.
12	This is the share of sinners forever,
	but those who fear the Lord shall rise up to eternal life,
	and their life shall be in the Lord's light, and it shall never end.

The psalm starts with a self-encouragement to praise the Lord (vv. 1-2), followed by a programmatic statement about what the righteous do (vv. 3-4). Verses 5-8 and 9-12 depict the contrast of the righteous and the sinner, how both react to the same situation of stumbling. The Greek text in both cases has past tense in the beginning, followed by a present

---

40. With regard to these historical questions all modern authors agree.

tense: 'The righteous stumbled and proved the Lord right, he fell and watches for what God will do about him' (v. 5), 'the sinner stumbled and curses his life...' (v. 9). That may reflect the underlying Hebrew grammar, but when we look at v. 9, it makes sense to look for someone who stumbled and cursed his life, the day of his birth and his mother's pains. Indeed there is such a sinner in the biblical tradition: 'After this opened Job his mouth, and cursed the day of his birth. And Job said: "Let the day perish wherein I was born, and the night which said: A man-child is conceived...Why did I not die at birth, come forth from the womb and expire? Why did the knees receive me? Or why the breasts, that I should suck?"' (Job 3.1-3, 11-12).

Indeed, Jeremiah too cursed his life (20.14-15), but I think the allusion to the Job of the dialogues is not accidental. If we read the first of the *Psalms of Solomon*, it sounds like the story of the first chapter of Job, though from the opposite point of view:

1   I cried out to the Lord when I was severely troubled,
        to God when sinners set upon (me).
2   Suddenly, the clamor of war was heard before me;
        He will hear me, for I am full of righteousness.
3   I considered in my heart that I was full of righteousness,
        for I had prospered and had many children.
4   Their wealth was extended to the whole earth,
        and their glory to the end of the earth.
5   They exalted themselves to the stars,
        they said they would never fall.
6   They were arrogant in their possessions,
        and they did not acknowledge (God).
7   Their sins were in secret, and even I did not know.
8   Their lawless actions surpassed the gentiles before them;
        they completely profaned the sanctuary of the Lord.

The interpreters of this psalm may be right in looking for historical events of the first century BCE and in referring to Pompey's siege and final conquest of Jerusalem and its temple in 63.[41] But the model for this story is Job's initial welfare and his care for his children, though now his fate is seen as that of one who falsely considered himself full of righteousness, but in fact was a sinner and whose children were sinners too. What the book of Job and the *Psalms of Solomon* have in common is the question of the qualitative difference between sin and

41. Cf. e.g. Schüpphaus, *Psalmen Salomos*, pp. 25-28.

righteousness, a question both share with a broad stream of Jewish
Wisdom literature.

According to v. 3 to be righteous means to acknowledge God's
righteousness, a theme constantly repeated throughout these psalms.[42]
This eventually is the solution of the problem in the book of Job too, but
not before Job had seen the Lord himself; until then he had only heard
of him (42.1-6). At the same time, however, Job's friends, who had tried
to convince him that he should repent for unknown sins, are rebuked by
the Lord, 'for they have not spoken of the Lord what is right' (42.7-8).
What is said about the righteous in *Pss. Sol.* 3 seems to be more in
accordance with the theology of those friends: Job should acknowledge
the Lord's judgments as right, he should take his fate as discipline from
the Lord and he should search for sins of ignorance.

The difference between sinners and righteous ones becomes clear
when both stumble. The paradigm for a sinner is Job who in such a case
cursed his life. The righteous, in contrast, even then prove the Lord
right, looking for salvation which comes from the Lord, again a major
theme of the book of Job, who looked for his salvation.[43] To deal with
the inevitable sins of ignorance means first of all to avoid them as far as
possible. However, to be righteous does not mean to be without sins:

> And whose sins will he forgive except those who have sinned?
>> You bless the righteous, and do not accuse them for the sins
>>> they have committed.
>> And your goodness is upon those that sin, when they repent
>>> (9.7).

So on the other side there is the question of atonement for these
inevitable sins. In the Old Testament we find regulations concerning the
'sin offering' in cases of sinning 'unwittingly' or 'through error' in
Leviticus 4: a young bull is to be offered.[44] This is not the way of
atoning proposed in our psalm. It does not refer to Leviticus 4, a possibility still open in the first century BCE when the people of Israel had
their temple in Jerusalem where it was possible to offer a young bull for
sins of ignorance whenever such an offering was needed.

By contrast, the wording of v. 8 refers to Leviticus 16's regulations
about Yom Kippur, the 'Day of Atonement':

---

42. Cf. Schüpphaus, *Psalmen Salomos*, p. 100.
43. Cf. the dominance of σώζειν, σωτηρία in Job LXX.
44. Lev. 4.14, cf. ἀγνοεῖν in v. 13.

In the seventh month, on the tenth day of the month, you shall afflict yourselves, and shall do no work, either the native or the stranger who sojourns among you: for on this day shall atonement be made for you, to cleanse you; from all your sins shall you be clean before the Lord (Lev. 16.29-30).[45]

In the written Law Yom Kippur is the only regular day of fasting, though we hear about four such days from post-exilic times (Zech. 8.19). The term for this fasting connected with Yom Kippur is not the usual Hebrew root צום, but ענה נפש, 'to humble or afflict one's soul or oneself', ταπεινοῦν τὴν ψυχήν in Greek.[46] German translations of Leviticus 16 and other passages where this phrase is used render it simply by 'to fast', making no distinction between the terms as, for instance, the RSV does. Our psalm explicitly interprets this 'humbling one's soul' by 'fasting', and that goes back to a possibly exilic or even post-exilic usage of the term: 'Then I proclaimed a fast..., that we might humble ourselves before our God' (Ezra 8.21).[47] In rabbinic times ענה became the technical term for fasting (cf. the tractate *Ta'anayot* 'On Fasting' in the Talmud).[48]

So v. 8 leads us back to one of the fundamental concepts of the Old Testament and to the greatest feast of Israel. In Leviticus 16, however, it is not fasting that atones, but the offering of the two goats. God's cleansing of the people is the result of Yom Kippur.[49] In *Pss. Sol.* 3, however, fasting itself is the means by which the righteous one atones and so 'the Lord will cleanse every devout person and his house' (v. 8).[50]

45. Cf. Lev. 23.26-32; Num. 29.7-11. Y. Yadin (*The Temple Scroll*, I [Jerusalem: Israel Exploration Society, 1983], p. 134) observes that the regulations for the 'Day of Atonement' in Temple Scroll 25.10–27.10 include many details from Lev. 4.8-9.

46. Cf. H.A. Brongers, 'Fasting in Israel in Biblical and Post-Biblical Times', *OTS* 20 (1977), pp. 1-21; E. Gerstenberger, ענה II, *ThWAT* VI/3-5 (1987), pp. 247-70, esp. 253-55.

47. Cf. Isa. 58.3, 5; Ps. 35.13: 'I afflicted my soul with fasting'; Sir. 31.21; frequently in the Qumran texts.

48. Here, however, Yom Kippur is mentioned only in 4.1 and 4.8. On the other hand the tractate *Yoma* has regulations on fasting in ch. 8 only, but is mostly concerned with the highpriest and the offerings.

49. The same is true for the Temple Scroll (cf. n. 46).

50. At least this passage does refer to the cult, and therefore I cannot agree with Sanders's statement that 'the failure to mention the sacrificial system as atoning is probably due to the nature of the Psalms and their immediate concerns' (*Paul and*

As far as we know regular fasting had been characteristic of one group of Judaism only, the Pharisees, twice in the week, as the Pharisee of Lk. 18.12 says, perhaps on Monday and Thursday (cf. *Did.* 8.1), though these proof-texts derive from the times after 70 CE. But the conflict story Mk 2.18-22 at least shows that as against the disciples of John the Baptist the question of fasting also marked a difference between Pharisees and early Christians; this story, however, presupposes that some Christians would fast again, after Jesus was taken away (cf. also Mt. 6.16-18; *Did.* 8).

Pss. Sol. 3 helps us to understand what fasting meant for the Pharisees: atonement for the inevitable sins of ignorance. That corresponds to their conception of the 'traditions of the fathers', for (a) nowhere in the written Law do we find regular fasting demanded, and (b) nowhere in the Old Testament is fasting by itself seen as a means of atonement.[51] So it also corresponds to their conception of transferring the Law from the cultic frame to everyday life.

III

Such a conception of atonement seems to be unique in comparable Jewish texts of those times. The Sadducees held to the written Law and as the party of the Jerusalem aristocracy they were connected with the temple. We do not know much about the Samaritans and their conception of atonement, but as they too followed the Pentateuch only, it was either Yom Kippur or the 'sin offering' of Leviticus 4 that could atone for sins of ignorance. With the Qumran documents the *Psalms of Solomon* share the sharp stress on the qualitative difference between sin and righteousness, but nowhere there is fasting a means of atonement.[52] So I think it is for good reasons that we can take these psalms as belonging to the Pharisees, that Jewish group for which regular fasting was characteristic.[53]

Palestinian Judaism, p. 398). By contrast: the concept of atoning is transferred from the cult to everyday life.

51. Cf. B. Janowski, *Sühne als Heilsgeschehen* (Neukirchen: Neukirchener Verlag, 1982), who, however, does not take into account the *Psalms of Solomon*.

52. Cf. P. Garnet, *Salvation and Atonement in the Qumran Scrolls* (Tübingen: Mohr [Siebeck], 1977).

53. Sanders (*Paul and Palestinian Judaism*, pp. 402-403) is right in rejecting Wellhausen's identification of the sinners as the Sadducees; but, I think, there is a lot

If we now go on to compare some aspects of Pauline theology with what we read in the *Psalms of Solomon*, we have to take into account that Paul is not *the* representative of early Christianity in general. We have seen already that there were Christians who did fast, though Jesus himself did not (Mk. 2.18-22). In Paul's letters the verb is absent: the noun νηστεία is used in the general sense of 'asceticism' (1 Cor. 7.5) or in the sense of 'lack of food' (2 Cor. 6.5; 11.27). This is also the meaning of ταπεινοῦσθαι in Phil. 4.12 in opposition to περισσεύειν 'to abound'.[54] Nowhere does fasting as such appear as a problem that arose from the controversies about the Law, though we hear about questions of which meals might be allowed.[55]

So it is not fasting that makes Paul and the *Psalms of Solomon* comparable. Rom. 3.24-26, however, also refers to Leviticus 16, as *Pss. Sol.* 3 does. Ever since Bultmann's *Theology* and Ernst Käsemann's short article, supporting Bultmann's interpretation, these verses have been taken as a pre-Pauline formula, going back to the Jewish-Christian tradition which Paul picked up here and elsewhere.[56] And indeed the vocabulary is not typical of Paul, nor are the christological concepts which describe Jesus' death as atonement according to Leviticus 16: 'whom God put forward as an expiation (through faith, perhaps a Pauline insertion) by his blood to show his righteousness because of the passing over of the sins committed before in the forebearance of God'. So atonement is given once and for all and no further offerings are needed, but at the same time there is no place for regular fasting. Paul's formula as well as *Pss. Sol.* 3 transfers the concept of atonement from the cultic frame of Yom Kippur—the *Psalms of Solomon* to everyday life, the Pauline formula to christology. As *Pss. Sol.* 9 shows, Paul shares

of internal evidence in the *Psalms of Solomon* to ascribe them to the Pharisees (cf. n. 64 below).

54. Cf. the parallelism with ὑστερεῖσθαι in the same verse.

55. The term 'Christians' I have used above perhaps needs some clarification. It comes from the end of the first century (Acts 11.26; 26.28; 1 Pet. 4.16) and may sound anachronistic for the first generation. However, it can be used in the sense that 'Christians' are those who believe that God's salvation expected by the righteous ones (cf. *Pss. Sol.* 3.5-6) has come in Christ. In this sense Paul was a 'Christian', though he himself, if asked to which religion he belonged, would have called himself a Jew.

56. Bultmann, *Theology*, p. 46; E. Käsemann, 'Zum Verständnis von Röm. 3.24-26', *ZNW* 43 (1950–51), pp. 150-54 = *idem, Exegetische Versuche und Besinnungen*, I (Göttingen: Vandenhoeck & Ruprecht, 1960), pp. 96-100.

with them the reference to Abraham and to God's promises given to 'Abraham our father'.[57] An adequate way to summarize Rom. 3.24-26 could be that in Jesus' death the covenant is re-established, and the covenant is fundamental for the theology of the *Psalms of Solomon* too. Paul himself, however, at least is quite cautious in using this concept, for even the 'new covenant' of Jer. 31.31 still has the Law as its content.

The 17th and the 18th of the *Psalms of Solomon* are our major sources for messianic expectations in Judaism, if one takes Messiah in the strict sense of the anointed king of Israel, son of David.[58] Again a probably pre-Pauline formula,[59] Rom. 1.3-4, speaks of Jesus 'who was of the seed of David according to the flesh'. This concept, incidentally, proves that the *Psalms of Solomon* cannot be of Essene origin, for in the Qumran documents we find the expectation of two Messiahs, the priestly Messiah of Aaron being superior to the Messiah of David.[60] This messianic concept of the *Psalms of Solomon* corresponds to what Josephus says about the Pharisees, that they were critics of the Hasmonaean dynasty who called themselves 'kings of Israel'.[61] Generations after, this question of earthly kingship split the Pharisees when under Roman occupation the Zealot Judas and the Pharisee Zadok denied that the Jews should acknowledge other rulers besides God himself.[62] *Pss. Sol.* 17 and 18 show that there could be an expectation of a future king of Israel while they were waiting for the kingdom of God himself. Neither in the psalms, however, nor in the Qumran documents, is the Messiah, the 'Christ', the one to atone by his death as the 'Christ' Jesus does according to Rom. 3.24-26.

That sin means transgressions of the Law is a presupposition of the psalm, not explicit here, but obvious from other passages.[63] So the contrast of sinners and righteous ones is primarily the contrast between Jews and Gentiles. But in accordance with a long tradition there is also the distinction between the righteous and the godless within Israel itself, the difference being established according to observance or

---

57. Cf. *Pss. Sol.* 9.9-10.
58. Cf. M. de Jonge, χρίω κτλ., *TDNT*, IX, pp. 513-14.
59. Cf. Bultmann, *Theology*, p. 49.
60. Cf. A.S. van der Woude, χρίω κτλ., *TDNT*, IX, pp. 517-20.
61. *Pss. Sol.* 17.5-6, cf. Josephus, *Ant.* 13.431.
62. Josephus, *Wars* 2.117-18; *Ant.* 18.2-4.
63. Cf. e.g. 14.2-3, quoted below; cf. ἀνομία 1.8; 2.3, 12; 9.2; 15.8, 10; παρανομία 4.1; 8.9; παράνομος 4.9, 11, 19, 23; 12.1; 14.6.

non-observance of the Law, or more precisely by observance or non-observance of a specific interpretation of the Law. So for the *Psalms of Solomon* it is the Gentiles who are sinners, the Romans who conquered the land; but sinners are also those Jews who transgress the Law.[64]

> For Israel is the portion and inheritance of God.
> But not so are sinners and criminals,
> who love (to spend) the day in sharing their sin (14.5-6).

The righteous ones by contrast are those who live 'in the Law' (ἐν νόμῳ):

> The Lord is faithful to those who truly love him,
> to those who endure his discipline,
> to those who live in the righteousness of his commandments,
> to the Law, which he has commanded for our life.
> The Lord's devout shall live by it forever (14.1-3a).

This reminds us of what Paul says with regard to his Pharisaic past: 'as to the righteousness which is in the Law, blameless' (Phil. 3.6)—not, however, without sins, but holding to the Law and its promises. And it reminds us of Lev. 18.5, quoted by Paul in Gal. 3.12 and Rom. 10.5:[65] 'he who does them (i.e. God's statutes and judgments), shall live in them'. But Paul takes Lev. 18.5 as a proof-text in an opposite sense: living in the Law does not mean righteousness; the righteous ones are those who live by faith, as is witnessed, he says, by Hab. 2.4.

Nevertheless, or perhaps precisely because of this, the qualitative difference between sin and righteousness is the general topic of Paul's letter to the Romans. I think that the discussions of Pauline theology have isolated the term 'righteousness of *God*' too much and therefore have neglected the general contrast of righteousness and sin. Paul has to defend his concept of righteousness not in the Law but by faith in Christ

64. Sanders (*Paul and Palestinian Judaism*, pp. 402-43) and others are right in arguing against Wellhausen, that the sinners are not the Sadducees and therefore the righteous ones the Pharisees (cf. n. 53 above). But when Sanders says (p. 403) that 'the two characteristic differences between the Pharisees and the Sadducees—the question of the oral law and the resurrection—are not mentioned' in the *Psalms of Solomon* one can refer for the second to 3.12 ('those who fear the Lord shall rise up to eternal life'; cf. 15.12-13); and for the first to Sanders himself, who speaks of 'a general halakic dispute'. So at least it is a specific understanding of the Law that makes the difference.

65. Cf. A. Lindemann, 'Die Gerechtigkeit aus dem Gesetz: Erwägungen zur Auslegung und zur Textgeschichte von Römer 10, 5', *ZNW* 73 (1982), pp. 231-50.

against those who report, as he says, 'slanderously' and affirm that he says: 'Let us do evil, that good may come' (Rom. 3.8; cf. 6.1, 12). So in Rom. 10.3 he denounces such 'righteousness in the Law' as 'their own righteousness', as he had created the contrast of 'a righteousness of my own, even that which is of the Law', in which he was found blameless, and 'the righteousness which is of God, by faith' (Phil. 3.9).

The accusations Paul had to encounter sound familiar if we remember that the Qumran-Essenes rebuked the Pharisees for 'justifying the wicked and condemning the righteous'.[66] Such accusations were common in intra-Jewish polemics, for the qualitative difference of sin and righteousness is the dominating question of early Jewish theology, and is the dominating question of early Christianity as well, perhaps of Judaism and Christianity up to this day.

The fact that Paul was attacked depends upon his conception that even Gentiles, the sinners *par excellence* of the Jewish tradition, could get access to righteousness, not because they are sinners, but because there is no distinction between Jews and Gentiles, for 'all have sinned and fall short of the glory of God', for 'the same Lord is Lord of all and bestows his riches upon all who call upon him' (Rom. 3.23; 10.12). To let even Gentiles be righteous can be nothing less than a consequence of what is said in *Pss. Sol.* 9.6:

> To whom will you be good, O God, except to those who call
>   upon the Lord?
> He will cleanse from sins the soul in confessing, in restoring,
>   so that for all these things the shame is on us, and (it shows)
>   on our faces

And this verse is repeated by what we know already:

> And whose sins will he forgive except those who have sinned?
>   You bless the righteous, and do not accuse them for the sins
>   they have committed.
>   And your goodness is upon those that sin, when they repent
>   (9.7).

Who, then, are the righteous ones in contrast to the sinners, if for Paul the Law no longer marks a qualitative difference between Jews and Gentiles[67] or the difference between those Jews who adhere to a specific interpretation of the Law and those who do not follow it? The righteous

---

66. See at n. 18 above.
67. Cf. Gal. 2.15-16.

for Paul are those—and this is quite in accordance with *Pss. Sol.* 3—who acknowledge God's righteousness.[68] After quoting his opponents in Rom. 3.8 who accused him of neglecting the qualitative difference of sin and righteousness, Paul gives a long confession, made up by texts especially from the Psalms. And this confession includes both Jews and Greeks, 'that they are all under sin' (Rom. 3.9-20).

What made the righteous righteous, according to *Pss. Sol.* 3.3-4, was to acknowledge God's righteousness. Paul's concept of righteousness at this point therefore does not leave its Pharisaic origins, though these are radicalized. Neither here nor there is it the fulfilment of the Law and the fulfilment of the commandments that makes the righteous righteous; even in the *Psalms of Solomon* the righteous one is a sinner, who needs remission of sins.[69]

IV

The *Psalms of Solomon*, I think, bring us nearer to Paul than do the other sources of Pharisaism discussed earlier. They can show us some of Paul's presuppositions, options and questions or even solutions and can lead us to understand what it meant to be a Pharisee in his day. So, why, according to Phil. 3.7-8, did he count all this a loss, even dung? He says: 'for Christ', 'for the excellency of the knowledge of Christ Jesus my Lord'. But this 'Christ' Jesus is neither a new interpreter of the Law nor a new 'Teacher of Righteousness'.

We have already touched on Paul's christology, more precisely pre-Pauline formulae which he took up. Bultmann drew the distinction between the 'kerygma', the proclamation, on the one side and 'theology' on the other, and he defined theology as explication of human existence before God in anthropological terms.[70] Here no Pauline christology seemed to be left; it was all pre-Pauline formulae or traditions. When we look at Bultmann's 'Theology of Paul' in his *Theology of the New Testament*, it is indeed built up on the basis of anthropological terms, with three exceptions:

68. *Pss. Sol.* 3.3; cf. 8.7, 26; 9.2, 6; 10.6; 15.2; 16.5.

69. For the relation between righteousness and resurrection cf. Rom. 6.12-13.

70. Cf. R. Bultmann, 'Das Problem einer theologischen Exegese des Neuen Testaments', *Zwischen den Zeiten* 3 (1925), pp. 334-57, reprinted in G. Strecker (ed.), *Das Problem der Theologie des Neuen Testaments* (Darmstadt: Wissenschaftliche Buchgesellschaft, 1975), pp. 249-93: 'Theologie bedeutet die begriffliche Darstellung der Existenz des Menschen als einer durch Gott bestimmten' (p. 272).

1. §33, where he tries to show how confused Paul's ideas on christology were; the conceptions come from Judaism, Gnosticism or from elsewhere and are contradictory in themselves;[71]

2. §34 dealing with the church and the sacraments, but preceded by 'the word';

3. and this is my major point, §27 'the Law', by no means an anthropological term, if it is not replaced by 'boasting'.

So two of the key-words of Philippians 3, my starting-point, do not fit in with Bultmann's definition of what theology should be, namely 'at the same time anthropology';[72] neither does 'Law' nor 'Christ'.

But to me it seems at least questionable whether 'righteousness' fits that definition either. Paul was not the first to make righteousness the fundamental question of theology—that goes back to a long tradition in Judaism, including the Pharisees. Nor is his conception of acknowledging God as righteous a new one—again the Pharisees were not the only ones who held this view. Nor, finally, was Paul the first to understand human righteousness in a forensic sense of 'being justified by God'—the *Psalms of Solomon* have the same idea when the righteous ones are those whom the Lord will cleanse, will declare clean (3.8).

So the *Psalms of Solomon* leave us with two questions, the question of christology and the question of the Law, both questions coming together in what for Paul is the contrast between the righteousness which is of the Law and that righteousness which is through faith in Christ, the righteousness which is of God by faith. How does christology supply something extra when compared with the Law? What is the deficiency of the Law compared with christology with regard to righteousness? The answer cannot simply be 'faith'. Though, surprisingly, the terms 'faith' or 'to believe' are not found in the *Psalms of Solomon*,[73] in other Jewish documents of those times these terms were used as self-definitions of those who held to the Law.[74] So 'faith' is not by itself the new 'self-understanding' of those who are justified in Christ, but for Paul to believe in Christ marks the difference over against those

71. Cf. my 'Christologie und Rechtfertigung', in *Rechtfertigung* (Festschrift Ernst Käsemann; ed. J. Friedrich *et al.*; Göttingen: Vandenhoeck & Ruprecht, 1976), pp. 351-63.

72. Bultmann, *Theology*, p. 191.

73. Only πιστός as an epithet of God (14.1; 17.10).

74. Cf. my 'Pistis im Judentum', *ZNW* 64 (1973), pp. 19-38.

who believe in the Law, trust in the Law, or set their faith in the Law of God, all of which are possible renderings of πιστεύειν τῷ νόμῳ .

Both Paul and the *Psalms of Solomon* are concerned with the qualitative difference between sin and righteousness, both of them following a long Jewish tradition. For Paul it was Christ in whom sin and righteousness came together: 'For our sake he made him to be sin who knew no sin, so that in him we might become the righteousness of God' (2 Cor. 5.21). So this fundamental and decisive difference of sin and righteousness is annulled in Christ, Christ's death according to Rom. 3.24-26 being the atonement for sins and at the same time the manifestation of God's righteousness, 'that he himself is righteous and that he justifies him who has faith in Jesus' (3.26).

Throughout his letters we find that Paul's christology is always one that annuls fundamental contrasts such as life and death,[75] freedom and slavery,[76] rich and poor,[77] spirit and flesh,[78] heaven and earth,[79] God and humanity.[80] We need differentiations of that kind to know who we are and where we are, but for Paul Christ is the reconciliation of such contrasts. This, however, is not only a question of pure theology, but also one of sociology, and therefore I cannot accept that theology and sociology are alternatives:[81] 'There is neither Jew nor Greek, neither slave nor free, neither male nor female...If you belong to Christ, then you are Abraham's seed, heirs according to promise' (Gal. 3.28-29). By this, Paul radicalizes what is said in the *Psalms of Solomon* about the righteous ones who trust upon belonging to Abraham's seed and trust upon being heirs of the promises.[82]

If ever we want to look back on Paul's past, the *Psalms of Solomon* can show us some of his presuppositions, can show us options he had and can lead us to the questions he raised not only in discussions with his Jewish fellows and his Jewish-Christian opponents, but which he even raised as his own questions. He had been a Pharisee before, perhaps already then a radical Pharisee. When he got to know Christ, 'the end of

75. Gal. 2.19-20.
76. Phil. 2.7.
77. 2 Cor. 8.9.
78. Rom. 8.3-4.
79. Rom. 1.3-4.
80. Phil. 2.6-7.
81. An again (see n. 7) unsatisfactory aside, this time to F. Watson, *Paul, Judaism and the Gentiles* (SNTSMS, 56; Cambridge: Cambridge University Press, 1986).
82. Cf. *Pss. Sol.* 9.9; 18.3.

the Law' as he says (Rom. 10.4), it was still the qualitative difference of sin and righteousness that structured not only his theology, but also the communities he founded: Jews and Greeks, slaves and free people, men and women sitting together at one table to remember the basis of their community, the death of the Messiah, 'Christ', which meant the annulment of the difference of sin and righteousness as it meant the annulment of other differences.

JSNT 24 (1985), pp. 3-23

ACTS AND THE PAULINE CORPUS RECONSIDERED

William O. Walker, Jr

Introduction

It is the 'nearly universal judgment' of contemporary New Testament scholarship, according to Werner Georg Kümmel, that the author of Acts did not know the letters of Paul.[1] The reasoning that supports this judgment is relatively simple and straightforward: If this author (hereafter to be referred to as 'Luke')[2] had known Paul's letters, he surely would have used them in the composition of his own narrative about Paul (Paul is, after all, the hero of the entire second half of Acts), or, at the very least, he would have given some indication that Paul wrote letters. There is very little, if any, evidence, however, that Luke did make use of the letters,[3] and, although he mentions and even 'quotes'

---

1.   W.G. Kümmel, *Introduction to the New Testament* (Nashville, New York: Abingdon Press, rev. edn, 1975), p. 186; cf. e.g. C.L. Mitton, *The Epistle to the Ephesians: Its Authorship, Origin and Purpose* (Oxford: Clarendon Press, 1951), p. 216: 'Those who have tried to demonstrate that the author of Acts was acquainted with Paul's epistles as a whole have failed to prove their case because of the almost complete absence of similarities of thought and phrase'; and his *The Formation of the Pauline Corpus of Letters* (London: Epworth Press, 1955), pp. 24-28.

2.   I very much doubt that Luke was the actual author, but I use the name simply for the sake of convenience.

3.   Luke fails to include a great deal of important information about Paul that, in the judgment of many, he surely would have included had he been aware of it: e.g. the episode involving the question of Titus' circumcision (Gal. 2.1-5), the confrontation with Cephas in Antioch (Gal. 2.11-14), the problems of the church in Corinth, Paul's catalogue of his own sufferings (2 Cor. 11.23-33), the story of Onesimus (Philemon), and Paul's reference to having 'fought with beasts at Ephesus' (1 Cor. 15.32); for other examples, see e.g. T. von Zahn, *Introduction to the New Testament* (Edinburgh: T. & T. Clark, 1909), III, pp. 119-21. Moreover, the portrayal of Paul in Acts, as

letters attributed to others,[4] nowhere does he so much as hint that Paul
ever wrote letters. It follows, therefore, that Luke cannot have known
Paul's letters. Such, apparently, has been the reasoning of most recent
scholarship.

This consensus, however, 'is a relatively recent conclusion, not shared
by earlier scholars'. Moreover, it appears to have emerged, 'with almost
no examination of the evidence', as part of a more general reaction
against the Tübingen school, which had simply assumed that Luke knew
the Pauline letters[5] and, indeed, 'that one of his strongest motives was to
contradict and neutralize them wherever they did not confirm his own
conception of early Christian solidarity and order'.[6] Noting this fact,
Morton S. Enslin proposed, in 1938, 'that a new and completely fresh
examination of this whole question be made', indicating, at the same
time, 'a few points that would appear to merit consideration in such a
study'.[7] Subsequently, John Knox took up the matter in a brief essay,[8]
Enslin contributed a second article on the subject, largely in response to
Knox's essay,[9] and C.K. Barrett entered the discussion.[10]

---

regards his thought, his activities, and his situation, is, in many respects, significantly
different from and even contradictory to the portrayal in Paul's own letters; on this
point, see e.g. E. Haenchen, *The Acts of the Apostles: A Commentary* (Philadelphia:
Westminster Press, 1971), pp. 112-16; and P. Vielhauer, 'On the "Paulinism" of
Acts', *Studies in Luke–Acts: Essays presented in honor of Paul Schubert* (ed.
L.E. Keck and J.L. Martyn; Nashville: Abingdon Press, 1966), pp. 33-50. Finally, in
the judgment of many, very few, if any, significant verbal parallels have been found
between Acts and the Pauline letters.

4.   Acts 15.23b-29; 23.26-30.
5.   M.S. Enslin, 'Once Again, Luke and Paul', *ZNW* 61 (1970), pp. 254-55; cf.
his '"Luke" and Paul', *JAOS* 58 (1938), pp. 81-82. Despite Enslin's assertion, there
were, as he acknowledged, at least two treatments of the evidence resulting in the
conclusion that Luke did know Paul's letters: A. Sabatier, 'L'auteur du livre des
Actes des Apôtres a-t-il connu et utilisé dans son récit les Epîtres de saint Paul?',
Bibliothèque de l'École des Hautes Études. Sciences religieuses 1 (1889), pp. 205-
29; and von Zahn, *Introduction to the New Testament*, III, pp. 118-26. More recently,
C.K. Barrett has suggested that Luke 'simply did not know' Paul's letters; see his
'Acts and the Pauline Corpus', *ExpTim* 78 (1976–77), pp. 2-5, esp. 4-5.
6.   J. Knox, 'Acts and the Pauline Letter Corpus', *Studies in Luke–Acts*, p. 281.
7.   Enslin, '"Luke" and Paul', p. 84 (81-91 for entire article).
8.   Knox, 'Acts and the Pauline Letter Corpus', pp. 279-87.
9.   Enslin, 'Once Again, Luke and Paul', pp. 253-71. It should be noted, at this
point, that this second article is essentially an expansion of the 1938 article, done

Thus far, at least to my knowledge, the 'new and completely fresh examination' of the matter, called for by Enslin, has not been made, nor is this the purpose of the present paper. What I intend is simply to summarize and evaluate the views of Enslin, Knox, and Barrett and, insofar as is possible at the present time, to advance the discussion somewhat by the introduction of some additional considerations.

Most of the debate (to the extent that the matter has been debated) has centered around three questions: (1) Did Luke know any of Paul's letters? (2) Did he make any use of these letters in the composition of his own work? (3) If he did know about the letters, and particularly if he made use of them, why did he fail to mention them or even to hint that Paul ever wrote letters?[11] Thus, my own discussion will be structured in terms of these three questions, although I shall reverse the order of the second and the third.

1. *Did Luke Know Paul's Letters?*

To the first question (Did Luke know any of the letters of Paul?), Enslin responded with an unequivocal affirmative: 'He may not have had copies of them, may not have had them, so to speak, open on the desk as he wrote, but that he had heard them, some at least, read in church services, and knew at least imperfectly their content appears to me inescapable'.[12] Enslin's conclusion, at this point, was based almost entirely upon what he regarded as the *a priori* improbability that an admirer of Paul, writing no earlier than the end of the first century[13] (at

primarily in the light of the intervening essay by Knox. Thus, much of the content of the two articles is identical.

10. Barrett, 'Acts and the Pauline Corpus', pp. 2-5.

11. Actually, the relevant questions are at least five in number: (1) Was Luke even aware that Paul wrote letters at all? (2) Was he aware of particular letters written by Paul? (3) Was he familiar with the contents of any or all of Paul's letters, and, if so, to what extent? (4) Did he have access to the actual text of any or all of the letters? (5) Did he make use of any or all of the letters (either their general contents or their actual text) in the composition of his own narrative? If the answer to even the first of these questions is affirmative, a sixth question then necessarily follows: (6) Why does Luke never so much as hint that Paul wrote letters?

12. Enslin, 'Once Again, Luke and Paul', p. 257; cf. '"Luke" and Paul', p. 84.

13. If Acts was written earlier, and particularly if it was written by an associate of Paul, it would be even less likely that the author would be unaware of Paul's activity as a letter-writer.

a time when other Paulinists certainly knew Paul's letters),[14] would have been ignorant of these letters. Speaking to the same point, Knox strongly agreed:

> ...this case is strong, indeed almost unanswerable...he must have known letters of Paul. How could he have escaped knowing them? I agree with Enslin that it is all but incredible that such a man as Luke, writing in any one of the later decades of the first century about Paul and his career, should have been 'totally unaware that this hero of his had ever written letters' and quite as hard to believe that he would have found it impossible, or even difficult, to get access to these letters if he had wanted to.[15]

In the past, various scholars had anticipated and challenged this type of *a priori* argument,[16] but the strongest and most plausible dissent, to date, has come from Barrett, who suggested five points 'not as a conclusive answer to the question—it may prove to be one to which no final answer is possible—but as possibly worthy of consideration and further discussion':[17] (1) At the time when Acts was written, the letters of Paul were not yet regarded as 'canon', some of them had certainly been lost (in some cases, perhaps, only temporarily), and some of them may have been intentionally suppressed because of 'remarks that were uncomplimentary' to particular individuals or groups. (2) Inasmuch as 'it scarcely shows any traces of the development of Frühkatholizismus, as this term is commonly understood',[18] Acts may well have been written earlier than is sometimes supposed, perhaps earlier even than any of the pseudo-Pauline writings (and, by implication, before Paul's letters became widely known). (3) It is highly unlikely that the author of Acts knew Paul personally; thus he cannot be assumed to have had personal knowledge regarding Paul's letters. (4) The so-called 'We Document', which is to be regarded as a simple itinerary rather than a journal, probably would not have made reference to letters of Paul. (5) Luke apparently reconstructed his story of Paul almost entirely upon the basis of this 'We Document' and 'traces that he could not overlook' (i.e.

14. This point, not specifically noted by Enslin, was made by Barrett ('Acts and the Pauline Corpus', p. 2).

15. Knox, 'Acts and the Pauline Letter Corpus', pp. 282-83.

16. For summaries and responses, see, e.g., Enslin, '"Luke" and Paul', pp. 83-84; 'Once Again, Luke and Paul', pp. 253-54, 256-57; and Knox, 'Acts and the Pauline Letter Corpus', p. 283.

17. Barrett, 'Acts and the Pauline Corpus', p. 4.

18. Barrett, 'Acts and the Pauline Corpus', p. 4.

'local recollections') of Paul, discovered 'again and again' by him in the course of 'his travels and study of the mission field'; thus, it is Luke's own 'non-Pauline (but not anti-Pauline)' theology, not that of Paul himself, that finds expression in the book of Acts (the implication being that this would be unlikely if Luke had actually known Paul's letters).[19]

Barrett's points are, to be sure, interesting and suggestive, but, in my own judgment, they are not finally convincing. In particular, if Luke did, as Barrett suggests, 'again and again' discover 'traces' of Paul, he almost certainly would have learned that Paul wrote letters, he very likely would have encountered at least some of these letters, and he might reasonably be expected to have looked for others. Thus, it is my conclusion that Enslin and Knox are correct as regards this first question: Luke surely knew, in some sense, at least some of the letters of Paul.[20] At this point, however, it would be premature to raise the further question of just how well or in what way he knew them; this can only be dealt with in connection with the later question, whether he made any use of the letters in the composition of his own narrative.[21]

2. Why Did Luke Not Mention Paul's Letters?

Regarding the second question (Why, if he knew them, did Luke not mention Paul's letters or, at least, the fact that Paul wrote letters?),[22] there is a basic agreement between Enslin and Knox, although it is Enslin who has dealt most comprehensively with the matter. Enslin suggested three lines of approach to the question:[23] (1) Inasmuch as Paul's letters contain very little narrative material, consisting primarily of 'reproofs, corrections, and long-winded theological arguments' which Luke perhaps failed to understand, there is little in these letters that

19. Barrett, 'Acts and the Pauline Corpus', pp. 4-5.

20. Barrett ('Acts and the Pauline Corpus', pp. 2-3) acknowledges that 'there appears to be a growing tendency' to accept this view, citing, as examples, the following: G. Klein, *Die zwölf Apostel: Ursprung und Gehalt einer Idee* (FRLANT, 59; Göttingen: Vandenhoeck & Ruprecht, 1961), p. 191; and C. Burchard, *Der dreizehnte Zeuge: Traditions- und kompositionsgeschichtliche Untersuchungen zu Lukas' Darstellung der Frühzeit des Paulus* (FRLANT, 103; Göttingen: Vandenhoeck & Ruprecht, 1970), p. 157.

21. See the first two paragraphs of my 'Conclusion', below.

22. This question becomes even more pressing, of course, if it is concluded that Luke not only knew but also used Paul's letters.

23. Enslin, 'Once Again, Luke and Paul', pp. 268-71.

would lend itself to direct use by the author of a narrative such as Acts. Rather, Luke, as a 'creative writer', apparently 'preferred to write his own story, utilizing as suggestions hints which he chose to write up, not to copy'.[24] Thus, there was no real reason, Enslin implied, for Luke to mention Paul's letters, because his purpose was quite different from that of the letters and he used them only indirectly and sparingly. (2) 'One of the most evident qualities of Acts is the attempt to tone down or omit mentions of clashes between Christian groups'.[25] It is not surprising, therefore, that Luke would not wish to call attention to such episodes as Paul's controversy with the church in Corinth and the collection for Jerusalem (which, according to Enslin, 'failed lamentably to accomplish what Paul had hoped that it would' and, indeed, was regarded by the Jerusalem Christians as an attempt by Paul to 'buy his way' into the inner circle), both of which figure prominently in Paul's correspondence. Even so much as a reference to the letters, it was implied, might well remind readers of such episodes or send them to the letters, where they would learn of the episodes. In short, Luke would not wish to call attention to Paul's letters because his own picture of early Christian history is so different from that implied in the letters. Thus, there may well have been a very positive reason for not mentioning the letters. (3) A strong case can be made, as Knox had suggested earlier,[26] that one of the principal reasons for the writing of Acts, with Paul as its chief character, was that Paul's letters had been 'appropriated' by 'pre-Marcionite, perhaps even Marcionite, Christians', who threatened 'to take exclusive possession of Paul himself as "the Apostle"'. Thus, it was implied, Luke would wish, on the one hand, to avoid reference to Paul's letters, which, in his

24. Enslin, 'Once Again, Luke and Paul', pp. 268-69.

25. Enslin, 'Once Again, Luke and Paul', p. 269; cf. 269-70. See also, e.g., C.H. Talbert, *Luke and the Gnostics: An Examination of the Lucan Purpose* (Nashville: Abingdon Press, 1966), p. 88: 'The author of Acts wanted to portray the church of the apostolic age as free from internal conflicts, possessing an inner unity. Because of this overall aim in Acts, the author omitted any reference to Paul's controversies in Galatia, in Corinth, in Philippi, and in Colossae. Moreover, it is almost certainly for the same reason that there is no reference in Acts to Paul as a letter writer. To have referred to Paul's letters to Corinth or Colossae would have necessitated a reference to the controversies out of which the letters sprang and to the solution of which they were directed...This silence is a part of Luke's purpose. It is part of his overall aim to idealize the apostolic age, portraying it as a period of almost absolute inner unity.'

26. Knox, 'Acts and the Pauline Letter Corpus', pp. 284-86.

view lent themselves to misunderstanding and misuse,[27] but he would also be eager, on the other hand, to re-present the great apostle, whose reputation and stature were such that he could not be overlooked or belittled, in a light more congenial and sympathetic to the emerging concerns of Christian 'orthodoxy'. Here, then, would be a second reason for not mentioning the letters of Paul.

Again, Barrett, while acknowledging that there is much truth in Enslin's arguments, has attempted to show that these arguments are not finally persuasive.[28] Barrett maintained, in the first place, that a great deal of material in Paul's letters would not have been at all problematic for Luke and that he, if he had known the letters, could have used such material, simply omitting any reference to the more controversial aspects. It would not have been necessary for him to ignore the entire corpus of letters. The problem, however, is that any direct use of or explicit reference to the letters at all might have served to call attention to the letters and thus to matters that, in the view of Luke, would better be left to sink into obscurity. In the second place, Barrett, quoting Philipp Vielhauer, suggested that it would be 'an undertaking as hopeless as it is improbable' to 'attempt to discredit Paul's letters by setting Paul himself in high esteem'.[29] Here, too, however, Barrett appears to have missed the real thrust of Enslin's argument. Luke is not attempting to 'discredit' Paul's letters; rather, he is seeking to 'rehabilitate' Paul as a spokesman for and a champion of 'orthodox' Christianity. In order to do this, he must direct attention away from Paul's letters, with their often controversial and problematic contents, in the direction of the apostle's activities as missionary and martyr. He is, in fact, attempting to build up the reputation of Paul for Christians who are suspicious of his theology and ethics, but he does this, not by 'discrediting' Paul's letters, but rather by setting Paul (and his letters insofar as they are known) within the larger context of early Christian history and faith, as he understands them, where Paul (and the letters) can be seen, not in isolation, but as an integral expression of apostolic Christianity.[30] In the

27. See, e.g., 2 Pet. 3.15b-17.

28. Barrett, 'Acts and the Pauline Corpus', pp. 3-4.

29. Barrett, 'Acts and the Pauline Corpus', pp. 3-4; cf. P. Vielhauer, *Geschichte der urchristlichen Literatur: Einleitung in das Neue Testament, die Apokryphen und die Apostolischen Väter* (Berlin: de Gruyter, 1975), p. 407.

30. I am even tempted, at times, to suggest that it was Luke (not the author of Ephesians, as E.J. Goodspeed and others have held) who 'published' the first

final analysis, therefore, it cannot be said that Barrett has successfully refuted Enslin on the matter of why Luke fails to mention Paul's letters. Enslin's arguments are, at the very least, highly plausible: There was no real need or reason for Luke to mention the letters of Paul, and he apparently had very strong reasons for choosing not to mention them.[31]

3. *Did Luke Make Use of Paul's Letters?*

Thus far, I have indicated my own basic agreement with Enslin and Knox, as over against Barrett, so far as the first two questions are concerned: I believe that Luke did know the letters of Paul, some of them at least, and that it is possible to show, with a high degree of plausibility, why he chose not to mention these letters. The crucial question, however, is whether Luke made any use of the Pauline letters in his own composition. If it can be shown that he did, then it necessarily follows that he must have known the letters, even if no satisfactory answer could be given as to why he never mentioned them. If, on the other hand, it cannot be shown that Luke used the letters, then any discussion of the other two questions necessarily remains highly speculative and inconclusive.

Before considering the third question, however, attention must be called to what Knox has termed 'the hidden major premise' in most discussions of the matter, namely: 'If Luke knew the letters of Paul, he

collection of Paul's letters and that he intended Acts (and perhaps his Gospel as well) as the 'introduction' to this collection—an 'introduction', that is, that would set the letters in the proper context.

31. The apparently liberal use of Paul's letters in the almost certainly pseudonymous Pastoral Letters, written to combat certain 'heretical' teachings perhaps promoted in the name of Paul, might be taken as evidence against such an attempt to 'rehabilitate' Paul without mention or overt use of the letters. The following points must, however, be noted: (1) Different writers may operate quite differently, even when dealing with essentially the same problem. (2) We do not know enough about the situation faced either by Luke or by the author of the Pastorals to say just how similar their situations (or purposes) were. (3) Even the Pastorals make no direct *mention* of the authentic Pauline letters. (4) Someone writing a *letter* in Paul's name would understandably seek to pattern the letter after other letters known or believed to have been written by Paul; such would not necessarily be the case, however, with someone writing a *narrative* about Paul, particularly if the principal motivation for writing the narrative was to put to rest certain apprehensions about Paul that could find support in the letters, by directing attention away from the letters or at least setting them in the 'proper' context.

must have used them'. Here, two distinct but related questions are confused: (1) Did Luke *know* Paul's letters? and (2) Did Luke *use* Paul's letters? As Knox insisted, the possibility must at least be kept open that Luke 'knew, or at least knew of, letters of Paul—even *the* (collected) letters of Paul—and quite consciously and deliberately made little or no use of them'.[32] Knox, in fact, argued that this apparently was the case: Luke knew but chose not to use the letters of Paul. Thus, the question of Luke's use of the Pauline letters must be considered separately from that of his knowledge of the letters.[33]

Enslin, in dealing with the question, whether Luke made any use of the letters of Paul, acknowledged that 'the evidence is very fragmentary' and scarcely conclusive but maintained, nevertheless, that there are 'a few cases which appear...easier of explanation on the assumption that Luke not only did know but made occasional use of at least some of these letters'.[34] Noting that 'many other passages would have to be considered in a complete study', he cited eleven points, which, he asserted, were 'chosen as examples, not as an all-inclusive list':[35] (1) Paul's missionary travels, as set forth in Acts, carry him to precisely those places, and only those places, to which we have Pauline letters or which could easily be inferred from references in these letters. (2) The perplexing statement in Luke 24.34, 'The Lord is risen indeed, and hath appeared

32. Knox, 'Acts and the Pauline Letter Corpus', p. 284.

33. If Luke did not know the letters of Paul, then, of course, the question of his use of them becomes meaningless.

34. Enslin, 'Once Again, Luke and Paul', p. 257. Indeed, in a slightly later work (*Reapproaching Paul* [Philadelphia: Westminster Press, 1972], pp. 26-27), Enslin went further: 'In my judgment Luke used them [Paul's letters] very fully. Back of almost every incident he paints is a statement or basis for inference in one or more of the letters quite sufficient for a writer who was an author, not a copyist or restricted editor...far from being unknown or unused, the letters of Paul...appear to have been the principal source used by Luke in reconstructing the activities of the man who brought to reality the Gentile mission.'

35. Enslin, 'Once Again, Luke and Paul', p. 267; cf. '"Luke" and Paul', p. 90. The eleventh point is not actually numbered in Enslin's articles, but it might well have been. As other possible examples, he mentioned the reference to Paul and Barnabas as 'apostles' (Acts 14.4, 14; cf. 1 Cor. 9.6) and the insistence that only those who have seen the Lord are eligible to be apostles (Acts 1.21; cf. 1 Cor. 9.1). An additional possible example, not mentioned by Enslin, is Paul's statement, before leaving Ephesus, that, after visits to Macedonia and Achaia, he intends to go to Jerusalem and then to Rome (Acts 19.21; cf. similar indications in the Corinthian correspondence and in Romans); see Knox, 'Acts and the Pauline Letter Corpus', pp. 281-82.

to Simon', which has no corresponding narrative, is best explained as based upon Paul's catalogue of resurrection appearances in 1 Cor. 15.5.[36] (3) The idea that Jesus was seen 'for many days' (Acts 13.31), that is, for forty days (Acts 1.3), after his resurrection, representing, as it does, a revision of Luke's earlier notion that the ascension occurred shortly after the resurrection (Lk. 24.50-53), is best understood as based upon Paul's repeated 'then...then...then' in his catalogue of resurrection appearances (1 Cor. 15.5-7). (4) There are several striking verbal similarities between Acts (or the Gospel according to Luke) and Paul's letters, coupled, in some instances, with remarkable parallels in concept, that suggest dependence of the former upon the latter.[37] (5) A strong case can be made that the report of Paul's escape from Damascus 'through' the wall (Acts 9.23-25) represents Luke's modification of Paul's own reference to the same occurrence (2 Cor. 11.32-33). (6) The several differences between Acts 15.1-29 and Gal. 2.1-10 (accounts of the so-called 'Jerusalem Conference')[38] are most easily explained by assuming that Luke has altered Paul's material in order to soften or eliminate the references to internal dissension among Christians. (7) The references to Paul having studied at the feet of Gamaliel (Acts 22.3), his involvement in the stoning of Stephen (Acts 7.58; 8.1), and his trip to Damascus (Acts 9.1-2) may well have been suggested by comments in Paul's own letters regarding his Pharisaic background, his zeal for the law, his persecution of Christians, and his conversion in or near Damascus (Phil. 3.5-6; Gal. 1.13-14, 17). (8) Various obscurities in the brief account of Paul's eighteen months in Corinth (Acts 18.1-17) are easily explainable on the assumption that the source for the account is Paul's own letter to the Corinthians (i.e. 1 Corinthians), and virtually all of the details in this passage could be inferred from the letter. (9) It is at least possible that the reversal of the order of the cup and the bread in Lk. 22.17-19a is based upon the same order in 1 Cor. 10.16, 21 (this order occurs elsewhere only at *Did.* 9.1-5). (10) The reference to Paul's

---

36. Enslin assumed, of course, as do I, that the same author wrote Luke and Acts.

37. For a discussion of these, together with other examples, see below.

38. Whether the gathering described in Acts 15.1-29 and that reported in Gal. 2.1-10 are the same continues to be matter of some debate among scholars; for a commentary based upon the assumption that they are the same, see e.g. Haenchen, *The Acts of the Apostles*, pp. 440-72; cf. also, e.g., K. Lake 'Note XVI. The Apostolic Council of Jerusalem', *The Beginnings of Christianity* (ed. F.J. Foakes Jackson, K. Lake and H.J. Cadbury; London: Macmillan, 1920–33), I/5, pp. 191-212.

last-minute change in plans regarding his route from Corinth to Jerusalem (Acts 20.3) may well have been prompted by an inexact recollection of Paul's words in 2 Cor. 1.15–2.12 and Rom. 15.31. (11) So far as the sometimes-noted argument from silence is concerned (Why, if he knew the letters of Paul, would Luke have omitted such items as Paul's catalogue of sufferings [2 Cor. 11.23-33], the story of Onesimus [Philemon], or Paul's reference to having 'fought with beasts at Ephesus' [1 Cor. 15.32]?), there may, in fact, be reminiscences or suggestions of some of these items in Acts,[39] and, 'after all, authors can omit what they do not want or what they feel unable to use for lack of space'.[40] In short, it was the contention of Enslin, although he acknowledged that he saw no way of proving it, that Luke did make use of the letters of Paul in reconstructing his own narrative about Paul.

Responding to Enslin, Knox asserted 'that the effort to demonstrate Luke's use of Paul with actual evidence fails, as all efforts to do this have previously failed, because every instance of his alleged dependence on the letters can be explained almost, if not quite, as plausibly by the hypothesis of his access to some independent tradition'.[41] Indeed, according to Knox, while it cannot be demonstrated that Luke did not use Paul's letters, 'so long as only a meager use is claimed', neither 'can one demonstrate that he did'.[42] The most interesting and potentially damaging aspect of Knox's critique, however, is his suggestion that 'the absence of adequate evidence of *verbal* dependence' may actually have the effect of reversing Enslin's argument, for, in effect, Enslin has asked one to believe 'that Luke used the letters of Paul as sources for *facts* or *data* but succeeded in avoiding...any trace of their actual language'. Thus, Knox concluded, in the absence of verbal parallels, 'every possible piece of evidence of Luke's having used the letters increases the probability that he did not use them'.[43]

In reply to Knox, five general points are to be noted; then some

39. See Enslin, 'Once Again, Luke and Paul', pp. 267-68, for the suggestions (1) that Luke did, in fact, make 'a very fair epitome' of Paul's catalogue of sufferings 'in his catena of trials and hardships encountered by his hero' and (2) that Luke understood Paul's reference to having 'fought with beasts at Ephesus' as 'a figurative reference to Paul's clash with the infuriated Ephesian mob'. Cf. '"Luke" and Paul', pp. 90-91.

40. Enslin, 'Once Again, Luke and Paul', p. 267; cf. '"Luke" and Paul', p. 90.

41. Knox, 'Acts and the Pauline Letters Corpus', p. 281.

42. Knox, 'Acts and the Pauline Letters Corpus', p. 284.

43. Knox, 'Acts and the Pauline Letters Corpus', p. 282.

additional evidence will be cited to support Enslin's contention that
Luke did not make use of Paul's letters; finally, specific attention will be
devoted to Knox's suggestion regarding the absence of verbal parallels
between Acts and the letters of Paul. The first general point is that, while
it may appear unlikely that an author would make use of a source for
facts or data and yet avoid any trace of this source's actual language,
this can by no means be accepted as an absolute principle of literary
criticism. An author may, for whatever reason, simply prefer a vocabulary more compatible with his/her own style, situation, or purpose, or
she/he may also be using another source or sources whose vocabulary is
viewed as more suitable. The second general point is that any
'independent tradition' used by Luke that would account adequately for
the various similarities between Acts and Paul's letters would, itself,
almost necessarily be dependent, at least to some extent, upon these
letters. Thus, Luke would still be at least *indirectly* dependent upon the
letters of Paul. The third general point is that, as Knox himself apparently recognized, the hypothesis of an independent tradition explains the
instances of alleged dependence upon the letters 'almost, if not quite, as
plausibly' as the hypothesis that Luke actually used the letters; in other
words, the latter hypothesis would appear, on the face of it, somewhat
stronger, all other beings being equal. The fourth general point, worthy,
at least, of consideration, is that an application of 'Ockham's razor' to
this matter would require a serious attempt to account for the similarities
between Acts and Paul's letters without appealing to unknown, hypothetical sources, allowing for the introduction of such sources only if the
matter could not be adequately resolved otherwise.[44] The fifth general
point is that it would be virtually impossible for any author who is
familiar with materials directly related to the subject matter of his/her
own composition not to make at least some use of these materials, either
directly or indirectly, intentionally or unintentionally, consciously or
unconsciously, in her/his own work. Even if such an author intends to

44. For a similar argument regarding, e.g., the Synoptic Problem, see
R.M. Frye, 'The Synoptic Problem and Analogies in Other Literatures', in *The
Relationships among the Gospels: An Interdisciplinary Dialogue* (ed. W.O. Walker,
Jr; Trinity University Monograph Series in Religion, 5; San Antonio: Trinity
University Press, 1978), pp. 285-86; cf. W.R. Farmer, *The Synoptic Problem: A
Critical Analysis* (New York: Macmillan; London: Collier-Macmillan, 1964), p. 209.
For a critique of the application of 'Ockham's razor' to such literary-historical
problems, see J.B. Tyson, 'Literary Criticism and the Gospels: The Seminar', in *The
Relationships among the Gospels*, pp. 325-27.

WALKER *Acts and the Pauline Corpus Reconsidered*   67

correct these materials, is writing in direct opposition to them, or wishes to conceal the very fact of their existence, they remain in his/her mind and influence both what she/he says and how it is said. Thus, if Luke knew the letters of Paul, as both Enslin and Knox agree that he did, he almost inevitably would have made some use of them (perhaps even unintentionally and unconsciously) in the writing of Acts.

So far as additional evidence supporting Enslin's contention that Luke used Paul's letters is concerned, two points can be noted. The first is this: As I have argued elsewhere, a rather strong case can be made that the account of the circumcision of Timothy in Acts 16.1-3 represents an altered version of Paul's reference to the question of the circumcision of Titus in Gal. 2.3-5. This case is based upon, among others, the following considerations: (1) Titus, who figures rather prominently in two of Paul's letters, is never mentioned in Acts. (2) Luke almost certainly would have known at least something about Titus. (3) There appear to be good reasons why Luke might have avoided mentioning Titus in his account of the early church. (4) The major differences between Gal. 2.3-5 and Acts 16.1-3 can all be accounted for on the basis of the general 'tendencies' of Luke. (5) There are such significant verbal, structural, and substantive similarities between Gal. 2.3-5 and Acts 16.1-3 as to suggest some type of literary relationship between the two passages.[45] The second point, then, is this: It can plausibly be argued, not only that the account of the so-called Jerusalem Conference in Acts 15 depends on Paul's reference to the same gathering in Galatians 2,[46] but also that, at least to some extent, the account in Acts is intended to correct impressions that might be conveyed by Paul's material.[47] For example, Paul claims that *he* has 'been entrusted with the gospel to the uncir-cumcised' and Peter with that 'to the circumcised' (Gal. 2.7-9), while in Acts, Peter claims it as God's choice that by *his* mouth 'the Gentiles should hear the word of the gospel and believe' (Acts 15.7). In the same context, *Paul* insists that 'God shows no partiality' (Gal. 2.6), while, in

45. W.O. Walker, Jr, 'The Timothy-Titus Problem Reconsidered', *ExpTim* 92 (1980–81), pp. 231-35.

46. See n. 38 above.

47. Cf., however, Knox, 'Acts and the Pauline Letter Corpus', p. 282: 'Actually, it would be more accurate to say that Galatians is correcting Acts—not Acts itself, of course, but that understanding of Paul's relation to the Jerusalem apostolate which happens to reach us in Acts but which was obviously prevalent in Paul's own time (since he is concerned in Galatians to deny its truth) and which undoubtedly left its traces in records to which Luke a generation or so later had access'.

Acts, it is *Peter* who asserts that God 'made no distinction between us and them' (Acts 15.9). Moreover, a few verses later, Paul claims that *he* accused Peter of seeking to 'compel the Gentiles to live like Jews', even though he, Peter, being a Jew, lived 'like a Gentile and not like a Jew' (Gal. 2.14), while in Acts, it is *Peter* who accuses others of 'putting a yoke upon the neck of the disciples which neither our fathers nor we have been able to bear' (Acts 15.10). Furthermore, in Galatians, it is *Paul* who insists, 'We...know that a man is not justified by works of the law but through faith in Jesus Christ' (Gal. 2.16), while, in Acts, it is *Peter* who says, 'But we believe that we shall be saved through the grace of the Lord Jesus, just as they will' (Acts 15.11). In short, Luke has Peter 'utter the same opinions about law and gospel as Paul, according to the epistle, expressed in Antioch'.[48] This is particularly remarkable in light of the fact that, in Galatians, it is precisely Peter to whom or about whom these views are expressed. Finally, where Paul has spoken of 'certain men' (τινας) who came from (ἀπό) James and created dissension in Antioch (Gal. 2.12), Acts refers to 'certain men' (τινες) who came from (ἀπό) Judea for the same purpose, thus eliminating Paul's clear implication that there was dissension within the leadership of the church (Acts 15.1). Thus, there are a number of indications that Luke's material in Acts 15 is, to some extent, based upon that of Paul in Galatians 2 and is intended, at least in part, to correct certain impressions that might otherwise be conveyed by the latter.

We move now to the question of verbal parallels. As was noted above, Knox was particularly impressed by what he took to be the absence of verbal parallels between Acts and the letters of Paul, regarding this as the most serious obstacle to any hypothesis that Luke actually made use of the letters in the composition of his own work. It is not really correct, however, as Knox suggested,[49] that the absence of verbal parallels is total. Enslin had already, in his first article on the subject, noted several instances of 'similarity of phrase', most striking of which is the use of the same rather unusual term, πορθεῖν, to describe Paul's activities in opposing the Christian movement (Gal. 1.13; Acts 9.21). Other examples included the somewhat unconventional idea, expressed in similar terminology in the two passages, that the law was given through the instrumentality of angels (Gal. 3.19-20; Acts 7.53), the phrase, ζηλωτὴς

48. K.H. von Weizsäcker, *The Apostolic Age of the Christian Church* (New York: Putnam, 1894–95), I, p. 211.
49. Knox, 'Acts and the Pauline Letter Corpus', p. 282.

ὑπάρχων (Gal. 1.14; Acts 22.3), the verbal similarity between Gal. 2.10 and Acts 11.30 (both apparently referring to the sending of aid), and certain similarities of vocabulary and concept between 1 Cor. 7.32-35 and Lk. 10.40-42 (both referring to the advantage of freedom from all 'cares' that would 'distract' attention from the Lord). In two of these instances (i.e. πορθεῖν and a word stem in 1 Cor. 7.32-35 and Lk. 10.40-42), the distinctive terminology occurs nowhere else in the New Testament.[50] In a different context, Enslin had also noted two verbal parallels in the reports of Paul's escape from Damascus (2 Cor. 11.33; Acts 9.25): both passages include the phrase, 'through the wall' (διὰ τοῦ τείχους), and both have a form of the verb χαλᾶν ('to let down') with the preposition 'in' (ἐν).[51]

In addition to these examples of verbal parallels already noted by Enslin, it can also be argued, again on the basis of striking verbal parallels, that, in at least two instances, the Lukan version of a saying of Jesus is dependent upon a Pauline saying.[52] For example, Mt. 5.44 has Jesus say, 'Love your enemies and pray for those who persecute you', while Lk. 6.27-28 has 'Love your enemies, do good to those who hate you, bless those who curse you, pray for those who abuse you' (there is no Markan parallel). The first clause in Luke's version is identical to that in Matthew's version, and Luke's final clause is similar to Matthew's second (final) clause. Luke's second and third clauses have no parallel in the Matthean version, but it is to be noted that the third clause ('bless those who curse you') has striking verbal similarities to Rom. 12.14 ('Bless those who persecute you: bless and do not curse them'), with the same word for 'bless' (εὐλογεῖν) and the same word for 'curse' (καταρᾶσθαι). (Elsewhere in the New Testament, εὐλογεῖν and καταρᾶσθαι are juxtaposed in this way only at Jas 3.9-10.) It is surely at least possible that Luke's third clause was suggested by Rom. 12.14. A second example is seen when Lk. 10.8b ('eat what is set before you'), missing from the Matthean parallel, is compared with 1 Cor. 10.27b ('eat whatever is set before you'), where the same word is used for 'eat' (ἐσθίειν) and the same word for 'set before' (παρατίθεναι) and, in both cases, παρατίθεναι is followed by ὑμῖν ('you'). Much more work needs to be done by way of comparing the Lukan version of

50. Enslin, '"Luke" and Paul', pp. 87-88; cf. 'Once Again, Luke and Paul', pp. 262-63.
51. Enslin, '"Luke" and Paul', pp. 88-89; 'Once Again, Luke and Paul', p. 263.
52. See n. 36 above.

dominical sayings with similar materials in the Pauline letters, and these two examples suggest that such work may prove extremely fruitful.[53]

On the basis, then, of the evidence cited by Enslin, the five general points noted above in response to Knox, the additional evidence brought in to support Enslin's view, and a number of specific verbal parallels between Luke–Acts and the letters of Paul, it is my own conclusion that Luke not only knew at least some of Paul's letters but also made some use of these letters in the composition of his own narrative.[54]

Conclusion

As I have already indicated, I am in basic agreement with Enslin, as over against Barrett and, to some extent, Knox, regarding the three questions at issue: Luke almost certainly knew, in some sense, at least some of the letters of Paul, he made some use of these letters in the writing of his own work, and there are plausible reasons why he, nevertheless, did not mention the letters or even indicate that Paul ever wrote letters. What now remains is to say something more about the nature and extent of Luke's knowledge and use of the letters, about his general purpose in writing Acts, and about specific ways in which his familiarity with the letters may have influenced the presentation in Acts.

I very much doubt that Luke had the text of Paul's letters before him

53. It could be argued, of course, that verbal parallels indicate, rather, Paul's knowledge of the Jesus tradition in its Lukan form, and, indeed, this is the usual approach; see, e.g., D.L. Dungan, *The Sayings of Jesus in the Churches of Paul: The Use of the Synoptic Tradition in the Regulation of Early Church Life* (Philadelphia: Fortress Press, 1971).

54. When speaking of the letters of Paul in this discussion, I have had in mind only those letters generally agreed to be authentically Pauline, namely, Romans, 1 and 2 Corinthians, Galatians, Philippians, 1 Thessalonians, and Philemon. C.L. Mitton, among others, has noted a special relation between Acts and Ephesians, suggesting that the author of Ephesians was familiar with Acts; see his *The Epistle to the Ephesians*, p. 220; and *The Formation of the Pauline Corpus of Letters*, pp. 27-28. For various theories regarding the relation between Acts and the Pastoral Letters, see, e.g., C.F.D. Moule, 'The Problem of the Pastoral Epistles: A Reappraisal', *BJRL* 47 (1964–65), pp. 430-52; A. Strobel, 'Schreiben des Lukas? Zum sprachlichen Problem der Pastoralbriefe', *NTS* 15 (1968–69), pp. 191-210; J.D. Quinn, 'The Last Volume of Luke: The Relation of Luke–Acts to the Pastoral Epistles', in *Perspectives on Luke–Acts* (ed. C.H. Talbert; Danville: Association of Baptist Professors of Religion/Edinburgh: T. & T. Clark, 1978), pp. 62-75; and S.G. Wilson, *Luke and the Pastoral Epistles* (London: SPCK, 1979).

as he wrote. He had read, or heard read, at least some of these letters, perhaps on numerous occasions, he was familiar with their basic content, and he had even absorbed some of their terminology. In writing his own work, it was almost inevitable that what he knew from the letters would influence what he wrote, even to the extent of affecting his vocabulary and the structuring of his materials. It may very well be that he was unaware of the extent to which he made use of the writings of Paul.

At certain points, however, it seems to me that he must have been writing in some sort of conscious dialogue with the letters (e.g. in his account of the Jerusalem Conference). At such points, I judge that he was not so much concerned to disagree with or to correct Paul as to reassure others who were inclined to reject the apostle because of his popularity among Christians whose 'orthodoxy' and perhaps morality were suspect. What Luke sought to do was to reclaim Paul for the main-stream of the Christian movement, by showing that Paul did, in fact, stand in the same apostolic tradition as Peter, James, and John (a point that Paul, himself, had somewhat contentiously attempted to make in his own letters) and that he, like they, also stood in the same tradition as did authentic Judaism. Paul, in other words, despite appearances to the contrary, was neither a Marcionite, a Gnostic, nor any other type of 'maverick'. In his own mind, Luke no doubt believed that he was, in a sense, rescuing Paul from himself (that is, from some of the hasty and provocative *ad hoc* statements in his letters) and from those who would mis-use Paul in the service of their own 'heresies' and 'lawlessness'.[55] To the success of this endeavor, the acceptance of Paul's letters into the canon of Christian scripture and the long-standing regard for Paul as apostle *par excellence* bear eloquent testimony. With Acts as an 'introduction', Paul's letters could become truly 'catholic', without such an introduction, they might well have remained purely 'sectarian'. When read with Acts as a 'preface', Paul's letters can be seen as 'orthodox'; standing alone, they risk the charge of 'heresy', or, at least, eccentricity.

It is not enough, however, merely to see Acts as providing the proper context in which the Pauline letters are to be read and understood. If Enslin is correct, as I believe him to be, regarding Luke's knowledge and use of the letters, then the influence of the letters on the narrative of

55. This is not necessarily to imply that Acts was written as late as the middle of the second century, although this can by no means be ruled out. There were certainly 'proto-Gnostic' and 'pre-Marcionite' tendencies within the Christian movement before the end of the first century.

Acts can be seen in various ways and at different levels. At one level, it appears simply in more-or-less unconscious echoes of Pauline terminology and thought: for example, the use of πορθεῖν in Acts 9.21 to describe Paul's activities in opposing the Christian movement (cf. Gal. 1.13) or the notion in Acts 7.23 of the law being given through the instrumentality of angels (cf. Gal. 3.19-20). At a more substantive level, it would determine the actual content of the story in Acts, particularly if, as Enslin suggests, the letters of Paul constitute 'the principal source used by Luke in reconstructing the activities of the man who brought to reality the Gentile mission'.[56] Examples here might include the account in Acts 9.23-25 of Paul escaping from Damascus in a basket (cf. 2 Cor. 11.32 33) and perhaps even the itineraries of Paul's various journeys in Acts. (This content would be somewhat modified, of course, to reflect Luke's own particular interests and concerns in writing his narrative.)

At the deepest level, however, the influence of the letters is to be seen in a strangely paradoxical way. As has already been noted, Paul strongly suggests in his letters that he is the real leader (and perhaps even the founder) of the Gentile mission (e.g. Gal. 2.6-9). He also insists that he is to be regarded as an 'apostle' (e.g. Gal. 1.1; Rom. 1.1-6). Furthermore, at least in Galatians and Romans, the doctrine of 'justification through faith' is an essential feature of Paul's gospel. In Acts, however, as has also been noted, it is Peter who is the real founder of the Gentile mission and the chief spokesman for the doctrine of justification through faith (although in a somewhat muted form); furthermore, except at Acts 14.4, 14, Luke never refers to Paul as an 'apostle'. Thus, it would appear that, while the Pauline letters have, at certain points, influenced the language and thought of Acts, as well as some of its actual content, this influence does not extend to the basic features of the Pauline message. In short, the external course of events in Acts may well reflect the influence of the letters of Paul, but apparently not the portrayal of Paul's theology and message; here, the influence seems to disappear. Such a conclusion is premature, however, for Luke does refer to Paul as an 'apostle' in the one passage already cited, thus indicating his familiarity with the notion, and he does, at one point (Acts 13.39), betray his awareness of the doctrine of justification through faith and, indeed, associate this doctrine with Paul. It is far from clear, from this passage, that Luke really understands the doctrine, and it is evident that the doctrine holds little real

56. See n. 34 above.

interest for him.[57] Nevertheless, there are clear, though distorted echoes of Galatians and Romans in the passage. Luke is aware of Paul's doctrine of justification through faith. What is significant, however, is the fact that, according to Acts, it is Peter, not Paul, who first gives practical expression to this doctrine in the conversion of the Gentile, Cornelius (Acts 10.1–11.18), and it is Peter who alone articulates the doctrine (although in diluted form) at the Jerusalem Conference—indeed, in language strikingly reminiscent of Paul's own language in Gal. 2.7-9, 14-16 (Acts 15.7-11), and this despite the fact that Paul portrays Peter as precisely the one who fails to understand fully and follow the implications of the doctrine (Gal. 2.11-14).

At this point, then, it might appear that the purpose of Luke here is to 'rehabilitate' Peter as a champion of the Gentile mission and of freedom from the law. Shortly after the conversion of Cornelius, however, Peter simply disappears from the narrative of Acts (12.17b: 'Then he departed and went to another place'), to reappear only for a moment at the Jerusalem Conference, where he emphasizes his own pioneering role as apostle to the Gentiles and endorses the work of Paul (Acts 15.7-11). It

---

57. The verse reads in the RSV: 'and by him every one that believes is freed from everything from which you could not be freed by the law of Moses'. The NEB has: 'It is through him that everyone who has faith is acquitted of everything for which there was no acquittal under the Law of Moses'. The Greek word translated as 'freed' in the RSV and as 'acquitted/acquittal' in the NEB is the passive of *dikaioun*, normally meaning 'to justify' (as it is, indeed, translated, in the KJV). Ernst Haenchen observes that the verse is 'evidently intended to reproduce Pauline theology', noting that 'Luke's contemporaries were still aware that Paul had preached "justification through faith"' (*The Acts of the Apostles*, p. 412). Cf. also F.J. Foakes Jackson and K. Lake, *The Beginnings of Christianity*, I/4, p. 157:

> Critics advocate two interpretations: (i) the ᾧ οὐκ ἠδυνήθητε etc. means that by the Law of Moses acquittal of some things was possible, but not of others, and Paul was announcing this possible method of going beyond what the Law could do; (ii) ὧν etc. merely qualify πάντων, "forgiveness for everything—which the Law never offered". The former view is possible, but the latter seems more natural. Nor can I resist the belief that this verse is an attempt to express Pauline doctrine. Whatever hypothesis be adopted, it is incredible that the author of Acts was ignorant of the main outlines of Paul's teaching, and it was surely a part of his message that salvation is open to everyone who believes, in a way which was not given by the Law, even though he may have been unfair to Judaism in so presenting it.

Particularly if the second interpretation suggested by Jackson and Lake is followed, the verse clearly echoes authentic Pauline theology as seen in Galatians and Romans (see, e.g., Gal. 2.16; 3.11, 21; Rom. 3.20). In either case, as both Haenchen and Jackson/Lake observe, it is intended to 'reproduce' or 'express' Pauline thought.

is clear, therefore, that the real object of Luke's interest is not Peter but rather Paul, who, for the remainder of the narrative, is the principal character. Indeed, it could even be said that, for Luke, Peter (like Stephen) serves as a kind of 'forerunner' for Paul. Thus, Paul is seen not as an innovator and certainly not as a rebel (as might be suggested by some passages in the letters), but rather as the legitimate successor of Peter as missionary to the Gentiles. Paul belongs to the 'church' (founded by Peter and the other apostles), not to some heretical or schismatic faction.

In short, the primary influence of Pauline theology as reflected in the letters is to be seen, not in Luke's portrayal of Paul's message, but rather in his portrayal of Peter's message and activity. Pauline language and ideas are placed on the lips of Peter, not (except at Acts 13.39) on the lips of Paul. This is done, however, for the sake of Paul. One can only surmise that Luke (like many others, both then and since) poorly understood and little appreciated Paul's doctrine of justification through faith, but he had great respect for Paul's activities as missionary to the Gentiles. The association of the doctrine, however, was too well known (from the letters?) to be denied or completely ignored, as was its relation to the Gentile mission. Unable, then, to deny or ignore the fact that Paul had preached justification through faith, the next best expedient for Luke was to attribute the doctrine (in muted form) initially and primarily to the one great rival of Paul for preeminence in the church, namely, Peter, thus making it impossible to reject Paul because of his espousal of the doctrine without, at the same time, rejecting Peter for the same reason. Similarly, by portraying Peter as the real founder of the Gentile mission, Luke set the missionary activities of Paul in the larger context of the primitive apostolic mission, thus legitimizing both the work of Paul and the churches founded by him. Finally, by virtually ignoring Paul's claim to apostleship, Luke emphasized the continuity and concord that, in his view, marked (or should have marked) the progress of the Christian movement in the apostolic age. The achievement of Luke was, indeed, remarkable: he succeeded in painting a picture of early Christianity that survived until the rise of modern critical scholarship.

PAULINE INTERPRETATION OF SACRED TRADITION

JSNT 31 (1987), pp. 51-72

TYPOLOGY, CORRESPONDENCE,
AND THE APPLICATION OF SCRIPTURE IN ROMANS 9–11

J.W. Aageson

I

In theological discussion, 'typology' has often been used as a term for expressing a category of scriptural use found in the New Testament. E. Earle Ellis, writing recently in the forward to the English translation of Goppelt's *Typos*, states:

> Unlike allegorical exposition, the typology of the NT writers represents the OT not as a book of metaphors hiding a deeper meaning but as an account of historical events and teachings from which the meaning of the text arises. Unlike a Judaizing hermeneutic, typology views the relationship of OT events to those in the new dispensation not as a 'one-to-one' equation or correspondence, in which the Old is repeated or continued, but rather in terms of two principles, historical correspondence and escalation...In typology, however, the OT type not only corresponds to the NT antitype but also is complemented and transcended by it.[1]

Writing in 1976, David L. Baker has also sought to provide working definitions of 'type' and 'typology':

> A *type* is a biblical event, person or institution which serves as an example or pattern for other events, persons or institutions; *typology* is the study of types and the historical and theological correspondences between them; the *basis* of typology is God's consistent activity in the history of his chosen people.[2]

---

1.   L. Goppelt, *Typos: The Typological Interpretation of the Old Testament in the New* (Grand Rapids: Eerdmans, 1982), p. x.

2.   D.L. Baker, 'Typology and the Christian Use of the Old Testament', *SJT* 29 (1976), p. 153.

While many have contributed to the discussion concerning typology over the years,[3] one further reference will suffice for our purposes. Gerhard von Rad has written: 'Indeed, one must see the basic ideas of typology less in the notion of "repetition" than in that of correspondence"'.[4] In addition, he asserts that the New Testament in many ways testifies to the impulse towards a heightening between 'type' and 'antitype'.[5]

Thus, there is no doubt that typology and the language of typology frequently have been used by theologians as a way of expressing the relationship between the old dispensation and the new, the Old Testament and the New. However, when we turn our attention to the Pauline epistles, we must address at the outset the question: does the language of 'type' and 'antitype' and of historical linkage and escalation provide an adequate basis for understanding the framework with which Paul approached the use and application of scripture?[6] To be sure, there

3.   See e.g. W. Eichrodt, 'Is Typological Exegesis an Appropriate Method?', in C. Westermann (ed.), *Essays on Old Testament Interpretation* (London: SCM Press, 1963), pp. 224-45; G.W.H. Lampe, 'Typological Exegesis', *Theology* 56 (1953), pp. 201-208 (he argues that the assumption which underlies typology is the recognition that the history of God's people and his dealings with them is a 'single continuous process'); K.J. Woollcombe, 'The Biblical Origins and Patristic Development of Typology', *Essays on Typology* (London: SCM Press, 1957), pp. 39-75 ('Typology, considered as a method of exegesis, may be defined as the establishment of historical connexions between certain events, persons or things in the Old Testament and similar events, persons, or things in the New Testament' [p. 39]); Goppelt, *Typos*; J. Barr, *Old and New in Interpretation: A Study of the Two Testaments* (London: SCM Press, 1966), pp. 103-48; R.T. France, *Jesus and the Old Testament* (London: Tyndale, 1971), pp. 38-43; H.D. Hummel, 'The Old Testament Basis of Typological Interpretation', *BR* 9 (1964), pp. 38-50; A.T. Hanson, *Studies in Paul's Technique and Theology* (Grand Rapids: Eerdmans, 1974), pp. 151-58.

4.   G. von Rad, 'Typological Interpretation of the Old Testament', in Westermann (ed.), *Essays on Old Testament Interpretation*, p. 20.

5.   Von Rad, 'Typological Interpretation', p. 21.

6.   It ought to be noted at the outset that Goppelt, whose work on typology and the New Testament was published in 1939 and which is still the most thorough treatment of the subject, has recognized that typology is limited in the Pauline epistles: 'But typology is not prominent in his epistles because they contain the doctrine of redemption primarily and include little redemptive history...The typology that is present is there for the sake of his doctrine' (pp. 128-29). But writing a quarter of a

is evidence for the typological use of biblical material in Paul's letters, but it is limited to only a few texts.

In Rom. 5.14, Paul uses the word τύπος. He writes: '... Adam who is the type of the one who is to come'. In this context, τύπος means 'model' or 'pattern';[7] and it is used to indicate the relationship between Adam and Christ and their respective representations of humanity. The element of historical linkage often associated with theological definitions of typology does appear to be present in Rom. 5.12-21 (especially vv. 18-19). Furthermore, the element of escalation is also present. Paul writes in 5.17: 'For if by the trespass of one man death reigned through the one, much more (πολλῷ μᾶλλον) shall those who receive the abundance of grace and the gift of righteousness reign in life through the one Jesus Christ'. Despite this rather straightforward example of escalation, it is not, however, inappropriate to ask: to what extent is this element of escalation simply inherent in the *qal waḥomer* method of argumentation and to what extent does it reflect Paul's view of history?[8] It is quite clear that these questions cannot be sharply differentiated, but they suggest that Paul's manner of argumentation has worked in tandem with his religious viewpoint to produce a typological statement which involves both analogy and contrast (see 1 Cor. 15.21-23, 45-49). Yet even in this text, perhaps the most vivid example of typology in the Pauline epistles, the use of scripture is limited to the use of names and allusions to the trespass of Adam and the giving of the Mosaic law. Goppelt may be right that the comparison between Adam and Christ is a basic element in Pauline theology,[9] but it cannot be argued meaningfully that it governs or is characteristic of his use of scripture.[10]

century later in an essay on 'Apocalypticism and Typology in Paul', Goppelt appears to have concluded that typology is more fundamental to Paul's use of scripture than his earlier statements may have suggested: 'Of the many references to the OT in the Pauline epistles, the typologies are only a small portion numerically, but they are characteristic of his overall use of scripture and set a pattern for it' (ET, p. 225).

7. Woollcombe, 'Typology', pp. 60-65. Cf. the use of τύπος in Rom. 6.17; 1 Cor. 10.6, 11; Phil. 3.17; 1 Thess. 1.7.

8. Cf. the discussion by H. Müller, 'Der rabbinische Qal-Wachomer-Schluß in paulinischer Typologie: Zur Adam-Christus-Typologie Rm. 5', *ZNW* 58 (1967), pp. 73-92.

9. Goppelt, *Typos*, p. 223. Cf. Eph. 4.22-23; Col. 3.9-10.

10. See above note 6.

Furthermore, Paul's use of Abrahamic material appears to reflect Jewish concepts of corporate solidarity and patriarchal descendancy rather than a typological view of scripture based on notions of redemption-history. Likewise, the use of τύπος and τυπικῶς in the sense of 'warning' or 'example' in 1 Cor. 10.6-13 provides little support for the view that Paul's use of scripture is fundamentally typological. In this text, the scriptural material is used didactically, and the 'end-time' viewpoint which is expressed does not necessarily imply notions of historical linkage. There is perhaps a eucharistic and baptismal typology in 10.1-4, but Paul does not elaborate this imagery. Other cases of alleged typology, for example the cult imagery in 1 Cor. 3.10-17 and 2 Cor. 6.16,[11] are equally vague and undeveloped. They indicate the limited role that typology, understood in terms of historical linkage and escalation, actually plays in Paul's epistles. Apart from Rom. 5.12-21 and perhaps 1 Cor. 10.1-13 the language of 'type', 'antitype', and historical linkage is neither adequate nor helpful in describing the basic framework with which Paul came to the use of scripture.

II

If the term 'typology', with its historical implications, is inadequate,[12] what then is appropriate terminology to describe the connection between scriptural persons or events and contemporary persons or events without implying some kind of underlying historical linkage? Before answering this question, it ought to be noted that in the epistles scripture is virtually always applied, and it is applied in basically two ways: (1) it is applied in order to illustrate and establish a religious principle; and (2) it is applied to contemporary individuals, groups, or events. As we shall see with respect to Romans 9–11, these are most often interwoven; but within the structure of the literary context of Paul's citations, these two aspects of scriptural application can usually be differentiated. Paul's use of scripture is fundamentally a theological enterprise,

11. Goppelt, *Typos*, p. 225. Goppelt says that Gal. 4.21-31 is a typology that passes over into allegory (p. 224). Hanson's statement that Romans 9–11 is replete with typology (e.g. 9.17) is highly questionable and is beside the point as far as Paul's use of scripture in these three chapters is concerned (*Paul's Technique*, p. 158).

12. Barr has shown the difficulty in using a view of history as a criterion in defining and identifying typology and allegory (*Old and New*, pp. 103-15).

but it is almost always related to people and circumstances in his own ministry.

In this discussion of terminology, it is primarily the second aspect of scriptural application which concerns us, for it is in this dimension that the issue of linkage comes to the fore. The connection between scriptural and contemporary persons or events, which we seek to describe in the Pauline epistles, is not made necessarily on the basis of a view of historical linkage, as is frequently implied in theological definitions of the term 'typology'. Paul often appears to have used scripture verbally or thematically to make an ethical or theological statement without linking scripture to the present according to a notion of redemption-history.[13] Rather than a view of history, the underlying assumption of Paul's application appears often to be that that which is 'true' in scripture (understood in light of his special religious and christological understanding, cf. 2 Cor. 3.4-18) is also 'true' in the present. The task for Paul is to discern (uncover) the verbal and thematic links between scripture and the circumstances of the present and thus to bring the 'truth' of scripture to bear both pastorally and theologically. This is not to deny that there is a prophetic element in Paul's understanding of scriptural application (cf. Rom. 1.2; 3.21; 1 Cor. 15.3-4; Gal. 3.8) or to minimize the fact that Paul understood something decisively new to have been inaugurated by God in Christ (cf. 2 Cor. 3.4-11). It is, however, to argue that Paul, the Jew, understood scripture as something sacred and holy (Rom. 1.2) and as such found it to be a source of inspiration for life, an expression of the will of God, and a basis for interpretation and religious argumentation.[14] In the process of uncovering the 'true' meaning of selected scriptural texts and applying them to the circumstances of his own ministry, Paul drew, sometimes only implicitly, connections and links between scriptural persons and events and contemporary persons and events. It is this feature of Paul's application of scriptural material which we wish to describe by the term *correspondence*.[15] As a technical

13. See my unpublished D.Phil. thesis, 'Paul's Use of Scripture' (Oxford, 1983), pp. 86-96, 147-51, and my article, 'Scripture and Structure in the Development of the Argument in Romans 9–11', *CBQ* 48 (1986), pp. 265-89.

14. My D.Phil. thesis, 'Paul's Use of Scripture', pp. 1-27.

15. The interpretations which the pesher commentators gave often involved an element of *correspondence* expressed in disguised language.

term, it is neutral regarding the issue of linkage based on a notion of redemption-history and the role this notion may have played in Paul's use of scripture. *Correspondence* does not presuppose it but neither does it preclude it in every instance. It is with this preliminary discussion in mind that we set out to examine the network of *correspondences* in Paul's application of scriptural material in Romans 9–11 and to highlight this one aspect of Paul's method of scriptural argumentation in these three chapters of Romans.

III

In Romans 9–11, the term 'Ἰσραήλ is used eleven times;[16] and the fact that it occurs nowhere else in the epistle is an indication of the significance which Paul attaches to it in these chapters. It is the key term for understanding scriptural application in this section of the epistle (see Rom. 9.6, 27, 31; 10.19, 21; 11.2, 7, 25, 26). In 9.6 Paul writes: 'not all those descended from Israel are (really) Israel'. He differentiates Israel as the historical people of God from Israel as the 'people of promise'; and this involves a theological distinction which enables Paul to differentiate two groups of people in the present.[17] The Jews who do not 'believe' are distinguished from the Jews and Gentiles who do. Since Paul uses the term 'Ἰσραήλ, however, to designate in the present both the historical people of God and the 'people of promise', the lines of correspondence which are developed must be examined individually.

Descendants
The first set of passages involving the term 'Ἰσραήλ concerns Israel as 'seed' and as 'children' (9.6-13). In this discussion, the pattern of scriptural correspondence is developed according to two incomplete but parallel lines.

16. Cf. the use of this term in 1 Cor. 10.18; 2 Cor. 3.7, 13; Gal. 6.16; Phil. 3.5; Eph. 2.12. 'Ἰσραηλίτης also occurs in Rom. 9.4; 11.1. See also 2 Cor. 11.22.

17. In Rom. 9–11, the term 'Ἰουδαῖος occurs in 9.24 and 10.12, whereas in the remainder of Romans and the other Pauline epistles, it is used frequently to refer to the people of Israel. See Rom. 1.16; 2.9, 10, 17, 28, 29; 3.1, 9, 29; 1 Cor. 1.22, 23, 24; 9.20; 10.32; 12.13; 2 Cor. 11.24; Gal. 2.13, 14, 15; 3.28; 1 Thess. 2.14; Col. 3.11. The different contexts in which Paul uses the terms 'Ἰσραήλ and 'Ἰουδαῖος reinforces the assertion that 'Ἰσραήλ is a theological concept with social and historical implications.

οἱ ἐξ Ἰσραήλ— historical Israel	Ἰσραήλ—Israel according to promise, faith τέκνα—Israel according to promise, faith
σπέρμα—Israel by physical descent[18]	σπέρμα—children of God
τέκνα τῆς σαρκός— Israel by physical descent	τέκνα τῆς ἐπαγγελίας Israel according to promise, faith[19] υἱός—Sarah's son/Israel according to promise, faith
ὁ μείζων—historical Israel	τῷ ἐλάσσονι— Israel according to the call of God
Ἡσαῦ—historical Israel	Ἰακώβ—Israel according to the love of God, faith

At the beginning of each column, we find a different use of the term Ἰσραήλ;[20] and implicit in each line is the connection between scriptural persons and persons (groups) from Paul's own time and situation. Israel according to the flesh and Israel according to promise are intended to correspond in the present to Israel according to physical descent and Israel according to 'faith'.[21] There is no suggestion in 9.6-13 that Paul

18. If, as C.E.B. Cranfield argues (*The Epistle to the Romans* [2 vols.; ICC; Edinburgh: T. & T. Clark, 1975–79], II, p. 473), σπέρμα in 9.7a corresponds to οἱ ἐξ Ἰσραήλ, then it refers to historical Israel whereas σπέρμα in the citation from Gen. 21.12 (9.7b) is clearly used to refer to Israel according to promise. Hence, Paul has used the word σπέρμα in two different senses. The syntax of 9.7a favors Cranfield's argument; but if Paul's use of Gen. 21.12 in its context in Rom. 9.6-7 is to be consistent, σπέρμα in both 9.7a and 7b would be required to correspond with Ἰσραήλ in 9.6. Cf. C.K. Barrett's translation, *The Epistle to the Romans* (HNTC; New York: Harper & Row, 1957), pp. 179-80. Despite this apparent inconsistency, σπέρμα in 9.7a has been included in the same line as οἱ ἐξ Ἰσραήλ. Cf. also Gal. 3.16.

19. The word σπέρμα is in the quotation from Gen. 21.12, whereas τέκνα τῆς ἐπαγγελίας is part of the inference which Paul draws from the scriptural citation.

20. Cf. the development of lines of correspondence in Gal. 4.21-31.

21. To argue, as Gaston has done, that it is impossible that Isaac and Jacob could refer to anybody but Israel (historical Israel) or that Ishmael (not introduced here), Esau, and Pharaoh could refer to anyone but the Gentiles is, to say the least, a forced interpretation of Romans 9 ('Israel's Enemies in Pauline Theology', *NTS* 28 [1982], pp. 411-18). It is more consistent with Paul's argument in Rom. 9 and Gal. 4.21-31 to argue that Ἰσραήλ as a religious and historical concept is being expanded to include not only Jews but also Gentiles. See Rom. 11.16-24.

understood the Christian community as having superseded Israel; on the contrary, he argues that the Christian community is the embodiment of Israel, that is, Israel understood as the 'people of promise'.[22] For Paul, the two groups designated by the term 'Ισραήλ correspond to Jacob and Esau. Only Jacob bears the promise. To confirm this, Paul in 9.13 cites two scriptural passages (Gen. 25.23 and Mal. 1.2-3).[23] In scripture, Israel is designated by the promise and the call of God; so too in the present Israel is designated by the promise and the call. Behind Paul's play on the term 'Ισραήλ stands a religious conviction, and this conviction determines the way he draws the lines of correspondence. According to Paul, God has called both Jews and Gentiles (see Rom. 3.29-30; 9.24; 10.10-13; Gal. 3.28-29).

In 9.6-13, Paul infers from the scriptural material two theological principles: (1) the children of God are the children of the promise and not the children of the flesh; and (2) God's plan of election remains not because of works but because of the call of God (see Rom. 9.8, 11; cf. Rom. 9.32; 11.6). The first of these is drawn from Gen. 21.12, and the second is inferred from the story of Rebekah and the birth of her two sons (Gen. 25.23). The statement that the plan of election remains not because of works but because of God's call is the claim that the citations from Gen. 25.23 and Mal. 1.2-3 are intended to substantiate. The elder shall serve the younger because God loved Jacob but hated Esau. According to Paul, the implication of these passages is that election depends on divine rather than human action. As a religious principle found in scripture, this is applied to the present situation between Israel as a national and religious entity and the people of promise. In 9.6-13, both elements of Paul's application of scripture are present; he has drawn from scripture religious and theological principles which have

22. See W.D. Davies, 'Paul and the People of Israel', *NTS* 24 (1977), pp. 4-39.

23. E. Käsemann's comment on Rom. 9.12b-13 (*Commentary on Romans* [Grand Rapids: Eerdmans, 1980], p. 264), that 'Paul is no longer concerned with two peoples and their destiny...but timelessly...with the election and rejection of two persons who are elevated as types' tends to obscure the basis which underlies the entire argument in 9.6-13. Paul's passing comment in 9.10—'Ισαὰκ τοῦ πατρὸς ἡμῶν—suggests that Paul in this segment of the argument is indeed concerned with historical individuals and not simply with timeless types (even in 9.12-13). See also the comments by Hans Hübner regarding the relation between Paul's scriptural argument and the contemporary situation (*Gottes Ich und Israel: Zum Schriftgebrauch des Paulus in Römer 9–11* [FRLANT, 136; Göttingen: Vandenhoeck & Ruprecht, 1984]), pp. 19-20, 45.

been understood to correspond to contemporary circumstances.[24] These principles which Paul has discovered in scripture enable him to account for the present division within Israel between 'believers' and 'unbelievers'.[25] From another perspective, it is the present situation that enables him to see in the patriarchal narratives features which appear to correspond to his experience as apostle to the Gentiles. In 9.6-13, Paul deals with religious concepts; but for him these are inseparable from the relationship between Jews and Gentiles in the present day.

Remnant

The second set of texts associated with the term 'Ισραήλ pertains to the use of remnant imagery. In 9.27, the words of Isaiah are said to be addressed to Israel;[26] and the scriptural citation which follows asserts that 'even though the sons of Israel be as numerous as the sand of the sea (only) a remnant will be saved'. The next citation in this series of references is from Isa. 1.9 (Rom. 9.29); although the term ὑπόλειμμα does not occur,[27] it is evident that Paul has used this citation to indicate that a remnant indeed has been allowed to remain.[28] The introductory formula in 9.29, καὶ καθὼς προείρηκεν 'Ησαίας, suggests that Paul has understood the words of Isaiah prophetically; the words of the prophet spoken beforehand apply to the present.[29]

The citations in 9.25-29 are used within the context of Paul's argument that both Jews and Gentiles have been called and prepared beforehand for glory. The remnant imagery, however, serves to make a distinction between Israel as the whole people of God and that group within Israel which will be saved. For Paul, the demarcation of a

24. See above.
25. The discussion in this segment of the discourse is not about faith primarily, but it clearly provides the context for the argument (Hübner, *Gottes Ich*, p. 46).
26. The citation in Rom. 9.27-28 is, however, taken from Isa. 10.22-23 and Hos. 2.1.
27. σπέρμα is used instead. Cf. Rom. 9.7-8; 11.1.
28. The assertion by Gaston ('Israel's Enemies', p. 416), that the citation in 9.27-28, as well as the reference in 9.29, is used in a positive sense to indicate that God will never abandon his people, may have some merit when viewed in light of 9.23-24. But to make sense of the quotation itself, a contrast between the whole of Israel and the remnant is necessary. Hence, the citation cannot be taken only in a positive light. Furthermore, a sense of threat appears to be intended by the use of the word κράζειν (see Cranfield, *Romans*, II, p. 501).
29. See Cranfield, *Romans*, II, p. 502.

remnant within Israel as described in scripture corresponds to the present division between those in Israel who 'believe' and those who do not. In the immediate context of 9.14-29, the issue is discussed in terms of divine sovereignty, but the distinction between 'believing' Israel and 'unbelieving' Israel undoubtedly provided the historical and social background for this argument. The discussion which began as an attempt to demonstrate that both Jews and Gentiles have been called concludes with a distinction between Israel as the whole people of God and the remnant.[30]

In 11.1-5, Paul again uses remnant imagery (1 Kgs 19.10[14] and 18). The scriptural statement that God kept for himself seven thousand men is applied explicitly to the present; and it is used to substantiate the claim that God has not rejected his people.[31] God has preserved a remnant. The correspondence between the remnant in the scriptural statement and the remnant in the present, the Jews who believe in Christ, confirms for Paul that God has not abandoned the people whom he foreknew.

Paul has used the concept of a remnant and the scriptural citations associated with it in two different contexts. In 9.25-29, the quotations are part of an argument which is intended to substantiate the claim that both Jews and Gentiles have been called by God (cf. Rom. 10.12). The scriptural material in 9.27-28 has been linked with the combined citation in 9.25-26 on the basis of the textual similarity between Hos. 2.1 LXX and Isa. 10.22 LXX. The remnant imagery in 9.27-28 is intended as a sign that God has placed Israel under judgment. Though the people of Israel be as many as the sand of the sea only a remnant shall be saved. In 9.29, however, the message of the citation is different from 9.27-28; Israel has not been entirely destroyed. She has not been made like Sodom and Gomorrah; descendants have been preserved. In 9.27-28, the contrast is between the vastness of the sand of the sea and the remnant, whereas in 9.29 it is between the destruction of Sodom and Gomorrah and the preservation of descendants. In the former, the contrast conveys a message of judgment, while in the latter it issues a message of assurance. From a scriptural argument designed to substantiate the claim that both

30. See also the pattern of scriptural correspondence in Rom. 10.19-21, in which the passages are also applied successively to the Gentiles and then to Israel.

31. In 11.1-2, Paul is speaking of the people of Israel as a whole. See Cranfield, *Romans*, II, p. 545 and Käsemann, *Romans*, p. 299. See also N.A. Dahl, 'The Future of Israel', in *Studies in Paul: Theology for the Early Christian Mission* (Minneapolis: Augsburg, 1977), p. 149.

Jews and Gentiles have been called and prepared for glory, Paul has developed a remnant theology based on scriptural citations from Hos. 2.1, Isa. 10.22-23 and Isa. 1.9.

In 11.1-6, the scriptural material is used to substantiate an explicit assertion: 'God has not rejected his people whom he foreknew'. Furthermore, the application of the Elijah story also includes the claim that the remnant in the present has received election by grace. In 9.27-29, the discussion of the remnant is incorporated into the presentation through the linking of scriptural passages; it is derived from the argument in 9.23-26. In 11.1-6, however, the discussion focuses on Paul's denial that God has rejected his people and on the claim based on scripture that a remnant has been preserved. The material from 1 Kgs 19.10 (14) and 18 is included directly into the discussion; it is not derived through the juxtaposition of scriptural passages. The fact that the scriptural material in 11.1-6 is integral to Paul's argument and not derived from it may be the reason that Paul has chosen to elaborate the discussion by applying the material explicitly to the present day and by interpreting it to mean that the remnant has been chosen by grace and not works (see also Rom. 9.12, 16, 32). In addition to support for his claim that God has not rejected his people, Paul apparently saw in this scriptural material ideas which he thought could be exploited to illustrate his conviction that election is by χάρις and not ἔργα. A remnant has been preserved, argues Paul, and it has been preserved because of χάρις. Despite the fact that the people killed the prophets and destroyed the altars, seven thousand men who have not worshipped Baal have been kept by God. That God did not respond to Elijah's denunciation of the people by destroying Israel but kept for himself a remnant is interpreted as evidence that the election of a remnant is according to grace. From the scriptural story, Paul has derived a theological concept and applied this concept to the relationship between Jews and Jewish Christians in the contemporary situation.

Those who Believe, Proclaim, and Confess
The third set of passages associated with Ἰσραήλ has to do with faith, proclamation, confession, and salvation made available to Jews and Greeks without distinction. In 10.10-13, Paul uses scripture to confirm two statements: (1) 'For a person believes with his heart and is justified and confesses with his lips and is saved'; and (2) 'For there is no distinction between Jew and Greek, for the same Lord is Lord of all and

bestows riches on all who call upon him' (Rom. 10.10 and 12). The scriptural citations used to support these statements are understood by Paul to apply universally to Jews and Greeks. The religious conception which underlies 10.1-13 is the relationship between the universal promise of salvation and the confession and belief that Jesus is Lord (see also 10.9); and the scriptural correspondence focuses on the claim that there is no distinction between Jews and Greeks in the present day, as far as the promise of salvation is concerned.[32] It may perhaps be argued that in 10.9-13 the theological dimension of Paul's scriptural argument predominates, but it cannot be argued that this segment of the discourse is not grounded also in his experience as apostle to the Gentiles.[33] For Paul, the soteriological dividing line between Jews and Greeks may have been removed; but the social and religious dividing line still remains. In social and religious affairs, Jews and Greeks most often are separated, and it is this reality that provides the background against which Paul's use of scripture in this context must be understood.[34] The universal character of salvation as a theological concept must be contrasted with Israel's historical claim that it has a special relationship with Yahweh (cf. Rom. 3.9-18, 22-23). In 9.4-5, Paul himself acknowledges this relationship.

In 10.14-18, the focus of the discussion is on hearing and believing the 'word of Christ'. The word has indeed gone forth, says Paul; preachers

32. See Rom. 3.21-23; 9.23-24; Gal. 3.27-29. The claim that there is no distinction in a soteriological sense between Jews and Greeks had definite social, and therefore historical, consequences for the Christian communities in Paul's sphere of missionary activity. In these communities, there were both Jews and Gentiles, and the practical as well as the religious consequences of this were undoubtedly manifold. Paul's claim that there is no distinction between Jews and Greeks, however, did not make it a social reality (cf. e.g. Gal. 3–4; 1 Cor. 12–14). The very fact that Paul was compelled to engage in an extended discourse (Rom. 9–11) which involved the relationship between Israel and the Gentiles testifies to the fact that this relationship was not only a matter of abstract, theological concern but was also a matter of profound practical concern. The historical fact was that the vast majority of Jews did not believe in Christ and did not believe that salvation had been extended to the Gentiles without distinction.

33. This is true even if, as Käsemann has suggested (*Romans*, p. 291), Rom. 10.19 is from a baptismal setting. See also Barrett, *Romans*, p. 200.

34. Dahl's comments on Rom. 10.4-17 support this observation ('Future of Israel', p. 148).

have been sent to proclaim the 'good news'.[35] Still it remains a fact that 'not all' (Israel) have believed: 'Lord, who has believed our report (Isa. 53.1)?' From the argument in 10.14-16 and in particular from the quotation of Isa. 53.1, Paul infers that 'faith comes from the message heard and the message comes through the word of Christ'. As can be seen in the introductory formula in 10.18, Israel's 'unbelief' cannot be attributed, according to Paul, to having never heard the 'word of Christ'. In light of 9.6, it can be said that Israel's 'unbelief' must not be ascribed to the failure of God's word. In 10.18, Paul cites Ps. 19.5: 'Their voice has gone out to all the earth, and their words to the ends of the world'.

Behind the theological argument in 10.14-18 stands the missionary work of the early Christian evangelists. Preachers have taken the message of Jesus to Jews as well as to Gentiles;[36] and this has enabled Paul to see in Isa. 52.7, 53.1 and Ps. 19.5 a series of ideas which appear to correspond to this early Christian mission.[37] First, preachers have proclaimed the 'good news'. Secondly, not all Jews have believed the message which these preachers have heralded. And thirdly, preachers have taken the word of Jesus to many parts of the world. Allowing for the hyperbole involved in Paul's use of Ps. 19.5, it is evident that this passage has been applied to the work of the early Christian apostles. By means of a perceived correspondence between the scriptural texts and the present circumstances, Paul has constructed a theological argument designed to deprive 'unbelieving' Israel of an excuse for its 'unbelief'.

Those who Have Been Disobedient and Hardened
The next set of texts concerns the disobedience or hardening of Ἰσραήλ. As part of the scriptural argument in 10.19-21, Paul cites Isa. 65.2. The introductory formula explicitly directs the words of Isaiah

35. Rom. 10.14-15, 18 (Ps. 19.5). Cf. Rom. 10.19-21 (Deut. 32.21; Isa. 65.1-2). The deliberative questions in 10.14-15 are, from a literary point of view, important in leading to this assertion.

36. On the basis of Rom. 9.30–10.13 and 10.19-21, it is reasonable to conclude that the argument in 10.14-18 refers to the Jews (Israel), specifically in 10.16-18 to those who do not believe in Christ. See Barrett, *Romans*, p. 205; Cranfield, *Romans*, II, p. 533; E. Dinkler, 'The Historical and the Eschatological Israel in Romans, Chapters 9–11: A Contribution to the Problem of Predestination and Individual Responsibility', *JR* 36 (1956), pp. 114-15.

37. Dahl, too, has emphasized the way scriptural passages and contemporary events have influenced each other in 10.4-17 ('Future of Israel', p. 148).

to Israel. On the basis of the epistolary context, it is evident that Paul has in mind that part of Israel which has rejected the 'word of Christ' (see Rom. 10.16-19). In Paul's application of Isa. 65.2, the scriptural passage is understood to correspond to the disobedience of contemporary Israel, as this has been expressed in the rejection of the gospel. In this text, the disobedience of the people is accompanied by the claim, stated in the first person, that God has stretched out his hand 'all the day'. In light of the discussion in 10.14-18, it is evident that the message of this citation is not understood by Paul to be an abstract theological point. For him, the scriptural statement has come to expression in the missionary work of the Christian apostles (cf. Rom. 1.1-6; 2 Cor. 11.22-23, Gal. 1.11-21).

In 11.7-10, the issue of Israel's rejection of the gospel is expressed in a different way. The distinction within 'Ισραήλ between the 'elect' and the 'rest',[38] implicit throughout the discourse, is here made explicit: "Israel failed to obtain what it sought. The elect obtained it, but the rest were hardened'.[39] This religious distinction, which for Paul has social manifestations in the present, is placed firmly in a theological context by reference to Isa. 29.10 and Deut. 29.3. God gave the λοιποί a spirit of stupor (cf. Rom. 9.30-33; 10.19). In 11.9-10, the citation from Ps. 69.23-24 continues the scriptural argument, but the change to third-person speech changes its theological impact. From a statement of what God has done in 11.8, it shifts in 11.9-10 to a statement of imprecation.

In 10.21, the emphasis is on the disobedience of Israel in the face of God's summons. In 11.8, it is on the hardening of those within Israel who do not believe. These are religious concepts which Paul has applied to the present; and they are designed to explain why some Jews believe the 'word of Christ' and others do not. The citations in 10.21 and 11.7-10 are intended to give a theological account of Israel's 'unbelief'. From Paul's perspective, they provide a theological description of the λοιποί and their rejection of the gospel. As one who implicitly claimed for himself special insight into the purposes of God, Paul used scripture to explain theologically the 'unbelief' of those outside his Christian

38. As Barrett says (*Romans*, p. 210), the 'rest' means Israel less the remnant. Käsemann also remarks that ἐκλογή and λεῖμμα (11.5) are synonymous (*Romans*, p. 301).

39. This distinction is present in a different way in Rom. 9.6-13; but in 11.7, it is given added force because of the differentiation between ἐκλογή and λοιποί. Cf. Rom. 9.14-23, 30-33; 10.16-21.

community, especially the 'unbelief' of the Jews who themselves claimed a special relationship with God.

Christ

The final set of texts pertaining directly to Ἰσραήλ involves a connection between Israel and Christ (Torah).[40] In 9.32, Paul makes the claim that Israel has stumbled on the stone of stumbling.[41] Barrett, among others, has suggested that in speaking of the stone of stumbling and the rock of offence Paul has Torah primarily in mind. Israel mistakenly pursued the law by works instead of by faith, and so stumbled.[42] Barrett, however, recognizes that there cannot be an unqualified equation drawn between the 'stone' and Torah, because αὐτῷ in 9.33b and 10.11 must refer to Christ. Nevertheless, the close connection between Christ and Torah in 9.32–10.8 is evident. In 10.4, for example, Christ is described as the τέλος of the law that those who believe may be justified. In light of the tradition which developed in the early church, however, it seems almost certain that Paul intended his readers to see Christ in the figure of the 'stone'.[43] In Christ, righteousness is shown to be according to 'faith' and not 'works'. Apart from Christ, this distinction is not perceived and 'stumbling' results.

For our purposes, however, this issue must be sharpened. What is the connection between Christ, stumbling, and the 'unbelief' of the Jews? Was belief in Christ as messiah the 'stumbling block' for the Jews or was belief in Christ which included a different understanding of the law the 'stumbling block'? At the outset, it must be said that Paul's understanding of Christ is not separated from his conviction that both Jews and Gentiles have been called and prepared beforehand for glory. Likewise, Paul does not perceive 'righteousness' and 'faith' to be separated from his understanding of Christ.[44] In 9.33b he quotes the prophet Isaiah: '...and he who believes in him shall not be put to shame'. For Paul, faith in Christ is distinguished from works of law. In the discussion

40. Rom. 9.30-33; 10.4-8; 11.26-27.

41. The subject of προσέκοψαν is Ἰσραήλ in 9.31.

42. Barrett, 'Romans 9.30–10.21: Fall and Responsibility of Israel', in *Essays on Paul* (London: SPCK, 1982), p. 144; C.E.B. Cranfield, 'Some Notes on Romans 9.30-33', in *Jesus und Paulus* (E.E. Ellis and Erich Gräßer; Göttingen: Vandenhoeck & Ruprecht, 1975), pp. 35-43.

43. Hübner, *Gottes Ich*, p. 69.

44. Cranfield, *Romans*, II, p. 512.

in 9.30-33, the issue is not 'belief' versus 'unbelief'. It is 'faith' versus 'works'. Hence, when Paul claims that Israel has stumbled over the 'stone of stumbling', he is not saying simply that it has refused to believe in Christ. Rather, Israel has not pursued righteousness according to 'faith' but according to 'works'. In 9.33b, the discussion is also given a soteriological dimension. Those who believe in Christ will be saved (cf. Rom. 10.10-11). Unlike 10.16, the focus of the discussion in 9.30-33 is not Israel's refusal to believe in Christ; it is its failure to distinguish two approaches to righteousness. According to Paul, Israel has stumbled because, apart from Christ, it did not understand that it pursued righteousness in the wrong way.[45] This is clearly a theological argument and not an historical description; but, when the primary issue for Paul is understood to be Israel's relationship to the law and its pursuit of righteousness, the *Sitz im Leben* in which this discussion appears to have emerged becomes clearer. The situation which precipitated the issues in 9.30-33 would have involved contention between Jews and Gentiles over the issue of obedience to Torah. It would not have been solely a matter of 'belief' or 'unbelief' but of the way belief in Christ was alleged to have affected a person's stance before the law and before God (cf. Rom. 10.4). According to Paul, Christ has brought to expression the true approach to the law and righteousness; and it was the consequence of this religious claim that caused tension between Jews and Gentiles. It was this that constituted a 'stumbling block' for many Jews. For Paul, the discussion in 9.30-33 was not simply a matter of whether or not Jesus was to be believed and confessed as the messiah who had been promised in the holy scriptures. The citation in 9.33 was used by Paul against the background of a particular kind of controversy. It was applied to Jews who reject Christ and Paul's understanding of the law.

In 10.5 and 6, the introductory statements or formulae illustrate once again the theological distinction which Paul has in mind in 9.30–10.8. Righteousness based on law is contrasted with righteousness based on faith. By citing Lev. 18.5, Paul argues that those who do the law shall live by the law. This quotation, which in its scriptural context encourages obedience to God's commands, has been used by Paul to argue against

---

45. It is not evident that in 9.30-33 Paul is speaking of the Jews during the early life of Jesus, as J. Munck has argued (*Christ and Israel: An Interpretation of Romans 9–11* [Philadelphia: Fortress Press, 1967], p. 81). In the context of 9.30–10.5, Paul is arguing against those who demand obedience to Torah.

the necessity of observing the law.[46] Paul's use of Lev. 18.5 reflects a situation in the early church in which obedience to Torah is at issue; it reflects Paul's polemic against those who object to his understanding of the law. If a person observes the requirements of the law, argues Paul, that person will live according to law. For him, life according to the law is in opposition to life according to faith. Once again, the controversy reflected in Paul's use of Lev. 18.5 is not simply about belief in Christ; it is about belief in Christ and the way this affects a person's observance of the law. Paul's use of Lev. 18.5 reflects a particular kind of situation in the early church. It was in the context of this type of situation that Paul developed a scriptural argument to support his contention that 'faith' is opposed to 'works'. Paul's application of Deut. 30.12-14 in 10.6 8 also involves a connection between Christ and the law. In effect, Paul has substituted Christ for the commandment of God in Deut. 30.12-14. Hence, that which is not 'far off' is applied to Christ, and the word which is 'near' corresponds to the word of faith which Paul preaches.

In 11.26-27, Paul uses scripture to make another reference to Christ.[47] In the epistolary context, the combined citation from Isa. 59.20-21 and 27.9 serves as substantiation for the claim or expectation that 'all Israel' will be saved. The fact that Jesus was a Jew serves as the link between the scriptural text and the statement which Paul intends to substantiate. The future tense of the verbs in Isa. 59.20-21 LXX enables Paul to project the message of the text into the future: '...he will turn ungodliness from Jacob, and this will be my covenant with them when I take away their sins'. From the perspective of the prophet, the coming of the savior was to take place in the future. But now Christ has come. In the future, Christ will turn Jacob from ungodliness and their sins will be forgiven. For Paul, the salvation of 'all Israel' is a future expectation (cf. Rom. 10.10-13). Paul's application of the scriptural passages in this text involves a correspondence between ὁ ῥυόμενος and Christ and between Ἰακώβ and contemporary Israel.

---

46. Cf. Gal. 3.11-12; Rom. 1.17. Because of the verbal link between Hab. 2.4 and Lev. 18.5 (ζήσεται), Paul has juxtaposed the two passages in Galatians. In them he has seen a contrast between life based on faith (or life as the result of faith) and life based on law.

47. See the discussion by Davies, 'Paul and the People of Israel', pp. 23-29.

Gentiles

Another group of applied scriptural texts corresponds directly to the Gentiles. In 9.25-26, the combined reference from Hos. 2.25 and 2.1 is intended to confirm the assertion that God has also called the Gentiles. In this discussion, Paul intends the readers of his epistle to make the connection between ἔθνη in 9.24 and οὐ λαόν μου/οὐκ ἠγαπημένην in the quotation from Hos. 2.25.[48] The sense of the scriptural argument requires that the term Gentiles be understood as only those who have been called. It refers to those Gentiles who believe or will believe in Christ. Since 'not my people', too, 'shall be called "sons of the living God"', it follows according to Paul's manner of argumentation that God has not only called the Jews but also the Gentiles. In 9.23-26, the theological principle at stake for Paul is the recognition that election is not restricted to the Jews. By inviting his readers to see the correspondence between 'Gentiles' and 'not my people'/'not beloved', Paul has attempted to confirm this theological assertion. The historical situation reflected in this scriptural argument is the debate in the early church concerning the place of the Gentiles in the plan of God and how they might obtain salvation. This, of course, is inseparable from the issue of Israel's place in the divine plan.

The citations in 10.19-20 are part of a scriptural argument in which the term Ἰσραήλ is included in the opening interrogative. The pronoun ὑμᾶς in 10.19 also refers to Israel (Deut. 32.21). But Paul intends the term ἔθνη, as well as the expressions 'those who did not seek' and 'those who did not ask', to correspond to the Gentiles. As understood by Paul, the scriptural references establish two religious principles: (1) God will use the Gentiles to make Israel jealous and angry; and (2) the Gentiles have come to know God. There is an important element of corporateness in Paul's use of the terms 'Israel' and 'Gentiles'; but to make sense of his argument in this context 'Israel' must refer specifically to those in Israel who do not 'believe' and 'Gentiles' must refer to

48. Dahl states that this citation refers to both Jews and Gentiles ('Future of Israel', pp. 145-46). While this cannot be ruled out (see also Cranfield, *Romans*, II, p. 500) it appears more likely that 9.25-26 refers to the Gentiles and 9.27-29 to Israel. Furthermore, it was the claim that God had called the Gentiles which needed scriptural substantiation and not that he had called Jews. Thus, it would seem that this reference has been placed first in order to establish the most contestable part of Paul's claim. But if Paul did intend the reference to apply to the Jews as well as the Gentiles, then, of course, the term Ἰουδαίων (perhaps referring to the Jews who do not presently believe in Christ) also corresponds to οὐ λαόν μου/οὐκ ἠγαπημένην.

those among the Gentiles who do. As groups within Israel and the Gentiles, Paul has used them to represent their respective segments of humanity. The Jews' present resistance to the gospel has been interpreted by Paul to be a phase which will lead eventually to the salvation of 'all Israel' (cf. Rom. 11.1-15). Furthermore, argues Paul, acceptance of the gospel by some Gentiles makes the 'Gentiles' an agent in this process. This is part of God's plan.

Pharaoh and Israel

The scriptural argument in 9.14-18 is primarily a theological discussion, but Paul's application of Exod. 33.19 and 9.16 may also reflect a correspondence between Pharaoh and Israel. Although Moses and Pharaoh are referred to in the introductory formulae in 9.15, 17, Paul does not develop the antitheses between these two figures.[49] But it is improbable that this contrast would have escaped the attention of a Jewish reader or perhaps a Gentile familiar with the Exodus narratives. It is difficult to establish whether Paul intended a correspondence between Pharaoh and Israel,[50] as the sense of 9.17-18 may suggest; but, if he did, it presumably would not have had a conciliatory impact on his Jewish readers.[51] It may be, however, that in 9.14-18 Paul is focusing primarily on the theological implications of the Exodus texts and does not intend his readers to connect them with any specific group of people in the present day. This is supported by the observation that 9.16, 18, the two explanatory statements, are theological assertions which do not emphasize the application of the scriptural texts to contemporary groups or individuals. Thus, in the scriptural accounts relating to Israel's history, Paul discerns a theological message, and he relates this message to the present without identifying directly the people about whom he is speaking. To see a line of correspondence between Pharaoh and Israel in 9.17-18 may imply more than Paul intends.

Evangelists

In 10.15-18, as indicated above, the scriptural references display a connection with those who proclaim the gospel. The emphasis in these verses is on the fact that the gospel has been proclaimed, but there is

---

49. See Cranfield, *Romans*, II, p. 485.

50. See Barrett, *Romans*, pp. 186-87; Hübner, *Gottes Ich*, p. 45.

51. This, however, does not rule out the possibility that Paul intended or implied this correspondence.

undoubtedly a correspondence between the scriptural citations and those responsible for this proclamation. It is not clear whether Paul is referring only to those who have proclaimed the gospel to the Jews or is also including himself, as an evangelist, who has worked among Jews in his missionary activity.[52] In either case, there are lines of correspondence between the quotations in 10.15, 16, 18 and those who proclaim the gospel. Furthermore, Käsemann and Munck have argued that in 11.2-4 Paul sees a correspondence between Elijah's situation and his own.[53] This possibility cannot be excluded, but it seems unlikely. In 11.1-4, Paul is concerned with establishing the claim that God has not rejected his people; it is not apparent that he intends his readers to see a connection between himself and Elijah (cf. Rom. 11.5-6).

Analogy and Metaphor
Finally, an examination of Paul's use of analogy and metaphor in Romans 9–11 indicates that correspondence also plays a role in these texts. In 9.20-24,[54] 11.16a, 16b, 17-24 Paul uses analogies to develop and illustrate his argument.[55] Implicit in the use of analogy, of course, is the similarity or correspondence between words and images in the analogy and the situation which the writer is describing or illustrating.[56]

---

52. Munck asserts that in 10.16 those who are portrayed as speaking are those who have been sent to the Jews (*Christ and Israel*, p. 93). This interpretation fits the sense of the discussion best, but because Paul probably also worked among Jews in the diaspora it cannot be ruled out that he included himself among those who had proclaimed the 'good news' to Israel. In 10.18, it is likely that Paul includes himself among those who have preached the gospel to the 'ends of the earth'.

53. Käsemann, *Romans*, p. 301; Munck, *Christ and Israel*, pp. 107-109.

54. Cf. Isa. 29.16 LXX; 45.9; Jer. 18.1-12; Sir. 33.12-13; Wis. 15.7.

55. See H.M. Gale, *The Use of Analogy in the Letters of Paul* (Philadelphia: Westminster Press, 1964), pp. 198-215; Hanson, *Paul's Technique*, pp. 104-25; S. Fujita, 'The Metaphor of Plant in Jewish Literature of the Intertestamental Period', *JSJ* 7 (1976), pp. 30-45.

56. Rom. 9.20-24: 'molder' and 'potter' = God; 'molded', 'clay', and 'lump' = humankind; 'vessels for honorable use' = those called and prepared for glory; and 'vessels for menial use' = those not called and not prepared for glory. Rom. 11.16a: 'dough'/'first fruits' = patriarchs (only Abraham?) or Adam (cf. various options and Hanson's own suggestion [*Paul's Technique*, pp. 104-16]); and 'lump' = Israel (totality?). Rom. 11.16b: 'root' = patriarchs (only Abraham?) (cf. Hanson, *Paul's Technique*, pp. 177-25); and 'branches' = Israel (totality?). Rom. 11.17-24: 'cultivated olive tree' (root) = Israel; 'wild olive tree' = Gentiles; 'branches cut off' = 'unbelieving' Jews; and 'branches grafted in' = 'believing' Gentiles. K.H. Rengstorf

Herbert Gale argues that Paul's analogies and the traditions from which they appear to be taken are subordinate to his argument. The traditions are shaped to fit the point which Paul intends to make.[57] To the extent that these analogies and metaphors have generated religious themes and images, they, too, have contributed to the development of the discourse in these three chapters.

IV

In light of the foregoing discussion, it is evident that the application of scripture in Romans 9–11 develops according to two interrelated but distinct patterns: (1) it is used to illustrate and substantiate religious principles; and (2) it is applied to individuals, groups, or events in Paul's own historical situation. To be sure, these are inseparable; but as they work together in the development of the discourse, they illustrate that Paul's method of scriptural application in Romans 9–11 does not collapse into theological abstraction. Through *correspondence*, his use of scripture is firmly anchored in the circumstances of his ministry among the Gentiles. Hence, for Paul, the use of scripture is theologically motivated and it is put in the service of a message which is undergirded by definite theological presuppositions (that God is faithful to his promises to Israel, that righteousness is by faith, and that in Christ God's redemptive purposes include Gentiles), but it is virtually never divorced from his own missionary work and those whom he encounters during the course of this work. In this sense, at least, Paul's application of scriptural material is grounded historically.

However, typology understood in terms of 'type', 'antitype', historical linkage, and escalation is of extremely limited usefulness in assisting us to understand the dynamic of Paul's application of scripture in the epistles. Moreover, with respect to Romans 9–11, this terminology is completely inadequate. Nowhere in these three chapters can it be demonstrated with any degree of precision that Paul is relating 'type' and 'antitype' according to a notion of redemption-history. This is even

argues that the 'first fruits' in 11.16a reflects Num. 15.20-21 and that in Jewish tradition this image is related to Adam and not Abraham ('Das Ölbaum-Gleichnis in Röm. 11.16ff.: Versuch einer weiterführenden Deutung', in *Donum Gentilicium: New Testament Studies in Honour of David Daube* [ed. E. Bammel, C.K. Barrett and W.D. Davies; Oxford: Clarendon Press, 1978], pp. 128-32).

57. Gale, *Analogy*, pp. 204-205, 213-14.

true in 11.11-24, which incidentally is the one section of the discourse in which Paul refrains from quoting scripture directly. Thus, we have suggested that the term *correspondence* is more appropriate than typology for describing this linkage in Paul's application of scripture. If our argument is correct, it is clearly without foundation to assert that typology, understood theologically, is characteristic of Paul's use of scripture and is formative in his method of scriptural argumentation.

JSNT 9 (1980), pp. 2-28

THE MIDRASH IN 2 CORINTHIANS 3:
A RECONSIDERATION

A.T. Hanson[†]

In this article I intend to defend and expound the theory that in his midrash on Exodus 34 in 2 Cor. 3.7-18 Paul understood Moses to have seen the pre-existing Christ in the tabernacle.[1] I would add to this the suggestion that according to Paul the pre-existent Christ appeared in the form of man. But before we begin to expound the midrash in 2 Corinthians 3 there are a number of preliminary questions to be considered.

I

The concept of man as the image (εἰκών) of God is of central importance for this enquiry, so we may well begin by noting the words which are used in Gen. 1.26 and 5.3, the two passages where this concept is most clearly expressed. In Gen. 1.26 God says: 'Let us create man in our image, after our likeness'; and in Gen. 5.3 Adam 'became the father of a son in his own likeness, after his image'. Presumably the second passage is intended to make it plain that the quality of being in God's image was not confined to Adam but belonged to his posterity, that is, to the whole human race. Here is a diagram showing both the MT and the way in which the MT was rendered in the LXX and in the two *Targums Pseudo-Jonathan* and *Neofiti I*, both of which have interesting translations:

---

1. I put forward this theory originally in my book *Jesus Christ in the Old Testament* (London: SPCK, 1965), pp. 25-35.

	Gen. 1.26	Gen. 5.3
MT	בצלמנו כדמותנו	בדמותו כצלמו
Targ. Ps.-J.	בצלמנא כדיוקננא	רדמי לאיקוניה
Targ. Neof.	בדמותן כדנפק(ב)	בדמותיה כדנפק בה
LXX	κατ' εἰκόνα, καθ' ὁμοίωσιν	κατὰ τὴν ἰδέαν, κατὰ τὴν εἰχόνα

Etheridge renders *Frag. Targ.* in 1.26 with 'in the likeness of the presence of the Lord' and R. Le Déaut with 'à l'image de devant Yahwé'.[2] It is interesting that by the time *Targum Pseudo-Jonathan* came to be written εἰκών had been adapted into Aramaic. The periphrasis in the *Neofiti I Targum* may be purely reverential. Judging by the variety of translation, it does not look as if there was any real difference in the meaning between צלם and דמות.

Next we may look at the rabbinic evidence about the possibility of seeing God. Since the scriptures certainly represent various individuals as having seen God on certain occasions, it was difficult to deny outright that such a thing was possible. But a study of how later exegetic tradition treated those passages where individuals are described as seeing God shows that they caused embarrassment. Such passages are Jacob's wrestling with the angel in Genesis 32, after which he declares: 'I have seen God face to face'; Moses' vision of God in the burning bush in Exodus 3; the narrative in Exod. 24.9-11 where Moses, Aaron, and the elders of Israel go to Mount Sinai 'and they saw the God of Israel...they beheld God, and ate and drank'; the occasion when the skin of Moses' face shone because he had been talking with God (Exod. 34.29-35); the incident of the challenge to Moses' authority made by Aaron and Miriam in Num. 12.1-8, where God says: 'With Moses I speak mouth to mouth...and he beholds the form of the Lord'; Isaiah's vision of God in the temple in Isa. 6.1-5; and above all Ezekiel's daring chariot vision, which culminates in Ezek. 1.26 with the words 'and seated above the likeness of a throne was a likeness as it were of a human form'. Strack-Billerbeck quote a number of rabbinic passages on the question of the visibility of God.[3] The general sentiment is that no man can see God in

2.   See J.W. Etheridge, *The Targums of Onkelos and Jonathan ben Uzziel on the Pentateuch* (London: Longman, 1862; new edn: New York: Ktav, 1968), I, p. 160; R. Le Déaut, *Targum de Pentateuque I Genèse* (Paris: Cerf, 1978), p. 80; A. Díez Macho, *Ms Neophyti* (Madrid–Barcelona: Consejo Superior de Investigaciones Cientificas, 1968), I, Genesis, pp. 7, 27.

3.   H.L. Strack and P. Billerbeck, *Kommentar zum Neuen Testament aus Talmud und Midrasch*, III (Munich: Beck, new edn, 1961), *in loc.* 1 Cor. 11.7.

this present age, but in the age to come the righteous will see him. There are various instances of Gentiles demanding to see God and rabbis responding by telling them to look directly at the sun. This implies that God cannot be seen because of his exceeding glory, not necessarily because he is metaphysically incapable of being revealed in the world of particulars. The natural conclusion to be drawn from this is that when God is described as being seen in the scriptures it must have been not God in his essence who was seen, but some sort of an image of God.

The *Targum Pseudo-Jonathan*'s rendering of Num. 12.6b-8 is significant. This is how Etheridge translates it:

> To those (prophets) the Word of the Lord hath been revealed in apparition, speaking with them in a dream. Not so is the way with Mosheh my servant; in all the house of Israel my people he is faithful. Speaker with speaker have I spoken with him, who hath separated himself from the married life; but in vision, and not with mystery, revealed I myself to him at the bush, and he beheld the likeness of my Shekinah.[4]

The last phrase is a translation of the Aramaic:[5] חזי שכינתי דבתר וחמו. The meaning here seems to be that prophets only saw God by indirect vision; Moses had a direct vision, but what he saw was an image or likeness, not the great Invisible himself. A very instructive passage in this respect is Exod. 24.10-11. Here in v. 10 the MT has ויראו את אלהי ישראל. LXX renders with καὶ εἶδον τὸν τόπον οὗ εἱστήκει ἐκεῖ ὁ Θεὸς 'Ισραήλ. This very Hebraic expression suggests that the modification goes back to a Hebrew original, perhaps an oral Targumic tradition. Similarly in v. 11 the MT ויחזו את האלהים is translated by the LXX with καὶ ὤφθησαν ἐν τῷ τόπῳ τοῦ θεοῦ.[6] In 24.10 Aquila boldly translates with καὶ εἶδον τὸν θεὸν 'Ισραήλ, but Symmachus compromises with εἶδον ὁράματι τὸν θεὸν 'Ισραήλ. Josephus in his *Antiquities* does not describe the Sinaitic theophanies in detail, but his treatment of the incident of wrestling Jacob in Genesis 32 is significant: he describes Jacob as wrestling with a phantom, φάντασμα.[7] This word is normally

4.   Etheridge, *Targums*, II, p. 377.

5.   See M. Ginsburger, *Pseudo-Jonathan* (Hildesheim–New York: Georg Olms, 1971), *in loc.*

6.   ὤφθησαν seems to render the reading of the Samaritan Pentateuch, which has ויראו. Philo made use of the tradition reflected in the LXX of Exod. 24.10; see *Conf. Ling.*, pp. 95-99.

7.   S.A. Naber (ed.), *Flavii Josephi Opera Omnia* (Leipzig: Teubner, 1888); *Ant.* 1.331-32. Cf. also Philo, *Mut. Nom.* 14, where the angel is described as being

used to describe some apparition that is regarded as essentially unreal; compare Plato, *Sophist* 236c, where the act which produces φάντασμα ἀλλ' οὐκ εἰκόνα is described as 'fictional' (φανταστικήν). It looks as if Josephus wishes to relegate Jacob's encounter with God to the realm of dream or imagination.

There is an interesting comment on the incident of Moses' skin shining to be found in *b. Ber.* 7a (quoted also by Strack–Billerbeck). An ingenious comparison is made between Exodus 3, Moses' encounter with the burning bush, and Exod. 34.29-34:[8] 'As a reward of those [pious acts] Moses was privileged to obtain three [favours]'. In reward of 'And Moses hid his face', he obtained the brightness of his face. In reward of 'For he was afraid', he obtained the privilege that 'they were afraid to come nigh him'. In reward of 'To look upon God', he obtained 'The similitude of the Lord doth he behold'. This implies that Moses did see the similitude of God in the tabernacle. See also *b. Yeb.* 49b, commenting on Isa. 6.1: '*I saw the Lord* [is to be understood] in accordance with what was taught: All the prophets looked into a dim glass, but Moses looked through a clear glass'.[9] The editor here quotes Rashi's comment on this: 'In their prophetic visions they, like Isaiah, only imagined that they saw the deity. In reality they did not.' This comment comes of course from a much later age, representing no doubt a more sophisticated philosophical outlook. In *b. Ḥag.* 13b Raba is reported as saying, 'All that Ezekiel saw Isaiah also saw. What does Ezekiel resemble? A villager who saw the king. And what does Isaiah resemble? A townsman who saw the king.'[10] The editor explains the meaning of this comparison: a villager has to give a full description (as Ezekiel did) in order to convince his bearers that he really has seen the king. A mere mention, such as we find in Isaiah 6, will suffice if it comes from an educated man.

This last reference brings us to the famous chariot vision in the first chapter of Ezekiel. The rabbis were extremely nervous about allowing

invisible. All Philo references are from L. Cohn and B. Wendland, *Philonis Alexandri Opera Quae Supersunt* (Berlin: Reimer, 1896).

8. M. Simon, 'Berakoth', in *The Babylonian Talmud* (ed. I. Epstein; London: Soncino, 1948), p. 34.

9. W. Slotki 'Yebamoth', in *The Babylonian Talmud* (ed. I. Epstein; London: Sonsino, 1936), p. 324.

10. I. Abrahams. 'Hagiga', in *The Babylonian Talmud* (ed. I. Epstein; London: Sonsino, 1938), p. 79.

anyone to expound this passage, perhaps because of the danger of anthropomorphism or even idolatry, but also perhaps in the Tannaitic period and after because the passage was being claimed by Christians as an appearance of the pre-existent Christ. See *b. Hag.* 13a, where the editor, I. Abrahams, points out that Ezek. 1.27-28 is the very passage which the rabbis said should never be expounded. We even find the opinion expressed that but for Rabbi Hananiah b. Hezekiah the book of Ezekiel might well have been declared uncanonical, 'for its words contradict the words of the Torah'. A great part of ch. 2 of *Hagiga* is concerned with deciding what may or may not be taught about 'the work of the chariot'.

Ezekiel himself is guarded in his language: in 1.26 on 'the appearance of the throne' he sees רמות כמראה אדם. In 1.28 this is identified with מראה דמות כבוד יהוה. This is very significant from the point of view of our study, because God appearing in the form of a man is identified with the appearance of the divine glory. That glory came later to be associated very closely with the εἰκών. But it must be pointed out that neither the LXX nor the *Targum* uses εἰκών in translating these verses. Jervell brings evidence to show that כמראה אדם in 1.26 was taken by the rabbis as a reference to εἰκών. What the prophet saw was a heavenly image which was identified with Israel.[11] Here is the suggestion that when God appears as man he appears both as the εἰκών of himself and of ideal humanity.

We can point to two other passages in rabbinic literature which are relevant: in *b. Roš Haš.* 24a-b[12] we read: 'why then has it been taught: all portraits are allowed save the portrait of man? R. Anna the son of R. Idi replied: From a discourse of Abaye I learned *Ye shall not make with me* (Exod. 20.20) [implies] "Ye shall not make me".' The editor comments: 'And, since man was made in God's image (Gen. 1.27), the reproduction of the human face is not allowed.' In other words, man actually looks like God. The other passage is Piska 33.11 in *Pesiqta Rabbati*.[13] God is represented as speaking:

11. See. J. Jervell, *Imago Dei* (Göttingen: Vandenhoeck & Ruprecht, 1960), p. 117.

12. M. Simon, 'Rosh Hashanah', in *The Babylonian Talmud* (ed. I. Epstein; London: Soncino, 1938), p. 106.

13. *Pesikta Rabbati* (ed. W.G. Braude; New Haven and London: Yale University Press, 1968).

In how many different guises did I come to you! At the Red Sea I appeared to you as a mighty man waging war, as it is written: 'The Lord is a man of war'(Exod. 15.3). Then at Sinai I appeared as an elder teaching Torah, for the Torah is most comely when it issues out of the mouths of the elders. In the tabernacle I appeared before you as a bridegroom entering the chamber.

Compare with this R.P. Martin's conclusion based on Ezek. 1.26-28 that 'God cannot be seen in his essence...but only in his image';[14] and see also his reference on p. 205 to O. Michel's conclusion that 'as if in the form of a man' language was appropriate for divine epiphanies. Thus there was in the Judaism of the first three centuries of our era a tradition that, if anyone in scripture is described as having seen God, he must have seen the image of God, and probably that image took the form of a man.

II

We now turn to Paul, and we begin by asserting the proposition that Paul believed in the pre-existence of Christ. There are not many modern scholars who deny this proposition in set terms. It is true that J.A.T. Robinson does so in his book *The Human Face of God*.[15] But he seems to me to ignore most of the evidence. The fact that the Pauline doctrine of Christ's pre-existence is one which it is very difficult to accommodate to the sort of Christology which we tend to favour today must not be made a reason for denying that Paul held this doctrine. O. Cullmann in his well-known book *The Christology of the New Testament* emphasizes very much Christ's soteriological function and deprecates the attempt to assign him an ontological status *vis-à-vis* God; but he does not deny that Paul held a doctrine of pre-existence.[16] Similarly Käsemann does not deny that the entry of a pre-existent being into the world is implied in Rom. 8.3, but he does not think this was originally a Pauline doctrine.[17] In his exposition of Phil. 2.6-11 Käsemann also emphasizes very much the functional as opposed to the ontological status of Christ: 'Philippians

14. R.P. Martin, *Carmen Christi* (SNTSMS, 4; Cambridge: Cambridge University Press, 1967), p. 111.

15. See J.A.T. Robinson, *The Human Face of God* (London: SCM Press, 1973), pp. 161-69.

16. O. Cullmann, *The Christology of the New Testament* (London: SCM Press, 1959 [German edn Tübingen: Mohr (Siebeck), 1957]), pp. 168-69, 181.

17. E. Käsemann, *An die Römer* (Tübingen: Mohr [Siebeck], 1973), *in loc.*

2 tells us what Christ did, not what he was'.[18] We should however heed Feuillet's insistence that we are not justified in claiming that Paul does not speculate about the ontological relationship of Christ to God: some ontological relation must be implied in what Paul writes on the subject.[19]

Schneider accepts a full doctrine of pre-existence in Paul, but maintains that there is no question of pre-existence in the image of man: 'Jesus, who was the full image of God, became fully the image of man'.[20] We shall have reason to question this presently. In the meantime we may note Eltester's conclusion: 'The eikon of God is a sort of heavenly being'.[21] Eltester, rightly no doubt, believes that Paul reached this conclusion via the tradition of the divine wisdom. Jervell claims that by the time of the book of Wisdom the divine wisdom had been identified as the εἰκών of God and had therefore become an hypostasis and no mere poetical personification (Wis. 2.23; 7.26).[22] He also says that in Paul at least δόξα and εἰκών are synonymous (p. 180). Larsson voices a similar view when he writes: 'Doxa and eikon belong very closely together in Paul'.[23] He believes with the majority of Pauline scholars that the pre-existence of Christ must be implied by the phrase ἐν μορφῇ θεοῦ ὑπάρχων in Phil. 2.6 (p. 237). Commenting on the same passage, Barrett concludes that ἁρπαγμός means both *res rapta* and *res rapienda* because Paul sees Jesus as both a pre-existent divine being and a man who had given up divine status.[24] We can also quote R.P. Martin in his magisterial treatment of the 'hymn of the incarnation' in Phil. 2.6-11 as writing of 'the pretemporal existence of the heavenly Lord in his unique relationship to God'.[25] Most recent of all is R.G. Hammerton-Kelly; he goes beyond anything we would wish to claim here in his identification of a lineage for the concept of the heavenly man, accepting the speculations about a connection with Son of Man Christology and

18. Quoted in R.P. Martin, *Carmen Christi*, p. 83.

19. A. Feuillet, *Le Christ Sagesse de Dieu* (Paris: Gabalda, 1966), p. 158.

20. J. Schneider, ὁμοίωμα, *TWNT*, V, pp. 191-92.

21. W. Eltester, *Eikon im Neuen Testament* (BZNW, 23; Berlin: Töpelmann, 1958), p. 133.

22. J. Jervell, *Imago Dei*, p. 50.

23. E. Larsson, *Christus als Vorbild* (Uppsala: Acta Seminarii Neotestamentici Upsaliensis, 1962), p. 185. See also H. Conzelmann, *Der Erste Brief an die Korinther* (Göttingen: Vandenhoeck & Ruprecht, 1969), *in loc.* 11.7.

24. C.K. Barrett, *From First Adam to Last* (London: A. & C. Black, 1972), p. 72.

25. R.P. Martin, *Carmen Christi*, p. 119.

the *Ur-Mensch* myth.[26] But he does emphasize throughout that Paul believed in a pre-existent being whom he identified with Jesus Christ.

The next step is to consider Paul's description of Jesus as 'the man from heaven' or 'the heavenly man' (1 Cor. 15.47-48). Perhaps it would be best at this point to lay down the principle that we do not need to assume any connection between Paul's doctrine of Christ as the heavenly man and either a transcendental conception of the Son of Man or a Gnostic myth of the *Ur-Mensch*. Both these figures have played a large part in the works of some of the scholars we have quoted, such as Jervell, Larsson, Käsemann, and Hammerton-Kelly. But recent scholarship has tended to deprecate efforts to find a lofty transcendental lineage for the Son of Man concept, and the *Ur-Mensch* myth is now more often relegated to the second century.[27] Though texts such as Mk 14.62 show that one tradition in the early church had developed the Son of Man title in a transcendental direction, it does not seem necessary to assume that Paul did so. Admittedly he comes near to mentioning the title in 1 Cor. 15.27 where he applies the Son of Man text Ps. 8.6 to Christ. This need not mean any more than that he understood this psalm in a messianic sense. The author of Hebrews uses it similarly without apparently committing himself to a Son of Man doctrine. We will restrict ourselves accordingly to examining the one undoubted precursor of Paul who uses the 'heavenly man' concept, Philo.

Philo of course distinguishes between the first man of Genesis 1 and the second man of the second creation narrative; the first man was the image of God because he had no part in the temporal and earthly.[28] It is

26. R.G. Hammerton-Kelly, *Pre-existent Wisdom and the Son of Man* (Cambridge: Cambridge University Press, 1973), pp. 123, 152, 270-71.

27. See for example G. Vermes, *Jesus the Jew* (London: Collins, 1973); R. Leivestadt, 'Exit the Apocalyptic Son of Man', *NTS* 18 (1972), pp. 243-67; C. Colpe, *Die Religionsgeschichtliche Schule* (Göttingen: Vandenhoeck & Ruprecht, 1961); R. McL. Wilson, *Gnosis in the New Testament* (Oxford: Basil Blackwell, 1968); E.M. Yamauchi, *Pre-Christian Gnosticism* (London: Tyndale, 1973); M. Hengel, *The Son of God* (ET London: SCM Press, 1976 [German edn Tübingen: Mohr (Siebeck), 1975]). My view of Paul's relation to speculations about the 'heavenly man' is very similar to that of J.D.G. Dunn in his 'I Corinthians 15.45: Last Adam, Life-giving Spirit', in B. Lindars and S. Smalley (eds.), *Christ and Spirit in the New Testament* (Cambridge: Cambridge University Press, 1973), pp. 127-41, though of course Dr Dunn differs from my view of the pre-existence of Christ.

28. See G. Kittel, εἰκών, *TWNT*, II, pp. 391-92. Philo discusses these matters in *Op. Mund.*, p. 134 and *Leg. All.*, I, p. 31.

not clear however whether the ideal man in Philo is identical with the Logos.[29] The οὐράνιος ἄνθρωπος is 'made (γεγονώς) according to the image of God (κατ᾽ εἰκόνα θεοῦ)'.[30] Philo distinguishes between the ὑπὲρ ἡμῶν λόγος, which as such is εἰκὼν θεοῦ, and the logos in us, which he calls an ἐκμαγεῖον (almost 'offprint') of the image. Lietzmann well compares Phil. 3.21, where the 'heavenly' and the 'earthly' bodies are compared. Paul here uses Philo-like language but handles it in his own way. Conzelmann says that whereas in Philo we can find a hierarchy God-Logos-man, in Paul it becomes God-Christ-man.[31] Jervell amusingly describes Philo as having 'demythologized' Gen. 1.26-27.[32] From all this it seems reasonable to conclude that Paul himself knew of the doctrine of the 'heavenly man' and of the 'earthly man' in Judaism, but not that he was necessarily aware of Philo's treatment of this theme. On the other hand there are a number of striking parallels between Col. 1.15-20 and Philo's doctrine: Philo describes his Logos as πρωτόγονος (corresponding to πρωτότοκος in Col. 1.15, 18); he is δεσμὸς ἁπάντων (cf. Col. 1.17); and is also described as εἰκών and ἀρχή (see Col. 1.15, 18).[33] The author of Colossians, faced as Paul was not by a form of teaching which placed Christ in a cosmological setting, though a subordinate one, is compelled to elaborate a cosmological christology himself.[34]

By identifying Christ with the 'heavenly man' how far was Paul committing himself to a speculative christology? Allo is most emphatic

29. Eltester, *Eikon*, p. 41, and below p. 49.

30. See H. Lietzmann, *An die Korinther* I/II (ed. W.G. Kümmel; Tübingen: Mohr [Siebeck], 1969), in loc. 1 Cor. 15.45-46.

31. H. Conzelmann, *Der erste Brief an die Korinther*, in loc. 11.7. For Philo's refs. to ἐκμαγεῖον see *Op. Mund.*, p. 146; *Rer. Div. Her.*, p. 57.

32. Jervell, *Imago Dei*, p. 60.

33. For references see Eltester, *Eikon*, pp. 35, 37, 138, 143; Conzelmann, *Der erste Brief au die Korinther*, in loc. 11.7; Feuillet, *Le Christ Sagesse*, p. 186. Philo calls his Logos υἱὸς θεοῦ, πρωτόγονος, and ἀρχή in *Conf. Ling.*, pp. 145-46, and cf. p. 63; and see *Somn.*, I, p. 215. For the Logos as δεσμός, see *Plant.*, p. 9; *Fug.*, p. 112, and cf. *Migr. Abr.*, p. 220. For the Logos as εἰκών, see *Leg. All.*, III, p. 96. In *Op. Mund.* 2.5 the Logos is called the stamp (χαρακτήρ) of God's seal. I cannot find that Philo anywhere describes his Logos as κεφαλή. In *Spec. Leg.*, IV, p. 92, he describes thought (λόγος) in man as κεφαλή, but that is not the same thing.

34. Though I believe that Col. 1.1–4.6 was written by a disciple of Paul's after his death, it seems to me that 4.5-18 is genuinely Pauline. For another possible example of a separate Pauline letter of greetings being attached to a work to which it did not originally belong, compare Rom. 16.

that according to Paul Christ did not exist as heavenly man before the incarnation,[35] but one cannot help wondering how far Allo has been influenced in this judgment by dogmatic presuppositions. In very much the same way G. Kittel, though he agrees that Paul identified Christ with the heavenly Adam, claims that the figure had no speculative interest for Paul.[36] How far is this judgment influenced by the Barthian tradition in theology? Cullmann holds that Paul encountered the doctrine of the heavenly Adam in rabbinical tradition, but not directly in Philo. He believes that Paul is deliberately inverting the order which we find in Philo. He too is nervous about attributing any speculation to Paul.[37] Eltester is content to say that Paul was not directly influenced by Philo, but drew on the tradition of Hellenistic Judaism.[38] Jervell denies that Christ as δεύτερος ἄνθρωπος (1 Cor. 15.45-46) is identical with Philo's ideal man: Paul held that man was made in the image of the pre-existent Christ, who is the image of God.[39] C.K. Barrett believes that Paul by the heavenly man meant the Son of Man, a conclusion which we have agreed to regard as not necessary for our argument.[40] Conzelmann cannot make up his mind whether Paul in 1 Cor. 15.45-46. is arguing with Jews who had brought Philo's tradition from Alexandria, or whether he has a quite independent tradition of his own. He emphasizes (as does Barrett also) the eschatological element in Paul's presentation of Christ as the heavenly man: Paul is not talking about a knowledge of Christ that brings salvation, but is offering an interpretation of the historical act of salvation.[41] Martin, like nearly all other scholars, holds that Paul was acquainted with speculations 'about a Heavenly Original Man in Hellenised Judaism'.[42] From all this I would be content for the moment to draw the conclusion that when Paul called Christ 'the man from heaven', he must have thought of him as having been always the man from heaven. Christ could hardly have only begun to be the man from heaven at the resurrection. In other words, the pre-existent Christ, image of God, was also the heavenly man. Dunn in his

35. E.-B. Allo, *Saint Paul: Première Épître aux Corinthians* (Paris: Gabalda, 2nd edn, 1956), *in loc* 15.45-46.
36. Kittel, εἰκών, pp. 391-92.
37. Cullmann, *Christology*, pp. 167-69.
38. Eltester, *Eikon*, p. 131.
39. Jervell, *Imago Dei*, pp. 259, 327.
40. Barrett, *From First Adam to Last*, pp. 75-76.
41. Conzelmann, *Brief au die Korinther, in loc.* 15.45-46.
42. Martin, *Carmen Christi*, p. 133.

article 'I Corinthians 15.45' states emphatically that according to Paul Jesus only became the Last Adam at the resurrection. 'Christ's role as "second man" does not begin either in some pre-existent state, or at incarnation' (p. 140). I find this view impossible to reconcile with Paul's describing 'the second man' as being ἐξ οὐρανοῦ, and very difficult to reconcile with his calling Christ ὁ ἐπουράνιος. I agree with him that the era of the Spirit only began with the resurrection, but I see nothing incongruous in the suggestion that Paul thought of Christ as the heavenly man from all eternity, to be described as 'the second man' because he was only fully revealed as such at the resurrection.

Perhaps we should at this point give some attention to the question of what Paul exactly meant by saying that Christ was the εἰκών of God, and in particular, was he a visible image of God? Plummer commits himself to the statement that according to Paul Christ was 'the one visible representative of the invisible God'.[43] One can see the force of this conclusion in view of Col. 1.15 'image of the invisible God', and of Paul's emphasis on the historical Jesus as the revelation of God. Feuillet agrees with this conclusion. He says that εἰκών must mean 'the visible image of the invisible' despite the efforts of Origen and other Platonists to argue otherwise.[44] But there are two objections to this conclusion: first, if Christ is the pre-existent image of God, we cannot simply identify his character as image with the incarnation. And secondly, in the post-incarnation period Christ can only be recognized as image *by faith*, not by sight. Eltester appreciates both these points, for he writes: 'The eikon of God is a sort of heavenly being', and a little later adds that Christ is not the sensible image of God, because for Paul he is known by faith.[45] Martin, in his exposition of Phil. 2.6, points out that translating μορφή there by 'image' was a help, since it brought the subject back to the status of pre-Lapsarian Adam, and he takes it as a reference to 'the pre-temporal existence of the heavenly Lord in his unique relationship to God'.[46] That is, both as image of God and as image of man Christ is pre-existent. We must assume, I think, that according to Paul Christ is the image of God from all eternity, and this means that he represents the action of God whenever that becomes apprehensible in human history.

43. A. Plummer, *A Critical and Exegetical Commentary on the Second Epistle of Paul to the Corinthians* (ICC; Edinburgh: T. & T. Clark, 1915), *in loc.* 4.4.

44. Feuillet, *Le Christ Sagese*, pp. 174-75.

45. Eltester, *Eikon*, pp. 133, 135.

46. Martin, *Carmen Christi*, pp. 107, 119.

His quality of being God's image is not confined to the period of the incarnation, though it was uniquely manifested during that period. He was also revealed as image during Israel's history as narrated in scripture; and he now exists as God's image to be apprehended by faith in the experience of the Church.

Some light is thrown on Paul's view of the visibility of Christ by the sentence in 2 Cor. 5.7: διὰ πίστεως γὰρ περιπατοῦμεν οὐ διὰ εἴδους. Paul is contrasting our present condition with what we may expect at the parousia. All editors agree that εἶδος must mean 'form seen' and not 'act of seeing'. εἶδος is a word which in the LXX is regularly used to translate מראה, where the latter refers to an appearance of God. See Gen. 32.31-32, where the LXX renders פניאל twice with εἶδος θεοῦ; Exod. 24.17; Num. 12.8; Ezek. 1.26. Num. 12.8 (quoted by all editors) is particularly relevant, since the LXX runs: στόμα κατὰ στόμα λαλήσω αὐτῷ, ἐν εἴδει καὶ οὐ δι' αἰνιγμάτων, καὶ τήν δόξαν κυρίου εἶδεν. This must mean that Moses saw an image of God. Everyone agrees that Paul is thinking of this passage in 1 Cor. 13.12, and almost everyone connects it also with 2 Cor. 5.7. The one notable exception is G. Kittel in his article εἶδος in *TWNT*, II, pp. 371-73, who denies that 1 Cor. 13.12 or Num. 12.8 is relevant to the interpretation of 2 Cor. 5.7. Kittel also insists, because of the context, that Paul is contrasting our present state with the bodies which we shall have at the parousia. Collange rightly contests this (p. 232, see n. 57 below). The phrase must refer to the appearance of Christ in view of the usage in the LXX. Nor can it be dissociated from either Num. 12.8 or 1 Cor. 13.12. Bultmann takes the same view as Kittel (in loc. 2 Cor. 5.7; see n. 58 below). But Héring well comments that διὰ εἴδους is 'synonymous with στόμα κατὰ στόμα' (on 2 Cor. 5.7, see n. 54 below). We must conclude therefore that Paul seeing Christ διὰ εἴδους while still in this life corresponds to Moses seeing the εἶδος of the pre-existent Christ in the tabernacle, and that therefore when Paul does see Christ διὰ εἴδους at the parousia it will be in some inconceivable way a clearer and more glorious vision than that which Moses enjoyed. At least we can reasonably claim that Paul's use of διὰ εἴδους in 2 Cor. 5.7 confirms our claim that Moses saw an εἶδος τοῦ θεοῦ in the tabernacle, and that that εἶδος was an appearance of the pre-existent Christ.

We are now able to take the final step and suggest that according to Paul the pre-existent Christ, whenever he revealed himself, appeared in human form. Scholars have not in fact drawn this conclusion explicitly, no doubt because it only becomes apparent when one applies general conclusions about Pauline christology to specific problems of Paul's interpretation of scripture. But Cullmann's conclusions about Paul's understanding of the heavenly man seem to imply this. The second Adam comes from heaven, he says, where he exists in the image of God. 'Jesus the divine heavenly man was divine already in his pre-existence.'[47] Similarly Larsson writes that 'the man from heaven' cannot apply only to the parousia; it must apply also to the earthly life and to Christ's origin in the heavenly world. In fact it must be attributed to 'the fact of Christ *in toto*'.[48] In this context it is relevant to refer to the evidence brought by Jervell to show that in rabbinic tradition unfallen Adam had a supra-human appearance: 'Adam war eine Lichtgestalt. Sein Gesicht leuchtete heller als die Sonne.'[49] This gives us a good idea of the way in which Paul must have thought of the appearance of the pre-existent Christ.

An objection to this conclusion might be brought on the grounds that in Phil. 2.7 Paul, referring specifically to the life of the historical Jesus, uses the phrase ἐν ὁμοιώματι ἀνθρώπων γενόμενος. If Christ as image of man always existed in human form, how can he be described as 'being born in the likeness of man', or indeed as 'being found in human form'? We may reply that the words are probably not Paul's own composition, but part of the hymn which he is using. In any case, any doctrine that regards the pre-existent Christ as liable to appear to men in the course of Israel's history must imply *both* that the pre-existent being could appear in human form (e.g. to Abraham at the oaks of Mamre) *and* that his appearance as Jesus of Nazareth on the stage of history for thirty years had something unique about it. Indeed the suggestion that in Paul's view the pre-existent Christ appeared in human form goes a considerable way to solving the question, how can he be at one and the same time the pre-existent image of God and the pre-existent image of man? Because, Paul would reply, God chose that at various points in Israel's history he should be manifested through the pre-existent Christ in the form of a man. We think of all those theophanies we listed at the beginning of this article, starting from the three men at the oaks of Mamre, and culminating in Ezekiel's mysterious vision of God 'in the likeness as it were of a human form'. Indeed we

47. Cullmann, *Christology*, pp. 169, 181.
48. Larsson, *Christus als Vorbild*, pp. 319-20.
49. Jervell, *Imago Dei*, p. 100.

may suggest that a passage such as Deut. 18.15-16 would point in this direction also. There Israel is reminded that they could not endure God speaking to them out of the midst of the fire, and they are promised instead a prophet like Moses. We know from the Qumran documents that there was interest in this eschatological prophet in Judaism during the first century. Early Christians might well claim that Jesus, who was at least in their view the fulfilment of that prophecy, was only carrying out God's proclaimed policy of normally appearing to his people in the form of man.

III

We must now consider 2 Cor. 3.7-18 on the provisional assumption that he whom Moses saw in the tabernacle as narrated in Exodus 34 was, according to Paul, the pre-existent Christ, in the form of man. It follows therefore that Moses' reason for putting the veil on his face was not because he wished to conceal the fact that the reflected glory on his face was fading away. The reason he put on the veil was to prevent the messianic glory of the pre-existent Christ from being seen by the Israelites. This in turn must have been motivated (again according to Paul) by Moses' knowledge of the divine plan. God intended that, when the Messiah should appear in the flesh, Israel should not believe in him. Or rather, God knew that Satan would blind their minds. But God had provided for this: the very blindness of Israel would give an opportunity for the Gentiles to believe and thus become members of God's people. The theology of all this is spelt out in Romans 9–11, but particularly in Rom. 11.11-32, where Paul uses the same language of πώρωσις as he uses in 2 Cor. 3.14. If we compare 3.14 with 4.4, we can see that in Paul's day the agency that blinded the minds of the Jews was Satan, not God. We have no reason to conclude that it was otherwise in Moses' day. It seems to me that this is a much more plausible motive to ascribe to Moses, given Paul's rabbinic background. The great majority of scholars, who assume that Moses put on the veil to hide the fading away of the glory, must ascribe this action to personal vanity or pique, quite literally a desire to save his face. This seems a most improbable rôle for Paul to assign to Moses.

At the same time we must conclude that even the messianic glory reflected on Moses' face was ultimately bound to be done away according to Paul. This is because it belonged to the old dispensation, which was temporary and less direct than the new dispensation of the incarnate and risen Lord. But this obsolescence itself was not to take place until the coming of Christ in the flesh, that is, not till hundreds of years after the time of Moses. With these preliminary remarks we may proceed to a more detailed examination of the text.

The first important point of exegesis occurs in v. 7. Paul describes the glory on Moses' face as τὴν καταργουμένην. A number of scholars render this in one way or another so as to give the sense 'the glory which was fading away'. The notion of the glory actually beginning to disappear while Moses spoke to the Israelites outside the tabernacle is one which has been imported into the text by editors. The word καταργουμένην does not mean 'fade away, disappear'. The verb is used in the LXX in the sense 'to be vain, to cease working'. Symmachus uses it at Eccl. 12.3 to render the verb בטל: the grinders 'cease working'. Another version uses it to translate the Hiph'il of פרר in Lev. 26.15, 44 where the verb is used of a covenant and means 'to invalidate'. This is very significant, since Paul's point here is that the old dispensation or covenant was invalidated by Christ's coming in the flesh. Liddell and Scott only give the sense 'cause to be idle, hinder, make of no effect'. They also add 'be abolished, cease', but only quote this passage and others from Paul! Delling in *TWNT* is not very enlightening; he can only suggest that the verb indicates 'a devaluation of something which at one time had a relative worth'.[50] At any rate it must be plain that when Paul refers to the glory on Moses' face as τὴν καταργουμένην, he must be referring to the passing away of the old dispensation, an event not destined to take place till centuries after Moses' time, not to any alleged fading away of the glory during Moses' lifetime. This is surely confirmed by his reference in v. 19 to τὸ τέλος τοῦ καταργουμένου. This must refer to the end of the old dispensation.

We must therefore reject the interpretation of Allo, Lietzmann (commenting on v. 13),[51] Le Déaut,[52] and Dunn,[53] all of whom assume that the glory was short-lived and began to fade as soon as Moses left the tabernacle. Héring translates the phrase in v. 7 with 'destinée à

50. G. Delling, καταργεῖν, *TWNT*, I, pp. 453-54.

51. H. Lietzmann, *An die Korinther* I/II.

52. R. Le Déaut, 'Traditions Targumiques dans le Corpus Paulinien', *Bib* 42 (1961), p. 43.

53. J.D.G. Dunn, '2 Corinthians III.17—"The Lord is the Spirit"', *JTS* 21 NS (1970), p. 311.

disparaître', which is not far from the mark, but later on he renders the phrase with 'qui n'était cependant qu'ephémère'.[54] A phenomenon which lasted hundreds of years can hardly be called ephemeral. C.K. Barrett has a precisely similar comment.[55] On the other hand in a previous work, commenting on τοῦ καταργουμένου in v. 13, Barrett wrote that it is not clear what is referred to: 'the gender shows that it is not simply the glory', and concludes that Paul must mean 'the whole religious system based on the law'.[56] Collange when commenting on v. 7 seems to appreciate the difficulty of translating καταργουμένης as if it meant 'fading'. He offers 'abolie, anéantie, rendue vaine', and he goes on to say that it was abolished by the cross.[57] In similar vein Bultmann well remarks that the word means not 'vergehend' (actually in process of passing away), but 'vergänglich' (transitory).[58]

The next point at which our interpretation becomes relevant is v. 12, where Paul says that he (meaning, I take it, himself and his fellow-missionaries) uses great παρρησία. Compare also his use of ἐλευθερία in v. 17. According to our interpretation the boldness consists in preaching the risen Christ. It requires boldness because it involves claiming that God has been uniquely revealed in the human form of Jesus Christ. The risk that Paul runs is that his bearers will be led to believe that God is essentially in the form of a man. But if you are ἐν πνεύματι, and therefore can know Christ ἐν πνεύματι, you will not fall into this error; you will realize that God in Christ is now to be known ἐν πνεύματι and not κατὰ σάρκα (cf. 5.17), and also that the man-like aspect of God is wholly expressed in Christ incarnate and risen.

The contrast with Moses implies that Moses did in the tabernacle see God in the form of man but, unlike Paul, did not let this be known. Larsson takes the παρρησία to mean freedom from a false understanding of scripture and also freedom from guilt.[59] It is true that this last detail might seem to be supported by the rabbinic evidence: Rabbi

54. J. Héring, *La Seconde Epître de Saint Paul aux Corinthiens* (CNT; Paris: Cerf, 1958).

55. C.K. Barrett, *The Second Epistle to the Corinthians* (BNTC; London: A. & C. Black, 1973).

56. C.K. Barrett, *From First Adam to Last*, pp. 51-52.

57. J.-F. Collange, *Énigmes de la Deuxième Epître de Paul aux Corinthiens* (SNTSMS, 18; Cambridge: Cambridge University Press, 1972), p. 76.

58. R. Bultmann, *Der Zweite Brief an die Korinther* (ed. E. Dinkler; Göttingen: Vandenhoeck & Ruprecht, 1976).

59. Larsson, *Christus als Vorbild*, p. 277.

Simeon ben Jonai is recorded as having said that, whereas before the incident of the golden calf Israel had not been alarmed at the appearance of God as devouring fire on Mt. Sinai, after it they dared not even approach Moses with the glory on his face.[60] But this detail is not incompatible with the view we are advocating: blindness to Christ is associated in Paul's scheme of things with a sense of guilt induced by the law. Van Unnik has an interesting and scholarly treatment of the concept of 'unveiled face' in v. 18.[61] He protests that Moses covering his face has no real connection with freedom of speech. But it has, if Moses' veiling his face was done so that the Israelites should not know and proclaim the true revelation of God. It follows, he says, that Paul's παρρησία is not towards God, but towards men, which is true enough as far as it goes. He concludes that Christians 'are therefore in the same position which Moses, according to Exodus 34, only temporarily enjoyed' (p. 167). This too is true, except that the temporary period lasted longer than most editors allow, the rest of Moses' life, not just a few moments.

Next we come to the central question of our study, which faces us in v. 13: why did Moses put the veil on his face? As we have already indicated, the great majority of scholars assume, often with very little discussion, that he put it on because he knew that the glory on his face was rapidly fading away as soon as he left the tabernacle, and he wished to conceal this from the Israelites. This is true of Plummer and Allo. The latter claims that Moses did not intend to mislead the Israelites, but that his behaviour was 'a prophecy in action'. We can continue the list with Jeremias,[62] Feuillet (p. 135), Lietzmann (he adds that Moses did not need to take this precaution since the Jews' minds were blinded), C.K. Barrett (Moses did it 'that they might not see the glory come to an end and thus be led to disparage Moses as being of no more than temporary importance'), Van Unnik (pp. 161-62), Ulonska (Moses actually deceived Israel),[63] Dunn,[64] and Collange. This last writes: 'Moise aurait donc volontairement caché au peuple que sa gloire était

60. See K.G. Kuhn (ed.), *Sifre zu Numeri Tannaitische Midrashim* (Stuttgart: Kohlhammer, 1959), p. 13.
61. W.C. Van Unnik, '"With Unveiled Face"; An Exegesis of 2 Corinthians iii, 12-18', *NovT* 6 (1963), p. 159.
62. J. Jeremias, Μωϋσῆς, *TWNT*, IV, pp. 873-74.
63. See H. Ulonska, 'Die Doxa des Mose', *EvT* 26 (1966), p. 386.
64. See Dunn, '2 Corinthians III.17', p. 311.

évanescent' (p. 97). This is however hardly consistent with his statement quoted above that it was the cross which put an end to the glory of the old dispensation. If the glory was only to come to an end hundreds of years after Moses' time, there would have been no need for a veil during Moses' lifetime. Finally we may add Bultmann to this list: he (or his editor) does mention the view that the glory which was concealed from Israel was Christ's glory, but they call this an 'abwegige Reflexion'. Jervell had also considered this idea, but he writes: 'that would be quite a strange concept in this context'.[65] Perhaps we should add that Collange's account of Moses' motivation is modified in the same passage of his work when he says that Moses did not want the Israelites to attribute too much importance to his glory because he knew it was bound to end ultimately. So Paul does not want too much importance given by the Corinthians to ecstatic visions. But this interpretation seems too much influenced by Collange's own view of the nature of Paul's opponents in Corinth. Quite recently P. Jones has suggested quite a different motivation for Moses' act: 'Moses had to hide his face because the people could not partake in his experience of the vision of God'.[66] This is interesting and if pursued further might well lead to our view. But I cannot agree with him that Paul saw himself as a second Moses.

We maintain, then, that the right explanation for Moses' veiling his face is, according to Paul, that he wished to hide the glory of the pre-existent Christ whom he had seen in the tabernacle. Moses, we would argue, must have been hiding Christ, otherwise there is little point in the contrast between what Moses did and what Paul and his companions do (v. 13). Certainly Paul was proclaiming Christ. The objection might be made that Paul would not describe the glory of the pre-existent Christ as doomed to pass away. But on any reckoning he is prepared to say this about the glory of God reflected in Moses' face, so why should he not say it about the glory of the pre-existent Christ? Of all the editors I have consulted, only Larsson comes anywhere near this conclusion; he writes: 'If the apostles see the glory of Christ, this means that they see Christ in the scripture.'[67] Strack-Billerbeck quote several passages in which the

65. Jervell, *Imago Dei*, p. 188. Plummer was aware of this view but dismissed it likewise.

66. See P. Jones, 'L'Apôtre Paul: un second Moise pour la Communanté de la nouvelle Alliance' *Foi et Vie* 75 (1976), p. 49.

67. Larsson, *Christus als Vorbild*, p. 291.

divine origin and permanence of the glory reflected on Moses' face are emphasized: it was the same glory as he saw from the cleft in the rock; it came from the Torah when he received it on the mountain; some of the fire with which he wrote the Torah ran from his pen onto his face. And the reflected glory lasted till after he was buried.[68] I do not think that Paul would have been disposed to reject any of this *haggada*. He would have still maintained that this glory was doomed ultimately to pass away.

Naturally one's conclusion as to why Moses veiled his face will influence how one understands the phrase τὸ τέλος τοῦ καταργουμέ-νου in v. 13. Those who are convinced that Moses veiled his face because the glory was already fading away will insist that τέλος here must mean 'terminus' and nothing else. This point is made by Plummer, C.K. Barrett, Bultmann (the glory of Moses 'ein Ende nahm...zu Ende war'). On the other hand several editors admit that τέλος may very well mean 'fulfilment' and compare Rom. 10.4, where Christ is described as τέλος νόμου, very probably in the sense of 'the goal of the law'. See Héring, Feuillet (who claims the word in 2 Cor. 3.13 means both 'terminus' and 'goal'),[69] and Larsson.[70]

Now in v. 14 Paul transfers the veil from the time of Moses to his own time and places it on the minds of contemporary unbelieving Jews. This indicates that Paul's typology, as so often happens, is getting out of hand and is verging towards allegory. As long as Moses lived, the veil could be described as a means by which the Israelites were prevented from seeing the glory of the pre-existent Christ. But when Moses died he is represented by the Torah, by reading which rightly, Paul maintained, one could have discovered Christ; but the figure of the veil no longer applies, so it must be transferred to the minds of the Jews. Lietzmann protests that, if the Jews' minds were hardened there was no need for Moses to put on the veil. This is a fair point and makes one suspect that there is much truth in Barrett's contention that Moses' act of veiling had a typological or prophetic significance. Anyway Paul has in mind the whole course of Jewish history up to the coming of the Messiah. Moses and his veil could not stay there indefinitely. Just as Israel is represented in Deuteronomy as requesting that God should not speak directly to them, but use Moses as a mediator, so Paul may have thought of the Israelites as requesting Moses to wear a veil: they

---

68. Strack-Billerbeck, *Kommentar*, III, *in loc*. 2 Cor. 3.7.
69. Feuillet, *Le Christ Sagesse*, p. 117.
70. Larsson, *Christus als Vorbild*, p. 278.

preferred the indirect communication which was the work of the legal dispensation. Dunn in his article makes much of the phrase 'the same veil' in v. 14 in order to emphasize the fundamentally allegorical nature of the figure.[71] But this detail fits quite well into our interpretation: Moses used the veil to prevent the Israelites seeing the (pre-existent) Christ. The same veil today prevents the Jews from recognizing (the proper meaning of the word ἀτενίσαι, as several editors point out)[72] the risen Christ. Bultmann sees a connection between the hardening here and the hardening in Rom. 11.7, 25; and Van Unnik makes an illuminating comparison with Rom. 11.8.[73] Only Collange entirely repudiates any connection with Romans 11, claiming that in Romans Paul is speaking of the Jews in corporate terms, and in 2 Corinthians 3 of any of his opponents who turn to Christ.[74] But his interpretation is strongly influenced by his own view as to the arguments of Paul's opponents.

The next point that concerns us comes at the very end of v. 14: it turns on the question: what is the subject of καταργεῖται there? We maintain, together with the majority of commentators, that the subject must be ἡ παλαιὰ διαθήκη and not κάλυμμα. In fact the verb καταργεῖν cannot be appropriately used for the removal of a veil. Only Plummer amongst those whom I have consulted holds that κάλυμμα is the subject of the verb. We need not spend much time on the very difficult phrase μὴ ἀνακαλυπτόμενον. Those editors are no doubt right who claim that the word cannot be a synonym for ἀποκαλυπτόμενον, and that the accusative absolute construction is therefore untenable.[75] Oepke cites a passage in the Testaments where the verb can mean 'lifting a veil'.[76]

The interpretation of vv. 16, 17 and 18 is all of a piece. Most editors who understand πρὸς κύριον in v. 16 of Christ also understand Christ to be referred to in ὁ δὲ κύριος in v. 17, as also by τὸ πνεῦμα κυρίου in that verse, and by τὴν δόξαν κυρίου in v. 18. The phrase ἀπὸ κυρίου πνεύματος is different. In this group are Plummer, Allo,

71. Dunn, '2 Corinthians III.17', p. 312.

72. Compare Collange, *Énigmes*, p. 75; he suggests 'fixer du regard, regarder intensement'.

73. Van Unnik, '"With Unveiled Face"', pp. 162-63.

74. Collange, *Énigmes*, pp. 93, 101-102.

75. See for example Bultmann.

76. A. Oepke, ἀνακαλύπτω, *TWNT*, II, pp. 562-63.

Héring, Barrett, Van Unnik,[77] and Ulonska.[78] This last scholar however suggests that Paul did not mean us to take him very seriously;
he writes: 'for Paul's imaginative treatment of the Old Testament
("alttestamentliche Anspielungen") only constituted material suitable for
parenesis'. This is a view which it seems to me is fundamentally mistaken: the scriptures were not regarded by Paul as 'the Old Testament'
at all; he did not treat them merely as material for parenetic allegories.
He believed that in them he could find genuine information about Christ.
Thus here Paul makes a perfectly comprehensible comparison: just as
Moses, when he returned to the tabernacle and saw the pre-existent
Christ there (ἐπιστρέφῃ πρὸς κύριον) removed the veil from his face,
so today when a Jew turns to the risen and glorifies Christ, the veil is
removed from his heart and he sees the Lord (Christ).[79]

There is however a group of scholars that insists on translating πρὸς
κύριον in v. 16 as 'to Yahweh' or at least as 'to the Lord' in the sense
of God the Father. Among these is Feuillet.[80] As he believes v. 16
applies to the Jews of Paul's day, he has to maintain that Paul can
describe a Jew becoming a Christian as his turning to God the Father,
not to Christ, a most unlikely conjecture. Similarly Collange claims that
in citations from the Old Testament Paul usually uses κύριος as meaning God not Christ. He refers to Cerfaux for confirmation of this view,
but makes it plain that Cerfaux regards v. 16 as an exception to his
rule.[81] A similar claim is made by Dunn, who says that normally in Paul
ὁ κύριος is Christ and κύριος is Yahweh.[82] Since he also maintains that
in v. 17 ὁ κύριος means the Spirit, not Christ, he has to argue that
there ὁ δὲ κύριος is 'anaphoric' and virtually conveys the meaning
'that Lord (in Exod. 34.34)'. He proceeds to go through all the
examples of Paul's use of κύριος and ὁ κύριος. But there are so many
doubtful instances or positive exceptions to his rule that by the end it has
collapsed altogether.

We now approach what could be called the Mount Everest of Pauline

---

77. Van Unnik, '"With Unveiled Face"', pp. 164-66.

78. H. Ulonska, 'Die Doxa', pp. 387-88.

79. I think Plummer is correct in his suggestion that Paul got the word ἐπιστρέφῃ
from the LXX of Exod. 34.31, where Aaron and the elders of Israel returned
(ἐπεστράφησαν) to talk to Moses.

80. Feuillet, *Le Christ Sagesse*, pp. 127-32.

81. Collange, *Énigmes*, pp. 103-104.

82. Dunn, '2 Corinthians III.17', pp. 317-19.

texts as far as difficulty is concerned—or should we rather call it the sphinx among texts, since its difficulty lies in its enigmatic quality rather than in its complexity? We take the phrase ὁ δὲ κύριος in v. 18 to refer to Christ. As such it fits in very easily to our interpretation: when Moses returned to the sanctuary to converse with the pre-existent Christ, he removed the veil. When a Jew in Paul's day turns to Christ, the veil is removed from his mind. But Christ is now known to us as Spirit (see 1 Cor. 15.45), and where the Spirit of the Lord (Christ) is, there is liberty. That is why we can freely proclaim Christ and know him in our experience. The difference between our situation and Moses' is that since the resurrection of Christ we have entered the era of the Spirit, so veils and restriction of proclamation can be done away with. In other words, we follow what might be called the theory of an 'economic' identity between Christ and the Spirit, an identity of experience though not of essence. This theory has been fully worked out by I. Hermann in his book *Kyrios und Pneuma*, and is, in one form or another, accepted by all editors who read ὁ δὲ κύριος in v. 17 as indicating Christ.[83]

In fact most editors follow this line. To interpret the phrase otherwise involves very great difficulties indeed. So we find an 'economic' solution adapted by Plummer, Allo, and Barrett. Barrett is in fact inclined to favour what might be called a 'pesher' classification of Paul's exegesis of scripture here. Just as in the Qumran documents the identification of the person or object referred to in scripture with a person or object in the history (contemporary or past) of the Qumran sect is made simply by saying 'A is B', so with Paul. So when Paul says in effect 'the Lord referred to in Exod. 34.29-35 *is* the Spirit', he only means that the narrative in Exodus is a prophecy of the figure who was to appear in the messianic era. He does not imply any substantial identity of the 'A' in scripture with the 'B' in Paul's day. This view is strongly espoused by Dunn,[84] and seems to be expressed in an extreme form by Vörster.[85] But surely this is a most unfortunate instance whereby to support this

83. I. Hermann, *Kyrios und Pneuma* (Munich: Kösel, 1961). This view of the relation of Christ to the Spirit in Paul is in fact accepted by Dunn (see 'I Corinthians 15.45, p.139), but he insists that 2 Cor. 3.17 is not an illustration of this. See below n. 84.

84. Dunn, '2 Corinthians III.17', *passim*. See also his book, *Unity and Diversity in the New Testament* (London: SCM Press, 1977), pp. 84-91.

85. W.S. Vörster, '2 Kor. 3.17: Eksegese in Toeligting' *Neot* 3 (1969), pp. 37-44. I have not read this article, but have only studied the epitome given in *New Testament Abstracts*.

'pesher' theory. The person 'A' here is none other than the Lord (whether God or Christ does not affect this particular argument), the one being who cannot be relegated to the past. To interpret Paul as saying 'When Moses turned back to the Lord (in the tabernacle) is an allegorical way of referring to the future conversion of any given Jew to Christianity' is surely to introduce a quite gratuitous complication of exegesis. We may well quote Greenwood: 'Surely "Yahweh" had christological connotations for St Paul from which he could not escape even when composing a pesher'.[86]

We revert therefore to the list of those who take v. 17 to refer to Christ and who accept an 'economic' identity between Christ and the Spirit. The list continues with Lindblom,[87] Larsson,[88] Bultmann, and Daniélou.[89] Daniélou actually suggests that the phrase ὁ δὲ κύριος τὸ πνεῦμά ἐστιν is a quotation from Lam. 4.20a. The LXX of this line runs: πνεῦμα προσώπου ἡμῶν χριστὸς κύριος. But there is a variant reading, κυρίου, and some of the Fathers read πρὸ προσώπου for προσώπου. These variants would presumably give the sense: 'The Lord Christ is Spirit before our faces', that is, for us whose faces are not veiled. Daniélou claims that the same line is echoed in Lk. 2.26 πρὶν ἢ ἂν ἴδῃ τὸν Χριστὸν κύριον. If Daniélou is right, it would confirm our interpretation since the clear implication would be that when Moses took off the veil the Lord Christ was before his face. But it seems rather a doubtful speculation. There does not seem to be much likelihood that Lam. 4.20a was in use as a proof text among the Christians of Paul's day.

Feuillet, in maintaining that ὁ δὲ κύριος in v. 17 must refer to God the Father and not Christ, asks pointedly whether anyone can say in the same phrase: 'Christ is the Spirit' and 'the Spirit of Christ' (p. 134). But in Rom. 8.9 Paul appears to identify 'the Spirit of God' with 'the Spirit of Christ', so, if Feuillet's interpretation of v. 17 here is correct, Paul could say that Christ was the Spirit of God, despite writing of 'the Spirit of Christ'. And later on in Romans 8 Paul attributes the same function of intercession to the Spirit (8.26) and to Christ (8.34), which looks very

86. See D. Greenwood, '"The Lord is the Spirit": Some Considerations of 2 Cor. 3.17', *CBQ* 34 (1972), p. 470.
    87. J. Lindblom, *Gesichte und Offenbarungen* (Lund: Gleerup, 1968), pp. 117-19.
    88. Larsson, *Christus als Vorbild*, p. 277.
    89. See J. Daniélou, *Études d'exégèse judéo-chrètienne* (Paris: Beauchesne, 1966), p. 92.

much like the sort of 'economic' identity for which we are arguing.[90]

In v. 18 we must understand the verb κατοπτριζόμενοι as meaning 'contemplating' not 'reflecting', since the point that Paul is making is that Christians, like Moses in the tabernacle, can see the Lord Christ. By contemplating we are transformed into his image. Only after this point, if at all, comes the parallel with Moses reflecting the glory on his face. Editors are very much divided between those who prefer 'contemplating' and those who prefer 'reflecting'. As far as usage of the word elsewhere is concerned, there is much more evidence for the meaning 'contemplating', though 'reflecting' cannot be absolutely ruled out on lexicographical grounds.[91] As one might expect, Feuillet (p. 136), Collange (p. 111), and Dunn (p. 318) all take τὴν δόξαν κυρίου in v. 18 to refer to God, not Christ, and so does Jervell (p. 189). But the first three of these agree in seeing this chapter not really as a christo-centric midrash, whereas we claim that this is exactly what it is. Plummer, Lindblom,[92] and Larsson (p. 185) all take the phrase as referring to Christ. Naturally scholars divide along the same line of interpretation as far as understanding τὴν αὐτὴν εἰκόνα is concerned. If you believe that πρὸς κύριον in v. 16 refers to Christ, you will interpret the image here as being Christ's. If you believe that Christ is not referred to in vv. 16-17, you will take it as God's image. Personally I find it impossible not to refer it to Christ, both because of my foregoing interpretation and because Christ is called 'the image of God' only four verses later.

This leaves us with the difficult phrase καθάπερ ἀπὸ κυρίου πνεύματος. Feuillet, consistently with his approach, takes this as a reference to Yahweh (p. 147), but either Plummer's rendering or Lietzmann's seems to make better sense. Plummer offers 'Even as from the Lord Christ who is spirit', and Lietzmann paraphrases with 'as naturally happens, since it comes from the Lord the Spirit'. Christ, he

90. We need not consider Héring's solution to the problem of v. 17 by arbitrary alteration of the text.

91. In favour of the meaning 'contemplating' are G. Kittel (κατοπτρίζομαι, *TWNT*, II, pp. 696-97, p. 254), Oepke (ἀγακαλύπτω, p. 563), Feuillet (*Le Christ Sagesse*, p. 138; he claims that the passage in Plutarch where the word appears to mean 'reflect' is doubtful), Barrett, Collange (*Énigme*, p. 117; he considers the usage in Philo, *Leg. All.*, III, p. 101 decisive), Larsson (*Christus als Vorbild*, pp. 279-80, for precisely the reasons we have given alone), and Bultmann. In favour of the rendering 'reflecting' are Plummer, Allo (but on the basis of the Plutarch ref.), Héring, Jervell (*Imago Dei*, p. 184), and Van Unnik ('"With Unveiled Face"', p. 167).

92. Lindblom, *Gesichte*, p. 119.

adds, can be called the Spirit, since he is the possessor of the Spirit. This seems the better of the two translations, since κυρίου πνεύματος is not a very natural way of expressing 'the Lord who is spirit'. The sense, if we follow out our interpretation consistently, must be: 'as Moses saw Christ in the tabernacle with unveiled face, so we today can see him and thereby be transformed into his likeness, a process of growing freedom, since freedom is the mark of the Spirit, and we know Christ as Spirit'.

* * * * *

In conclusion we have three remarks to make about our interpretation of this famous midrash. First, 2 Cor. 4.1 6 seems to confirm our exegesis: in these verses Paul makes clear his belief that Christ is the image of God and as such he mediates to Christians the glory of God. Eltester well points out how the δόξα τοῦ Χριστοῦ in v. 4 corresponds to the δόξα τοῦ θεοῦ in v. 6.[93] Similarly Jervell, though he believes that δόξαν κυρίου in 3.18 refers to Yahweh, concludes that the δόξαν κυρίου is Christ because he is the image of God.[94] Feuillet says equally explicitly that Christ is the image or mirror of the Father, who is essentially invisible.[95] Thus we seem to have in 2 Corinthians the doctrine which is certainly present in the Fourth Gospel, that Christ is the visibility of God. Better perhaps to say that he is the apprehensibility of God, since, as we have noted above, Christ is only knowable now by faith. This means that the statement in Col. 1.15 that Christ is 'the image of the invisible God' is only making explicit by a disciple of Paul's what was certainly an element in Paul's christology.

Secondly, it might be as well to repeat what we have said before, that this midrash is an example of Paul's typological use of the scriptures. The narrative in Exod. 34.29-30 is not a mere cipher to Paul. He believes it really did happen, but the pattern of events has to some extent been reproduced in the circumstances of the early Church. Paul therefore traces a parallel between a set of events in the old dispensation and in the new. Admittedly Paul's use of the figure of the veil becomes confused when he applies it to his own day: the veil has to stand for *both* Moses' determination that Israel should not see the glory of the pre-existent Christ *and* the failure of Jews in Paul's day to acknowledge

93. Eltester, *Eikon*, p. 133.
94. Jervell, *Imago Dei*, p. 180.
95. Feuillet, *Le Christ Sagesse*, p. 149.

Jesus Christ. The result is a tendency towards allegory. But this is not Paul's intention, which is firmly based on his concept of salvation history.

Thirdly, we might make some attempt to set the midrash as understood by us in its context. In the beginning of ch. 3, and in ch. 4, Paul is apparently vindicating his ministry and that of his colleagues against those in Corinth who are traducing it. He makes two essential points about this ministry: (a) it is a ministry which is centred on Christ, and (b) it is a ministry of open proclamation. Both these principles come out clearly in the midrash, and indeed it could reasonably be said that the midrash was composed in order to defend these two principles. From this one might be justified in conjecturing that Paul's critics in Corinth had emphasized the Torah rather than Christ as the centre of their gospel, and also that they claimed to possess a secret *gnōsis* and perhaps also to know mysteries which would only be disclosed to the elect. This sort of teaching might be traced later perhaps in the heresy which afflicted the church in Colossae. But here we enter the realm of mere speculation. It seems to me to be more satisfactory to interpret Paul primarily on the basis of what he says himself rather than attempting to start from what we think we can reconstruct of what his opponents were saying.

JSNT 16 (1982), pp. 64-78

'AND ROSE UP TO PLAY':
MIDRASH AND PARAENESIS IN 1 CORINTHIANS 10.1-22

Wayne A. Meeks

The logic of Paul's counsel to the Corinthian Christians about 'meat offered to idols' has long troubled interpreters. A particularly difficult problem has been the relation of 1 Cor. 10.1-22 to the rest of chs. 8–10. In these verses Paul appears to adopt an absolute prohibition of contact with pagan cults, but that accords ill with his more lenient stand in ch. 8 and in 10.23-31. Moreover, the sequence of thought in 10.1-22 has not been completely clear, either. How are the scriptural examples connected with the paraenetic warnings? How is the consoling statement about temptation in v. 13 to be squared with the general warnings that precede it and the specific warning against idolatry that follows? What is the connection between the example of the wilderness experience of Israel and the dangers of pagan society in the city of Corinth?

Several modern commentators have sought a key to the exegetical problems by supposing that Paul depended on Jewish aggadic traditions and that he used interpretative techniques like those found in rabbinic midrash. Johannes Weiss called vv. 1-5 'a midrash',[1] and he has been followed by many subsequent interpreters. Attempts to describe this 'midrash', however, have focused mostly on the intriguing matters of the first four verses: the following Rock, the meaning of 'spiritual food' and 'spiritual drink', and the 'Wisdom Christology' suggested to many by the fact that Philo had treated both manna and rock as symbols of the divine wisdom.[2] As a result, the scriptural texts alluded to in vv. 1-4

1. Johannes Weiss, *Der erste Korintherbrief* (KEK, 5; Göttingen: Vandenhoeck & Ruprecht, 9th edn, 1910), p. 250.
2. E.g., J.W. Doeve, *Jewish Hermeneutics in the Synoptic Gospels and Acts* (Assen: van Gorcum, 1954), pp. 110-11; Peder Borgen, *Bread from Heaven: An*

and the Jewish targums and interpretations of those texts have been repeatedly examined, while little attention has been paid to the allusions in vv. 6-10, including the one explicitly cited quotation in v. 7.[3] Consequently the unity of vv. 1-13 has often been overlooked or ignored.

In fact vv. 1-13 are a literary unit, very carefully composed prior to its use in its present context. For convenience's sake I shall call it a homily, without wishing to beg the question of its pre-epistolary *Sitz im Leben*. By analyzing its construction, we will be able both to understand its own meaning better and to see more clearly how Paul has adapted it to his epistolary admonition.

The passage is divided neatly in half by a simple contrast between 'all' of the Israelites, who enjoyed God's salvation at the Sea of Reeds and his protection in the wilderness, and 'some [most] of them', who rebelled against God and were punished for it. To the five parallel clauses signalled by the repeated πάντες in vv. 1-4 correspond five statements about 'some of them' in vv. 6-10.[4] The five positive and the five negative *exempla* are both punctuated and linked with the paraenetic conclusion in vv. 12-13 by means of an *inclusio*, vv. 6 and 11:

ταῦτα δὲ τύποι ἡμῶν ἐγενήθησαν κτλ.
ταῦτα δὲ τυπικῶς συνέβαινεν ἐκείνοις, ἐγράφη δὲ πρὸς
    νουθεσίαν ἡμῶν κτλ.

The summary warning in v. 12, in the generalizing third person imperative, draws together the five warnings of vv. 6-10, which in the commonly accepted text alternate between first and second person plural.[5]

Exegetical Study of the Concept of Manna in the Gospel of John and the Writings of Philo (NovTSup, 10; Leiden: Brill, 1965), pp. 21-22, 91-92; E. Earle Ellis, *Prophecy and Hermeneutic in Early Christianity* (WUNT, 18; Tübingen: Mohr [Siebeck]/ Grand Rapids: Eerdmans, 1978), pp. 156, n. 36, 168, 209-12, 226, n. 11; Gustave Martelet, 'Sacrements, figures et exhortation en 1 Cor., X, 1–11', *RSR* 44 (1956), pp. 323-59, 515-59. On the other hand, Roger Le Déaut, *La nuit pascale* (Rome: Pontifical Biblical Institute, 1963), pp. 320-21, regards the exhortation as a spontaneous composition by Paul, but based on the Passover seder.

3.   An exception is the second half of Martelet's essay cited in n. 2 above.

4.   Four times καθώς (καθάπερ) τινες αὐτῶν. But the first of the series, καθὼς κακεῖνοι, is no exception, for the antecedent is οἱ πλείονες in v. 5.

5.   The textual witnesses are divided, however. The first plural has strong support in v. 10, and γίνεσθε in v. 7 could possibly have been an early auditory error for γίνεσθαι (pronounced the same), parallel to εἶναι in v. 6 (a reading actually attested in the bilingual mss F G and presupposed by the Armenian, according to Tischendorf).

Thus it is not only vv. 1-4 that exhibit a 'strenger Aufbau',[6] but the whole section, vv. 1-13.

There are some elements that perturb this rigorous symmetry, however. 'And the rock was Christ' reads like a gloss. It is very likely Paul's addition; a possible reason for it will emerge as we look more closely at the ways he adapted the homily. The clause, 'And all received baptism[7] into Moses by means of the cloud and by means of the sea', has also seemed problematic to many readers. Because no real analogy can be found in Jewish texts, commentators all but universally agree that it is a Christian construction by analogy with 'baptized into Christ'. If this whole sentence were eliminated, the *exempla* would be simply the cloud-pillar, the sea-crossing, the manna, and the miraculous spring, and the whole homily might be Jewish rather than Christian. However, the double five-fold structure would thereby be broken. Furthermore, while it is conceivable that another Jewish eschatological sect could believe itself to have encountered already 'the end of the aeons',[8] v. 11 expresses a view of scripture's fulfillment that is also stated by Paul in Rom. 15.4. On the whole, it requires fewer assumptions to regard the homily as Christian. In that case, the variant reading χριστόν in v. 9 may well be original, as the *UBSGNT* and Nestle–Aland texts now suppose.

To be sure, there is no dearth of Jewish models for this kind of composition. Space does not permit here a rigorous form-critical analysis, which would reveal several related *Gattungen*. However, the general pattern is obvious: a list of God's gracious acts for Israel, especially connected with the Exodus and the wilderness pilgrimage, followed by a list of Israel's sins in despite of that grace, committed especially by the

---

6.   Georg Braumann, *Vorpaulinische christliche Taufverkündigung bei Paulus* (BWANT, 82; Stuttgart: Kohlhammer, 1962), p. 20 n. 46.

7.   Although the *UBSGNT*[3] and Nestle–Aland[26] have returned to the passive ἐβαπτίσθησαν, the arguments made for the middle by Georg Heinrici, *Kritisch exegetisches Handbuch über den ersten Brief an die Korinther* (KEK, 5; Göttingen: Vandenhoeck & Ruprecht, 7th edn, 1888), p. 269 n., still seem persuasive. So does his interpretation, that the middle here does not necessarily imply self-baptism, but perhaps merely emphasizes 'den receptiven Sinn' (p. 271). Apparently C.K. Barrett agrees, for he translates 'accepted baptism' (*A Commentary on the First Epistle to the Corinthians* [Black/Harper NTC; London: A. & C. Black; New York: Harper, 1968], pp. 219-21, 234). See also H.W. Bartsch, 'Ein neuer Textus Receptus für das griechischen Neue Testament?', *NTS* 27 (1981), pp. 585-92.

8.   Cf. e.g., 1QpHab 7.1-4.

wilderness generation, culminating in warnings to the contemporary audience to respond to God's grace and not to follow the bad example of the wilderness Israelites. Several of the so-called 'historical Psalms' exhibit this pattern, especially Psalm 78. Psalm 105 is similar, but scarcely mentions Israel's rebellions, while Psalm 136 mentions them not at all. Both Psalm 106 and the great prayer of Ezra recorded in Neh. 9.9-37 use the pattern in a confession of sins rather than an exhortation. A similar prayer may have been used by the Alexandrian Jews on Yom Kippur in the first century of our era, for Philo quotes just such a prayer, although he describes it as a silent prayer of the souls of those fasting and omits all reference to sins.[9] The admonitory form recalls some of the judgment oracles of the classical prophets, for example, Hos. 13.4-8; Amos 2.9-16; 3.2. The pattern is implicit in several strands of the Hexateuch narratives, and it is a leitmotif of Deuteronomy. It is particularly clear in the 'Song of Moses', Deuteronomy 32, a passage which, as we shall see later, has special importance for understanding 1 Corinthians 10. It is interesting that the fourth-century Samaritan midrash on sections of the Pentateuch, the *Memar Marqah*, devotes an entire book to the exposition of the Song of Moses, elaborating just the pattern I am describing by means of cross-references to the narratives of Exodus and Numbers.[10]

Paul was not the last Christian author to adapt this pattern for Christian exhortation. The principal theme of the Epistle to the Hebrews turns upon the superiority of the new covenant established through the new High Priest to the old covenant enacted through Moses, and the consequently greater dangers of neglecting it. This theme is announced in 2.1-4 and summed up in 12.18-29. Heb. 3.7–4.13, an exposition of Ps. 95.7-11, particularly resembles our text in 1 Corinthians. A similar homiletic pattern may be found in Jude, as E. Earle Ellis has observed.[11] Jude 5, indeed, is a terse summary of the point made in 1 Cor. 10.1-12.

9. *Spec. Leg.* 2.199.

10. *Memar Marqah: The Teaching of Marqah* (ed. and trans. J. Macdonald; BZAW, 84; Berlin: Töpelmann, 1963). See especially 4.4 and 4.8. Note the introduction to 4.4, which would be better translated as follows, rather than as Macdonald does: 'A faithful God [Deut. 32.4]. The word pertains to kingship. There is no succession [to the kingship] forever. Yet there were rebellions against it ten times [cf. Num. 14.22, quoted and expounded in 4.8], and no one quelled these but Moses the prophet.'

11. Ellis, *Prophecy and Hermeneutic*, pp. 221-36; for comparison with 1 Cor. 10.1-13, see p. 226, n. 11.

The careful construction of our passage is evident not only in its logical structure, but also in a subtle use of the scripture that underlies that structure. That is what Weiss and others meant by calling the first portion 'a midrash'. The 'midrashic' character of vv. 6-11 is even more complex. Since the aggadah about the wandering well, spring, or rock has been so often explored, I shall concentrate rather on the five *exempla* of the wilderness generation's sins. The question of what that generation did which was so heinous that they were forbidden to enter the promised land already exercised the biblical writers, and it was frequently discussed by later interpreters. The basic text is Num. 14.20-35; it will be helpful to have two of its sentences before us:

> None of the men who have seen my glory and my signs which I wrought in Egypt and in the wilderness, and yet have *put me to the proof* these ten times and have not harkened to my voice, shall see the land which I swore to give their fathers; and none of those who despised me shall see it (vv. 22-23).

> Say to them, 'As I live', says the Lord, 'what you have said in my hearing I will do to you: *your dead bodies shall fall in this wilderness*; and of all your number, numbered from twenty years old and upward, who *have murmured against me*, not one shall come into the land where I swore that I would make you dwell, except Caleb the son of Jephunneh and Joshua the son of Nun (vv. 28-30).

(I have italicized the elements to which Paul makes direct allusion in 1 Cor. 10.5, 9, 10). The rabbis disagreed about precisely which incidents were to be counted among the ten 'tests'. Mishnah Aboth 5.4 compares them with the ten wonders in Egypt, ten at the sea, and ten plagues, but does not specify the rebellions. Version 'A' of *Aboth de Rabbi Nathan*, however, offers two lists. In ch. 9, the ten are '[two] at the Red Sea, one when the manna began to fall, one when the manna ceased to fall, one when the first quail were seen, one when the last quail were seen, one at Marah, one at Rephidim, one at Horeb, and one when the spies (returned)'.[12] In ch. 34 there are seven derived from Deut. 1.1—the calf,

---

12. *ARNa* 9, in Judah Goldin (trans.), *The Fathers According to Rabbi Nathan* (Yale Judaica Series, 10; New Haven: Yale University Press, 1955), p. 54. The same list appears in *b. 'Arak.* 15a, and Goldin has restored the text of *ARNa* 9 from there (p. 186 n. 7). *Midr. Teh.* on Ps. 95.3 (ed. Buber, pp. 420-21; in the trans. by William G. Braude, *The Midrash on the Psalms* [Yale Judaica Series, 13; New Haven: Yale University Press, 1959), II, pp. 137-38) has a related but not identical list: 'twice at the Red Sea; twice with the quail; once with the manna; once with the golden calf; once at Paran, this one being the most provoking'.

the clamor for water (Exod. 17.3), the Red Sea complaint (Ps. 106.7), the spies (Num. 13.3ff.), the complaint about manna (Num. 21.5), the Korah rebellion (Num. 16), the quail (Num. 11)—and three from Deut. 9.22 (Taberah, Massah, and Kibroth-hattavah, not further explained in the text). Since Deut. 1.1 can be read as a list of eight items, a glossator has added a further explanation of the one omitted, Di-zahab, making it a second allusion to the golden calf. The second version of *Aboth de Rabbi Nathan* contains a further list, attributed to Rabbi Judah, and a fragment of yet another.[13]

Paul or his *Vorlage* has been content to mention five of the wilderness sins. Four of the five are allusions to texts in Numbers. 'Craving evil things' probably is suggested by Num. 11.4, καὶ ὁ ἐπίμικτος ὁ ἐν αὐτοῖς ἐπεθύμησαν ἐπιθυμίαν. The 'mixed crowd' craved flesh, remembering the abundant fish of Egypt. The fornicators of v. 8 are those who succumbed to the wiles of the daughters of Moab, Num. 25.1-9—though Paul has somehow reduced the twenty-four thousand of Num. 25.9 to only twenty-three thousand. The 'testing' of God that led to punishment by the serpents (v. 9) is described in Num. 21.4-9. The verb πειράζειν, to be sure, does not appear in this account, though it is used in the partly parallel story in Exod. 17.1-7, as well as in the summary of the wilderness sins discussed above, Num. 14.22. The 'grumbling' of v. 10 is more difficult to pin down, since the verb γογγύζειν is used frequently in the wilderness traditions: Exod. 16.7; 17.3; Num. 11.1; 14.27, 29; 16.41; 17.5. Destruction of malcontents by plague occurs after the 'craving' (Num. 11.33) and after the rebellion of Korah (16.49). The latter is most likely the occasion to which Paul refers.[14]

One of the named sins is different from the other four in that it is identified by means of a direct quotation, introduced by the formula ὥσπερ γέγραπται, and that quotation is from Exod. 32.6 rather than from Numbers. We might suppose that, since 'idolatry' is the immediate issue under discussion in the letter, Paul himself has added this reference. The Golden Calf episode was the classic instance of Israel's idolatry. *Aboth de Rabbi Nathan* preserves a saying attributed to Rabbi Eliezer ben Jacob, 'For this iniquity there is enough to punish Israel from now until the dead are resurrected'.[15] It was sometimes passed over in silence

13. Ch. 38, ed. Schechter, pp. 98-99.
14. Cf. Heinrici, *Kritisch exegetisches Handbuck*, p. 278.
15. *ARNa* 34, trans. Goldin.

by interpreters.[16] For this very reason, however, it is hard to imagine a list of the wilderness generation's sins without this one. Moreover, the cited text may have a more intimate connection with the structure of the whole homily than first appears. It may be that it is quoted verbatim because it provides the midrashic basis for the antithesis we found to be central to the whole passage's logic:

> 'They sat down to eat and drink'—that is, they 'ate the spiritual food and drank the spiritual drink'—
>
> 'and rose up to play'—that is, to commit the five sins listed.

This possibility will seem more likely if we can find in Jewish tradition some analogous exegetical move that would permit the verb παίζειν to imply all these sins: ἐπιθυμεῖν, εἰδωλολάτραι γίνεσθαι, πορνεύειν, ἐκπειράζειν τὸν Χριστὸν, γογγύζειν. As a matter of fact, rabbinic midrash does take an interest in the variety of nuances of the corresponding Hebrew verb *śḥq*. The troublesome text that produces the midrashic problem for the rabbis, however, is Gen. 21.9, 'But Sarah saw the son of Hagar the Egyptian, whom she had borne to Abraham, playing [*mᵉsaḥēq*]. So she said, "Cast out this slave woman with her son".' Why would a child's play provoke such anger from Sarah and such punishment from Abraham? Obviously *mᵉsaḥēq* must have a more serious meaning, and several traditional explanations are handed down. One of the earliest collections is in the Tosefta, reported in the name of Rabbi Simeon ben Yohai:

> Rabbi Akiba interpreted [the verse], 'And Sarah saw the son of Hagar the Egyptian, whom she had borne to Abraham, *mᵉsaḥēq*', [as follows:] *Śaḥôq* as used here means only idolatry ['*abodah zarah*], as it is said, 'The people sat down to eat and drink and rose up *lᵉsaḥēq*'—thus teaching that our mother Sarah saw Ishmael building pedestals [*bêmôsin* = Greek βήματα], catching locusts, and making burnt offerings with incense for idolatry.
>
> R. Eliezer, son of R. Jose the Galilean, said: *Śaḥôq*[17] as used here means only sexual immorality [*gᵉluy 'aryôt*], as it is said, 'This Hebrew slave came in to me…*lᵉsaḥēq bî*' (Gen. 39.17), teaching that our mother

---

16. *m. Meg.* 4.10 directs that when the two accounts of the calf (Exod. 32.1-20; 32.21-25, 35) are read in synagogue, only the first is to be translated; so it is in *Targum Neofiti I.* Josephus, *Ant.* 3.95-98, omits both (cf. Thackeray's note *ad loc.* in the LCL edition).

17. The orthographic variants are of no significance for our purposes.

Sarah saw Ishmael 'seizing the gardens'[18] and assaulting the women. R. Ishmael said: The word *sahôq* means only bloodshed, as it is said, 'And Abner said to Joab, "Let the youths arise now *wîsaḥ*ᵃ*qû* before us", and they arose...' (2 Sam. 2.14-17), teaching that our mother Sarah saw Ishmael taking bow and arrows and shooting them toward Isaac, as it is said, 'Like a madman who throws firebrands, [arrows, and death is the man who deceives his neighbor and says, "I am only joking (*m*ᵉ*saḥēq*)]"' (Prov. 26.18).[19]

There are several variants of this tradition elsewhere in rabbinic literature. In *Gen. R.* 53.11, for example, all four of these explanations are repeated, but the attributions are different: Akiba, immorality; Ishmael, idolatry; Eleazar, bloodshed; Azariah in the name of R. Levi, the threat to Isaac's life derived from Prov. 26.18. The Palestinian targums on Gen. 21.9 all explain Ishmael's sin as idolatry.[20] Some of the other interpretations appear singly in other midrashic collections.[21]

These rabbinic variations on the possible meanings of the verb *ṣhq/śhq* yield two of our five Pauline examples: idolatry and sexual immorality. There is no need to suppose, however, that Paul (or his *Vorlage* if there was one) was using only the Hebrew text. The Septuagint usually renders *ṣhq/śhq* by παίζειν or ἐμπαίζειν (occasionally by γελᾶν), so the texts employed by the rabbis in their midrash would also work for

18. The phrase *mkbš 't hgnwt*, in the Vienna codex here and in the generally accepted text of the parallel passage in *Gen. R.* 53.11, is difficult. The variant reading in the Erfurt codex of Tosefta and in 'the best manuscript' of *Gen. R.*, which Lieberman prefers, is even more obscure: 'seizing roofs' (*ggwt*). Both seem to be sexual metaphors, however. For *gan* as a euphemism for a woman, see Marcus Jastrow, *Dictionary of Talmud Babli, Yerushalmi, Midrashic Literature and Targumim* (New York: Pardes, 1950), s.v. *gan*. For 'roofs' as an allusion to homosexual activity, see Saul Lieberman, *Tosefta ki-Fshutah: A Comprehensive Commentary on the Tosefta* (New York: Jewish Theological Seminary of America, 1955–73), VIII, p. 670.

19. *t. Soṭ.* 6.6.

20. 'Playing in foreign worship and bowing to the Lord', *Targ. Ps.-J.*; 'Doing evil works which are not proper, playing in foreign worship', *Frag. Targ.*; 'Doing actions that are not proper, playing in foreign worship', *Targ. Neof.* (the last clause restored by the editor from v. 8, where a longer version of v. 9 appears, presumably by scribal error).

21. E.g. *Exod. R.* 1.1., idolatry; *Pes. R.* 48.2, the threat to Isaac's life; *Sifre* §31 (ed. Finkelstein, p. 50), idolatry (attributed to R. Akiba, as in *t. Soṭ.* 6.6). *Exod. R.* 42.1 applies three of these interpretations to Exod. 32.6: idolatry, immorality, and bloodshed; also in *Midr. Tanḥ., Ki-tiśśa'* (ed. Buber, p. 113).

the Greek reader. At the same time, the semantic range would be altered somewhat. Thus παίζειν and ἐμπαίζειν frequently mean 'to joke, mock, make fun of'.[22] That would immediately suggest the fourth and fifth sins, 'testing Christ [or, the Lord]' and 'grumbling' (1 Cor. 10.9, 10).

It is more difficult to see how the first and more general of the sins, 'craving for evil things', could be read into the verb παίζειν. Philo's interpretation of the Golden Calf gives us the needed clue. For him the calf is 'the Egyptian vanity', symbol of the body.[23] Thus in his *Life of Moses* he expatiates on the 'play' of the calf-worshippers:

> Then, having fashioned a golden bull, in imitation of the animal held most sacred in that country, they offered sacrifices which were no sacrifices, set up choirs which were no choirs, sang hymns which were very funeral chants, and, filled with strong drink, were overcome by the twofold intoxication of wine and folly. And so, revelling and carousing the livelong night, and unwary of the future, they lived wedded to their pleasant vices, while justice, the unseen watcher of them and the punishments they deserved, stood ready to strike.[24]

Philo consistently understands the sin of the Golden Calf to be a turning of the soul away from higher things and becoming embroiled in the material world, with the things that concern the body rather than the mind. Paul's phrase, ἐπιθυμία κακῶν, is an apt expression of that view, which was hardly unique to Philo among Jews of Hellenistic culture.[25]

---

22. LSJ, s. vv. παίζω, ἐμπαίζω. The LXX prefers ἐμπαίζειν for *ṣḥq/śḥq* in this sense, e.g. Exod. 10.2, God mocking the Egyptians; cf. 1 Kdms 6.6; Num. 22.29, Balaam accuses the ass of mocking him; 1 Kdms 31.4 = 1 Chron. 10.4, Saul fears the Philistines will mock him; 2 Chron. 36.16, Israel 'kept mocking the messengers of God despising his words, and *scoffing* at his prophets, till the wrath of the Lord rose against this people'. Cf. Hab. 1.10. Note, too, Philo's interpretation of the calf episode in *Spec. Leg.* 3.125. He understands παίζειν as 'to dance', but also recognizes the nuance 'to mock', which he expresses by χλευάζειν: 'They [the calf-makers] *mocked* at the most excellent and admirable injunctions which bade them honour the truly existing God' (trans. Colson).

23. *Ebr.* 95; *Sacr.* 130; *Fug.* 90–92; cf. *Spec. Leg.* 3.125 and *Vit. Mos.* 2.162.

24. *Vit. Mos.* 2.162, trans. Colson; cf. *Spec. Leg.* 3.125.

25. There is another possible midrashic connection between Num. 11.4 and Exod. 32.6: the idolaters '*sat* to eat and drink'; the grumblers '*sat* and wept'. Cf. *Exod. R.* 41.7, where the midrash tells us, 'Wherever you find the expression "sitting" (*yᵉšibah*), you will find that some great sin occurred there'. The scriptural examples cited are, beside Exod. 32.6, Gen. 11.1; 37.25; Num. 25.1. The same tradition is

We are thus able to follow the way in which Paul or some anonymous predecessor constructed the homily he has used in 1 Cor. 10.1-13. The form is one that is common in both biblical and post-biblical exhortations. Each of the individual components of the Pauline composition has close parallels in contemporary, Hellenistic Jewish documents, in later Christian expositions, or in later rabbinic midrash. Above all, these parallels, especially the rabbinic ones, help us to perceive the interpretative techniques that connect the logical structure of the homily with the scriptural texts that support it. The elegant symmetry of the piece is not adventitious, but is founded on a quite subtle exegesis of the one scriptural verse that is formally quoted, Exod. 32.6.

It remains for us to see whether our reconstruction of the earlier homily can help us to understand better the force of Paul's argument in the letter. The homily's moral is drawn in vv. 12-13. On the one hand it warns against overconfidence—in language that could well be Paul's own (cf. Rom. 11.20-21; 14.4; 1 Cor. 15.1-2)—on the other, it offers the consolation that God does not permit temptation beyond the strength of the faithful. Paul, however, begins his exposition of the homily's implications in v. 14, which states a rule that was evidently widespread in early Christianity.[26] 'Idolatry' is the central issue being debated between 'the weak' and 'the strong' at Corinth, and the subject of this part of Paul's reply to their letter. Hence the central place of Exod. 32.6 in the homily made it particularly suitable for the occasion, even though the homily itself makes a rather different point, about resistable temptations. Then, in vv. 15-22, Paul further supports the prohibition of any engagement in pagan cults by inferences he draws from the Lord's Supper. There are signs in these verses that he has not entirely finished with the 'midrash' of vv. 1-13.

Among the biblical texts that show a formal resemblance to the homily, Deuteronomy 32 is especially similar, as I pointed out earlier. Perhaps Paul, too, noticed this resemblance, for he twice alludes to the Song of Moses in his application to the Corinthian situation. In v. 20 he quotes Deut. 32.17 directly, except for a change of tense, from the aorist to the present. Verse 22 is a clear allusion to Deut. 32.21. Perhaps it is

---

found in *Midr. Tanḥ., Ki-tiśśa'* (ed. Buber, p. 113), and a related one in *Sifre* §43 (ed. Finkelstein, p. 92).

26. Cf. the 'Apostolic Decree' Acts 15.20, 29; 21.25; and 1 Jn 5.21; also the rules and vice catalogues quoted in the Pauline corpus, Gal. 5.20; 1 Cor. 5.10-11; 6.9; Col. 3.5; Eph. 5.5.

not accidental, too, that, in the Hebrew text of the Song, 'Rock' (*ṣûr*) is the preferred name for God, though the Septuagint abandons it for the colorless θεός (vv. 15, 18, 30, 31). Since it seems likely that Paul added the gloss in 1 Cor. 10.4, 'The rock was Christ', it may well be that 'putting Christ to the test' in v. 9 (if that is the original text) is a midrashic cross-reference to Deut. 32.15, 'He [Jeshurun = Israel] scoffed at the Rock of his salvation'. To be sure, the Septuagint renders the Hebrew verb *nbl* (pi'el) by the stronger verb ἀφιστάναι, but it will not have escaped Paul's ken that the Hebrew ('to play the fool, mock') could be yet another synonym for our now familiar παίζειν. Be that as it may, he did find in Deuteronomy 32 phrases that were suggestive for his admonition to the Corinthian Christians.

The change of tense in v. 20 generalizes and actualizes the Deuteronomic text. This suggests a solution to the age-old problem whether Paul meant the subject of the verb to be 'pagans' (as most manuscripts have it) or 'Israel according to the flesh' (v. 18, the nearest logical subject if we read, with most modern critics, the text of B D F G, Ambrosiaster, and pseudo-Augustine). Since the quoted text refers again to the Golden Calf debacle, it is still 'Israel according to the flesh' that is the bad example, as in vv. 5-11. By changing from the aorist to the present tense, however, Paul wants to say, 'Everyone who engages in pagan festivals'—whether Israelites in the wilderness or a Corinthian Christian eating in a pagan shrine—is 'sacrificing to demons and not to God'.

If I am correct in seeing the whole of vv. 1-13 as a previously composed homily, and Paul's application as still controlled to some extent by scriptural texts related to that homily, then the apparent *aporiae* between it and the rest of Paul's argument in chs. 8–10 are easier to understand. However, the sequence of thought in these chapters is not so disjointed as it is sometimes said to be. Paul is responding to a question put to him in the letter from Corinth, whether one is allowed to eat 'meat offered to idols' (8.1). The question has been sent to him because there is a division of opinion among the Corinthian Christians. Paul labels the two sides of the controversy 'the strong' and 'the weak'. 'The strong' adopt a weak-boundary position in their understanding of the relationship between the Christian community and the larger society. Taboos against idolatry are not needed to protect their Christian faith, because they know that the idols are not real. 'The strong' are proud both of their 'knowledge' (γνῶσις) and of the 'power' (ἐξουσία) and 'freedom' (ἐλευθερία) which this knowledge, the grace they have received as believers in Christ, gives them. 'The weak', on the other hand, are accustomed to associate the eating of meat with participation in the cults of pagan gods. 'Idolatry' for them is real and dangerous.

Chapter 8 sketches out the problem and Paul's dialectical answer in lively, diatribal style, using slogans and phrases from the Corinthians' internal debate. Chapter 9 and 10.1-22 provide backing for Paul's answer in the form of examples drawn first from his own missionary practice (ch. 9), then from the biblical account of Israel in the wilderness (the homily we have just analyzed, 10.1-13) and, in the light of that account, from an implication of the Eucharist (10.14-22). Finally, Paul sums up with a series of rules, formulated in imperatives, introduced by his modification of a Corinthian slogan (10.23–11.1).

Paul's response is addressed to 'the strong', speaking to 'the weak' only obliquely. He affirms the intellectual position of 'the strong': the idols are non-existent (8.4)—though he qualifies this statement in 8.5-6 and 10.19-20. Eating and drinking are matters of ultimate indifference (8.8). Therefore a Christian may eat anything sold in the market without scruples of conscience, 'for the earth and its fulness are the Lord's' (10.25-26). So, too, one may accept invitations by pagans and eat any-thing served by them, so long as the eating is not explicitly designated a cultic act by someone else (10.27-28). However, the enlightened believer must be prepared to sacrifice this freedom to avoid harming the 'weak' brother, for whom the association of meat with pagan sacrifices is still a serious matter (8.7-13; 10.24, 28-29).

The first of the examples Paul offers fits admirably with this general rule. The apostle's 'rights' (ἐξουσία), for example to be accompanied by a wife or to receive financial support, are by no means abolished by his decision not to assert them. He has not ceased to be 'free' (ἐλεύθερος) by freely 'enslaving' himself to others. So also 'the strong' will not deny their freedom of conscience if on occasion they relinquish their rights for the sake of 'the weak'; on the contrary, they will 'become imitators of me [sc. Paul] as I am of Christ' (11.1). The second example does not fit the context so well, but as we have seen, that is partly because it was composed for another purpose. From the homily Paul draws out the central warning against idolatry and restates it in the form of the common rule (10.14). Then he backs this rule by connecting an interpretation of the Lord's Supper, evidently known to the Corinthians, with a further deduction from the Golden Calf story.

The cup of blessing and the broken bread represent 'partnership' with Christ. In Israel, too, those who ate the sacrifices were 'partners in the altar', but by the same principle those who participated in the sacrifices to the Golden Calf became 'partners of demons' (vv. 18-20). Notice that the diatribal question that Paul inserts in v. 19 reveals that he is aware that he seems to be contradicting his agreement with the 'strong' (8.4) that the idols are not real. He wants to say that the pagan gods are not what their worshippers think they are; they are 'by nature not gods' (Gal. 4.8). Nevertheless, they have some reality, as 'demons', and any participation in their cults is absolutely excluded for those who belong to the one God and one Lord.

The result of the argument leaves the issue of the Christian group's boundaries—and that is the policy question behind the immediate concern about eating meat—somewhat ambiguous.[27] On the one hand, social intercourse with outsiders is not discouraged. Paul desacralizes the mere act of eating meat, in order to remove a taboo that would prevent such interaction. It is thus not 'idolatry'; in this respect Paul agrees with 'the strong'. On the other hand, any action that would imply actual participation in another cult is strictly prohibited. Thus the exclusivity of cult, which had been a unique mark of Judaism, difficult for pagans in the Hellenistic cities to understand, would remain characteristic also of Pauline congregations. The emphasis in Paul's paraenesis, however, is not upon the maintenance of boundaries, but upon the solidarity of the Christian community: the responsibility of members for one another, especially of the strong for the weak, and the undiluted loyalty of all to the one God and one Lord.

27. I have dealt with this question at some length in one chapter of *The First Urban Christians: The Social World of the Apostle Paul* (New Haven: Yale University Press, 1983), pp. 74-110.

JSNT 33 (1988), pp. 41-56

THE ROLE OF THE TENTH COMMANDMENT IN ROMANS 7

J.A. Ziesler

It must be suspected that the confusions concerning the correct interpretation of Romans 7 must be blamed, at least in part, on Paul himself, unless we are to hold that almost all his interpreters have been miraculously and incurably obtuse. The old issues continue to be debated as much as ever: is the passage vv. 7-25 autobiographical, or partly autobiographical, or not at all autobiographical?[1] Clearly vv. 7-12 are about life without Christ, but are vv. 13-25 on the contrary about Christian experience, or are they too about pre-Christian life, whether Jewish or universal?[2] Despite periodical announcements that an issue has been settled,

---

1.   The classic case against an autobiographical interpretation was made by W.G. Kümmel, *Römer 7 und die Bekehrung des Paulus* (Leipzig: Hinrichs, 1929), now republished in *Römer 7 und das Bild des Menschen im Neuen Testament* (Munich: chr. Kaiser Verlag, 1974). An impressive case for allowing at least an autobiographical element has now been made by G. Theissen, *Psychologische Aspekte Paulinischer Theologie* (Göttingen: Vandenhoeck & Ruprecht, 1983), ch. 3, pp. 181-268.

2.   Most exegetes now seem to favour some sort of pre-Christian view, though nearly always with the proviso that the chapter is retrospective, i.e. looking at life without Christ from a strictly Christian standpoint, and does not describe how it seemed at the time: see, for example, Theissen, *Aspekte*, pp. 185-87; U. Wilckens, *Der Brief an die Römer*, II (Zürich: Benziger; Neukirchen: Neukirchener Verlag, 1980), p. 86; E.P. Sanders, *Paul and Palestinian Judaism* (London: SCM Press, 1977), p. 443; S. Lyonnet, 'L'histoire du salut selon le chapitre VII de l'épître aux Romains', *Bib* 43 (1962), pp. 117-51, at 118-19. A 'Christian' view, however, is still defended, notably by J.D.G. Dunn, 'Rom. 7,14-15 in the Theology of Paul', *TZ* 31 (1975), pp. 258-73; see also C.E.B. Cranfield, *The Epistle to the Romans*, I (ICC; Edinburgh: T. & T. Clark, 1975), pp. 340-47, and C.K. Barrett, *The Epistle to the Romans* (BNTC; London: A. & C. Black, 1957), pp. 151-53.

one way or the other, different answers continue to be given to these questions.

Still further issues have been raised, the most well-known being the degree to which the story of Adam in the Garden of Eden lies behind vv. 7-13, and that too has been both strongly advocated and firmly denied.[3] Most recently, Professors Sanders and Räisänen[4] have pointed out that there is something about the relation between sin and the Law in Romans 7 that is unique in Paul: the Law has been 'hijacked' by sin, with the result that no one can fulfil the Law *at all*. It is not just that everyone sins, which has been said earlier in the letter (e.g. 3.9, 23). Nor is it just that Law increases the trespass, perhaps by making implicit sin overt, in order that in the end grace may be seen to reign (5.20). Here, and only here, sin exploits the Law to bring about total moral paralysis. Sin can no longer be seen as within the long-term beneficent provision of God, and must instead be regarded as another and hostile power, capable of perverting even the Law of God.[5]

It is the contention of this article that there is another confusing feature in the passage, a feature which may, however, go some way in explaining those confusions which have led to the debates already mentioned. This feature is a confusion between the Law as a whole, and the particular exemplification of it in the tenth commandment, the command against coveting, on which Paul focuses. We concentrate on this commandment, therefore, in the hope that we may be able to return to some of the familiar issues of the chapter, with something by way of illumination.

> If it had not been for the law, I should not have known sin. I should not have known what it is to covet if the law had not said, 'You shall not covet'. But sin, finding opportunity in the commandment, wrought in me all kinds of covetousness. Apart from the law sin lies dead. I was once

---

3.   Proposers include S. Lyonnet, *Les Étapes de l'histoire du salut selon l'Épître aux Romains* (Paris: Gabalda, 1969), especially pp. 113-37; M.J. Lagrange, *Épître aux Romains* (Paris: Gabalda, 1950), pp. 167-68; Theissen, *Aspekte*, pp. 204ff., 253-68. Opposers include Kümmel, *Römer* 7, pp. 86-87; G. Schrenk, *TDNT*, II, pp. 550-51; R.H. Gundry, 'The Moral Frustration of Paul before his Conversion', in D.A. Hagner and M.J. Harris (eds.), *Pauline Studies* (Festschrift F.F. Bruce; Exeter: Paternoster Press, 1980), pp. 228-45, at 230-32.

4.   E.P. Sanders, *Paul, the Law and the Jewish People* (Philadelphia: Fortress Press, 1983), p. 78; H. Räisänen, *Paul and the Law* (Tübingen: Mohr [Siebeck], 1983), p. 110.

5.   See Sanders, *Paul*, pp. 70-73.

alive apart from the law, but when the commandment came, sin revived (or, 'sprang to life') and I died; the very commandment which promised life proved to be death to me. For sin, finding opportunity in the commandment, deceived me and by it killed me. So the law is holy, and the commandment is holy and just and good (Rom. 7.7b-12, RSV).

My thesis is that the choice of precisely *this* commandment, the tenth, was crucial for what followed, for both vv. 7-12 and vv. 13-25. This is not a new suggestion, and we begin by looking at two interpretations which do concentrate on the role of the tenth commandment in Romans 7, but arguably do so incorrectly.

First, R. Bultmann[6] argued that the word ἐπιθυμία ('covetousness' or 'desire') should be taken in a nomistic way as well as, or even instead of, in an antinomistic way. That is to say, ἐπιθυμία is not (or not only) the desire for what is forbidden or for what is not properly one's own, but is also the lust for self-righteousness, for an achieved status before God, the supposed besetting sin of the Pharisees. In effect, it is the sin of wanting to be God-like. It has further been argued by S. Lyonnet[7] that in the background is Numbers 11 and the strong craving for food other than the divinely provided manna, and that in 1 Corinthians 10 Paul interprets this strong craving in nomistic terms, that is, as a wanting to become God-like by having fully kept the Law. It must be confessed that this is hardly a natural or convincing reading of either Numbers 11 or 1 Corinthians 10, and indeed recently such a reading, together with the supposed relevance of it to Romans 7, has been refuted (for once, not too strong a word) by Heikki Räisänen. Moreover he has in the same article demolished the whole nomistic interpretation of ἐπιθυμία in Romans 7.[8] He has shown that in Paul the word *never* means the thirst to establish one's own righteousness before God, and that there is, moreover, nothing in the chapter to require or even render plausible such an interpretation. It can now, surely, be given a decent burial. One

6.   'Romans 7 and the Anthropology of Paul', in *Existence and Faith* (ET London: Collins, 1961), pp. 147-57; see also his *Theology of the New Testament* (ET London: SCM Press, 1952), I, pp. 247-49. See also G. Bornkamm, *Das Ende des Gesetzes* (Munich: Chr. Kaiser Verlag, 2nd edn, 1958), p. 55; H. Hübner, *Law in Paul's Thought* (ET Edinburgh: T. & T. Clark, 1984), pp. 72-76, and many others.

7.   ' "Tu ne convoiteras pas" ', *Neotestamentica et Patristica* (Festschrift O. Cullmann; NovTSup, 6; Leiden: Brill, 1962), pp. 157-65 at 160-61.

8.   'Zum Gebrauch von ΕΠΙΘΥΜΙΑ und ΕΠΙΘΥΜΕΙΝ bei Paulus', in *The Torah and Christ* (Helsinki: Finnish Exegetical Society, 1986), pp. 148-67; see especially pp. 156-67.

aspect of the Bultmannian treatment does, however, remain suggestive, and that is his making ἐπιθυμία have a decisive influence on the meaning of what follows: all that is said about being unable to control one's behaviour and one's desires, is strictly about ἐπιθυμία.[9] This is a point to which we must return later.

A dramatically different interpretation is offered by R.H. Gundry in an article which is richly suggestive even if its main contention is not to be found credible.[10] Gundry argued in 1980 that Romans 7 is strictly auto-biographical, in the sense that only a Jew could have written it. Like Bultmann, he concentrates on the tenth commandment, on ἐπιθυμία and its cognate verb in vv. 7-8, but unlike Bultmann takes them to refer strictly and solely to sexual lust. It is this that controls the rest of the chapter, which is thus all concerned with inability to manage one's sexual desires. He rejects any reference to Adam in vv. 7-13, and takes v. 9, 'I was once alive apart from the law', to refer to Paul's becoming *bar mitzvah* at the time of puberty. Once this connection has been made, between the onset of puberty and sexual desire on the one hand, and the entry into responsibility for the observance of the Law on the other hand, clearly only a Jew can be the 'I' of the chapter. Paul writes in the first person singular precisely because what he says applies to him, as it does to other Jews, but does not apply to his mainly Gentile readers. They, of course, had entered puberty, but had never become *bar mitzvah* (Gundry is aware that the term is anachronistic, but the assumption of responsibility for Torah-keeping which it represents is not, and he uses the term for convenience). So then, in Paul's own experience it was just at the time that he became aware of stirrings of sexual desire which he could not control, that he also became personally responsible to God for obedience to his Torah. He found that although he could (and according to Phil. 3.6, did) keep the Law in general, his sexual desires were not subject to him, and that in this one, but thoroughly crucial matter, he was quite powerless. The whole of the rest of Romans 7 is then to be read as being specifically about his inability to keep the Law in this particular. It was only in Christ that he found a power which enabled him to be free of this uncontrollable lust, and that was because

---

9.   *Theology*, I, pp. 247-49.

10.   'Moral Frustration', cf. n. 3 above. Gundry's view has recently been given support by F. Watson, *Paul, Judaism and the Gentiles* (SNTSMS, 56; Cambridge: Cambridge University Press, 1986), pp. 151-56.

in Christ and in his Spirit, the very heart of his existence, including his desire, was changed.

I wish to argue that, for all its daring character, this solution of Gundry's comes close to being correct. His critical mistake, in my view, is that he limits the reference of the tenth commandment and ἐπιθυμία to *sexual* desire. Of course one cannot object that if Gundry is right, Paul would have done better to choose the seventh commandment, against adultery, because that is about actions and not just desires. Nevertheless, we must doubt if the tenth commandment can be restricted as Gundry supposes. He argues for the restriction partly on the ground that it is precisely sexual desire that 'springs to life' at puberty and the time of *bar mitzvah*, and partly that elsewhere in Paul, Rom. 1.24 and 1 Thess. 4.5, ἐπιθυμία does occur with strongly sexual connotations. The verb ἐπιθυμέω has no object in v. 7 not because it is intended to have a wide reference, but simply for reasons of brevity, as in 13.9. Moreover, he links Romans 7 with the rabbinic 'evil impulse' which, he says, was understood largely in sexual terms.[11] So then, it was sexual lust which sprang to life when the commandment came, and 'apart from the law' in 7.8, 9 refers not to the Law as a whole, but strictly to the tenth commandment as forbidding sexual lust, so that it was not 'an instrument of sin and death in Paul's prepuberal boyhood'; it became that only at puberty.

Now Gundry is not the only scholar to have observed the temporal conjunction of the onset of sexual consciousness at puberty and the assumption of responsibility for Torah-obedience.[12] Certainly a sexual aspect cannot be excluded from the tenth commandment either in Exod. 20.1, where it occurs in second place, or in Deut. 5.21, where it comes first. Moreover, in discussing ἐπιθυμία Philo too includes a sexual element, sometimes prominently and sometimes not: *Quaest in Gen.* 1.47-48; *Spec. Leg.* 4.84ff.; *Dec.* 142, 150, 173. The rabbinic tradition to be found variously in *b. Šab.* 145b-146a, *Yeb.* 103b, and *'Abod. Zar.* 22b, that the snake injected Eve with lust, would be further support

---

11. Some connection between Rom. 7 and the rabbinic *yēṣer hārā'* is not infrequently suggested; cf. W.D. Davies, *Paul and Rabbinic Judaism* (London: SCM Press, 2nd edn, 1955), pp. 24-26, 30-31, who notes that the battle between the good and evil impulses was indeed held to begin at the age of 13, and that the evil impulse was largely sexual, though not exclusively so (see pp. 20-23).

12. See Lyonnet, 'L'histoire du salut', p. 122 n. 2. It is also implied in Davies, *Paul and Rabbinic Judaism*, p. 25.

for Gundry's case if he were prepared to allow at least some Adamic background to Romans 7, but the same tradition adds that lust departed from Israel and Israel alone at Sinai, perhaps because of the coming of the tenth (or even the seventh) commandment. In all this, however, we so far lack evidence of a strong Jewish tradition which took the tenth commandment in a strictly or even predominantly sexual fashion, and that is what Gundry's case needs.

If, unlike Gundry, we were to allow some fusion of the tenth commandment with the command not to eat in the Garden, then sexual interpretations of the Fall Story would lend support. *4 Macc.* 18.8 seems to presuppose that Eve's fall consisted in sexual seduction, and the dubiously relevant *Apoc. Abr.* 23 has Adam and Eve embrace while eating the forbidden fruit (though in the context, cf. 24; it is bold to claim that the sin was exclusively sexual). In *Apoc. Mos.* 19.3 (cf. v. 25) there are sexual overtones but not an exclusive focus on sex. As for Philo, although in *Op. Mund.* 152 the wrong desire of Adam and Eve is sexual (though ἐπιθυμία is not used), in *Quaest in Gen.* 1.47-48, *Leg. All.* 2.72, 74 and indeed *Op. Mund.* 157-60, desire is in terms of food and drink, as well as sex. In short, although we can find relevant traditions which stress the sexual element, it is hard to find much that justifies taking Rom. 7.7 in an entirely or even predominantly sexual sense.

Of course, Gundry's linking of puberty with *bar mitzvah* in 7.9 means that 'I was once alive apart from the law' must be taken at least partly autobiographically. Perhaps this is not impossible: although there was an important sense in which, because of circumcision and simply because of living within an Israelite family and community, no Jewish boy was ever 'apart from the law',[13] nevertheless there was a tradition (see *m. Nid.* 6; *b. Nid.* 52; *b. Ber.* 44a, 88a)[14] according to which a boy was 'exempt from the commandments' until puberty, in the sense that he was not personally responsible for their observance. Though attested later than Paul's time, this tradition could be reflected in Rom. 7.9. However, a reference to Adam as now so often proposed seems more likely: it fits the idea of the commandment's 'coming' (v. 9), as well as the statement

13. Kümmel (*Römer 7*, pp. 81-82) points to Philo, *Leg. Gai.* 115; Josephus, *Apion* 2.178; 2 Tim. 3.15. Theissen (*Aspekte*, p. 253) quotes Philo, *Leg. Gai.* 210, for the assertion that a child learns the Law from earliest days, and a gravestone on which a νήπιος is described as φιλόνομος.

14. I am indebted to Dr Maurice Casey for these references, and for the observation which they support.

that sin deceives (v. 11), which seems slightly odd unless it echoes the serpent's deception of Eve in Gen. 3.13. At best, therefore, making 7.9 refer to Paul's *bar mitzvah* is possible, but it is not likely.

The most serious objection to Gundry's view is v. 8b, 'wrought in me all kinds of covetousness' (πᾶσαν ἐπιθυμίαν), which is not mentioned at all by Gundry. This must tell very strongly against his solely sexual interpretation. Moreover, it is obvious that neither Exod. 20.17 nor Deut. 5.21 limits 'desire' to sexual desire, and throughout the New Testament and LXX the words ἐπιθυμία and ἐπιθυμεῖν lack a specifically sexual reference unless the context requires it. There is not a single instance in the LXX of the verb's referring to sexual ἐπιθυμία as a bad thing,[15] though out of about seventy-five occurrences of the noun, about ten may have such a reference.[16] Both words are used for all sorts of desires, good, bad, and neutral, so that if the usage of the LXX is any guide to Paul's, we ought not to give either word a specifically sexual reference unless indicated by the context. The New Testament evidence, whether Pauline or non-Pauline, provides a closely similar picture.[17] Paul does indeed use the noun for wrongful sexual desire in Rom. 1.24 and 1 Thess. 4.5. Yet he can also use it for good or neutral desires in Phil. 1.23 (for death) and 1 Thess. 2.17 (to see the Thessalonian Christians). Elsewhere his use is negative, for bad things, but they are in every case unspecific: Rom. 6.12; 13.14; Gal. 5.16, 24; Col. 3.5, if by Paul. In each instance, sexual lust may be taken to be included, but in no

15. The four passages which do have a (positive) sexual reference are: Jdt 16.22; Ps. 44.11; Cant. 2.3; Sus. 8. There are about 30 occurrences for perfectly justifiable desires, e.g. for the necessities of life, or for wisdom; about 22 for bad desires, e.g. for forbidden foods or someone else's land, but of these only 2 (*4 Macc.* 2.5, 6) specifically include a sexual element.

16. About 24 occurrences are neutral or positive (for e.g. food, or wisdom); 31 are unspecified bad desires; 4 are lust for possessions; 2 are good sexual desire (Cant. 5.16; Sir. 36.22); 10 are bad sexual desire (Prov. 6.25; Sir. 20.4; Jer. 2.24; Sus. 32, 56; Dan. 11.37; *4 Macc.* 1.3; 2.1; 3.2, 22).

17. For the New Testament apart from the acknowledged Paulines, the verb is neutral or positive 9 times (Mt. 13.17; Lk. 15.16; 16.21; 17.22; 22.15; 1 Tim. 3.1; Heb. 6.11; 1 Pet. 1.12; Rev. 9.6). It is for bad desire only 3 times: Mt. 5.28 (sexual); Acts 20.33 (gold etc.); Jas 4.2 (possessions?). The noun is used positively only once (Lk. 22.15). It is negative but unspecified in Eph. 2.3; 4.22; 2 Tim. 2.22; 3.6; 4.3; Tit. 2.12; 3.3; Jas 1.14, 15; 1 Pet. 1.14; 2.11; 4.2, 3; 2 Pet. 1.4; 3.3; Rev. 18.14. It is negative about riches or possessions in Mk 4.19; 1 Tim. 6.9; negative about the will of the Devil in Jn 8.44. Six times it is negative-sexual: 2 Pet. 2.10, 18; 1 Jn 2.16, 16; Jude 16, 18.

case does it exhaust or dominate the reference. Paul uses the verb rather seldom: apart from Rom. 7.7, there is 13.9 in which it is non-specific: 1 Cor. 10.6 where it is primarily connected with idolatry, though the allusion to Num. 11.4 may indicate that the desire is more generally for anything that is neither right nor God-given;[18] Gal. 5.17 ('the flesh desires contrary to the Spirit, and the Spirit to the flesh'), where the context shows that sexual desires are included, but again neither exhaust nor dominate the reference. There is, therefore, either in Paul or in the New Testament generally, no case for assuming a solely sexual reference for verb or for noun, without clear warrant in the context. In the absence of a stated object in Rom. 7.7-8, the presumption must then be that all sorts and objects of wrong desire are in principle included.

Suggestive and ingenious though it is, Gundry's interpretation of Romans 7 cannot stand. If we take ἐπιθυμία non-specifically, as is more natural, then his hypothesis cannot survive, and the supposed link between becoming *bar mitzvah* and the awakening of desire cannot bear the required weight. It can hardly be supposed that *all* desires awoke at puberty! Nevertheless, although his hypothesis must be rejected as it stands, he has hit upon something of critical importance when he concentrates on Paul's choice of just this commandment and no other, and in proposing that the choice had a decisive effect on what follows in the rest of the chapter. In this respect, Gundry and Bultmann are entirely right, or so I wish to argue.

We cannot read Paul's mind. All we have is the text, and therefore we do not know why he chose precisely the tenth commandment in Romans 7 to make his point about the Law's inability to deliver what it commands. Yet, so long as we remember that we cannot know, there may be some point in noting possible reasons for his choice.

1.	The tenth commandment was chosen because there already existed in some Jewish tradition a fusion of the Adam story and the story of the giving of the Law on Mount Sinai.[19] In this

18. See Räisänen, 'Zum Gebrauch', pp. 164-65. See also his account of Paul's general use of the noun, pp. 160-66. Lyonnet, '"Tu ne convoiteras pas"', pp. 143-44, also rejects a sexual meaning in 1 Cor. 10.6; for him it refers to refusing what God provides and wanting something else.

19. See Lyonnet, *Étapes*, pp. 129ff.; *ibid.*, '"Tu ne convoiteras pas"', p. 162; A. Feuillet, 'Loi de Dieu, loi du Christ et loi de l'Ésprit d'après les épîtres pauliniennes', *NovT* 22 (1980), pp. 29-65, at 32-35. Cf. also Gundry, 'Moral Frustration', p. 230.

fusion the tenth commandment had an important place because of its similarity to the command in the Garden: both concerned desire for the forbidden. For the fusion in general see *Targum Neofiti I* on Gen. 2.15 (Adam was put into the Garden to observe the Law) and on Gen. 3.24 (the tree of life is the Law); see also Sir. 17, especially vv. 7 and 11-12, where there is no clear demarcation between the time of creation and the time of the giving of the Law. For the fusion of the commands not to eat and not to covet see *b. Šab.* 145b-146a; *Yeb.* 103b; *'Abod. Zar.* 22b; *Apoc. Mos.* 19.3; Philo, *Quaest. in Gen.* 1.47-48, and perhaps *Op. Mund.* 157-60; *Leg. All.* 2.72, 74. The evidence is not extensive, and for reasons of geography as well as dating, we cannot be sure that Paul used or even knew this tradition.

2. The tenth commandment was used because in some Jewish tradition covetousness, or wrong desire, was held to be the sin from which all others flow.[20] There is reasonably substantial evidence for this: Philo, *Spec. Leg.* 4.84-94; *Dec.* 142, 150, 173; *Apoc. Mos.* 19.3; *Apoc. Abr.* 24.10; *Targum Neofiti I*; Exod. 20.17 and Deut. 5.18; Exod. 20.17 Mekilta.

3. Paul chose the tenth commandment deliberately because it, and it alone, could give him the argument he needed in order to show that the Law could command, but not produce what it commanded.

There is no obvious reason why some combination of these reasons could not have operated. However that may be, it is the contention of this article that, whatever the reason for his choice, *the result was an argument in Rom. 7.7-25 that worked for the tenth commandment but would not work for almost any other commandment.* To that extent we must agree with both Bultmann and Gundry, though we disagree with the way in which they understand the tenth commandment. The tenth

---

20. For much illustrative material, see K. Berger, *Die Gesetzauslegung Jesu*, I (Neukirchen: Neukirchener Verlag, 1972), pp. 346-49. See also Theissen, *Aspekte*, p. 207; Räisänen, 'Zum Gebrauch', pp. 154, 156; Lyonnet, '"Tu ne convoiteras pas"', pp. 144-46. It is sometimes also said that the tenth commandment could be used in Jewish tradition to represent the whole Law: so Hübner, *Law*, p. 78; Theissen, *Aspekte*, pp. 207-208; E. Käsemann, *Commentary on Romans* (ET London: SCM Press, 1980), p. 194. The passage most often cited is *4 Macc.* 2.6, but it is not clear from the context that the tenth commandment in particular stands for the whole Law, at least any more than forbidden meats do in 1.33-35.

commandment is to be taken as in Exodus and Deuteronomy, as covetousness in all its aspects. It is wanting what is not one's own, and especially wanting it at the expense of one's neighbour (but see n. 26 below).

There are two major features of Rom. 7.7-25 that 'work' for the command against coveting but do not work for almost any other. Working backwards, the first is the divided self of vv. 14 (or 13)-25. It is just not true, and Paul must have known it was not true (cf. Phil. 3.6), that for most people, most of the time, in most matters of the Law, intention or will was at odds with performance. Most devout Jews doubtless kept most of the Law most of the time without agonizing difficulty, just as *mutatis mutandis* most of us keep vast areas of the law ninety per cent of the time without a second thought. If we work through vv. 14-25, with, say, murder, or keeping the Sabbath, or robbery, or even adultery, in the forefront of our minds, the thing becomes absurd. It is untrue to most experience, this note of agonized, struggling impotence that pervades the passage. One can think of whole lists of commands for which it is totally inappropriate, and indeed, it is difficult to think of many for which it *is* appropriate (the love commands could be rather obvious candidates, but there are not many more). The point of the tenth commandment is that it is about desires, and the point of Rom. 7.13-25 is the difficulty of matching right desire with right performance, of conflicting desires, and of having right desire in the first place. So then, the tone and the argument of this passage match the tenth commandment well, but very few others, for most people most of the time (there are, of course, some people who have this sort of struggle about some particular thing, e.g. stealing).

It would, needless to say, be possible to import into Romans 7 the sort of interpretation of other commands in terms of intentions that we find in Matthew 5, but there is no warrant for doing so. In any case, that would, in effect, be to import the matter of right desire which *in the Law* is found explicitly in the tenth commandment, so that we would be back where we started. Indeed Paul is, consciously or not, using as a model in this passage a widespread ancient insight into the difficulty of matching intentions with performance,[21] but the crucial matter is that he

---

21. Best known in the saying of Ovid, *Video meliora, proboque; Deteriora sequor* (*Metamorphoses* 7.20). On this ancient insight as a whole, see especially the full treatment in Theissen, *Aspekte*, pp. 213-33; also Feuillet, 'Loi de Dieu', pp. 35-36.

is applying it specifically to *Law*, and the only laws for which it is appropriate are laws which concern the inner springs of action, intentions. Once more we are brought back to the tenth commandment as the most suitable candidate, at least in the Decalogue. As soon as we try to cast into legal terms matters of will, intention, and the divided self, this is where we are returned.

The second major feature of the chapter which works for the tenth commandment but not for most others, is the argument about the provocative nature of the Law in vv. 7-11. The point is made clearer if we try inserting another commandment into the passage in place of the tenth. I take the sixth as an example:

> If it had not been for the law, I should not have known sin. I should not have known what it is to kill if the law had not said, 'You shall not kill'. But sin, finding opportunity in the commandment, wrought in me all kinds of killing. Apart from the law, sin lies dead. I was once alive apart from the law, but when the commandment came, sin sprang to life and I died.

It just does not work.

Now it is because covetousness heavily involves desire and intentions, that it can be said that the Law not only unmasks what was already there (though unrecognized as evil), but actually makes it worse. It makes it worse, it may be suggested, because it condemns something to which we customarily give more respectable names, like 'an insistence on fairness', or 'justifiable resentment'. However, after giving it a bad name, the Law does nothing more about it, and we continue to covet, but now in full awareness that we sin in doing so. Our position is by that much the worse. It is not that the command invents desires that I otherwise would not have, but rather that having named and condemned the desires I already have, the Law makes my position worse and not better. In that sense the Law is used by sin as a base of operations (vv. 8, 11). The point is still not altogether straightforward, but it is easier to grasp than if we suppose that the whole Law, in all its parts, is at stake. Of course, if we suspect that behind vv. 8 and 11 lies the story of the Garden, in which the coming of the command gives the serpent a handle for temptation, then the interpretation now being suggested is a way of translating that from mythology into ordinary experience.

From what has gone before up to 7.7, we should naturally have expected Paul to be talking about the whole Law without exception or differentiation. The present argument is that, whatever his reason for doing so, Paul has taken the tenth commandment as the paradigm of the

Law's inability to deliver what it demands, indeed as the paradigm of the way in which it makes things worse rather than better. Unfortunately it is a faulty paradigm, faulty because it is not representative, so that by using it Paul is able to (or is led to) say things about the Law and sin that he could not readily have said if he had used a different commandment as paradigm. (Of course, it is just possible that from v. 7 onwards 'the law' is to be understood not as the Torah as a whole, but as the tenth commandment in particular,[22] and that this is what is meant in vv. 8, 9, 12, 14, 16. However, in view of the conjunction of 'the law' with 'the commandment' in vv. 9, 12, it is more likely that 'the law' is the Torah as a whole, and 'the commandment' is the tenth commandment as the paradigm).

One rather obvious objection to the interpretation here proposed is that throughout the chapter Paul uses *doing* words[23] in relation to the Law, and how can one *do* or *not do* coveting? The answer is that in the LXX although 'keep' the commandments is often found,[24] so also are 'doing' words, even where the command in question is not literally about doing or not doing anything:[25] e.g. Lev. 19.37 (which includes loving and not hating, vv. 17-18), and the places where 'doing' refers to the whole Decalogue, including the tenth commandment, Exod. 24.3, 7; Deut. 5.1, 31, 32; 6.1, 24; 28.58; 31.12. One *does* the commandments, whether or not any literal doing is involved. It is therefore not strange that in Romans 7 Paul should speak of doing the Law, even though his paradigm is the tenth commandment which concerns desires rather than actions.[26] He was simply following normal usage.

22. Certainly in Rom. 7.2, 3 one particular law, or at least one area of Law, is to be understood, and νόμος for *a* law occurs in Heb. 8.10; 10.16, and even perhaps Gal. 5.23. There are also plenty of instances in LXX where νόμος is one particular law and νόμοι are a plurality of such laws, e.g. Exod. 12.43; 13.10; Lev. 6.9, 14, 25, 31, 37; Num. 5.29; 6.13, 21; Ezek. 43.12. However, in Rom. 7.4-6 we clearly have to do with the Law as a whole, and it therefore seems perilous to restrict νόμος in v. 8 etc. to the tenth commandment alone.

23.   κατεργάζεσθαι   7.15, 17, 18, 20
         πράσσειν   7.19
         ποιεῖν   7.16, 19. 20, 21

24. E.g. Deut. 6.17, 25; 7.9; 8.2, 6, 11; 10.13. We also often find φυλάσσειν καὶ ποιεῖν, e.g. Lev. 26.3; Deut. 7.11; 8.1; 12.1. The terms in fact appear to be interchangeable.

25. Oddly enough, 'do' is almost invariably ποιεῖν. Rarely indeed does πράσσειν occur (though see Josh. 1.7), and never κατεργάζεσθαι.

26. Although the point is sometimes disputed, it is widely held that in Exod. 20.17

There is one final matter which lends support to the present proposal about the crucial role of the command against coveting, and that is the appearance of the singular δικαίωμα (RSV 'just requirement') in 8.4. What follows can be only a résumé of a case presented at more length elsewhere.[27] There are two outstanding oddities about this verse (8.4). The first and more often noticed is that having talked in 7.1-6 about dying to the Law, Paul now in a notably bald statement appears to bring us back to life again in relation to the Law, if not under it. We died to the Law in order to keep it better. Of course interpreters have found ways to deal with this strange sequence, but strange it remains. The second oddity, not always fully recognized, is that δικαίωμα is in the singular. Whether we go by Paul's own usage, that of the New Testament in general, or that of the LXX, where this word means a requirement or ordinance of the Law,[28] we should expect it to mean not the Law's requirements collectively, but one particular requirement. If the Law as a whole were meant here, we should have expected the plural, τὰ δικαιώματα. It is in just this sense that we find the plural in Rom. 2.26. The initial presumption, therefore, must be that in 8.4 the singular refers

and Deut. 5.21 *ḥmd* means not just bad desire, but an active scheming to fulfil that desire. See D. Patrick, *Old Testament Law* (London: SCM Press, 1986), pp. 58-59; B.S. Childs, *Exodus: A Commentary* (London: SCM Press, 1974), pp. 425-28; J.J. Stamm, *The Ten Commandments in Recent Research* (trans. M.E. Andrew; London: SCM Press, 1967), pp. 101-107. In Deut. 5.21 the verb *ḥmd* is partnered by *'wh* and it is possible (so A.D.H. Mayes, *Deuteronomy* [London: Marshall, Morgan & Scott, 1979], pp. 171-72) that the two are synonymous, both meaning wrongful desire only. However, the Rabbis tended to take the first as meaning actively scheming desire, and the second the desire itself even without any scheming (see J.Z. Lauterbach, *Mekilta de-Rabbi Ishmael*, II [Philadelphia: Jewish Publication Society, 1976], pp. 264-66; see also Maimonides, *The Commandments*, II [ed. C.B. Chavel; London: Soncino, 1967], pp. 250-52, where Mekilta Exod. 20.14 is discussed). Professor E.P. Sanders points out to me that in Romans 13 it certainly appears that not only love but also coveting is interpreted 'objectively', i.e. as a way of acting, in line with what appears to be a normal understanding in Judaism. In the light of all this, the at least predominantly interior understanding in Romans 7 is the more noteworthy, though of course the use of Greek (cf. LXX) might have facilitated this. Cf. also Philo, *Dec.* 173.

27. 'The Just Requirement of the Law (Romans 8.4)' *AusBR*. See now also Watson, *Paul, Judaism and the Gentiles*, pp. 156-57, though he thinks, with Gundry, that the tenth commandment is to be taken in a sexual sense.

28. This is leaving aside instances where δικαίωμα means 'justification', as probably in Rom. 5.16, or 'righteous deed', as usually proposed for Rom. 5.18.

to one particular ordinance of the Law.[29] If so, it is overwhelmingly probable that the ordinance in question is the tenth commandment and not, as is sometimes supposed, the love command, which is not mentioned in Romans until 13.8-10. The only specific commandment of the Torah to have been cited in the letter so far is the command against coveting.

If this identification is correct, we thus have the long discussion of the Law in 7.7–8.4 within an *inclusio*, namely the tenth commandment.

Conclusion

We must now try to indicate the consequences of the present thesis for the interpretation of the chapter in some crucial respects. How is Rom. 7.7-25 affected by the choice of this particular commandment as the paradigm, and a faulty one, for the relation between sin and the Law?

1.   It reinforces the suspicion that in this chapter Paul is not at his clearest. Indeed it is possible that his choice of a faulty paradigm lies at the root of some of the confusion.

2.   It helps to explain why Paul can, for the first time, claim in Romans 7 that one cannot obey the Law *at all*. In itself this is a highly implausible claim, but it is understandable if the real point at issue is the control of one's desires.

3.   It may help to reconcile Romans 7 with Phil. 3.6. One of the main reasons why many scholars have been uneasy about allowing an autobiographical element in this chapter (which is not the same as making it strictly autobiographical) is precisely the difficulty of making this reconciliation. On the other hand, a typical or general picture in Romans 7 that did not, as it happened, include Paul himself, has always been more than a little hard for some commentators to swallow.[30] If our argument is correct, then it is possible that in observable matters, matters subject to the control and scrutiny of the community, the Law

29.   It is difficult to find *any* occurrences in the New Testament or LXX where δικαίωμα in the singular could conceivably denote the Law's requirements collectively. The only possibilities, and not strong ones at that, are Prov. 8.20; 19.28.

30.   Moreover, Theissen (*Aspekte*, pp. 181-268) has shown that Kümmel's argument for a rhetorical 'I' that does not include the speaker, is highly unlikely in this case, and that an Adamic model as the basis for vv. 7-12 does not mean that an autobiographical element is altogether excluded.

may be fully kept (Phil. 3.6), while secret desires are out of
control. 'All is in the hand of heaven except the fear of
heaven.'

4.   It makes a pre-Christian interpretation of vv. 13-25 more likely
than a Christian one, because it is precisely one's desires that
have to be dealt with, not by commands, but by moving from
σάρξ to Πνεῦμα, from 'flesh' to 'Spirit' (ch. 8), that is to say
by dealing with the inner person by a total transformation.

5.   It helps to answer the question recently raised,[31] why it is only
the Law and not also the Pauline ethical teaching (or the ethical
teaching of Jesus) that prompts sin. It is not in fact the Law as
a whole that works in such a way, but only the one particular
commandment. Moreover, Pauline ethical teaching is based on
the assumption that the believer has already moved from σάρξ
to Πνεῦμα.

6.   It removes the absurdity of the passage vv. 13-25 if it is transferred from a timeless and universal human dilemma to a discussion about the Law.[32] It is absurd about most of the Law,
but not at all absurd about the command against coveting.

Finally, having said that Paul took a faulty paradigm, we must also say
that in a sense it was a very apt paradigm, simply because covetousness,
a basic sin in some Jewish thought, *is* something that cannot be dealt
with by the Law as such, but only by the sort of fundamental change of
direction that Paul envisages. Certainly this is true of its sexual aspect,
but it is equally true of all other aspects of it. In vv. 13-25 Paul talks
about a conflict of desires, about a mismatch between desires and
actions, and about a conflict of norms or laws. It is an odd mixture of
language, but an understandable one if the immediate subject is one particular command of the Torah, which is strictly concerned with human
desires.

Perhaps there is another sense in which the paradigm is not faulty but
apt, apt at least for the argument at this point in Romans (cf. above the
third reason hazarded for Paul's choice of the tenth commandment as
paradigm). No other command could make the case for the powerlessness of the Law to enable what it commands as well as this one does. It
is true, as I have tried to show, that what he says could not in detail have

31.   See Räisänen, *Paul and the Law*, pp. 148-49.
32.   Räisänen, *Paul and the Law*, p. 113; also 'Zum Gebrauch', p. 151.

been said using most other commands of the Law as a model. Nevertheless it may be that the command against coveting constitutes an extreme case which is needed in order to reveal the powerlessness of the Law, as he sees it. As it were, it is the highest hurdle which cannot be overcome, and thus shows that the whole of that race cannot be won.

PAULINE THEOLOGY

JSNT 32 (1988), pp. 93-113

SPHERES OF INFLUENCE:
A POSSIBLE SOLUTION TO THE PROBLEM OF PAUL AND THE LAW

Klyne Snodgrass

Of the many areas of disagreement among New Testament scholars, the explanation of Paul's understanding of the law is probably the topic about which there is the most debate. Presuppositional and methodological differences are magnified to such an extent by ecclesiastical traditions and existential concerns that what Paul actually said is difficult to determine. However, New Testament scholars are not wholly to blame for the disagreements over Paul's view of the law. The statements from Paul have caused the difficulty, for they are often enigmatic and at times appear contradictory. What is the meaning of 'I through the law died to the law' (Gal. 2.19)? How can Paul on the one hand claim that he does not abolish the law ($\kappa\alpha\tau\alpha\rho\gamma\epsilon\hat{\imath}\nu$, Rom. 3.31) and on the other hand say that we have died to the law and been cut off ($\kappa\alpha\tau\alpha\rho\gamma\epsilon\hat{\imath}\nu$) from the law (Rom. 7.4, 6)? How can he say 'For all the law has been fulfilled in the one statement "You will love your neighbor as yourself"' (Gal. 5.14), obviously expecting people to fulfill that command, and four verses later say 'you are not under law'? How is it that the same law can be both $\gamma\rho\alpha\phi\dot{\eta}$ (Gal. 3.22) and $\gamma\rho\dot{\alpha}\mu\mu\alpha$ (Rom. 7.6)? Citations of such 'anomalies' could be multiplied easily.

1. *Unsatisfying Solutions*

The scholarly writings on Paul have offered various explanations of his view of the law. While these writings provide insight into Paul's discussion, I find none of the explanations satisfying. There is, however, benefit in listing the attempted solutions and commenting briefly on them. The following suggestions have been made:

1   A supposed distinction between ὁ νόμος as the law of Moses and νόμος as the qualitative idea of law.[1] Paul was just not consistent in making such a distinction (see e.g. Gal. 3.21-24), and few people would support this view today.

2.   That there were two ways of salvation, an earlier way based on the law and a new way based on faith. Dispensationalism traditionally has held such a view, and various New Testament scholars also have fallen into this language.[2] Paul, however, seems to reject this option with his focus on Abraham being acquitted by faith (Rom. 4 and Gal. 3). For Paul, the only way to salvation is faith. He would never have agreed that there was a time when salvation was obtainable through 'works of the law'.

3.   That part of the law was annulled—the ritual and civil elements—while the moral law continues in force. New Testament scholars rightly have insisted that neither Judaism nor the early Christians made such distinctions in the law.[3] That the law was viewed as a unity is not to be questioned. Still, it is clear that various persons or groups did make implicit distinctions in the law: the prophets focused on justice rather than the cult;[4] Qumran focused on spiritual sacrifices rather than physical ones;[5] Jesus, according to such texts as Mt. 9.13 and 12.7, followed the prophetic lead and drew conclusions different from

1.   See e.g. J.B. Lightfoot, *St Paul's Epistle to the Galatians* (London: Macmillan, 1880), p. 118; Ernest De Witt Burton, *The Epistle to the Galatians* (ICC; Edinburgh: T. & T. Clark, 1921), pp. 455-56; see the discussions in Richard N. Longenecker, *Paul: The Apostle of Liberty* (New York: Harper & Row, 1964), pp. 117-19; Edward Grafe, *Die paulinische Lehre vom Gesetz nach den vier Hauptbriefen* (Tübingen: J.C.B. Mohr [Paul Siebeck], 1884), pp. 2-11.

2.   See the discussion in Daniel P. Fuller, *Gospel & Law: Contrast or Continuum?* (Grand Rapids: Eerdmans, 1980), pp. 1-64. Heikki Räisänen, *Paul and the Law* (Tübingen: J.C.B. Mohr [Paul Siebeck], 1983), p. 178, argues Paul ascribes saving value to the law within the Jewish system. See also Rudolf Bultmann, 'Christ the End of the Law', in *Essays Philosophical and Theological* (New York: Macmillan, 1955), p. 54.

3.   Bo Reicke, 'Paulus über das Gesetz', *TZ* 41 (1985), p. 241; James D.G. Dunn, 'Works of the Law and the Curse of the Law (Galatians 3.10-14)', *NTS* 31 (1985), p. 531; Douglas J. Moo, '"Law", "Works of the Law", and Legalism in Paul', *WTJ* 45 (1983), p. 85.

4.   Hos. 6.6; 8.11-13, 9.4; Amos 4.4-5; 5.21-22; Jer. 7.22; Mic. 6.6-8; Ps. 50.

5.   1QS 8.5-10; 9.3-6.

his contemporaries about the law;[6] and Paul clearly had made distinctions in the law when he did not include circumcision among the commands of God (1 Cor. 7.19).[7] The problem, of course, is that none of these persons says explicitly that there are distinctions or tells us on what basis they were being made. Even if the distinctions are granted, this will not explain Paul's theology, for in Rom. 7.7-10 it is the moral law that works death for him.

4.   That expectations concerning the messianic age included the belief that the law would no longer be in force or would be replaced by a new law.[8] Although such claims are often made, the evidence for such a belief is weak. This does not appear to be the reason Paul argued Christians are no longer under law.[9]

5.   That the law of God in Paul refers to more than the Torah since it includes the teaching of Jesus. On this view, which was argued by C.H. Dodd, Christians are free from the Torah, but loyal to the law of God.[10] Paul did refer to the teaching of Jesus on occasion, but that 'law of Christ' in Gal. 6.2 refers to the teaching of Jesus or that other positive references to the law should be interpreted this way seems very unlikely.

6.   That Paul only argued against a misunderstanding of the law, not the law itself. This view has been argued by—among others—C.E.B. Cranfield,[11] but as attractive as parts of the

6.   See the discussions in Marcus J. Borg, *Conflict, Holiness & Politics in the Teaching of Jesus* (New York: Edwin Mellen, 1984) and E.P. Sanders, *Jesus and Judaism* (Philadelphia: Fortress Press, 1985), pp. 245-69, although this is a complicated discussion which needs further treatment. In particular, I do not think Sanders's treatment is satisfactory.

7.   E.P. Sanders, *Paul, the Law, and the Jewish People* (Philadelphia: Fortress Press, 1983), pp. 104-105.

8.   H.J. Schoeps, *Paul: The Theology of the Apostle in the Light of Jewish Religious History* (trans. Harold Knight; Philadelphia: Westminster, 1974), p. 171; Albert Schweitzer, *The Mysticism of Paul the Apostle* (trans. William Montgomery; London: A. & C. Black, 1931), pp. 191-93. Cf. W.D. Davies, *Torah in the Messianic Age and/or the Age to Come* (Philadelphia: Society of Biblical Literature, 1952).

9.   See Peter Schäfer, 'Die Torah der messianischen Zeit', *ZNW* 65 (1974), pp. 27-42; George Foot Moore, *Judaism in the First Centuries of the Christian Era* (Cambridge, MA: Harvard University Press, 1927), I, pp. 269-74.

10.   C.H. Dodd, 'ΕΝΝΟΜΟΣ ΧΡΙΣΤΟΥ', in *Studia Paulina* (Haarlem: De Erven F. Bohn, 1953), pp. 98-99.

11.   C.E.B. Cranfield, 'St Paul and the Law', *SJT* 17 (1964), pp. 43-68; see also

theory are, in the end it is not convincing. Paul does not merely argue against a misunderstanding of the law, and the phrase 'under the law' cannot be confined to the meaning 'under the curse of the law'.[12] Paul is negative in his view of the law itself in some respects and by 'under the law' at times means 'under the tyranny of the law' (Rom. 6.14).

7. That Paul's view of the law changed from a largely negative view in Galatians to a more balanced view in Romans. Such a development hypothesis has been argued most recently by Hans Hübner and John Drane.[13] Galatians is clearly more polemical than Romans, and certainly we should expect that Paul's views developed over the course of the years. Still, the development hypotheses are not convincing. Paul's letters are not of such a character that they allow us to trace a straight-line development. Furthermore, the problem of the law is present in both Galatians and Romans individually. Hübner's explanation founders on his inability to treat the positive statements on the law in Galatians, especially 5.14.[14]

8. That Paul preached a law-free gospel only to Gentiles and never encouraged Jews to abandon the Torah. This approach concludes that there were two religions and two peoples of God.[15] But this does not fit Paul's discussion in Romans, where

Dunn, 'Works of the Law and the Curse of the Law', p. 536.

12. As Cranfield ('St Paul and the Law', p. 56) suggests. For a better understanding of this phrase, see Peter von der Osten-Sacken, *Römer 8 als Beispiel paulinischer Soteriologie* (Göttingen: Vandenhoeck & Ruprecht, 1975), p. 188; and Herman Ridderbos, *Paul: An Outline of his Theology* (trans. John Richard De Witt; Grand Rapids: Eerdmans, 1975), p. 148.

13. Hans Hübner, *Law in Paul's Thought* (trans. James C.G. Greig; Edinburgh: T. & T. Clark, 1984); John W. Drane, *Paul, Libertine or Legalist?* (London: SPCK, 1975); see also the earlier argument of Charles Buck and Greer Taylor, *Saint Paul: A Study of the Development of his Thought* (New York: Scribner's, 1969) and the critique by Victor Furnish, 'Development in Paul's Thought', *JAAR* 38 (1970), pp. 289-303.

14. Hübner (*Law in Paul's Thought*, p. 136) does not see Gal. 5.14 as referring to the Torah at all.

15. Lloyd Gaston, 'Paul and the Torah', in *Antisemitism and the Foundation of Christianity* (ed. Alan Davies; New York: Paulist, 1979), pp. 48-71.

he offers his gospel to the Jew first and explicitly discusses the Jewish rejection of his message.[16]

9. That Paul is inconsistent and illogical. This position has been argued forcefully by H. Räisänen and E.P. Sanders.[17] One can sympathize with this position because of the difficulty of understanding Paul's statements about the law. But there are too many texts where the arguments of Räisänen and Sanders either take an unnecessarily negative view of Paul's comments or do not do justice to his point.[18]

There are other solutions that have been proposed,[19] but these should suffice to demonstrate that we have not yet attained a satisfactory explanation of Paul's teaching on the law.

2. *Guidelines for a Solution*

Even if there is not a convincing explanation of Paul's treatment of the law, it should be possible to establish certain points that are clear. If they could be established, such points might provide a basis for a more suitable treatment of Paul's teaching on the law.

The first such clear point, I would suggest, is that Paul never saw himself as rejecting or calling into question the Hebrew scriptures. Those scriptures functioned for him authoritatively even when he was making a negative point about the law. At times his use of a text may cause difficulty for us (e.g. Rom. 10.5-8), but he obviously thought his position was validated by scripture. He knew of a greater glory revealed in the gospel (2 Cor. 3.11), but that did not negate his commitment to the scriptures.

16. Rom. 1.16; cf. 15.19; chs. 9–11.

17. Räisänen, *Paul and the Law*; Sanders, *Paul, the Law, and the Jewish People*, pp. 3-167.

18. The interpretation of Rom. 2 by both Räisänen and Sanders is a clear case in point. See my 'Justification by Grace—to the Doers: An Analysis of the Place of Romans 2 in the Theology of Paul', *NTS* 32 (1986), pp. 72-93. See also Jerome Hall, 'Paul, the Lawyer, on Law', *The Journal of Law and Religion* 3 (1985), pp. 1-49.

19. See the solutions listed by James A. Sanders, 'Torah and Paul', in *God's Christ and His People* (ed. Jacob Jervell and Wayne A. Meeks; Oslo: Universitetsforlaget, 1977), pp. 133-35; Räisänen, *Paul and the Law*, pp. 3-15. Note also Peter Stuhlmacher's attempt (following H. Gese) to distinguish between a Sinai Torah and a Zion Torah in his 'Das Gesetz als Thema biblischer Theologie', *ZTK* 75 (1978), pp. 257-76.

Similarly, he did not see himself as undermining obedience to the will of God revealed in the law or as advocating antinomianism. Others may have charged him with antinomianism (Rom. 3.8; 6.15), but he had no sympathy with such a stance. As E.P. Sanders has correctly pointed out, Paul expected the law to be lived by Christians[20] (cf. e.g. 1 Cor. 7.19;[21] Rom. 8.4). Obviously Paul had also made distinctions on some basis so that we should say he expected the law to be lived by Christians *except* for circumcision and certain other items. He does not tell us how he arrived at the exceptions, but he expected the law to be lived. Paul's focus on obedience to the law deserves much more attention than it usually receives. In fact, I doubt that Paul would have agreed that he had a negative view of the law.

'Works of the law', however, are not to be equated with godly obedience in Paul's thinking. The identification of the meaning of this expression is crucial for understanding Paul, and attention will be given to this issue below.

We may also be certain that Paul did not see himself as breaking with Judaism. The recent discussion between H. Räisänen and J. Dunn underscores the importance of this point.[22] Räisänen, following Sanders,[23] insists on speaking of Paul's break with Judaism, even though he admits that Paul saw himself as a loyal Jew.[24] Räisänen also recognizes that there are various degrees of discontinuity with Judaism evidenced in people like Matthew or Philo and that Paul did not initiate the break with Judaism. Such a break was inherent already in the claims of the gospel and was implied by John the Baptist, if proselyte baptism is pre-Christian. To maintain his belief that Paul broke with Judaism, Räisänen must argue that Abraham was a special case for Paul. For both Räisänen

20. Sanders, *Paul, the Law, and the Jewish People*, pp. 93-122.

21. Some deny that Paul refers to the Torah in 1 Cor. 7.19, but this is not acceptable. See Drane, *Paul: Libertine or Legalist?*, p. 65; W.D. Davies, 'Paul and the Law: Reflections on Pitfalls in Interpretation', in *Paul and Paulinism* (ed. M.D. Hooker and S.G. Wilson; London: SPCK, 1982), p. 9. 1 Cor. 7.19 is surprising in view of what Paul says elsewhere, but this passage is important for understanding the positive aspects of his view of the law.

22. Heikki Räisänen, 'Galatians 2.16 and Paul's Break with Judaism', *NTS* 31 (1985), pp. 543-53; reacting against James D.G. Dunn, 'The New Perspective on Paul', *BJRL* 65 (1983), pp. 95-122.

23. E.P. Sanders, *Paul and Palestinian Judaism* (Philadelphia: Fortress Press, 1977), p. 550; and *Paul, the Law, and the Jewish People*, pp. 171-72, 207-10.

24. Räisänen, 'Galatians 2.16 and Paul's Break with Judaism', pp. 544-50.

and Sanders Paul did not suggest that the possibility of faith was there all along.[25] However, that seems to be precisely Paul's point in Romans 4. How can Abraham be viewed as a special case when the example of David is used as well (Rom. 4.6-8) and when Abraham is viewed as the father of faith for both Jews and Gentiles (Rom. 4.12)? Others may question the legitimacy of his belief, but Paul saw himself as in line with Abraham and in line with a proper understanding of Judaism.[26] The 'transfer' terms are important for Paul, but he never speaks of transferring from Judaism to Christianity (cf. the analogy in Rom. 11.17-24).[27]

The element of discontinuity ought not to be minimized, however. Circumstances are different for Paul now that Christ has appeared. His orientation changed dramatically in response to God's act in Christ. Whereas formerly the center of gravity or dominating force for Paul and other Jews was the law, now he found that center of gravity in Christ. The spotlight has been turned from the law and placed on Christ, and accordingly one must turn to Christ (2 Cor. 3.16). The cross and resurrection, the giving of the Spirit, and the presence of the new age constitute a decisive turning point and require a salvation-historical shift. But turning to Christ is done *in keeping* with Old Testament faith, not in rejection of it. With the focus on Christ there is correspondingly a diminishing of the role of the law. Justice must be done both to continuity and discontinuity if we are to understand Paul.

I would affirm two other established points that are important for the discussion of Paul and the law. They relate, not to Paul, but to our approach to him. Paul's letters are not systematic discussions of the law or any other theological topic. They are *ad hoc* documents dealing with pastoral issues. At times Paul does focus specifically on the law, especially in Rom. 7.7ff., but nowhere do we get a complete discussion. Anything that we say about the law is an extrapolation from Paul's teaching on other subjects. All of us grant the *ad hoc* character of the letters, but we still too frequently treat them as if they were theological statements.

The remaining point concerning our approach to Paul relates to the broader question of the relation of Judaism and Christianity. Too

25. Räisänen, 'Galatians 2.16 and Paul's Break with Judaism', p. 552 n. 41; Sanders, *Paul, the Law, and the Jewish People*, p. 207.

26. See Rom. 4.9-11.

27. Against Räisänen, 'Galatians 2.16 and Paul's Break with Judaism', p. 549, who speaks of a 'third tree'. Cf. the later descriptions of Christians as a third race.

frequently when we have approached Paul, we have had other agendas on our minds. At times people have been apologetically motivated to demonstrate the superiority of Christianity to Judaism. At other times people have been concerned for healthy Jewish–Christian dialogue. While the one group painted Judaism in a negative way, the other group defended Judaism from any charge. Both approaches can lead to a skewing of our understanding of Paul. Our primary task—as important as the relation of Christianity to Judaism is—must be the descriptive task of understanding Paul and the situation to which he addresses himself.

3. *Toward a Possible Solution*

No doubt there will continue to be some texts in Paul's treatment of the law that defy our attempts to explain them. Without thinking that one theory will account for all the difficulties, I would suggest that there is a way forward that helps to explain many of the statements Paul makes. The suggestion is not new, but it deserves more emphasis than it has received.

The starting point for a solution is a holistic view of Paul's theology of participation in Christ. The presentation of his theology using participationist categories is well known.[28] The tendency, however, is to set his participationist language over against his forensic terms as if the two approaches were mutually exclusive. It seems to me that the forensic terms have their significance in the participationist language. One is justified only *in* Christ (Rom. 8.1; Gal. 2.17). Accordingly, Paul's understanding is based on 'spheres of influence' or 'power fields'.[29] Salvation is described as the transfer from one sphere of lordship to another.[30]

Surprisingly, Paul's understanding of the law has not been treated very frequently from the standpoint of spheres of influence. We have discussed salvation in terms of spheres of influence, but have forgotten this framework when we discuss the law. Seeing Paul's statements about the law within the context of his assumption of spheres

28. Schweitzer, *The Mysticism of Paul the Apostle*, pp. 101-102, Sanders, *Paul and Palestinian Judaism*, pp. 435-36; James Stewart, *A Man in Christ* (London: Hodder & Stoughton, 1936), pp. 147-48.

29. See Robert C. Tannehill, *Dying and Rising with Christ* (Berlin: Töpelmann, 1967), pp. 11-24 and *passim*; Stewart, *A Man in Christ*, pp. 169-70, 185, 193.

30. Tannehill, *Dying and Rising with Christ*, p. 7 and *passim*; Sanders, *Paul and Palestinian Judaism*, pp. 463-64.

of influence changes our perspective and increases our understanding of him considerably.

The sphere of influence that controls life before conversion is sin. Sin is personified by Paul and viewed as a tyrant. But there are lesser tyrannies—death, flesh, and principalities and powers—that function under the tyranny of sin. Surprisingly, law also is one of these lesser tyrannies and becomes a sphere of influence in which people live. Therefore, Paul can speak of being ἐν τῷ νόμῳ or ὑπὸ νόμον (Rom. 3.19; 6.14). The difficulty is that sometimes these expressions seem to be circumlocutions for being Jewish (Rom. 2.12; and 1 Cor. 9.20), while at other times at least ὑπὸ νόμον means under the tyranny of the law (Rom. 6.14; Gal. 4.5).[31] Rom. 7.1ff. describes the tyranny of the law more directly than any other text.

The law was not supposed to function as a tyrant, however. Paul's point in Rom. 7.13 is that sin has co-opted law and pressed it into a service for which it was not intended. Sin is the real culprit and has commandeered law by bringing it into the sphere of sin and the flesh to accomplish death. Law does not belong in this sphere, since it is good, just, holy, and spiritual (Rom. 7.12-14). Therefore, law also can be viewed as belonging to the sphere of Christ, the Spirit, and faith. *The determinant for the law is the sphere in which it is placed.* As F. Hahn, C.F.D. Moule, and Bo Reicke have pointed out, in Paul the law does not stand for itself; it occurs in a context and in connection with something else. It refers to the law as *used* in various specific ways.[32] νόμος obtains its function from the sphere in which it is placed. The qualitative genitive forms express not the nature of the law, but the context in which law works.[33] The law can be either the law of sin and death or the law of the Spirit of life (Rom. 8.2). Therefore, Paul's view of the law was

31. Should ἐν νόμῳ in Gal. 3.11; 5.4 be interpreted 'by law' or 'in the sphere of law'? See the discussion of ὑπὸ νόμον by Linda L. Belleville, '"Under Law": Structural Analysis and the Pauline Concept of Law in Galatians 3.21–4.11', *JSNT* 26 (1986), pp. 53-78.

32. Ferdinand Hahn, 'Das Gesetzverständnis im Römer- und Galaterbrief', *ZNW* 66 (1975), p. 49; C.F.D. Moule, '"Justification" in its Relation to the Condition κατὰ πνεῦμα (Rom. 8.1-11)', in *Battesimo e Giustizia in Rom 6 e 8* (ed. Lorenzo De Lorenzi; Rome: Abbazia S. Paolo fuori le mura, 1974), p. 181; Reicke, 'Paulus über das Gesetz', pp. 243-44. See also Osten-Sacken, *Römer 8 als Beispiel paulinischer Soteriologie*, pp. 209-210; Irene Beck, 'Altes und neues Gesetz', *MTZ* 15 (1964), pp. 127-42.

33. Reicke, 'Paulus über das Gesetz', p. 243.

positive, but the law was like a tool. It did not contain power within itself (Rom. 8.3); rather, it could be taken over and used by sin or it could have its rightful use in the sphere of Christ, the Spirit, and faith. In the sphere of sin the law is a sub-tyrant, is negative, and causes death, but in its intended sphere it is the expression of the will of God and is for life (Rom. 8.7; 7.10).

E.P. Sanders is one of the relatively few people who have recognized that the law functions in the sphere of sin and in the sphere of Christ. His diagram of the spheres is helpful in that it lists terminology describing the spheres, the transfer from one sphere to the other, and the results of life in each realm.[34] One of the largest drawbacks to Sanders's discussion is that he leaves out of consideration those texts where νόμος could mean 'principle'.[35] However, it seems to me that these texts are among the most important for discussing the law within Paul's assumption of spheres of influence.

With this preliminary statement before us, we may look once again at Paul's use of νόμος in key passages in Romans to see how law viewed from the standpoint of spheres of influence helps us understand the epistle.

a. *Rom. 3.27-31*

The obvious question in this text is whether νόμος has the same meaning in each occurrence or whether with νόμος πίστεως Paul is only playing with words so that we must translate this phrase as 'principle of faith',[36] 'religious system of faith',[37] or 'order of faith'.[38] G. Friedrich has challenged this 'metaphorical' interpretation and argued instead that νόμος πίστεως is the Old Testament law which witnesses to the righteousness of faith.[39] Hans Hübner and Peter von der Osten-Sacken

34. Sanders, *Paul, the Law, and the Jewish People*, p. 7.

35. Sanders, *Paul, the Law, and the Jewish People*, p. 10.

36. C.H. Dodd, *The Epistle of Paul to the Romans* (London: Hodder & Stoughton, 1932), p. 86; *The Bible and the Greeks* (London: Hodder & Stoughton, 1954), p. 36, but on p. 37 Dodd grants that Paul had in the back of his mind the thought of νόμος = תורה; Sanders, *Paul, the Law, and the Jewish People*, p. 15 n. 26.

37. C.K. Barrett, *A Commentary on the Epistle to the Romans* (HNTC; New York: Harper & Row, 1957), p. 83.

38. Räisänen, *Paul and the Law*, p. 52; Ernst Käsemann, *Commentary on Romans* (trans. Geoffrey W. Bromiley; Grand Rapids: Eerdmans, 1980), p. 103; Heinrich Schlier, *Der Römerbrief* (Freiburg: Herder, 1979), p. 116.

39. Gerhard Friedrich, 'Das Gesetz des Glaubens Rom. 3.27', *TZ* 6 (1954), pp. 401-17.

have adapted his view and extended his critique of the 'metaphorical' approach to other texts as well.[40] Friedrich's strongest argument is that νόμος occurs eleven times in 3.19-31 and all the other occurrences refer to the Mosaic law. His weakest (and I think unacceptable) point is his suggestion that νόμος πίστεως means the same as ἐπαγγελία in ch. 4.

H. Räisänen has argued against Friedrich's interpretation and thinks to have excluded a reference to the Mosaic law by the following points:

1.	There are various meanings given to νόμος in 7.21–8.2, which Friedrich granted, and therefore the argument that there could not be various uses in 3.19-31 is invalid.

2.	As is shown by the aorist passive, the 'law of faith' is a one time act of God by which boasting is excluded. How could the Torah be presented as the once for all exclusion of boasting?[41]

Räisänen does grant the possibility of Cranfield's interpretation by which God is understood to have shown boasting to be futile and absurd through the Old Testament scriptures. The result would be that 'law of faith' refers to the Old Testament law in so far as it locks all under sin. But Räisänen rejects this option and concludes that 'law of faith' is the same as 'for a man to be justified by faith'.[42]

Räisänen's argument has force, but it also has its weak points. It assumes that there are various meanings of νόμος in 7.21–8.2, but that is a debated issue itself. On his view, for all intents and purposes, the word νόμος could just as easily have been omitted in 3.27. Further, Räisänen ends up claiming that Paul sees the order of the Torah being replaced by another law, which is the *opposite* of what Paul claims to be saying in 3.31.[43] Räisänen has to conclude that Paul makes the positive comment on the law in 3.31 *blitzartig*.[44]

Clearly Paul's point is that boasting has been excluded by God's act in Christ.[45] We would have expected a statement like 'Boasting has been

40.	Hübner, *Law in Paul's Thought*, pp. 137-48; Osten-Sacken, *Römer 8 als Beispiel paulinischer Soteriologie*, pp. 245-46.

41.	Heikki Räisänen, 'Das "Gesetz des Glaubens" (Rom. 3.27) und das "Gesetz des Geistes" (Rom. 8.2)', *NTS* 26 (1980), especially pp. 106-10.

42.	Räisänen, 'Das "Gesetz des Glaubens"', pp. 111-12. See C.E.B. Cranfield, *The Epistle to the Romans* (ICC; Edinburgh: T. & T. Clark, 1975–1979), I, p. 219.

43.	Räisänen, *Paul and the Law*, p. 52. No wonder that Räisänen finds Paul inconsistent.

44.	Räisänen, 'Das "Gesetz des Glaubens"', p. 113.

45.	This is established by the context, but not just because the verb is in the aorist,

excluded by the cross' (cf. 1 Cor. 1.18-19) with no reference to the law at all. Why is the law mentioned in connection with boasting? Paul's thought builds on 2.23 where he implies that Jews boast in the law. Earlier, in 2.17, he had described the Jew as one who boasts in God. Boasting is an important theme in Paul's theology in that he excludes any boasting in 'the flesh', but encourages boasting in what God has done in Christ. 'Boasting in God' I understand to be a positive expression similar to 'boasting in the Lord' in 1 Cor. 1.31. 'Boasting in the law' is potentially positive in view of the advantage of the Jews in having the oracles of God (Rom. 3.1-2), but it could be understood negatively if it resulted in Jewish exclusivism, the position that Paul argues against.

In rejecting Jewish exclusivism Paul appeared to be rejecting the law, a charge to which he responds in 3.31. It is because of this charge and the connection of boasting with law in 2.23 that Paul asks 'By what kind of law' has boasting been excluded? The law is an actor, but it is not on the stage alone. *It is not the sphere and qualifier Jewish exclusivism thought it was.* It is always qualified by another entity. Moule rightly points to 'Paul's notoriously flexible and pregnant uses of the genitive'.[46] The words in the genitive are not incidental 'add-ons' for Paul, but often carry as much or more force than the noun they qualify. When Paul asks 'What kind of law?', the options he offers are 'law characterized by works' and 'law characterized by faith'. I do not think that we can avoid a reference to the Torah with these expressions.[47] It is through the law that Paul died to the law. The law characterized by faith does not merely refer to the witness function of the law, although that may be

as Räisänen asserts ('Das "Gesetz des Glaubens"', p. 110). The aorist tense does not mean a 'once for all act'. See Frank Stagg, 'The Abused Aorist', *JBL* 90 (1972), pp. 222-31.

46. Moule, '"Justification" in its Relation to the Condition κατὰ πνεῦμα (Rom. 8.1-11)', p. 181. Cf. Friedrich Lang, 'Gesetz und Bund bei Paulus', in *Rechtfertigung* (ed. Johannes Friedrich, Wolfgang Pohlmann, and Peter Stuhlmacher; Tübingen: J.C.B. Mohr [Paul Siebeck], 1976), p. 318, who points out that with expressions like Rom. 3.27, etc. the content of the saying lies in the idea expressed in the genitive. He does not, however, follow through with the implications of this in his interpretation.

47. Ulrich Wilckens, *Der Brief an die Römer* (Cologne: Benziger Verlag, 1978), I, p. 245; Moule, '"Justification" in its Relation to the Condition κατὰ πνεῦμα (Rom. 8.1-11)', p. 181; Cranfield, *The Epistle to the Romans*, I, p. 220; C. Thomas Rhyne, *Faith Establishes the Law* (Chico, CA: Scholars Press, 1981), pp. 68-70.

included.[48] It means the law brought into the sphere of faith where it was intended to function. Boasting has been excluded when the law is placed in its proper sphere: faith. Any boasting that is done in the sphere of faith is not boasting in self, but is boasting in the Lord (cf. 5.2-11).

A second issue in this section I consider to be one of the most difficult and determinative factors in interpreting Paul: What is the meaning of the expression ἔργα νόμου? In the New Testament the phrase 'works of the law' only occurs eight times in Paul's letters and hardly occurs, if at all, in Jewish literature until after the tannaitic period.[49] All eight of Paul's occurrences show that God's saving activity comes from some other source than 'works of law'.[50] It is important to note that the plural ἔργα is nearly always negative in the Pauline letters,[51] while the singular ἔργον is always positive except for two times which the context clearly marks as negative. The usual explanation is that ἔργα νόμου refers to actions performed in obedience to statutes (often with the connotation of legalism)[52] or works done as human achievement to present oneself to God.[53] Recently the term has been the focus of renewed debate. Following E. Lohmeyer and J. Tyson,[54] several scholars have begun to

48. The witness function of the law is the interpretation of Friedrich, 'Das Gesetz des Glaubens Rom. 3.27', pp. 413-17; Hahn, 'Das Gesetzesverständnis im Römer- und Galaterbrief', p. 41; and Rhyne, *Faith Establishes the Law*, pp. 65, 74-75.

49. Markus Barth, *Ephesians* (AB, 34; Garden City: Doubleday, 1974), I, p. 245. Some such as Moo, '"Law", "Works of the Law", and Legalism in Paul', p. 91, point to 4QFlor 1.7, but others read מעשי תורה instead of תורה מעשי. See Lloyd Gaston, 'Works of Law as a Subjective Genitive', *SR* 13 (1984), p. 40 n. 8; J. Strugnell, 'Notes en marge du volume V des "Discoveries in the Judean Desert"', *RevQ* 7 (1970), p. 221. The plate in *DJD*, V, is not clear.

50. Gaston, 'Works of Law as a Subjective Genitive', p. 42. However, his conclusion that 'works of law' is a subjective genitive—meaning that the law works a curse, wrath, and death—does not fit Paul's usage.

51. The exceptions are Rom. 2.6, which is an Old Testament quotation, and the expression 'good works' in Eph. 2.10 and the Pastorals.

52. Burton, *The Epistle to the Galatians*, p. 120; C.K. Barrett, 'Romans 9.30–10.21: Fall and Responsibility of Israel', in *Essays on Paul* (Philadelphia: Westminster Press, 1982), pp. 141-42; Hübner, *Law in Paul's Thought*, p. 116.

53. Moule, '"Justification" in its Relation to the Condition κατὰ πνεῦμα (Rom. 8.1-11)', p. 181; Moo, '"Law", "Works of the Law", and Legalism in Paul', pp. 90-98.

54. Ernst Lohmeyer, 'Gesetzeswerke', in *Probleme paulinischer Theologie* (Stuttgart: Kohlhammer, n.d.), pp. 33-73 (originally in *ZNW* 28 [1959], pp. 177-207); J.B. Tyson, '"Works of Law" in Galatians', *JBL* 92 (1973), pp. 423-31.

argue that 'works of law' refers to those obligations prescribed by the law that identify a person as belonging to the people of God. These works are boundary and identity markers separating the people of God from others, particularly circumcision, food laws, and sabbath observance.[55]

As a result, ἔργα νόμου has become an important issue in the debate as to whether Paul was writing against boasting in works righteousness. Does the phrase refer to self righteous activity to present oneself to God or does it refer to sociological identity markers? The difference in the two affects how we see the Judaism of Paul's day. I find increasingly that there is an attraction to the view that ἔργα νόμου refers to identity markers, but the end result with regard to boasting may not be that different. As Dunn indicates, ἔργα νόμου is a shorthand way to refer to that in which the typical Jew placed his confidence.[56] Boasting is very much the issue. How different is it if confidence is placed in works that are identity markers or if works are viewed as human achievement to present oneself to God (cf. Rom. 10.3)? ἔργα νόμου then reflect identity markers, but they are a particular 'sub-set' of ἔργα in general, by which people seek to present themselves to God.[57]

What Paul attacks here and elsewhere is the traditional understanding of covenant and election.[58] 'Getting in' does not seem to have been an issue for Jews; obedience was, and 'staying in' may have been to some extent. For Paul, 'getting in' was relevant for Jews as well. No one is 'saved' merely because of nationality. Both Jew and Gentile entered the same way and stayed in the same way—by faith.[59] Still, the sociological exclusivism of ἔργα νόμου is not the only negative aspect of the law, for that would not do justice to texts like Rom. 7.7ff. But this does seem to be the focus in 3.27-31.

If we are correct, Paul's thought in these verses may be summarized as follows. Boasting has been excluded, not by the law characterized by exclusivism, but by the law characterized by faith (i.e. the law

---

55. Dunn, 'Works of the Law and the Curse of the Law (Galatians 3.10-14)', pp. 524-31; Sanders, *Paul, the Law, and the Jewish People*, pp. 46, 102.

56. Dunn, 'Works of the Law and the Curse of the Law (Galatians 3.10-14)', p. 528.

57. Cf. Moo, '"Law", "Works of Law", and Legalism in Paul'.

58. Sanders, *Paul, the Law, and the Jewish People*, p. 46.

59. Cf. R.H. Gundry, 'Grace, Works, and Staying Saved in Paul', *Bib* 66 (1985), pp. 1-38.

functioning within the sphere of faith). People are acquitted before God by faith, not by exclusivistic works. God is not the God of the Jews only, but he is also the God of the Gentiles. There is only one God and he acquits both Jew and Gentile on the basis of faith. The law is not destroyed by the focus on faith; rather, as a law of faith it is established.

Comparison should be made between 3.27-31 and 9.30-33, where again works and faith are contrasted, focus is placed on the inclusion of the Gentiles, and νόμος is used positively. Space will not permit consideration of 9.30-33 in detail, but one should note that νόμος is again qualified by another entity. Here Israel is said to have pursued a law qualified by righteousness (νόμον δικαιοσύνης), but did not attain to that law. As in 3.27, where the law excluded boasting, law again appears in an unexpected role. The law of righteousness was the *legitimate* goal Israel pursued.[60] Israel's goal was not wrong, but the path she chose to get there—works—was. The only way to the goal of a law characterized by righteousness or in a sphere of righteousness is faith.[61]

b. *Rom. 4.13-16*

Although our concern is primarily with texts where νόμος is sometimes (erroneously, I think) taken as 'principle', brief comment will be made on other texts relevant to the discussion of the law and Paul's theology of spheres of influence.

If the law is viewed as a sphere in keeping with Paul's participationist language, the statements in Rom. 4.13-16 become clearer. Paul's point here is that law is not the sphere from which the promise and salvation come. In 4.16 the promise does not belong only to those in the sphere of the law. It is also addressed to those having faith. It is worthy of note that Paul does not deny the validity of the promise to those who are in the sphere of law. The primary point, of course, is that he will not allow

---

60. C.E.B. Cranfield, 'Some Notes on Romans 9.30-33', in *Jesus und Paulus* (ed. E. Earle Ellis and Erich Grässer; Göttingen: Vandenhoeck & Ruprecht, 1975), pp. 36-40; C. Thomas Rhyne, 'Nomos Dikaiosynes and the Meaning of Romans 10.4', *CBQ* 47 (1985), pp. 489-90; Barrett, 'Romans 9.30–10.21: Fall and Responsibility of Israel', p. 140. But the attempt by Barrett and others to see in the stone a reference to the law, rather than a reference to Christ, will not work. Clearly Isa. 28.16 is understood christologically in Rom. 10.11 and is too established as a primitive christological testimonium for this suggestion to have merit.

61. Sanders (*Paul, the Law, and the Jewish People*, pp. 36-37) admits that Rom. 9.30-33 is the strongest text against his position on legalism.

it to be limited to those people either. The advantage of the Jews in having the law does not nullify the necessity of faith.

c. *Rom. 5.20*

This verse requires comment because so many people interpret Paul's words here in an excessively negative fashion. This is among the most negative statements that Paul makes, but conclusions should not be drawn that preclude any possibility of bringing this text into line with what Paul says elsewhere. Paul does bring the law into connection with sin, but the statement is enigmatic. It is important to notice Paul's method in Romans. Frequently he introduces a point briefly only to return to it later for detailed treatment. In 3.1-4 he raises issues that are not dealt with in detail until chs. 9–11. In 3.8 he asks a question that is dealt with in 6.1ff. In 3.31 he makes a statement that is explained in chs. 7–8.[62] Accordingly in 5.20 Paul brings law into connection with sin, but what he means by that statement is not clear until 7.7-13.[63] The most that we should say is that God permits the connection between sin and law in order that the true nature of sin may be displayed.

d. *Rom. 7.1-6*

This is the most obvious text in which the law functions as a tyrant. There can be no question that the law is viewed negatively nor that Christians are transferred from a sphere where law is a tyrant to another sphere where all is determined by Christ. The purpose of this transfer in 7.4, 6 should be noted. Christians have died to the tyranny of the law to be joined to Christ for the purpose of bearing fruit to God and serving in newness of the Spirit. One would have thought this was the purpose of the law as well. However, 7.5 introduces another sphere which we have not met before in Romans, the sphere of the flesh. In this sphere sinful passions evoked by the law worked in people to bear fruit for death. From 7.6 it is clear that the law is viewed as a tyrant that prevented the

62. Rhyne (*Faith Establishes the Law*, pp. 60-61) argues that 3.31 is explained in ch. 4, but it seems to me that Paul's claim to establish the law must include more than merely the witness function of the law.

63. Sanders (*Paul, the Law, and the Jewish People*, p. 71) recognizes that 7.7-13 is an explanation of 5.20, but still distinguishes between the meaning of the two passages (p. 80). Nor would I see Gal. 3.19 as an attempt to deny the divine origin of the law by interpreting angels as evil angels (*contra* Hübner, *Law in Paul's Thought*, pp. 27-31).

kind of service to God which, we know from elsewhere, the law itself was intended to promote.

This unexpected result calls forth Paul's most extended treatment of the law. He will not grant that there is anything negative about the law itself. Instead, sin works through the flesh and uses the law to cause death. This explanation is already implied in 7.5, but Paul works it out in detail in 7.7-25. Rom. 7.13 may be the most important part of his explanation. H. Räisänen argues that nothing happens to the law in 7.7–8.4; there is neither abolition of the law nor a new interpretation of it.[64] Clearly, however, in 7.13 something has happened to the law; it has been taken over by sin and a corresponding positive act will be required involving the law in salvation. Enough, I hope, has been said about sin co-opting the law and forcing it to function negatively in a sphere where it was not supposed to be, that a detailed treatment of 7.7ff. is not necessary. Paul's point is clear. The law is negative and functions as a tyrant when it is placed in the sphere of sin.

e. *Rom. 7.21–8.7*

Paul's use of νόμος in these verses is among the most difficult of all his discussions, and the use in 7.21 is particularly enigmatic. Some have argued that νόμος in 7.21 means 'rule', 'necessity', or possibly 'principle',[65] and such a meaning would fit well. U. Wilckens, however, points out that this meaning does not appear in classical or hellenistic literature, nor elsewhere in Paul.[66] Others understand νόμος in 7.21 as a reference to the Torah,[67] which is attractive, but not obvious. Moule describes this occurrence of νόμος as an anomaly caused by the use of analogy,[68] and P. von der Osten-Sacken takes it as the law restraint

64. Räisänen, 'Das "Gesetz des Glaubens"', p. 116.

65. Cranfield, *The Epistle to the Romans*, I, p. 362; Käsemann, *Commentary on Romans*, p. 205 (who argues there is no reflection on the Torah).

66. Wilckens, *Der Brief an die Römer*, II, p. 89.

67. See the discussion in Cranfield, *The Epistle to the Romans*, I, pp. 361-62. A plausible attempt to see a reference to the Mosaic law is that of H.A.W. Meyer, *Critical and Exegetical Handbook to the Epistle to the Romans* (trans. John C. Moore and Edwin Johnson; New York: Funk & Wagnalls, 1889), pp. 281-82. He connected νόμον to τῷ θέλοντι and takes ποιεῖν as an infinitive of purpose. He paraphrased the text, but a translation based on this understanding would read: 'I find then, for me, the one willing the law in order to do the good, that evil is present with me'.

68. '"Justification" in its Relation to the Condition κατὰ πνεῦμα (Rom. 8.1-11)', p. 180.

(*Gesetzmäßigkeit*) of man under the law.[69] While possibly νόμον in 7.21 is a reference to the 'other law' in 7.23,[70] the problem would be solved if this word is an accusative of reference. The verse could be translated, 'I find then with reference to the Torah, for me who wills to do good, that evil is present with me'.

Of more importance is the meaning of νόμος in the remainder of the text. In the next few verses the following expressions occur:

7.22	With respect to the inner being, I delight in the law of God.
7.23a	I see another law in my members warring against
7.23b	the law of my mind and taking me captive
7.23c	in the law of sin which is in my members.
7.25b	Therefore, I myself with the mind am serving the law of God,
7.25c	but with the flesh the law of sin.
8.2	The law of the Spirit of life in Christ Jesus has freed me from the law of sin and death
8.3	For the inability of the law in that it was weak through the flesh...
8.4	...in order that the righteous requirement of the law might be fulfilled in us who live not according to the flesh, but according to the Spirit.
8.7	For the thinking of the flesh...does not submit to the law of God, for it is not able to.

Do all the uses of νόμος refer to the Torah as viewed from various perspectives or do some of the occurrences not refer to the Torah at all? Often people interpret three of the references in 7.21–8.2 of the Torah and the rest as metaphorical. For example, Cranfield equates νόμος in v. 21 with 'the other law' and the 'law of sin' in v. 23 and understands all three as referring to the power of sin exercised over us. The 'law of sin' and the 'law of sin and death' in 7.25 and 8.2 refer to the same power. 'The law of the Spirit' in 8.2 is then understood as the authority and constraint exercised upon believers by the Holy Spirit. Apparently in 7.21–8.2 only 'the law of God' in 7.22, 25 and 'the law of my mind' in 7.23 (which Cranfield sees as equivalent to the law of God) refer to the Old Testament law.[71] The approach of H. Räisänen is essentially the

---

69. *Römer 8 als Beispiel paulinischer Soteriologie*, p. 212.

70. Wilckens, *Der Brief an die Römer*, II, p. 89, and Cranfield, *The Epistle to the Romans*, I, p. 362, although Cranfield does not see a reference to the Torah with ἕτερον νόμον while Wilckens does.

71. Cranfield, *The Epistle to the Romans*, I, pp. 361-87. I agree with Cranfield that

same.[72] Both Cranfield and Räisänen have balked at taking νόμος literally in 8.2, for they cannot imagine that Paul would say that the law freed. They conclude that νόμος means *power*. If that is true, Paul has stretched the word almost beyond recognition. Both Cranfield and Räisänen have forced a logic on the uses of νόμος, but the word has lost its force. Also they have created the difficulty of moving from one meaning of νόμος in 8.2 to a different meaning in 8.3. That is not impossible, but neither is it a convincing explanation.

Other scholars such as Moule, Osten-Sacken, and Wilckens argue that all the uses of νόμος in 7.22ff. refer to the Torah.[73] This line of argument is much more convincing than that of Cranfield and Räisänen. The occurrences in 7.22, 25b, 8.3, 4, 7 are clear references to Old Testament law.[74] The references to 'the law of sin' and 'the law of sin and death' in 7.23c, 25, 8.2 refer to God's law which has been commandeered by sin to effect death.[75] They refer to the law after it is in the hands of sin as described by 7.5, 13. 'The law of sin (and death)' is the law abducted into the sphere of sin. If 7.5, 13 are given their due, the necessity of freedom from the law abducted by sin makes perfectly good sense. 'The law of my mind' (7.23b) I understand as God's law in which the mind has found delight. The meaning of 'the other law' of 7.23a is not so obvious, but apparently it is to be equated with the law of sin.[76]

The remaining occurrence in 8.2, 'the law of the Spirit of life', is the most striking, but 7.14 ('the law is spiritual') provides a framework for understanding. The law belongs to the realm of the Spirit.[77] It is

the rearrangement theories for this section are not convincing.

72. Räisänen, 'Das "Gesetz des Glaubens"', pp. 113-17.

73. Moule, '"Justification" in its Relation to the Condition κατὰ πνεῦμα (Rom. 8.1-11)', pp. 181-87; Osten-Sacken, *Römer 8 als Beispiel paulinischer Soteriologie*, pp. 209-12 and 226-35; Wilckens, *Der Brief an die Römer*, II, pp. 90-91 and 122-23.

74. Against Käsemann, *Commentary on Romans*, p. 205.

75. Barrett, *A Commentary on the Epistle to the Romans*, p. 155, but not agreeing with his interpretation on the 'law of the Spirit' as the religion of the Spirit.

76. Cf. Moule, '"Justification" in its Relation to the Condition κατὰ πνεῦμα (Rom. 8.1-11)', p. 182, who understands 'the law of my mind' in 7.23b as 'the Law of God *as accepted* by my conscious self' and 'the other law' in 7.23a as 'God's Law *as used*...by self-will, or by sin and lust' (italics his).

77. I cannot accept that 'the law of the Spirit of life' is an oxymoron as does Joseph A. Fitzmyer ('Paul and the Law', in *To Advance the Gospel* [New York: Crossroad, 1981], p. 195).

surprising to see νόμος as the agent effecting freedom, but Räisänen's exclusion of a reference to the Torah on this ground is unjustified.[78] By now we should be accustomed to finding νόμος in unexpected expressions. In 9.31 the law of righteousness was Israel's legitimate goal. In 3.27 the law of faith excluded boasting. Now in 8.2 the law functioning in the sphere of the life-giving Spirit frees. Again it is the genitive in each case that must be emphasized, but the law is still an actor on the stage. It is not the law itself that frees; 8.3 precludes such a thought. But the law is not left out of the picture. It has been too important in the discussion just to be forgotten. If the law is not involved in salvation, then sin is a victor because it defeated God's law which was for life (7.13, 10). But now the law is placed within the sphere of the Spirit (cf. 8.4), where it belongs (7.14). The law in the right sphere frees us from the tyranny of the law in the sphere of sin. I do not think we can ignore a reference to the Old Testament law. It is through the law that Paul died to the law.

4. *Final Remarks*

Obviously on such an approach I would not interpret τέλος in Rom. 10.4 as the cessation of the law.[79] The law still has its proper role in the sphere of Christ, the Spirit, and faith; or, stated differently, Christ is the goal of the law for righteousness to everyone believing.

The theory of the law functioning in spheres of influence is not as obvious in the Epistle to the Galatians because of the character of that letter. However, the same theology of contrasting spheres of influence is present and operative in Galatians. Jesus is born under the law to redeem those under the law (4.4-5). Paul can expect the law to be fulfilled (5.14), but still knows that Christians are not under its tyranny (5.18). The works belonging to the sphere of the flesh are contrasted with the fruits belonging to the sphere of the Spirit. Paul can say Christians fulfill the law of Christ (6.2) and, similar to Rom. 8.4, mean that the law's legitimate requirements are lived out in the sphere of Christ by the work of the Spirit. The statements about the law are much more complete in Romans, but the basic ideas are already present in Galatians.

---

78. Räisänen, 'Das "Gesetz des Glaubens"', p. 115.

79. See the recent discussion by Robert Badenas, *Christ the End of the Law: Romans 10.4 in Pauline Perspective* (JSNTSup, 10; Sheffield: JSOT Press, 1985).

I do not want to leave the impression that I think all the problems surrounding Paul's statements about the law are solved by a focus on his participationist theology with the law operating within spheres of influence. A number of the difficulties, however, are alleviated. The negative statements about the law describe the usurped law in the sphere of sin, flesh, and death. The positive statements describe the law in its proper sphere where God intended it, the sphere of faith, Spirit, and Christ. No doubt there are other factors—such as misunderstanding of the law—that should be included in any comprehensive treatment of Paul and the law. Still the spheres of influence go a long way toward helping us deal with some very difficult material.

JSNT 7 (1980), pp. 2-32

THE DEMONSTRATION OF THE RIGHTEOUSNESS OF GOD
IN ROMANS 3.25, 26

John Piper

1. *The Problem and the Thesis*

This study rose out of a dissatisfaction with the widely accepted
assumption in contemporary Pauline studies that the righteousness of
God consists most basically not in any sort of 'distributive justice' but
rather in God's saving 'covenant faithfulness'[1] or (more universally with
Käsemann's school) 'the faithfulness of the creator to his creation'.[2] I
have come to the conclusion that these one-sided views (which focus
wholly on *iustitia salutifera*)[3] do not provide the key for interpreting

1.   Leonhard Goppelt, *Theologie des Neuen Testaments*, II (Göttingen:
Vandenhoeck & Ruprecht, 1976), p. 468.
2.   Wolfgang Schrage, 'Römer 3.21-26 und die Bedeutung des Todes Jesu
Christi bei Paulus', in *Das Kreuz Jesu* (ed. Paul Rieger; Göttingen: Vandenhoeck
& Ruprecht, 1969), p. 86. Also Ernst Käsemann, *An die Römer* (Tübingen:
J.C.B. Mohr [Paul Siebeck], 1974), pp. 74, 78; Peter Stuhlmacher, *Gerechtigkeit
Gottes bei Paulus* (Göttingen: Vandenhoeck & Ruprecht, 1966); Christian Müller,
Gottes Gerechtigkeit und Volk Gottes (Göttingen: Vandenhoeck & Ruprecht, 1964),
p. 111. For an excellent survey of the Käsemann–Müller–Stuhlmacher direction see
Manfred T. Brauch, 'Perspectives on "God's Righteousness" in Recent German
Discussion', in E.P. Sanders, *Paul and Palestinian Judaism* (Philadelphia: Fortress
Press, 1977), pp. 523-42.
3.   This one-sidedness is based mainly on recent interpretations of God's
righteousness in the Old Testament (see n. 51): 'In short, Yahweh's righteous
judgments are saving judgments', says E. Achtemeier, 'Righteousness in the Old
Testament', *IDB*, IV, p. 83. 'This *ṣᵉdāqā* (righteousness) bestowed on Israel is
always a saving gift. It is inconceivable that it should ever menace Israel. No
references to the concept of a punitive *ṣᵉdāqā* can be adduced. That would be a

some of the texts where Paul refers to God's righteousness (e.g.
Rom. 9.14-15, 3.5; 3.25-26; 2 Thess. 1.5, 6). This essay is an attempt to
demonstrate that Paul's view of the righteousness of God should be
differently conceived in Rom. 3.25, 26. All the exegetical problems in
these two verses will not be considered, but only those which weigh
heavily in our investigation of the reality behind δικαιοσύνης αὐτοῦ in
vv. 25, 26 and δίκαιον in v. 26.

Rom. 3.21-26 is 'the center and heart'[4] of the book of Romans.
Accordingly 'the central concept of Pauline theology',[5] the righteousness of God, is used here in a unique concentration (vv. 21, 22, 25, 26).
But 'the concept of God's righteousness in Rom. 3.25, 26 carries a new
and special accent as over against vv. 21, 22'.[6] It is not to be equated
with the gift of God received by the believer in justification nor is it
merely God's power laying rightful claim on his creature. Instead I
would like to argue that the righteousness of God in Rom. 3.25, 26
refers most basically to the characteristic of God's nature or the
unswerving inclination of his will (see note 89) which precedes and
grounds all his acts and gifts. It is his inviolable allegiance to act always
for his own name's sake—to maintain and display his own divine glory.
This is my general thesis which I will try to support and explain. I will
use the following sub-division of the verses:

(3.21a)   But now apart from the law the righteousness of God has been mani-
           fested (21b) being attested by the law and the prophets, (22a) that is,
           the righteousness of God through faith in Jesus Christ for all who
           believe. (22b) For there is no distinction, (23a) for all sinned (23b) and
           lack the glory of God, (24) being justified freely by his grace through
           the redemption which is in Christ Jesus; (25a) whom God put forth as
           a propitiation through faith, in his blood, for a demonstration of his
           righteousness (25b-26a) on account of the passing over of sins done
           beforehand in the forebearance of God; (26b) for a demonstration, I
           say, of his righteousness in the present time, (26c) in order that he
           might be righteous even in justifying the man who believes in Jesus.

contradictio in adiecto.' So Gerhard von Rad, *Old Testament Theology*, I (New
York: Harper & Row, 1962), p. 377.

    4.   C.E.B. Cranfield, *The Epistle to the Romans* (ICC; Edinburgh: T. & T. Clark,
1975), I, p. 199; Schrage, 'Römer 3.21-26', p. 65.

    5.   Käsemann, *An die Römer*, p. 307.

    6.   Otto Kuss, *Der Römerbrief* (Regensburg: Pustet, 1957), p. 117.

2. *The Use of Tradition in Romans 3.24-26*

Since the rise of form-criticism we have been much more sensitive to the so-called 'deep dimension of Scripture',[7] that is, the traditions out of which the scriptures grew. It is generally recognized that Paul's disclaimer in Gal. 1.12 does not mean that he rejected all tradition. On the contrary he preserved, handed on, and adapted much early Christian tradition in various forms (cf. 1 Cor. 15.3; 11.2, 23; 2 Thess. 2.15; 3.6).[8] The form-critical judgment that in Rom. 3.24-26a Paul is using a 'traditional statement which perhaps can be traced back to the earliest church' begins with Rudolf Bultmann. He reckons the following to be pre-Pauline (with Pauline additions in parentheses):

(24)   ...justified (by his grace as a gift) through the redemption that is in Christ Jesus, (25a) whom God put forward as an expiation by his blood (to be received by faith); (25b) this was to show God's righteousness, because he passed over former sins (26a) in his divine forebearance.

His arguments for this judgment are that (1) the designation of Christ as the ἱλαστήριον occurs only here in Paul; (2) it is not Paul's habit elsewhere (except Rom. 5.9 and the traditional passages, 1 Cor. 10.16; 11.25, 27 [if one rejects Eph. 1.7; 2.13; 6.12; Col. 1.20 as non-Pauline]), to speak of 'the blood' of Christ but rather of the cross; (3) 'the idea found here of the divine righteousness demanding expiation for former sins is otherwise foreign to him'.[9]

It was Ernst Käsemann's development of Bultmann's position in a 1951 article entitled 'Zum Verständnis von Römer 3.24-26'[10] which caused this form-critical judgment to prevail in German scholarship. Here and in his recent commentary he supplements Bultmann's arguments with the following: (1) the participial construction in v. 24 is such a 'harsh breaking off' from the syntax of v. 23 that 'it can be explained

7.   'Die Tradition, aus der die Schrift erwachsen ist, ist *die Tiefdimension der Schrift.*' So Leonhard Goppelt, 'Tradition nach Paulus', *KD* 4 (1958), p. 232.

8.   For a recent summary in English, see Ralph Martin, *New Testament Foundations*, II (Grand Rapids: Eerdmans, 1978), pp. 248-75.

9.   Rudolf Bultmann, *Theology of the New Testament*, I (New York: Scribner's, 1951), p. 46.

10.   *ZNW* 43 (1950–51), pp. 150-54. Now in *Exegetische Versuche und Besinnungen*, I (Göttingen: Vandenhoeck & Ruprecht, 1960), pp. 96-100.

only by assuming Paul is now quoting a hymnic fragment'.[11] (2) This assumption accounts for the piling up of terminology which is not characteristic of Paul: πάρεσις, προγεγονότα, ἁμαρτήματα, προτίθεσθαι in the sense of manifesting, δικαιοσύνη as a divine attribute (v. 25), and ἀπολύτρωσις as a designation for an accomplished redemption (Rom. 8.23 refers to the future, and 1 Cor. 1.30; Col. 1.14 are traditional).[12] (3) The 'overladen style of the verses with their genitive constructions and prepositional connections...is the characteristic of hymnic, liturgical tradition'.[13] (4) In v. 25 διὰ πίστεως interrupts the flow of the sentence and reveals itself as a Pauline insertion.[14]

(5) The fifth argument to support a traditional formula in Rom. 3.24-26a is, for Käsemann, decisive: a different conception of the righteousness of God is found in this unit than we have in v. 26b, where Paul, through the parallel construction beginning with πρὸς τὴν ἔνδειξιν, 'corrects' the tradition. In the tradition 'one sees himself standing in continuity with the old people of God, holding to the history of Israel as one's own, and counting the new covenant as the restitution of the old one'.[15] Thus the righteousness of God is here (v. 25) God's faithfulness to his covenant. But this is precisely what moves Paul to add his 'correction', since

> for him the righteousness of God is not primarily, if at all, the restitution of the old covenant...The present καιρός (v. 26b) is not viewed in relation to the redemptive history begun by Moses but rather over against the fallen world which is under God's wrath...Since he is thinking universalistically and no longer in terms of the covenant people, he speaks immediately at the end of v. 26 of the individual believer.[16]

In this way Paul gives his own interpretation to the 'righteousness of God': 'it becomes God's faithfulness to his whole creation and the execution of his rightful claim over it'.[17]

---

11. *An die Römer*, p. 88; 'Römer 3.24-26', p. 96.
12. 'Römer 3.24-26', p. 96.
13. 'Römer 3.24-26', p. 96.
14. *An die Römer*, pp. 90-91.
15. 'Römer 3.24-26', p. 99.
16. 'Römer 3.24-26', p. 100.
17. *An die Römer*, p. 94. Günther Klein, 'Gottes Gerechtigkeit als Thema der neuesten Paulus Forschung', in *Rekonstruktion und Interpretation* (Munich: Chr. Kaiser Verlag, 1969), p. 230, goes even further when he says that Paul was critical of the tradition 'nicht nur im Sinne einer Ausweitung des Motivs der Bundestreue zu dem der Schöpfungstreue...Die Korrektur ist vielmehr qualitativ: aus einem

It is precisely this fifth argument of Käsemann that makes the whole form-critical issue relevant for my specific question concerning the righteousness of God. If Käsemann is right, then vv. 25-26a cannot be used, as they have been traditionally, to interpret Paul's own understanding of the demonstration of God's righteousness, since Paul's own view is given in a 'korrigierenden Zusatz' in v. 26b. So we turn now to an assessment of this form-critical position.

First, the inclusion of v. 24 in the traditional unit has been widely rejected. Eduard Lohse pointed out that not only the words δωρεὰν τῇ αὐτοῦ χάριτι were from Paul (which Käsemann recognizes) but also the designation Χριστῷ Ἰησοῦ, 'since this phrase is not found prior to Paul'.[18] Gerhard Delling argues further that δικαιούμενοι is a good Pauline word and need not come from the tradition.[19] That leaves only the unPauline character of ἀπολυτρώσεως and the awkward syntactical connection with v. 23 as arguments for including v. 24 with the tradition. But Klaus Wengst, in explicit opposition to Käsemann, argues that the coordination of participles with finite verbs (as in vv. 23, 24) is something Paul 'loves' to do.[20] Heinrich Schlier in support of this gives 2 Cor. 5.6, 7.5, 8.18 as examples.[21] Finally Wengst argues that ἀπολυτρώσις is *not* so unusual for Paul (Rom. 8.23; 1 Cor. 1.30; Eph. 1.7, 14; 4.30; Col. 1.14) that it can definitely be ascribed to the tradition; nor has Käsemann proven that Paul's use of it in 1 Cor. 1.30 is a 'geprägte Formel'.[22] I regard these arguments as weighing heavily in favor of not counting v. 24 as part of the early Christian 'traditional formulation'.

But the traditional character of Rom. 3.25, 26a has been much more widely accepted[23] though not universally. While sporadic voices try to

---

Seinsbegriff (εἰς τὸ εἶναι αὐτὸν δίκαιον) wird ein forensischer (καὶ δικαιοῦντα)'. See n. 31 below for an alternative view.

18. *Martyrer und Gottesknecht* (Göttingen: Vandenhoeck & Ruprecht, 1955), p. 149 n. 4. Also Werner Kramer, *Christos Kyrios Gottessohn* (Zürich: Zwingli-Verlag, 1963), p. 140 n. 509.

19. *Der Kreuzestod Jesu in der urchristlichen Verkündigung* (Göttingen: Vandenhoeck & Ruprecht, 1972), p. 12.

20. *Christologische Formeln und Lieder des Urchristentums* (Gütersloh: Gerd Mohn, 1972), p. 87.

21. *Der Römerbrief* (HTKNT, 6; Frieburg: Herder, 1977), p. 107.

22. *Christologische Formeln*, p. 87.

23. Recently, Peter Stuhlmacher, 'Zur neueren Exegese von Röm. 3.24-26', in *Jesus und Paulus* (ed. E.E. Ellis and Eric Grässer; Göttingen: Vandenhoeck &

solve the syntactical unevenness and parallel structure of these verses by reference to later glosses or interpolations,[24] a number of scholars have seen good reasons for reckoning all of Rom. 3.24-26 as Paul's own work. First of all, Heinrich Schlier argues that the relative clause which begins v. 25 *could* (as in Rom. 4.25; Phil. 2.6; Col. 1.3) signal a traditional unit, but that one ought not draw this conclusion in the absence of clear stylistic and rhythmic features which set the unit off from Paul's own way of writing. This corroborating evidence is missing here.[25] The quotation is too short to reveal any rhythm and the grouping of prepositional phrases is not so distinctive as to argue strongly against Pauline origin.

Secondly, with regard to the argument from non-Pauline terminology, since πάρεσιν and προγεγονότων are *hapax legomena* in the New Testament and ἱλαστήριον occurs only here and in Heb. 9.5, it is an argument from silence that they belonged to the earliest Christian tradition. Moreover other important terms in these verses are not foreign to Paul. Delling points out that the key term ἔνδειξις is found in the New Testament *only* in Paul (Rom. 3.25, 26; 2 Cor. 8.24; Phil. 1.28) and with a sense similar to the one here.[26] The word ἀνοχῇ is found only here (v. 26a) and in Rom. 2.4. ἁμάρτημα is genuinely Pauline in 1 Cor. 6.18, and, while προέθετο has a meaning in v. 25 different from its use in Rom. 1.13 and Eph. 1.9, this is also true of προγράφω in Gal. 3.1 (in contrast to Rom. 15.4; Eph. 3.3) which no one denies to be Paul's. In short, the argument from non-Pauline terminology is not as strong as some have thought. Word statistics are too ambiguous to settle the issue.[27] And even if we grant the presence of traditional terms that are

Ruprecht, 1975), p. 316; George Eichholz, *Die Theologie des Paulus im Umriss* (Neukirchen–Vluyn: Neukirchener Verlag, 1972), p. 191 (who still includes v. 24); Wengst, *Christologische Formeln*, p. 87; Hartwig Thyen, *Studien zur Sündenvergebung* (FRLANT, 96; Göttingen: Vandenhoeck & Ruprecht, 1970), p. 164; Schrage, 'Römer 3.21-26', p. 86; Dieter Zeller, 'Sühne und Langmut: Zur Traditionsgeschichte von Röm 3.24-26', *TP*, 43 (1968), pp. 51ff.; Lohse, *Martyrer*, p. 140; Müller, *Gottes Gerechtigkeit*, pp. 110-11.

24. Gottfried Fitzer, 'Der Ort der Versöhnung nach Paulus', *TZ* 22 (1966), pp. 161-83; Charles Talbert, 'A Non-Pauline Fragment at Romans 3.24-26?', *JBL* 85 (1966), pp. 287-96.

25. *Römerbrief*, p. 109.

26. *Der Kreuzestod Jesu*, p. 13.

27. Schlier, *Römerbrief*, p. 107 n. 8: 'Methodischgrundsätzlich: Muss das

not *uniquely* Pauline, this would not betray the quotation of a pre-Pauline *formulation* but only the adoption of familiar traditional terminology.[28]

Thirdly, and most decisive in my judgment, Otto Kuss and C.E.B. Cranfield have objected that it is highly unlikely that in this 'vital and central paragraph' Paul would have proceeded in the way Käsemann suggests. Cranfield argues that

> to accept Käsemann's account of these verses requires a very great deal of credulity. In the construction of a paragraph as vital and central to his whole argument as this paragraph is, Paul is scarcely likely to have gone to work in the way Käsemann would have us envisage. It is very much more probable that these verses are Paul's own independent and careful composition reflecting his own preaching and thinking (cf. Cambier, *L'Évangile de Dieu*, 784) and that the overladen style is the result, not of the incorporation of a *Vorlage* and the need to provide it with connectives, but of the intrinsic difficulty of interpreting the Cross at all adequately and perhaps also, in part, of the natural tendency to fall into a more or less liturgical style when speaking of so solemn a matter.[29]

Otto Kuss shows even more precisely why Käsemann's 'purely hypothetical construction' is to be rejected. 'Absolutely nothing in the context points up an intention in v. 26b to correct vv. 25-26a'.[30] How are we to imagine that Paul intended his Roman readers (lacking contemporary form-critical tools, like concordances and other New Testament documents for comparison) to discover that Rom. 3.25-26a is corrected in v. 26b? The issue at stake in these verses (the ground of justification) is simply too important that Paul should omit some kind of adversative particle in v. 26b if he intended his readers to *contrast* it with vv. 25-26a. As it stands it is far more probable that εἰς ἔνδειξιν τῆς δικαιοσύνης αὐτοῦ διὰ τὴν πάρεσιν τῶν προγεγονότων ἁμαρτημάτων ἐν τῇ ἀνοχῇ τοῦ θεοῦ (vv. 25, 26a) gives the reason in the past why such a demonstration was necessary (see below p. 198) and v. 26b (πρὸς τὴν ἔνδειξιν...) gives the present purpose for the demonstration. There is no need to assume that Paul is correcting a limited Jewish-Christian view of righteousness. Therefore I conclude with

Auftauchen eines von Paulus sonst nicht oder selten gebrauchten Begriffs auf Übernahme einer Tradition weisen?'

28. So Schlier, *Römerbrief*, p. 109.

29. *Romans*, I, p. 200 n. 1.

30. *Der Römerbrief*, p. 161.

Kuss and others that even if Paul was using tradition here 'doubtless in this central text he presents theological sentences which to an especially high degree he has made his own'.[31]

Accordingly in the rest of this essay I will not assume that the righteousness of God in Rom. 3.25 has a different meaning from the same term in v. 26b. I am no longer interested in distinguishing between 'faithfulness to the covenant' and 'faithfulness to creation'. For my purposes these may be taken together since they both define the righteousness of God as an unswervingly saving action or gift, and rule out the concept of vindicatory righteousness. This, however, is what I am challenging.

3. *Critique of the Prevailing View*

There are two *fundamentally* different views of the demonstration of God's righteousness in Rom. 3.25, 26. The one is associated with Anselm's satisfaction view of the atonement (*Cur Deus Homo?*). It distinguishes between the righteousness of God in vv. 21, 22 and the righteousness of God in vv. 25, 26. The latter is an attribute of God's nature (usually equated with his strict distributive justice), the former is the imputed, divine righteousness appropriated by the believer in the event of justification or the action of God in justifying. For the other view, which rejects any identification with Anselm and which claims to have more biblical, hebraic presuppositions than he, the demonstration of the righteousness of God is his eschatological *saving action* in accomplishing redemption through the death of Jesus.

While this second view has, to be sure, gained the ascendancy in recent decades,[32] the dispute is by no means at an end. By way of

---

31. *Der Römerbrief*, p. 160. Eduard Lohse, 'Die Gerechtigkeit Gottes in der paulinischen Theologie', in *Die Einheit des Neuen Testaments* (Göttingen: Vandenhoeck & Ruprecht, 1973), p. 222: 'Paulus nimmt dieses Bekenntnis mit voller Zustimmung auf, gibt ihm aber eine Auslegung, die seine Aussage mit ungleich grösserem Nachdruck hervortreten lässt'. Stuhlmacher, 'Römer 3.24-26', p. 331, concludes that Paul's interpretation of the tradition must be understood 'nicht einfach als Kritik, geschweige denn als qualitative Korrektur, sondern mit Lohse als konsequente Weiterführung und Aufweitung'. Walter Maier, 'Paul's Concept of Justification and Some Recent Interpretations of Romans 3.21-23', *Springfielder* 37 (1974), p. 254 concludes that Rom. 3.24-26 is not a pre-Pauline formulation.

32. The following representatives do not necessarily agree in all exegetical details: A. Schlatter, *Gottes Gerechtigkeit* (Stuttgart: Calwer Verlag, 1935), pp. 148-49;

example: Hermann Ridderbos argues in his book on Paul that the righteousness of God in Rom. 3.25-26 refers to 'the vindicatory righteousness of God'.[33] And, on the other side, Peter Stuhlmacher takes him to task for 'brushing aside not only any attempt at an analysis of the tradition but also the whole newer discussion of the semitic background of the expression "Righteousness of God"'.[34] My aim is not to defend Ridderbos, even though I think his view is not as wrong as Stuhlmacher does. But, while avoiding the criticisms leveled against Ridderbos, I do want to argue for an alternative to the prevalent view of the righteousness of God in Rom. 3.25-26.

One of the most seminal studies of Rom. 3.25, 26 which interprets God's righteousness as his saving action in justification is W.G. Kümmel's 'Πάρεσις und ἔνδειξις, ein Beitrag zum Verständnis der paulinischen Rechtfertigungslehre'.[35] Subsequent studies regard this work as foundational. Therefore I will examine Kümmel's arguments in some detail and allow my alternative position to emerge if the evidence points in that direction.

Kümmel's interpretation may be summed up as follows: the demonstration of the righteousness of God in Rom. 3.25, 26 is 'an exact exposition' of the manifestation of God's righteousness in vv. 21, 22 (p. 160). The twofold ἔνδειξις of vv. 25, 26, which refers to an active showing (*Erweis*) rather than to a factual proof (*Beweis*), corresponds exactly to the active manifestation (πεφανέρωται) of God's righteousness in vv. 21, 22 and to the justification (δικαιούμενοι) of v. 24 (pp. 160-61). Consistently with this view the prepositional phrase, διὰ τὴν πάρεσιν... is rendered not as a causal clause ('*on account of* the passing over of sins done beforehand'), but rather as an instrumental clause

A. Nygren, *Commentary on Romans* (Philadelphia: Muhlenberg Press, 1949), p. 365; O. Michel, *Der Brief an die Römer* (Göttingen: Vandenhoeck & Ruprecht, 1966), p. 107; J.A. Ziesler, *The Meaning of Righteousness in Paul* (SNTSMS, 20; Cambridge: Cambridge University Press, 1972), p. 194; Goppelt, *Theologie*, II, p. 194.

33. *Paul: An Outline of his Theology* (Grand Rapids: Eerdmans, 1975), pp. 167, 189: 'In Christ's death the righteousness of God thus reveals itself in the demanding and vindicatory sense of the word. His blood as atoning blood covers the sin which God until now had passed over, when as yet he kept back the judgment. All that men wish to detract from the real character of Christ's propitiatory death signifies a devaluation of the language of Rom. 3.25, 26, which is unmistakable in its clarity.'

34. 'Römer 3.24-26', p. 317.

35. *ZTK* 49 (1952), pp. 154-67. The page numbers in the text refer to this essay.

('*through* the pardon of sins done beforehand'). Therefore, we are not to think that the passing over of sins calls God's righteousness into question so that he now must prove himself righteous by punishing sin in the death of Jesus; on the contrary God's righteousness is shown forth precisely in the pardon (*Erlass*) of those sins.[36] Accordingly the righteousness of God in vv. 25-26 refers not to a quality or attribute of God which must be preserved but rather to the saving action of God which justifies sinners. 'Therefore the satisfaction theory of Anselm does not even have a starting point in Paul's teaching' (p. 166).[37]

Now let us examine Kümmel's key arguments in support of this interpretation. After doing a lexical study of the key words πάρεσις and ἔνδειξις outside Rom. 3.21-26 Kümmel concludes with regard to both words that 'only the context can decide' which of the possible meanings Paul intends here (pp. 158-59). Thus all his arguments are based on grammatical and theological considerations of the immediate and wider Pauline context.

Kümmel's first and main argument is that up to this point in Romans, and most importantly in the near context of 3.21, 22, the righteousness of God has referred to the *action* of God in justifying sinners—to 'Gottes rechtfertigendes, Gerechtigkeit schaffendes, den Menschen gerecht sprechendes Handeln' (p. 161). Therefore to construe the righteousness of God in 3.25, 26 as an *attribute* of God would be 'contrary to the preceding usage' (p. 161). A serious flaw in this argument is Kümmel's omission of any reference to the meaning of God's righteousness in Rom. 3.5 and his consequent assumption that the term δικαιοσύνη θεοῦ has a uniform meaning throughout. Bultmann[38] and others[39] have warned against the contemporary tendency to limit this term to only one meaning—a tendency especially prevalent in the Käsemann school (notably P. Stuhlmacher's dissertation).[40] More

36. In his own words the phrase means 'dass Gott seine den Sünder rettende Gerechtigkeit sich auswirken lassen wollte dadurch, dass er die nicht endgültig bestraften Sünden der Zeit vor der Sendung Christi vergab' ('Πάρεσις', p. 165).

37. Goppelt (*Theologie*, II, p. 424) and Stuhlmacher (*Gerechtigkeit*, p. 88) also make explicit their rejection of Anselm's view.

38. 'ΔΙΚΑΙΟΣΥΝΗ ΘΕΟΥ', *JBL* 83 (1964), pp. 12-13.

39. For example, Lohse, 'Die Gerechtigkeit Gottes in der paulinischen Theologie', p. 223. See also Cranfield, *Romans*, I, p. 97.

40. For a critique of Stuhlmacher's *Gerechtigkeit Gottes bei Paulus* which brings this out, see Karl Kertelge, *Rechtfertigung bei Paulus* (Münster: Aschendorf, 1967), pp. 307-309. See also Klein, 'Gottesgerechtigkeit als Thema der neuesten Paulus

specifically Bultmann points out what is commonly accepted (though not by Käsemann and Stuhlmacher[41])—namely, that the meaning of the righteousness of God in Rom. 3.5 does not refer to God's gracious saving action but rather to God's attribute of strict distributive justice.[42] While it is probably not accurate to equate God's righteousness in Rom. 3.5 precisely with distributive justice (see note 80), yet I do think that Bultmann, with most exegetes, is correct at least in denying that the righteousness of God in Rom. 3.5 can refer (with 1.17 and 3.21-22) to the action of God in justifying sinners, since there it is the *wrath* of God which Paul is claiming to be just. Therefore Kümmel's argument from the uniformity of the meaning of God's righteousness in Romans 1–3 is weak since the meaning of the term in 3.25 may be more similar to the meaning in 3.5 than it is to the meaning in 3.21-22.

The rest of Kümmel's arguments are attempts to show the error of the alternative '*Anselmische*' interpretation. But I question whether the precise form of that interpretation which he defeats is really his strongest opponent. He argues that the interpretation of ἔνδειξις as 'proof' (*Beweis*) is untenable 'because it is not at all clearly expressed to whom God should want to prove his righteousness' (p. 161). Moreover 'in view of Rom. 9.19-20 it is foreign to Paul's theology that any man could put God's action into doubt and that God could see himself obligated to *prove* that such doubt is unfounded' (pp. 162-63). Here he is arguing against the view which says, in the words of John Murray, that 'the forebearance exercised in past ages [3.25b, 26a] tended to obscure in the apprehension of men the inviolability of God's justice' and this 'passing over' of sin 'made it necessary for [God] to demonstrate his inherent justice' by punishing sin in the death of Jesus.[43]

In response to Kümmel one could argue, in view of Rom. 2.24 where

---

Forschung'. But it is only fair to note that Stuhlmacher recognized this weakness and has expressed his 'Präzisierung und Selbstkorrektur' in 'Das Ende des Gesetzes', *ZTK* 67 (1970), p. 26 n. 28, and 31 n. 39, and in 'Römer 3.24-26', p. 331 n. 62.

41. On the righteousness of God in Rom. 3.5, Stuhlmacher (*Gerechtigkeit*, p. 86) says 'δικαιοσύνη θεοῦ ist an unserer Stelle also keineswegs, wie fast allgemein angenommen wird Gottes richterliche iustitia distributiva...sondern seine bisher über Israel waltende, fortan Israels Hoffnung begründende Treue zu dem von ihm einmal verkündeten (und in Christus verifizierten) Bundesrecht und Bund'. Similarly Käsemann, *Au die Römer*, pp. 73-74.

42. 'ΔΙΚΑΙΟΣΥΝΗ ΘΕΟΥ', p. 13.

43. John Murray, *The Epistle to the Romans*, I (NICNT; Grand Rapids: Eerdmans, 1959), pp. 119-20.

Paul picks up the Old Testament theme of how God's name is held in derision among the nations (cf. Ezek. 36.20; 22.16; Isa. 52.5), that it would accord perfectly with God's holy zeal for his own name if he should act to clear his name and *prove* that such derision is folly. This would not contradict Pauline theology at all.

But such an argument is unnecessary because the alternative to Kümmel's interpretation does not necessarily involve the concept of *proof* which he chides. One could translate ἔνδειξις as 'a showing forth' or 'an expression' and not lose anything essential to the 'satisfaction theory' which he is opposing.[44] One would simply argue that what was showing itself in the death of Christ is God's exacting demand of a recompense for sin. Therefore Kümmel does not strengthen his view by trying (unsuccessfully I think) to eliminate the idea of 'proof' from the term ἔνδειξις in Rom. 3.25-26.

Perhaps the best response to Kümmel's argument comes from C.E.B. Cranfield who draws attention to the very important grammatical fact that the ultimate object of God's 'showing' his righteousness is given with the words 'in order that he himself might *be* righteous' (3.26c). Cranfield argues that 'The words εἰς τὸ εἶναι αὐτὸν δίκαιον mean not "in order that He might show that He is righteous" [contra Barrett[45]], but "in order that He might be righteous."...Paul recognizes that what was at stake was not just God's being seen to be righteous, but God's *being* righteous.'[46] If the purpose of God in the ἔνδειξις of his righteousness is that he might be righteous then the ἔνδειξις is not a mere 'proof' or a mere 'showing' but an *establishment* of righteousness. Without the death of Christ as a propitiation[47] for sins the problem

44. 'Ob man hier von einem "Beweis" oder einem "Erweis" spricht, tut nicht viel zur Sache', so Kuss, *Römerbrief*, p. 158.

45. C.K. Barrett, *The Epistle to the Romans* (HNTC; New York: Harper & Row, 1957), p. 80.

46. *Romans*, I, p. 213.

47. It is not necessary for my present purpose to enter the debate over the precise meaning of ἱλαστήριον. The older controversy between Roger Nicole ('C.H. Dodd and the Doctrine of Propitiation', *WTJ* 17 [1955], pp. 117-57) and C.H. Dodd ('ΙΛΑΣΚΕΣΘΑΙ, its Cognates, Derivatives and Synonyms in the Septuagint', *JTS* 32 [1931], pp. 352-60) has recently been revived: see R. Nicole, 'Hilaskesthai Revisited', *EvQ*, 49 (1977), pp. 173-77. For a recent and thorough examination of whether the Old Testament Day of Atonement (Lev. 16) or the atoning death of Jewish Martyrs (*4 Macc.* 17.21-22) provides the history-of-religions background for Paul, see Stuhlmacher, 'Römer 3.24-26'. I find Barrett's view very sound: '"Propitiation" is

would not have been the false accusations of men but the real unrighteousness of God. (More on this below, page 200).

The next argument which has to do with the meaning of πάρεσις (v. 25b) seems also to miss the target. Kümmel rejects the meaning 'passing over' or 'letting go' (*Hingehenlassen*) or 'overlooking' (*Übersehen*) and opts for 'pardon' or 'forgiveness' (*Erlass*)—a forgiveness granted in the death of Christ for the sins of old. He argues, 'It is in no way the opinion of Paul that during the time of God's ἀνοχή [v. 26a] he overlooked sins' (p. 163). Rather from Rom. 1.24, 2.4, 6.23, and 7.13 he concludes, 'The ἀνοχή of God in the period before the sending of Christ consisted not in an overlooking (*Übersehen*) of sins but in a punishment which did not destroy but aimed to bring about repentance (Rom. 2.4)...' (p. 163).

With this criticism Kümmel does not weaken his opponent at all. For these reasons: Kümmel's and Käsemann's[48] insistence that Paul views the time before Christ not as a time of leniency but as a time of wrath (1.18–3.20) is an oversimplification of Pauline theology. To be sure in Rom. 2.4, 5 (the only other use of ἀνοχή in the New Testament) men are storing up wrath for themselves in the patience of God, but Paul still calls this period a period of the 'kindness of God' (χρηστὸν τοῦ θεοῦ, 2.4). Kümmel himself refers to the sins of this period as 'not completely punished' (*nicht endgültig gestraft*). This concession is all that is required to validate the interpretation he is opposing. For the scholars who hold to a 'satisfaction theory' do not claim that the period of God's ἀνοχή was all leniency and that sins were ignored. What is argued, in the words of Leon Morris, is that 'God had not always punished sin with *full* severity in the past'.[49] The 'kindness' of withholding full judgment (not to mention the blessings given, cf. Acts 14.16; 17.30; Mt. 5.45) was not deserved by sinful man and precisely this provides the

---

not adequate, for this means that the offender does something to appease the person he has offended, whereas Paul says that God himself put forward Christ. Propitiation is truly there, however, for, through the sacrifice of Christ, God's wrath is turned away; but behind the propitiation lies the fact that God actually wiped out (*expiated*) our sin, and made us right with himself.' *Reading through Romans* (Philadelphia: Fortress Press, 1977), p. 16.

48. *Au die Römer*, p. 92: '1.18–3.20 haben die Vergangenheit nicht unter das Thema der Nachsicht übenden Geduld, sondern der Zornesoffenbarung gestellt...'

49. *The Apostolic Preaching of the Cross* (Grand Rapids: Eerdmans, 1965), p. 278.

basis of the satisfaction theory which claims that God's apparent injustice must be rectified.

But even more can be said to show the weakness of Kümmel's argument. Suppose πάρεσις does mean 'pardon' or 'forgiveness' in v. 25. Even this does not contradict, but accords with, the satisfaction theory. The Old Testament is replete with the mercies of God 'who forgives iniquity and transgression and sin' (Exod. 34.7) and, for example, angers his prophet Jonah with his mercy toward Ninevah. It may well be the justifying forgiveness shown to the Old Testament saints which constitutes the πάρεσις of 3.25. Paul certainly thought that men of faith like David (Rom. 4.6-8) and Abraham (Rom. 4.9) had received forgiveness before Christ. But this remitting of sins creates the same problem for justice that leniency of punishment does. Therefore the 'satisfaction theory' cannot be refuted by showing that πάρεσις means pardon. One would have to go further and demonstrate that διὰ τὴν πάρεσιν does not have its usual causal force ('on account of [past] pardon') but rather has a rare instrumental force ('through the [present] pardon [in Christ]'). I will discuss this problem further on.

The *basic reason* why Kümmel and others view the righteousness of God in Rom. 3.25, 26 as God's saving action is not any exegetical detail or contextual clue. The factor that weighs most heavily in their exegesis is the conviction that has been growing ever since Hermann Cremer enunciated it in his book *Die Paulinische Rechtfertigungslehre* (1899), namely that the righteousness of God in the Old Testament is not his conformity to an ideal ethical norm (like strict retributive justice) but is his faithfulness within the dictates of a given relationship, especially his covenant with Israel.[50] This view has been supported by most Old Testament scholars.[51] Together with the conviction that 'the pauline

50. Schrage ('Rom. 3.21-26', p. 74) represents a host of scholars when he comments on the righteousness of God in our text: 'Gerechtigkeit ist im Alten Testament gerade nicht die Respektierung einer ideellen ethischen bzw. rechtlichen Norm oder eine sittlichen Qualität, sondern im strengen Sinn ein Relations-begriff, konkret: das dem *Bund* entsprechende, durch den Bund bestimmte Verhalten... Inhaltlich heisst dass: seine Gerechtigkeit ist sein heilschaffendes rettendes Eingreifen zugunsten seines Bundespartners.'

51. The literature is almost endless, but several recent works provide good overviews of the history of the investigation: Frank Crüsemann, 'Jahwes Gerechtigkeit (ṣᵉdāqā/ṣädäq)', *EvT* 36.5 (1976), pp. 427-50 (see especially his n. 2); Klaus Koch, *Theologisches Handwörterbuch zum Alten Testament*, II (Munich: Chr. Kaiser Verlag, 1975), cols. 507-530; Rafael Gyllenberg, *Rechtfertigung und Altes Testament*

doctrine of righteousness can be understood only against an Old Testament background',[52] this conviction has exerted tremendous power in the interpretation of the righteousness of God in Paul. Accordingly Anselm and all his contemporary followers are accused of importing Greek[53] or Germanic[54] concepts of law into the Hebraic-biblical view of God's righteousness.

Since Kümmel's 1952 article, in which he treated this relational view of God's righteousness as a 'presupposition' (*Voraussetzung*, p. 162) for the interpretation of Rom. 3.25, 26, Käsemann has provided the foremost illustration of how strongly the findings of history-of-religions research influence the interpretation of Paul. He has stressed that late Jewish apocalyptic had a profound influence on Paul. It is 'the mother of Christian theology'[55] and it is 'the driving element of pauline theology and practice'.[56] The specific concept of righteousness out of which Rom. 3.25-26 grew, he claims, is summarized in two key texts. The first is from Qumran (1QS 11.12-15):

> And if I stagger, God's mercies are my salvation forever; and if I stumble because of the sin of the flesh, my justification is in the *righteousness of God* (*mišpāṭî bᵉsidqat 'ēl*) which exists forever...He has caused me to approach by his mercy. And by His favors He will bring my justification (*mišpaṭî*). He has justified me by *His true justice* (*bᵉsidqat 'ămitô šᵉpaṭanî*) and by His immense goodness he will pardon all my iniquities. And by *his justice* (*ûbᵉsidqātô*) He will cleanse me from the defilement of man and of the sins of the sons of men, that I may acknowledge *His righteousness* (*sidqô*) unto God and His majesty unto the Most High.[57]

bei Paulus (Stuttgart: Kohlhammer, 1973); Hans Schmid, *Gerechtigkeit als Weltordnung* (BHT, 40; Tübingen: J.C.B. Mohr [Paul Siebeck], 1958); Gerhard von Rad, *Theology*, I, pp. 370-83; David Hill, *Greek Words and Hebrew Meanings* (SNTSMS, 5; Cambridge: Cambridge University Press, 1966), pp. 82ff.

52. George Ladd, 'Righteousness in Romans', *Southwestern Journal of Theology* 19 (1976), p. 6.

53. Stuhlmacher, *Gerechtigkeit*, p. 88 n. 6.

54. Goppelt, *Theologie*, II, p. 424.

55. E. Käsemann, 'On the Subject of Primitive Christian Apocalyptic', in *New Testament Questions of Today* (Philadelphia: Fortress Press, 1969), p. 137.

56. Käsemann, *Au die Römer*, p. 294.

57. The translation comes from A. Dupont-Sommer, *The Essene Writings from Qumran* (Oxford: Basil Blackwell, 1961), pp. 102-103. The Hebrew text comes from E. Lohse (ed.), *Die Texte aus Qumran* (Darmstadt: Wissenschaftliche Buchgesellschaft, 1971), p. 40.

The second text providing a summary statement of the Jewish-apocalyptic background of Paul's understanding of God's righteousness is *4 Ezra* 8.31-36:

> For we and our fathers have passed our lives in ways that bring death: but thou because of us sinners art called compassionate. For if thou hast a desire to compassionate us who have no works of righteousness then shalt thou be called 'the gracious One'. For the righteous who have many works laid up with thee, shall out of their own deeds receive their reward. But what is man that thou shouldest be wroth with him? Or what is a corruptible race that thou canst be so bitter towards it? For in truth there is none of the earth-born who has not dealt wickedly, and among those who exist who has not sinned. For in this, O Lord, shalt thy *righteousness* and goodness be declared, if thou wilt compassionate them that have no wealth of good works.[58]

It is fairly obvious from these texts as well as many in the Old Testament[59] that the righteousness of God in Jewish literature does not always mean strict retributive justice: it embraces mercy. This view of righteousness as *iustitia salutifera* has come to be seen as the peculiarly Jewish-biblical view and thus functions for many scholars as an *assumption* in dealing with Pauline texts.

More than a few scholars, however, have seen the hermeneutical pitfalls of such a use of the history of a concept. Käsemann and Stuhlmacher especially have come in for methodological criticism on this point. In reaction to the Käsemann–Stuhlmacher interpretation of God's righteousness Hans Conzelmann and Günther Klein have both stressed 'the priority of interpretation over any deductions from history-of-religions research or history-of-tradition research... Decisive is not the history of a concept but the pauline context.'[60] 'The evidence in Paul should be assessed on the basis of his own usage.'[61] Because of his doubt that the righteousness of God is a technical term in the late Jewish literature (as Stuhlmacher maintains[62]) and because he is alert to a peculiar, Pauline usage of the term, Conzelmann admits that in Rom. 3.25-26 the righteousness of God 'can (as in the Jewish usage) mean the

---

58. The translation is from *APOT*.

59. E.g. 1 Sam. 24.17; Ps. 51.14; 143.1-2; 69.27. See the word associations in Ps. 33.4; 36.5, 6, 18; 40.10; 88.11, 12; 116.5; 145.17; Hos. 2.19.

60. Klein, 'Gottesgerechtigkeit', p. 227.

61. H. Conzelmann, *An Outline of the Theology of the New Testament* (New York: Harper & Row, 1969), p. 218.

62. *Gerechtigkeit*, p. 175.

covenant faithfulness of God. But that is not certain. It can also be understood as *iustitia distributiva*.'[63]

Thus the interpretation of God's righteousness in Rom. 3.25, 26 which Kümmel and others espouse is in my judgment based mainly on the assumption that Paul stands in the stream of the Old Testament-Jewish tradition and that the Old Testament-Jewish view of God's righteousness, as a relational term embracing mercy, rules out the satisfaction theory of the atonement in which God's righteousness demands punishment for sins. The implicit danger here of minimizing Paul's originality[64] has already been mentioned. But now a greater objection must be registered: the relational, saving aspect of God's righteousness may not go to the heart of the Old Testament concept of divine righteousness and may not be the aspect that Paul picks up and applies in his interpretation of Christ.

4. *The Righteousness of God in the Old Testament*

At the risk of great presumption I must here distill my work on the righteousness of God in the Old Testament into a few pages in order to suggest a corrective to the current relational understanding of God's righteousness as *iustitia salutifera*. First, we must admit, I think, that it is inadequate to define God's righteousness in the Old Testament as his conformity to the norm of distributive justice. One need only to read Ps. 143.1, 2 to see the deficiency of such a definition:

> Hear my prayer, O Lord,
> Give ear to my supplications!
> Answer me in thy faithfulness, in thy *righteousness*;
> And do not enter into judgment with thy servant,
> For in thy sight no man living is righteous.

63. 'Die Rechtfertigungslehre des Paulus: Theologie oder Anthropologie?', in *Theologie als Schriftauslegung* (Munich: Chr. Kaiser Verlag, 1974), p. 198 n. 39. Also in *EvT* 28 (1968), p. 396. Similarly Bultmann, *Theology of the New Testament*, I, p. 46.

64. Cranfield, *Romans*, I, p. 97: 'While it is of course true that the righteousness language of the OT and of late Judaism is the background against which Paul's expression δικαιοσύνη θεοῦ must be understood, there is no reason to assume that he must have used the language he took over just precisely as it had been used. We must allow for the possibility of his having used what he took over with freedom and originality.'

This petition would make no sense if God's righteousness referred to his rendering strictly to each man his due. Clearly from this text and many others (see note 59) the righteousness of God must be so defined as to include the dimension of mercy. It cannot be simply opposed to mercy. It is common therefore to speak of God's righteousness as his 'covenant faithfulness' and to eliminate from the concept any punitive or vindicatory idea (see note 3).

But several problems have emerged with this definition. First, Klaus Koch[65] and Frank Crüsemann[66] have pointed out how seldom the concept of God's righteousness is found in context with the term 'covenant'. Secondly, Koch has called attention to the occasional reference to God's righteousness in the context of creation prior to any covenant with Israel: 'The arrival of *sedeq* on the earth had happened first in the event of creation without any pre-conditions (Ps. 33.4-6; 89.11-17)'.[67] Thirdly, and most importantly, von Rad's claim that 'no references to the concept of a punitive $s^e d\bar{a}q\bar{a}$ can be adduced—that would be a *contradictio in adiecto*' (note 3) cannot hold up.

The detailed support for this thesis cannot be developed here. There is only room for the barest outline of the argument. Frank Crüsemann[68] (who agrees with von Rad) and Hans Schmid[69] have recently come to opposite conclusions on the question of a punitive divine righteousness. Some of the texts on which there is disagreement, but which, in my view, support a punitive righteousness include Lam. 1.18; Neh. 9.33; 2 Chron. 12.6; Isa. 5.16; 10.22; Dan. 9.13-19. Von Rad acknowledges that such texts are problematical for his view but he does not do them justice.[70] Peter Stuhlmacher who wants to preserve a 'basically positive' sense for *sedāqā* as 'saving might' (*heilschaffende Macht*), nevertheless admits that 'according to the present wording the character of *sedāqā* in Isa. 5.16; 10.22, namely as dividing judgment, can scarcely be disputed'.[71] I would say that same conclusion applies also to the other texts cited above.

65. *ThWAT*, II, p. 516.

66. 'Jahwes Gerechtigkeit', p. 430. He can only cite five texts; Ps. 50.6/5, 16; 89.15, 17/4, 29, 35, 40; 11.3/5, 9; 132.9/12; 103.6/17, 18.

67. *ThWAT*, II, p. 520.

68. 'Jahwes Gerechtigkeit', pp. 448-49. (See the secondary literature here.)

69. *Gerechtigkeit als Weltordnung.* See the chapter: 'Is there a "punitive righteousness" in the Old Testament?' and the literature there.

70. *Theology*, I, p. 377 n. 17.

71. *Gerechtigkeit Gottes*, p. 135 n. 8; cf. p. 131 n. 7.

Therefore the question to be raised is: How can divine righteousness refer both to merciful acts of salvation and to acts of punishment upon unbelieving Israel? To put it another way: What aspect of God's righteousness provides the explanation for how this one concept can refer both to acts of mercy and to acts of punishment and still be a unified concept?

At one level the answer to this question may simply be that righteousness still means 'loyalty to a covenant', but that, since the covenant was conditional upon Israel's faithfulness, this loyalty could be expressed in punishment as well as salvation. Whether this is an acceptable answer will depend in part on one's view of the covenant's conditionality.

But, rather than taking up that problem here, I want to suggest that the concept of God's righteousness finds its *ultimate* unity and its main link with Rom. 3.25, 26 not in God's loyalty to an historical covenant but in his loyalty to his own name: to the preservation of his honor and the display of his glory.[72] To be sure, God's commitment to the covenant is the central manifestation of God's commitment to act always for his own name's sake. But the former is penultimate, the latter is ultimate. Covenant loyalty is grounded in a deeper loyalty, and my argument is that this deeper loyalty is the most fundamental aspect of the righteousness of God in the Old Testament, or, at least, that this deeper loyalty is so intimately connected with God's righteousness that they legitimately come to be regarded (by Paul) as overlapping concepts.[73]

Briefly in support of this thesis several texts should be cited. In Ps. 143.1, 2 the Psalmist prayed,

---

72. See *ThWAT*, II, p. 958 for the relationship between the name and glory of God.

73. Surprisingly von Rad's (OTL; *Genesis* [Philadelphia: Westminster Press, 1961], pp. 208-209) penetrating discussion of Gen. 18.25 ('Shall not the judge of all the earth do right?') leads me in this direction. His point is that since righteousness 'is always defined by a communal relationship', therefore 'Yahweh has a communal relationship with Sodom too' (p. 208). But what is this relationship which God has even with those outside of Israel? It must be a universal relationship which God has with creation. But what are the terms of this relationship? Could it not be shown from Genesis 1 and elsewhere (e.g. Isa. 43.7) that the terms of God's relationship with humanity are that they image-forth his glory and honor his name by faithful obedience? And would this not imply that the righteousness of God has as its root God's allegiance to his own name?

> Answer me in thy faithfulness, in thy *righteousness*;
> And do not enter into judgment with thy servant,
> For in thy sight no man living is righteous.

To what is the Psalmist really appealing—to God's allegiance to Israel? Verse 11 suggests, I think, how the Psalmist conceived of God's righteousness in delivering the unrighteous:

> *For the sake of thy name*, O Lord, revive me;
> *In thy righteousness* bring my soul out of trouble.

The parallelism here suggests that for the Psalmist an appeal to God's righteousness was most basically (or at least included) an appeal to God's allegiance to his own name. God's commitment to revive his servant (v. 12) who trusts in him (v. 8) is a penultimate commitment and is grounded in the ultimate commitment to his name. It is precisely with this commitment that the Psalmist aligns God's righteousness (v. 11). 'If God cared nothing for His name...we might have doubts of His salvation.'[74] For a similar use of 'righteousness' compare Ps. 31.1 and 3.

Next we consider the instructive passage in Daniel (9.7, 13-19) where Daniel confesses the sins of Israel, ascribes righteousness to God, and appeals to him for his anger to turn away from the exiles and from his holy city:

> (7) *Righteousness* belongs to Thee, O Lord, but to us open shame, as it is this day...(13) As it is written in the law of Moses, all this calamity has come upon us; yet we have not sought the favor of the Lord in turning from our iniquity and giving attention to thy truth. (14) Therefore the Lord has kept the calamity in store and brought it on us; for the Lord our God is *righteous* with respect to all his deeds which he has done, but we have not obeyed his voice. (15) And now, O Lord, our God who has brought this people out of the land of Egypt with a mighty hand and hast *made a name for thyself* as it is this day—we have sinned, we have been wicked. (16) O Lord, *in accordance with all thy righteous acts*, let now thy anger and thy wrath turn away from thy city Jerusalem, thy holy mountain; for because of our sins and the iniquities of our fathers, Jerusalem and thy people have become a reproach to all those around us. (17) So now our God listen to the prayer of thy servant and to his supplications, and *for thy sake*, O Lord, let thy face shine on thy desolate sanctuary. (18) O my God incline thine ear and hear! Open thine eyes and see our desolations and the city which is called by thy *name*; for we are not presenting our supplications on account of our *righteousness* but on account of *thy great*

---

74. Derek Kidner, *Psalms 73–150* (TOTC; Leicester: Inter-Varsity Press, 1975), pp. 476-77.

compassion. (19) O Lord, hear! O Lord, forgive! O Lord, listen and take action! *For thine own sake*, O my God, do not delay because thy city and thy people are called by *thy name.*

Concerning the meaning of God's righteousness in this text Hans Schmid writes, 'Yahweh is in the right; what he has wrought upon Israel it deserved. The nation is not *ṣādîq*; it has no *ṣᵉdāqā*. The connection here with judicial ideas is clear...What is remarkable is that in the same context, after Yahweh's *ṣᵉdāqā* designates his "right" [*Recht*] in v. 7 [cf. v. 14], it refers to "divine mercy" in v. 16 and is used parallel to *rhm* in v. 18b.'[75] In other words here we have in a single prayer a capsule of the contrast we saw earlier between a punitive and a merciful righteousness. But Daniel does not apparently feel any tension. One could argue that the tension is resolved in the concept of covenant loyalty, if God's punishment is seen as an expression of his loyalty to the conditionality of the covenant, and his future mercy is seen as an expression of his loyalty to the promise to forgive the repentant. But in fact when Daniel asks that God's anger be turned away 'in accordance with all thy righteous acts' his explicit and repeated ground for this is that *the honor of God's name is in jeopardy* (vv. 15, 17, 18, 19). Therefore, we are led to believe that a fundamental aspect of God's righteousness is his commitment to preserve and display the honor of his glorious name.

This aspect of God's righteousness provides a unity between its punitive and merciful manifestations. By punishing Israel he magnified his glory by showing that idolatry is a dreadful evil worthy of destruction. On the other hand, since Jerusalem and Israel are 'called by thy name' (vv. 18, 19), to save them and restore their prosperity after a time of punishment will magnify God's name and remove the reproach into which it has fallen among the nations (v. 16). Thus 'the Lord is righteous in *all* his deeds' (v. 14): he has never swerved from acting for his own name's sake, even when his people have acted as if his name were worthless.

Finally we may take a brief look at the righteousness of God in Isaiah 40–66. It is generally recognized that here the righteousness of God

---

75. *Gerechtigkeit als Weltordnung*, p. 143.

signifies his 'predicted new and eschatological saving act'.[76] God's righteousness and his coming salvation are almost interchangeable:

> I bring near my *righteousness*, it is not far off;
> And my *salvation* will not delay (46.13a).
> My *righteousness* is near,
> My *salvation* has gone forth
> And my arms will judge the peoples (51.5).
> Do not fear the reproach of man…
> For the moth will eat them like a garment…
> But my *righteousness* shall be forever
> And my *salvation* to all generations (51.7b, 8).

On what grounds may Israel expect to benefit from this salvific righteousness? Hermann Cremer argued rightly that it is grounded in the divine election: 'Not the fulfilling of God's commandments is the final ground that God upholds his election (Isa. 14.1), but rather only the election itself. For its sake God forgives his people at the decisive hour Isa. 43.20–44.2…'[77] Cremer's insight is valuable because it points us behind the covenant to God's freedom in election—in establishing the covenant. It thus leads us to ask whether the *ground* of the covenant should be considered in defining what God's allegiance to the covenant (righteousness) involves. Cremer says that God's election of Israel is itself the only reason God upholds this election. But more can be said about the ground of this election. God declares to his dispersed people in Isa. 43.6, 7:

> I will say to the north, Give them up!
> And to the south, Do not hold them back!
> Bring my sons from afar,
> And my daughters from the ends of the earth:
> Everyone who is called by my name
> And *whom I have created for my glory*
> Whom I have formed, even whom I have made.

Similarly, Isa. 49.13:

> And he said to me, You are my servant, Israel,
> *In whom I will show my glory.*

---

76. Crüsemann, 'Jahwes Gerechtigkeit', p. 444; Hill, *Greek Words*; W. Eichrodt, *Theology of the Old Testament*, I (Philadelphia: Westminster Press, 1961), p. 245; von Rad, *Theology*, I, p. 372.

77. *Die Paulinische Rechtfertigungslehre* (Gütersloh: Bertelsmann, 1899), p. 80.

According to these texts and others (Isa. 43.21; 44.23; 46.13 etc.) the ground of Israel's creation, i.e. election, is God's will to act for his own glory. Moreover the ground of God's *initiating* his relation with Israel is also the ground of its continuation. It is a distortion of large portions of the Old Testament when the impression is given that the ground of God's saving action and the touchstone of his righteousness is his faithfulness to Israel's welfare. Note the different focus in the following texts:

> *For the sake of my name* I delay my wrath
> And for my praise I restrain it for you
> In order not to cut you off.
> Behold I have refined you but not as silver;
> I have tested you in the furnace of affliction.
> *For my own sake, for my own sake* I will act;
> For how can (my name) be profaned?
> And *my glory I will not give to another* (Isa. 48.9-11).
> I, even I, am the one who wipes out your transgressions
>   *for my own sake,*
> And I will not remember your sins (Isa. 43.25).

Since, as we have seen, Israel's salvation is an expression of God's righteousness (Isa. 46.13; 51.5, 7, 8), and since the ground of this salvation is traced back not explicitly to a *covenant loyalty*, but to a deeper *loyalty of God to his own name*, therefore there is a clear implication that the righteousness of God is at least closely coordinate with God's unwavering commitment to act for his own name's sake.[78]

One could argue that a loose coordination of these concepts is all we have in the Old Testament. But on the basis of the texts assembled from the Psalms, Daniel and Isaiah (which could be greatly supplemented) I am inclined to see these two concepts as essentially related such that the most fundamental aspect of God's righteousness in the Old Testament is his loyalty to his own name. The righteousness of God does not consist in a strict distributive justice according to which each person must

---

78. Commenting on God's righteousness in Isaiah 40–66, W. Eichrodt gives expression to a needed emphasis: 'The close connection between God's righteousness and his holiness, of which the righteousness is a revelation, anchors Yahweh's intervention for the restoration of the covenant people firmly in the nature (*Wesen*) of God as Lord of the Universe. In this way Yahweh's [righteous] intervention is freed from all egoistic limitations of national self-interest and is given its proper place within the world-wide purposes of the divine sovereignty (*Walten*).' *Theologie des Alten Testaments*, I (Berlin: Evangelische Verlagsanstalt, 1948), p. 117 (my translation. Contrast *Theology*, I, p. 245).

receive his due, nor does it consist merely in a saving commitment to Israel. Both of these may be the outworkings of God's righteousness, but they are so only as they give expression to (and find their unity in) God's inviolable allegiance to maintaining his honor, displaying his glory, and always acting for his own name's sake.

Even if one should cautiously say that in the Old Testament there are only seeds for such an understanding of God's righteousness, nevertheless the possibility would still be open that this understanding was pursued in Jewish apocalyptic[79] and found expression also in Paul. In either case we would expect to find some clues that Paul shares this conception of divine righteousness and we may ask if such a conception might help us grasp Paul's meaning in Rom. 3.25, 26.

I can only mention in passing that I think such clues are present in Paul: (1) in Rom. 3.5, 7 where 'God's righteousness and glory are interchanged';[80] (2) in Rom. 3.8 where God's judgment upon unbelieving *Israel* is 'just' (τὸ κρίμα ἔνδικόν ἐστιν); (3) in Rom. 2.5 where the 'righteous judgment of God' (δικαιοκρισίας τοῦ θεοῦ) renders to those who disobey the truth—*to the Jew first* and also to the Greek—wrath and fury; (4) in 2 Thess. 1.6 where it is δίκαιον παρὰ θεῷ ἀνταποδοῦναι τοῖς θλίβουσιν ὑμᾶς θλῖψιν and where the persecutors very probably included Jews (cf. Acts 17.5). These clues all support (Rom. 3.1-8 can even be developed into a full scale demonstration) that 'covenant faithfulness' or 'faithfulness to creation' is not an adequate

79. A case could be made that the conception of God's righteousness I have developed has left traces in the apocalyptic literature which Käsemann sees as the background of Paul's conception. 1QS 1.26 reflects a punitive divine righteousness which has to be correlated somehow with the saving righteousness in 1QS 10.11, 12; 11.3, 5, 10, 12-15. The key may lie in the parallel between glory/majesty and righteousness (1QS 11.6, 7, 15). When *4 Ezra* says, 'For this, O Lord, shall thy *righteousness* be declared, if thou wilt compassionate them that have no wealth of good works', the next verses picture God *refusing* to do all that Ezra asks: he will rejoice only over the righteous (8.39). And who are they? 'Them that have always put their trust in thy *glory*' (8.30). 'Them who...search out the *glory*' (8.51). But not those who 'have themselves defiled the *Name* of him that made them'.

80. Käsemann, *Au die Römer*, p. 78. But I disagree strongly with the way he handles the quotation from Ps. 51.4 in Rom. 3.4. I agree that the righteousness of God in 3.5 cannot refer to '*iustitia distributiva*' but I am dissatisfied with the definition: 'jene Macht, welche ihr Recht auf das Geschöpf durchsetzt' (p. 78) since I was not able to decipher the place of punishment in this execution of power.

conception of the righteousness of God in Paul. But now we must return to Rom. 3.25, 26.

5. *An Alternative Interpretation of Rom. 3.25, 26*

There are two pivotal clauses in Rom. 3.25, 26 which receive their most coherent and least strained interpretation against the Old Testament background I have developed. The first is διὰ τὴν πάρεσιν τῶν προγεγονότων ἁμαρτημάτων: 'on account of (or through) the passing over (or pardon) of sins done before'. One can at least say from this clause that man's sins have created the need for God to put Christ forth as a propitiation by his blood.

What is the essential character of these sins? Rom. 1.21-23 together with 3.23 give the best answer to this question. 'All sinned and are lacking the glory of God' (3.23). Most recent commentators are probably right that this loss of glory reflects the Jewish tradition[81] in which Adam was divested of his glory when he sinned. But how *Paul* conceives of this loss is seen in Rom. 1.21-23. 'Although they knew God they did not *glorify* him as God or thank him...they exchanged the *glory* of the incorruptible God for the likeness of the image of corruptible man and birds and four-footed beasts and reptiles.' One can hear an echo of Jer. 2.11, 'Has a nation changed its gods, even though they are no gods? But my people have changed their glory for that which does not profit' (cf. Ps. 106.20). *Not* to glorify him as God and thank him is the primal sin: the esteeming of the creature above the creator and the consequent belittling of the creator's glory. This 'foolish' exchange results, as 1.24ff. show, in a swell of dishonorable and demeaning attitudes and acts. Thus, according to Rom. 1.24ff. all sins are an expression of dishonor to God, stemming as they do from the evil inclination of man's heart to value anything above the glory of God.

For God to condone or ignore the dishonor heaped upon him by the sins of men would be tantamount to giving credence to the value judgment men have made in esteeming God more lowly than his creation. It is not so much that he would be saying sins do not matter or justice does not matter; more basically, he would be saying that *he* does not matter. But for God thus to deny the infinite value of his glory, to act persistently as if the disgrace of his holy name were a matter of

81. Schlier, *Römerbrief*, p. 107; C.E.B. Cranfield, *Romans*, I, p. 204; Käsemann, *An die Römer*, p. 88. Cf. Apoc. Mos., p. 20; *3 Bar.* 4.16; *Gen. R.* 12.5 (on 2.4).

indifference to him—this is the heart of unrighteousness. Thus if God is to be righteous he must repair the dishonor done to his name by the sins of those whom he blesses. He must magnify the glory men thought to deny him.[82]

It is pointless to object here that God never is trapped in a situation where he *must* do something. This is pointless because the only necessity unworthy of God is a necessity imposed on him from causes not originating in himself. To say that God *must* be who he is, that he must value what is of infinite value and delight in his infinite beauty, this is no dishonor to God. On the contrary what would dishonor God is to deny that he has any necessary identity at all and that his acts emerge willy-nilly from no essential and constant nature.

Nor is it a legitimate objection here to say that 'Greek' or 'Germanic' ideas of justice are being brought in (see notes 53, 54) and that the semitic background is being ignored. The point is not that God is somehow forced to conform to an ideal ethical norm. The point—in good Old Testament fashion—is simply that God must be God and will brook no belittling of his glorious name.

In view of the nature of sin as dishonor to the glorious name of God and in view of the most basic Old Testament aspect of God's righteousness as his unswerving faithfulness to act always for his own name's sake in preserving and displaying his glory, there is no reason whatever to construe the prepositional phrase beginning with διά (v. 25b) any way but in its usual causal sense.[83] Given this perfectly Jewish thought connection we need not follow Kümmel[84] and Käsemann[85] in the unlikely view that here διά with the accusative is instrumental and means 'through'. Thus the sense of the prepositional phrase is that since God has not required from all individual sinners a loss of glory commensurate with their debasement of God's glory, therefore to preserve and display the infinite value of his own glory, God set forth

82. That this complex of ideas so closely echoes the teaching of Anselm is not due to any vested interest I have in defending him. It is due I suppose to the fact that his insights are more biblical than many of his critics (who seldom show specific errors) think. See St Anselm, *Basic Writings* (trans. S.N. Deane; La Salle, IL: Open Court, 1962), specifically pp. 201-10.

83. Nigel Turner, *A Grammar of New Testament Greek*, III (Edinburgh: T. & T. Clark, 1963), p. 263; C.F.D. Moule, *An Idiom-Book of New Testament Greek* (Cambridge: Cambridge University Press, 2nd edn, 1959), p. 54.

84. 'Πάρεσις', p. 164.

85. *An die Römer*, p. 92.

Christ as a propitiation whose death for sinners so glorified God (Rom. 15.7-9) that God's righteousness was preserved and made known.

The second pivotal clause in Rom. 3.25-26 is v. 26c εἰς τὸ εἶναι αὐτὸν δίκαιον καὶ δικαιοῦντα τὸν ἐκ πίστεως Ἰησοῦ. The interpretation by Käsemann,[86] following C. Blackman,[87] to the effect that the καί here is explicative (or intensive) and that God is δίκαιος precisely as he is ὁ δικαίων, is very awkward in view of what precedes. The awkwardness of this interpretation stems from its failure to distinguish clearly (1) the *demonstration* (ἔνδειξις, v. 26b) of God's righteousness, (2) his *being* (εἶναι, v. 26c) righteous and (3) his justifying believers (v. 26c). According to Käsemann, the first and third of these—the demonstration of God's righteousness at the present time and the justification of the one who trusts Jesus—refer to the same thing: 'the eschatological saving *action*' of God. But Käsemann does not say how we are to understand God's *being* righteous in distinction from this active demonstration.[88] It may be that he sees no distinction. But that would involve not taking Paul's purpose construction (εἰς τό plus the infinitive εἶναι) seriously. For Paul the demonstration of God's righteousness and God's being righteous are not the same; the latter is the outcome and *purpose* of the former. But this means that the *action* of God in justifying believers (v. 26c) is also not interchangeable with God's *being* righteous. Therefore the καί is not intensive and one should not construe v. 26c to mean that God is 'just' *in so far as* he is 'justifier' or that his righteousness consists in justifying.

If we grant full force to the purpose construction (εἰς τὸ εἶναι) and thus to the distinction between demonstration and being, a coherent interpretation emerges against the backdrop of the Old Testament view of divine righteousness sketched above. In putting Christ forth as a propitiation God acts for the sake of his glory, that is, he actively demonstrates inviolable allegiance to the honor of his name *in order that* his inexorable love of his own glory may not be weakened, that is, in order that he might remain and *be* righteous.[89]

86. *Au die Römer*, p. 93.

87. 'Romans 3.26b: A Question of Translation', *JBL* 87 (1968), pp. 203-204.

88. He comments innocuously, 'Finale Deutung ist der Konsekutiven vorzuziehen, weil mit εἰς τὸ εἶναι auf das Motiv der ἔνδειξις zurückgegriffen wird' (*Au die Römer*, p. 93). But in what sense are the εἰς τὸ εἶναι and the ἔνδειξις related? How are they different, if they are? He does not say.

89. It should be noted that when I speak of God's *being* righteous I am not

In this context the justification of sinners through faith (v. 26c) and the passing over (or pardoning) of former sins (v. 25b) both *seem* to imply that God is disregarding his glory (and would indeed imply this if it were not for God's setting Christ forth as a propitiation by his blood). 'Therefore the καί [of v. 26c] must be understood...as an adversative and is to be translated "it was to prove at the present time that he himself is just and *yet* the justifier of him who has faith in Jesus".'[90] Or as Cranfield translates it: 'that God might be righteous even in justifying'.[91] Understood in this way this pivotal purpose clause at the end of v. 26 is a fitting and perfectly clear climax to vv. 25, 26a. God has accomplished his twofold purpose of sending Christ: he has manifested and preserved his own righteousness and yet[92] has justified the ungodly merely through faith. The glorification of God and the salvation of his people are accomplished together.

In conclusion, therefore, I find confirmed that in Rom. 3.25, 26 the concept of God's righteousness as his absolute faithfulness always to act for his own name's sake and for the preservation and display of his glory provides the key which unlocks the most natural and coherent interpretation of this text. That this interpretation takes full account of Paul's Hebraic milieu and yet supports a traditional 'satisfaction theory' of the atonement should be of keen interest for dogmatics.

referring to metaphysical substances but to conditions of will. God's being righteous is properly described in terms of faithfulness, allegiance, commitment, devotion, loyalty, etc. He *is* righteous in that his inclination or will is inexorably committed always to preserve and display his glory. This eternal and unswerving inclination precedes and grounds all his acts of demonstration.

90. George Eldon Ladd, *A Theology of the New Testament* (Grand Rapids: Eerdmans, 1974), p. 432.

91. *Romans*, I, p. 213.

92. This 'yet' must not be construed to mean that the mercy of justification is contrary or adverse to the righteousness of God. What the adversative signifies is the *apparent* conflict between letting sins go unpunished and God's commitment always to preserve and display his glory. The putting Christ forth as a propitiation reveals how *in fact* there is no conflict: God is *just* and (with no tension at all) *justifier* of the one who trusts Jesus.

JSNT 22 (1984), pp. 19-35

EARLY ESCHATOLOGICAL DEVELOPMENT IN PAUL:
THE EVIDENCE OF 1 CORINTHIANS

Christopher L. Mearns

This article seeks to establish that a radical change may be discerned in Paul's eschatology, a change which took place before he came to write 1 Corinthians.[1] The method used is to reconstruct the stages of the arguments which underlie and precede the existing text, a method of 'backward extrapolating' as John Hurd expresses it in *The Origin of I Corinthians*.[2] But the attempt is here made to show that the content of some of the eschatological arguments in Hurd's reconstruction need to be revised.

1 Corinthians offers some evidence for the view that the earliest form of the Christian hope would have centred on the continuing process of present judgment, and expected its imminent coming to a climax. Jesus

1. For attempts to discern changes in Paul's eschatology in the course of epistles, see C.H. Dodd, 'The Mind of Paul', in *New Testament Studies* (Manchester: Manchester University Press, 1953), pp. 67-128; W.L. Knox, *St Paul and the Church of the Gentiles* (Cambridge: Cambridge University Press, 1939), p. 141. For a series of footnotes reviewing the literature on development as a whole within Paulinism, see J.C. Hurd, *The Origin of I Corinthians* (London: SPCK, 1965), pp. 8-11. See also H. Koester and J.M. Robinson, *Trajectories through Early Christianity* (Philadelphia: Fortress Press, 1971), p. 65; P. Benoit, *Apocalypses et Théologie de l'Espérance* (Paris: Cerf, 1977); M. Thrall, 'Christ Crucified or Second Adam? A Christological Debate between Paul and the Corinthians', in *Christ and the Spirit in the Church* (ed. B. Lindars and S.S. Smalley; Cambridge: Cambridge University Press, 1973), pp. 145-56.

2. Hurd, *Origin*. A serious defect of H. Conzelmann's commentary, *I Corinthians* (Philadelphia: Fortress Press, 1975 [German 1st edition of 1969]), is that while referring to Hurd for small points of detail, he fails to deal with his methods and conclusions.

was already perceived to be vindicated and exalted as Messiah and Lord by the earliest communities of Christians, and their hope was that in the near future this would be publicly and conclusively manifested to all. Since Jesus had been instituted as the eschatological judge by his resurrection and ascension, the process of judgment had already begun; and the future general judgment would bring to a climax before the world the revelation of Jesus Christ as the eschatological judge. Paul makes it clear that he, together with his living Corinthian converts, expected to take an active part in this climax of judgment (1 Cor. 15.51-52). This is shown by two of the ten questions which Paul puts to the Corinthians beginning with the formula οὐκ οἴδατε ὅτι. Paul thereby reminds them of what he expects them to have known since the days of his mission to found the church at Corinth: 'Do you not know that the saints will judge the world?', and, 'Do you not know that we are to judge angels?' (1 Cor. 6.2-3). The climax of judgment had been delegated by God to his 'holy ones', according to the probable translation of τὴν κρίσιν ἔδωκε τοῖς ἁγίοις τοῦ ὑψίστου (LXX for the Aramaic of Dan. 7.22). The 'one like a Son of man' or 'man-like figure' was the originally corporate figure representing these 'holy ones' (Dan. 7.13, 18, 27). The climax of judgment, therefore, had been envisaged as a future event from the first. But this climax of a judgment already in process would probably have been conceived of at first as a universalized revelation from heaven, of the already glorified and exalted Lord, on the analogy of a public and universal version of the appearance to Stephen at his martyrdom (Acts 7) and to Paul on the Damascus road (Acts 9). For it was not until the apocalypticizing movement of late first- and early second-generation Christianity that second adventism would have been formulated.[3]

Earliest Christian belief about the general resurrection would probably have been that it was largely accomplished already through adult believers' conversion–baptism, which we may infer was the belief among the Corinthians.[4] This was the main obstacle to the reception of teaching

3.   On the apocalyptic reinterpretation of 'parousia', see C.L. Mearns, 'Early Eschatological Development in Paul: The Evidence of 1 and 2 Thessalonians', *NTS* 27 (1980–81), pp. 137-57, especially pp. 142-45. A similarly tactful strategy in treading gently before the full future apocalyptic scheme is repeated in 1 Cor. 15 may be detected in Paul's cautious language in 1.7-8 about waiting for the revealing of our 'Lord Jesus Christ' on the 'Day of our Lord Jesus Christ'.

4.   See J. Héring, 'Saint Paul a-t-il enseigné deux resurrections?', in *RHPR* 12

about a future final resurrection. The notion of a future resurrection was taken from later Jewish apocalyptic (Dan. 12.2; Isa. 26.19; Tob. 13.2; 2 Macc. 7.9), and adopted in a Christian futurist sense by Paul and others after its earlier radical reinterpretation in a present baptismal sense.

Paul's new apocalyptic programme was the product of his creative response to several pressures. First, there was the desire to include growing numbers of deceased first-generation believers within the scope of the Christian hope (cf. 1 Thess. 4.13). Secondly, there was the desire to provide an 'eschatological reservation' in order to counter over-enthusiasm (cf. Phil. 3.12). Thirdly, Paul needed to help himself and others to come to terms with present bodily weakness, infirmities and sufferings, through developing the Christian hope (cf. 2 Cor. 5.2, 8). Fourthly, it was necessary to help Christians to cope with accumulating threats of a crisis of impending evil and with possibly imminent persecutions (cf. 2 Thess. 2.9). The answer to these pressures was to present the hope of a final resurrection in the future. This Paul did in 1 Thessalonians 4 and in his 'previous letter' to the Corinthians; he reinforced it with his teaching in 1 Corinthians 15. For he came to realize that many of his converts might have died, and even he himself might also have died, by the time the Day of the Lord came. Therefore a future resurrection would be required to ensure they were present at the final judgment.

The Last Judgment could be conceived as happening either on earth or in heaven. Whether the resurrected were taken to heaven along with the rapt living for judgment or assembled on earth, the general resurrection itself could only take place on earth. Therefore, once belief in a future final resurrection was accepted by Christians, the Lord of that resurrection was conceived as coming dramatically to earth, in order to superintend this aspect of the eschatological drama. He was to gather from the earth to himself the elect saints from among the living, and also those who were newly resurrected from their graves. When a future final resurrection took precedence over present baptismal resurrection, the notion of a second advent was developed to go with it, and to provide for a fulfilment in the future of such prophetic 'theophany'

(1932), p. 318 (cited by W.D. Davies, *Paul and Rabbinic Judaism* [London: SPCK, 1948], p. 292).

passages of the Old Testament, as Psalm 18, 29, 97, Habakkuk 3, Joel 3, Zech. 14.5.[5]

The case for detecting an early development in Paul's eschatology is strengthened by the firm impression which Paul gives that his apocalyptic scheme is a recent revelation to him. He is passing on new teaching to his converts which they have not previously been familiar with. A solemn formula which introduces a new revelation of divine truth granted through prophetic power of the Spirit is used by Paul in 1 Cor. 15.51. Paul then proclaims the apocalyptic scheme of the second advent and general resurrection. J. Ruef assumes that the reason for Paul's use of the term 'mystery' is simply the fact that 'the gentile would have been acquainted with none of their apocalyptic ideas. Therefore it is for him a mystery which Paul has to tell him.'[6] But the questions arise: Why had Paul evidently not delivered this teaching at his first preaching on the founding mission, and why does it now emerge as a new revelation? This is knowledge that had been hidden, but it is now revealed, Paul means, by telling the 'mystery' publicly. This supports the impression that here is new teaching, which affirms something that has only recently been made clear in the providence of God. There is a parallel to this in that the place of the Gentiles in the Kingdom of God had only become clear after some time had passed (cf. Eph. 3.4-5; cf. Col. 1.26-27). The Holy Spirit had only after a lapse of time made clear new understandings, so that inspired new teachings became available, especially about the Gentiles and the return of Christ. Paul had used a similar formula to 'Lo, I tell you a mystery' when he said to the Thessalonians: 'This we declare to you by the word of the Lord...', referring to a Spirit-inspired utterance or 'oracle' of the risen Lord (1 Thess. 4.14).[7]

---

5.   See T.F. Glasson, *The Second Advent* (London: Epworth Press, 1945), pp. 162ff.

6.   J. Ruef, *Paul's First Letter to Corinth* (London: Pelican/SCM Press, 1977), p. 176.

7.   This interpretation of 'word of the Lord' is endorsed by R.F. Collins in 'Tradition, Redaction and Exhortation in I Th. 4.13–5.11', in *L'Apocalypse Johannique et L'Apocalyptique dans le Nouveau Testament* (ed. J. Lambrecht; Leuven: Duculot, 1980), p. 330. See also D.C. Allison, 'The Pauline Epistles and the Synoptic Gospels: The Pattern of the Parallels', *NTS* 28 (1982–83), p. 26 n. 18, concluding with the verdict of B. Henneken (in 1969), 'ein Wort des erhöhten Herrn'. We may follow L. Hartmann, *Prophecy Interpreted* (Lund: Gleerup, 1966), pp. 181-90, in tracing it to a Christian midrash on verses in Daniel, while suspending judgment on his suggestion that 'Paul used a form of the eschatological discourse'

This phrase introduces the block of newly revealed teaching about the parousia in the sense of 'return' in 1 Thessalonians. The similar phrase does the same here in 1 Cor. 15.51.[8]

John Hurd's method of extrapolating backwards from the text of 1 Corinthians to reconstruct Paul's first preaching works in the following manner. First, Hurd identifies the points which the Corinthians made by letter and by messages to Paul in reply to his 'previous letter' to them (1 Cor. 5.9). Secondly, Hurd reconstructs the points Paul made in that 'previous letter'. Then he reaches behind the 'previous letter' to infer what Paul's teaching would have been before it, at the founding mission. Hurd maintains that by his 'previous letter' Paul sought to introduce rules and regulations based on an agreement to impose provisions of the Apostolic Decree from the Council of Jerusalem upon the churches of the Gentile mission (Acts 15). But even if this aspect of his argument is rejected, Hurd's reconstruction of the main stages of Paul's teaching still stands, as does most of the content of that reconstruction.[9]

Hurd outlines the stages of Paul's eschatological teaching, with special reference to the resurrection body, starting from his founding mission and finishing with the text of 1 Corinthians, in the following chronological sequence. Hurd supposes that at the founding mission Paul would

(p. 190). The 'thief in the night' simile of 1 Thess. 5.2//Lk. 12.39//Mt. 24.43//*Gos. Thom.* 100 could be explained if Paul knew Q, as suggested by V.P. Furnish, *Theology and Ethics in Paul* (Nashville: Abingdon Press, 1968), p. 54. Although Alfred Resch in his work of 1904 claimed to identify 925 parallels with the synoptic Gospels in 9 Pauline letters, V.P. Furnish says 'there are only 8 convincing parallels to the synoptic gospels' in the ethical teaching of Paul (p. 53). Six of these could reasonably be argued to derive from Paul's knowing Q (Rom. 12.14, 17; 14.13; 1 Thess. 5.2, 15). The parallel between 1 Thess. 5.13 and Mk 9.50 is not striking enough in itself to compel us to assume Paul was dependent on Mark. Paul could have derived Rom. 14.14 from the *Gos. Thom.* 14, which is a more primitive version of the saying in Mk 7.15 and Mt. 14.14. This suggestion receives some support because in 1 Cor. 2.9 Paul cites the *Gos. Thom.* 17, showing he could have known this sayings-source as well as Q.

8.   Paul also uses the phrase, 'We do not wish you to be ignorant' (οὐ θέλομεν δὲ ὑμᾶς ἀγνοεῖν), when he introduces new information or unfolds the basic proclamation of the gospel in a new way (Rom. 11.25; 1 Cor. 10.1; 12.1). He uses the same phrase to introduce his apocalyptic scheme (1 Thess. 4). See P. Ellingworth and E.A. Nida, *A Translator's Handbook on Paul's Letters to the Thessalonians* (London: United Bible Societies, 1979), p. 92.

9.   N.A. Dahl, *Studies in Paul* (Minneapolis: Augsburg, 1977), p. 58.

have taught that the End is at hand, and that Christians will enter the Kingdom soon; meanwhile the communion of the body and blood of the Lord is preserving Christians until that day comes. Later, in his 'previous letter', Paul would have taught the Corinthians that they were not to mourn for those who had died, since at the return of Christ they would be resurrected as Christ had been resurrected and would enter the Kingdom together with Paul. Apparently the Corinthians were disconcerted by this new teaching and objected both by letter and by messenger. Moreover, Hurd asserts that they repudiated belief in a bodily, fleshly resurrection, as the idea was gross and unspiritual. Finally, when writing 1 Corinthians, Paul insisted that the Corinthians do believe in the resurrection of Christ (1 Cor. 15.1-28), but he qualified the mode of the future resurrection of believers by affirming that it would be a spiritual, not a fleshly resurrection (1 Cor. 15.35-57). As against this reconstruction it will be argued in the present paper that a more probable reconstruction of Paul's eschatological teaching on his founding mission would be that the End had come, that believers had entered the Kingdom, and that the communion of the body and blood of the Lord kept reminding them that they were living in the age of the messiah's eschatological banquet.

Hurd proposed his futurist scheme of Paul's first eschatological teaching at Corinth in spite of having listed a series of 'characteristics of the Christian community [which] may be taken as reflecting a belief that they were living proleptically in the Kingdom'.[10] The first four items in Hurd's list are: (a) Spiritual marriages;[11] (b) Women unveiled (or 'with

10. Hurd, *Origin*, p. 285.

11. The evidence for the Corinthians' practice of 'spiritual marriages' is sometimes contested. But in view of 1 Cor. 7.1-5, it does not seem unreasonable to suppose that there was a practice of converting, at least for a while, ordinary marriages into 'spiritual marriages'. This fits in with late Jewish expectations about marriage in heaven as reflected in Jesus' reply to the Sadducees' question in Mk 12.23ff., and with the atmosphere of charismatic enthusiasm at Corinth, which ran to strenuous ascetic zeal in trying to conduct some marriages as if in 'heaven now'. This explanation may well mitigate the scandal of the apparent case of 'incest' in 1 Cor. 5.1-5, and explain the otherwise puzzling pride with which Paul says the Corinthians were regarding it. For the arrangement probably involved a 'spiritual marriage' between a son and his step-mother, in this instance, which Paul nevertheless felt compelled to deal with very harshly because of the danger to the whole Christian community from popular misunderstanding and ensuing discredit. References to sexual immorality among the Corinthian Christians may reflect Paul's reactions not so much to survivals

short hair'), and speaking in church; (c) Speaking in tongues by the power of the Spirit (i.e. the language of the angels in heaven; 1 Cor. 13.1);[12] (d) Freedom from law (cf. 1 Cor. 6.12).[13]

Four supporting items may be added to this list from the Pauline letters, indicating that the earliest Christians believed they were living proleptically in the Kingdom. First, when Paul protests, 'We hear that some of you are living in idleness', we may presume that the giving up of regular work in the case of many Thessalonians probably stemmed from the enthusiastic motive of living in 'heaven now' and enjoying a proleptic paradise (cf. 1 Thess. 4.11; 5.14; 2 Thess. 3.10-11). Secondly, enthusiasm may well have motivated the sort of person whom Paul criticizes as 'the weak man' who 'eats only vegetables' (Rom. 14.2), and may account for those who 'enjoin abstinence from foods which God created to be received with thanksgiving' (1 Tim. 4.3). For vegetarianism was a diet which not only circumvented the problems arising from Jewish dietary laws, but which also was appropriate to enthusiasts who perceived themselves as living in the harmonious, non-predatory and non-violent situation of 'paradise restored'. The third item to be added to Hurd's list of signs is the coming of Gentile nations to join God's people at the eschaton. The coming of these nations had been predicted as one of the signs of the Day of the Lord in Micah 4, Zech. 8.20ff., Isa. 49.6, and 60.3. It is implied in 1 Cor. 1.26, and 12.13, but Paul does not make it a theme of that letter. We shall not therefore treat it further here. The fourth item is life in Christ as a corollary of Christians being now the messiah's followers in the present messianic age. This is prominent in 1 Corinthians, though its relation with justification has been much in

of pagan practices among converts as to a radical re-appraisal of conventional ethics, both Gentile and Jewish, in this area, under the impetus of charismatic 'liberation-theology' (cf. 1 Cor. 6.12). 1 Cor. 11.4ff. may imply some Corinthians had begun to tolerate some cases of variant sexual self-identification—a suggestion prompted by J. Murphy O'Connor, 'Sex and Logic in 1 Cor. 11.2-16', *CBQ* 42 (1980), pp. 482-500, esp. p. 499.

12. The gift of the Holy Spirit (Joel 2.28; Zech. 12.10) is closely associated with the 'new covenant' prophecies in Ezek. 11.19, 36.27, and Jer. 31.31.

13. For the vexed question of the status of the law in the new age, see W.D. Davies, *Torah in the Messianic Age and/or Age to Come* (SBLMS, 7; Philadelphia: Society of Biblical Literature, 1952). For a view less 'Pauline', see the same author's *The Setting of the Sermon on the Mount* (Cambridge: Cambridge University Press, 1964), pp. 157-90. See also L. Baeck, 'The Faith of Paul', *JJS* 3 (1952), pp. 93-110, esp. pp. 105-107.

dispute, particularly since the writing of Albert Schweitzer.[14] Schweitzer may have erred both in assuming an unchanging parousia-concept in the early church and also in saying that Paul must have upheld two resurrections and two judgments (messianic and final).[15] But this does not dim the clarity and accuracy of his recognition of Paul's central perception, that is, that for those who confess Jesus as Christ and Lord, the eschatological situation has momentously changed: the messianic age has actually begun.[16] Therefore the life of the followers of the messiah in closest unity with him and with one another is 'life-in-Christ', lived in the Spirit in a situation of realized eschatology.[17]

If our general hypothesis is correct, it follows that the eucharist in churches like that at Corinth would have been interpreted as a dramatic sign of realized eschatology. Thus our reconstruction of Paul's eucharistic teaching at his founding mission differs from Hurd's futuristic one. Our reconstruction is that the communion of the body and blood of the Lord kept reminding the Corinthians that they were living in the age of the messiah's eschatological banquet. On the assumption that realized eschatology and charismatic enthusiasm prevailed at Corinth, it is obvious that this alternative reconstruction fits that situation more appropriately than Hurd's reconstruction. Some evidence for this reconstruction may be inferred from 1 Corinthians. Paul's modifying of this aspect of his first teaching can be detected in 11.23-25, where he delivers the tradition of the words and actions of Jesus at the Last Supper as the authority for the Church's eucharist. The main significance of the

14. A. Schweitzer, *The Mysticism of Paul the Apostle* (London: A. & C. Black, 1931), p. 166.

15. For Schweitzer's reconstruction of Paul's eschatological scheme, see *Mysticism*, pp. 90-95, and for a convincing critique of the double resurrections and judgments postulated by Schweitzer, see Davies, *Paul and Rabbinic Judaism*, pp. 288-98.

16. 'Christianity is for Paul no new religion, but simply Judaism with the centre of gravity shifted in consequence of the new era.' So A. Schweitzer, *Paul and his Interpreters* (London: A. & C. Black, 1912), p. 227.

17. It is vain to complain against Schweitzer's subordination of christology to eschatology, for eschatology is inescapably basic to the development of christology. E. Schillebeeckx rightly begins his survey of New Testament christology with the historically prime category of eschatological prophet: *Jesus* (London: Collins, 1979), pp. 439ff., although he disagrees (p. 541) with G. Fohrer's view that christology is grounded in eschatology (Fohrer, 'Das Alte Testament und das Thema "Christologie"', *EvT* 30 [1970], pp. 281-98).

eucharist in the context of prevailing realized eschatology would have been the celebration of the messianic banquet in the present messianic kingdom. First-generation Christians probably understood in this sense Jesus' words: 'I tell you that from now on I shall not drink of the fruit of the vine until the Kingdom of God comes' (Lk. 22.18; cf. Mt. 26.29; Mk 14.25). But when futurist eschatology was assuming dominant importance Paul added v. 26 to the tradition of the Lord's sanction for the eucharist: 'For every time you eat this bread and drink the cup, you proclaim the death of the Lord, until he comes'. This verse is not part of the tradition which Paul was delivering; it reads as Paul's own redactional comment. He thus gives an interpretation of the eucharist which accommodates the then new conception of a second advent. This goes together with a move away from celebrating the presence now of the resurrected Lord in the midst of his church. Instead Paul stresses that the eucharist proclaims the cross, passion and death of Jesus—it remembers the past, and also proclaims the return of Christ in glory—the future hope.[18]

From what Paul says in 15.13, it looks as if he thought that the Corinthians were denying any resurrection for Christians, either a past baptismal or a future final one. However that may be, a future general resurrection loomed so large in the foreground of Paul's thinking and arguing at the time 1 Corinthians was written that it temporarily prevented Paul from counting the Corinthians' continued belief in baptismal resurrection as proper resurrection belief. Paul then assumed that the Corinthians' denial of future final resurrection amounted to denying 'the resurrection'. Paul's words, 'If in this life we who are in Christ have only hope, we are of all men most to be pitied' (15.19), shows that when he wrote 1 Corinthians 15 his mind was almost entirely focused on resurrection considered as future and final.[19] The baptismal resurrection

18. For New Testament indications of a realized eschatological interpretation of the first day of the week to coincide with the resurrection and also of the eucharist as celebrating the resurrection and held on that day, see Jn 20.19; Luke 24.1, 13, 30, 36; Acts 20.7; Rev. 1.10.

19. J. Lambrecht conservatively says, 'we remain rather hesitant in the face of such daring positions' ('Paul's Christological Use of Scripture in 1 Cor. 15.20-28', *NTS* 28 [1981–82], pp. 502-27). For a survey of alternative views, see A.J.M. Wedderburn, 'The Problem of the Denial of the Resurrection in 1 Cor. 15', *NovT* 23 (1981), pp. 230ff. Wedderburn himself concludes: 'Paul in a sense both misunderstands and misrepresents the Corinthians' (p. 240). But for a view possibly favourable to that of the present article, see J.M. Robinson, 'Jesus—From Easter to

belief however was soon to re-emerge in Pauline writings, as in
Col. 2.12, 3.1, and (more guardedly), in Rom. 6.3-11; it is also implied
by Rom. 8.19, 'The creation waits with eager longing for revealing of
the sons of God', where 'revealing' is used rather than resurrection,
probably because Paul has in mind again the already experienced
baptismal resurrection, by which God has made believers his adopted
sons. The Corinthians do not protest that the notion of physical resurrection is repulsive, which is what Hurd supposes. Paul's opponents had not
adopted the refined rationalism of Greek philosophy, preferring the
immortality of the soul to the resurrection of the body, as many have
supposed. Rather, they clung to their prior belief in baptismal resurrection under the influence of the 'fanaticism of those who have already
risen and are living it up in glory'.[20] The Corinthian enthusiasts felt they
were 'at ease in Zion' and boasted about it.[21] Paul ironically reproved
the Corinthians, 'Already you are filled...Without us you have become
kings! And would that you did reign...' (1 Cor. 4.8).[22]

Valentinus (or the Apostles' Creed)', *JBL* 101 (1982), pp. 5-37. In commenting on
the Valentinian Treatise *On Resurrection* (to Rheginos) 46.2, Robinson says: 'Here it
is made clear that a future physical resurrection has become superfluous, having been
replaced by the spiritual resurrection. The doctrine of baptismal resurrection surely
deserves at least by this time the Pauline characterization that there is no (future
bodily) resurrection of the dead.'

20. Koester and Robinson, *Trajectories*, p. 33. E. Earle Ellis dissents from this
position: 'Even if [the denial of the future resurrection] is a precursor of the teaching
of Hymenaeus [that "the resurrection is past already", 2 Tim. 2.18], it probably
reflects more a Platonic anthropology than a "realized" eschatology: the immortal
soul, released to eternal life at death, has no need of resurrection' ('Christ Crucified',
in *Reconciliation and Hope* [ed. R. Banks; Exeter: Paternoster, 1974], p. 73).

21. For the first interpretation of the opponents of Paul in 1 Corinthians as
enthusiastic charismatics, see W. Lütgert, *Freiheitspredigt und Schwarm geister in
Korinth* (BFCT, 12.3; Gütersloh: Bertelsmann, 1908). He was followed by
A. Schlatter, *Die Korinthische Theologie* (BFCT, 18.2; Gütersloh: Bertelsmann,
1914).

22. Cf. C.K. Barrett, *The First Epistle to the Corinthians* (BNTC; London: A. &
C. Black, 1968), p. 109. Barrett quotes H.D. Wendland, *Die Briefe an die Korinther*
(NTD; Göttingen: Vandenhoeck & Ruprecht, 1946): 'They misinterpret gospel and
faith, and change both into gnosis and enthusiasm, by believing that the consumma-
tion is already realized'. Hurd refers to the similar view taken by J. Héring, H. von
Soden and J.S. Schniewind, in *Origin*, pp. 198, 269. For other advocates of this
position, see J. Moffatt, *The First Epistle of Paul to the Corinthians* (London:
Hodder, 1938), pp. 234ff.; W. Schmithals, *Gnosticism in Corinth* (New York:
Abingdon Press, 1971), p. 269; N.A. Dahl, 'Paul and the Church at Corinth,

The Corinthians would have objected by reminding Paul of the original terms in which he had preached to them a gospel of predominantly realized eschatology stressing baptismal resurrection.

This over-realized eschatology of Paul's Corinthian opponents was a view Paul attempted to restrain by developing apocalyptic to serve as an 'eschatological reservation'.[23] It is notable how the author of the Fourth Gospel, in spite of the emphasis on realized eschatology (cf. Jn 5.25), seems deliberately to avoid the terminology of baptismal resurrection, and instead prefers to speak in terms of baptismal regeneration (e.g. 3.5). This probably reflects the same kind of reaction as Paul signals in 1 Corinthians, that is, reaction against the incipiently 'heretical' tendencies experienced from over-emphasis upon baptismal resurrection.

J. Ruef[24] maintains that the reason for which the Corinthians were able to deny a resurrection of the dead was because they understood 'Christ is risen' in terms of exaltation upon translation or assumption into heaven 'rather than as a resurrection in the Jewish sense...In the mind of the Corinthians, resurrection meant that Jesus avoided death. In the thought of Paul, of course, resurrection meant that Jesus overcame death.' But there is no argument in Paul that Jesus really did die before his exaltation (cf. 1 Jn 5). This one would expect if the Corinthians had been interpreting Jesus' rising as a bodily assumption or ascension into heaven, escaping a real death. Ruef assumes that the impression which the Corinthians might be held to have given, 'that they believed that the resurrection had, somehow, already occurred',[25] would have to be attributed to 'a communications problem; either he had misunderstood them or they had misunderstood him, or both'. But it is not necessary to

according to 1 Cor. 1–4', in *Christian History and Interpretation* (ed. W.R. Farmer, C.F.D. Moule, and R.R. Niebuhr; Cambridge: Cambridge University Press, 1967), p. 332. The first to suggest that the Corinthians believed they were already resurrected may have been Aquinas; see B. Spörlein, *De Leugnung der Auferstehung: Eine historisch-kritische Untersuchung zu I. Kor. 15* (Regensburg: Pustet, 1971), p. 3. For 19th century upholders of the view, see J.H. Wilson, 'The Corinthians who Say There is No Resurrection of the Dead', *ZNW* 59 (1968), pp. 94-96.

23. E. Käsemann, 'On the Topic of Primitive Christian Apocalyptic', in *Apocalypticism* (ed. R.W. Funk; New York: Herder and Herder, 1969), p. 126.

24. Ruef, *Paul's First Letter to Corinth*, p. xxii.

25. Ruef, *Paul's First Letter to Corinth*, p. 163. He refers for this to J.H. Cadbury, 'Over-conversion in Paul's Churches', in *The Joy of Study* (ed. S.E. Johnson; New York: Macmillan, 1951), pp. 43-50. But Cadbury merely says: 'Like other teachers he [Paul] faces the problem of pupils overdoing his own viewpoint'.

suppose any misunderstanding, only that Paul was dominated by the concept of resurrection as future and final at the time of writing 1 Corinthians, and may also have wanted to place his opponents at Corinth at a disadvantage by making their denial of future resurrection appear to involve a denial of any resurrection at all. Ruef upholds Bultmann's view that 'Paul had spoken, in his original preaching to the Corinthians, only of the resurrection of Jesus and had not included the idea of the resurrection for ordinary men'.[26] But, given the pneumatic enthusiasm predominating at Corinth, rather than believing 'Christ is risen but the dead do not rise', it is more probable that the Corinthians asserted: 'Christ is risen, and we are risen too'.[27]

So when the Corinthians replied to the apocalyptic 'orthodoxy' of Paul's arguments in his 'previous letter' (at about the same time as he was writing 1 and 2 Thessalonians), they objected by saying, not as Hurd supposes, that bodily resurrection is gross and unspiritual, but by reaffirming what they honestly (and probably correctly) believed they

26. Ruef, *Paul's First Letter to Corinth*, p. 163, in reference to R. Bultmann, *Exegetische Probleme des zweiten Korintherbriefes* (Uppsala: Wretmans, 1947), pp. 3-12.

27. See the similar conclusions about the Thessalonians drawn by R. Jewett, 'Enthusiastic Radicalism and the Thessalonian Correspondence', *SBLSP* (1972), pp. 181-232. See also A.C. Thiselton, 'Realized Eschatology at Corinth', *NTS* 24 (1977–78), pp. 510-26. Thiselton concludes: 'We have tried to show that at several specific points in the epistle an exegesis in terms of eschatological and spiritual enthusiasm is preferable to one in terms of gnosticism'. The foundation study for this position was by W. Lütgert, in 1908; see n. 21 above. For the influence of gnosis on the Corinthians, see R. Mc.L. Wilson, 'How Gnostic were the Corinthians?', *NTS* 19 (1972–73), pp. 65-74. R. Horsley has weakened the case that Paul's opponents in 1 Corinthians were inspired by early gnosticism, by showing that the strongest parallels to Paul's vocabulary are in Philo and Hellenistic Jewish Wisdom literature. But it may be observed that Jewish Hellenistic 'enlightenment' religion shares the same matrix as gave birth to Gnosis. See R.A. Horsley, 'Gnosis in Corinth: 1 Cor. 8.1-6', *NTS* 27 (1980–81), pp. 35-51; 'Pneumatikos v. Psychikos, Distinctions of Spiritual States among the Corinthians', *HTR* 69 (1976), pp. 269-88; 'Wisdom of Words and Words of Wisdom in Corinth', *CBQ* 39 (1977), pp. 224-37; 'Consciousness and Freedom among the Corinthians', *CBQ* 40 (1978), pp. 574-89. There is an interesting analogy with the work of Horsley in that of R. Williamson, who detects terminology held in common between Philo and the author of the letter to the Hebrews ('Philo and New Testament Christology', *ExpTim* 90 [1978–79], pp. 361-65). Gnosis favoured a realized eschatology, and went on in gnosticism to develop an individualized eschatology of the 'pilgrimage' of the immortal soul beyond death, which was inhospitable to corporate future apocalyptic.

had heard Paul saying at his founding mission: 'Christians are already experiencing the putting on of the resurrection body and do now share in Christ's risen body'. In 1 Corinthians 15, Paul reaffirmed his belief in resurrection, but the resurrection is now regarded as a mainly future event in conjunction with his recently formulated re-interpretation of parousia.[28] The conquest of death lies still in the future, towards the end of a programmed sequence of end-events and signs leading to the final consummation where God becomes 'all in all' (1 Cor. 15.28).

Paul is evidently arguing a case throughout 1 Cor. 15.20-28. It is not something he can take for granted that the congregation at Corinth shares with him, in spite of his having announced a message very like it in the 'previous letter'. Paul is giving another slant to previous teaching, modifying it fairly extensively. The notes of time sequence for the end-events are almost as marked in these verses as they are in Jesus' eschatological discourse in Mark 13. A quick scrutiny of 1 Cor. 15.20-28 will make it abundantly clear that Paul is deliberately concerned to impose a new order, a programmatic 'tagma', upon the eschatological events.[29]

He spaces those events in an orderly fashion, in order to re-shape the expectations of the congregation at Corinth about the future events. Paul concludes his newly formed futurist eschatological emphasis in 1 Corinthians 15 with the insistence that the conquest of death will only come at the end of the order of eschatological events (cf. 15.54). The emphatic Greek construction, ὅταν δὲ...τότε, implies: 'Only at the time when [i.e. in the future apocalyptic events]...then shall come to pass...' Paul was again countering his Corinthian critics who had contended that death was already swallowed up for them in victory now.[30] The thrust of Paul's argument in 1 Corinthians is explained if he is contradicting the notion of the first-generation Christians that death was already abolished for believers because the eschaton had arrived, with the exaltation of Christ and the incorporation of believers by baptism into him.

28. See n. 3.
29. Barrett, *The First Epistle to the Corinthians*, p. 354, prefers to translate τάγμα as 'rank', i.e. Paul is referring to different groups of people, rather than to a sequential order of events. But Barrett admits that 'in later Greek (including the LXX) its use is widened, so that it could be applied to any sort of group, military or civilian, and could mean place or position or even ordinance'.
30. Wilson, 'The Corinthians who Say There is No Resurrection of the Dead', comments that H.W. Bartsch, in 'Die Argumentation des Paulus in 1 Cor. 15.3-11', *ZNW* 55 (1964), pp. 270-73, agrees with K. Barth that the point of 1 Cor. 15.6 is that even some of the five hundred brethren who have seen the risen Lord have died.

It is significant that there is no hint of anxiety in Paul that where the agreed rule, 'It is well for a man not to touch a woman' (7.1), was adopted (at any rate in the matter of relations between husband and wife) Christians would become depleted in number. This is probably because it had been assumed that the rule of death would not apply to the majority; it had been the general expectation that they would not physically die. Statements like 'Christ Jesus has abolished death, and brought life and incorruption to light through the gospel' (2 Tim. 1.10), and 'We know that we have passed from death to life' (1 Jn 3.14) may well have been understood literally in the first generation of Christianity. Death was the main form in which the threat of meaninglessness and despair was present to the mind of the ancient world.[31] The earliest Christians doubtless assumed that the powers of salvation were so eminently manifested and communicated in their experience of Jesus as the exalted Christ that disease and even death itself were abrogated when they entered the Kingdom of God through baptismal resurrection.[32] Evidence of the shock produced by the deaths of first-generation Christians, and a reappraisal of the earliest assumption that resurrection/eternal life was a present possession is provided by a number of New Testament passages (Mt. 16.18; 27.51-53; Acts 5.1-11; 1 Cor. 5.8; 11.30; 15.6, 26; 2 Cor. 3–5; 1 Thess. 4.13; 2 Tim. 2.17-18[33]). Although

31. See e.g. P. Tillich, *The Courage to Be* (London: Nesbit, 1952), p. 53.

32. For the hymn book of some Christians who maintained a strong emphasis on baptismal resurrection and a wholly realized eschatology, see the Odes of Solomon, probably from the late first century AD, and from the region of Eastern Syria. There is no reference to baptism as a 'sealing' for the future return of Christ or the future coming of the Kingdom. For a first-century AD dating of the Odes, see J.R. Harris and A. Mingana, *The Odes and Psalms of Solomon* (Manchester: Manchester University Press/London: Longmans, Green, 1916–20). See also *Odes of Solomon* (ed. T.M. Bernard; Texts and Studies, 8.3; Cambridge: Cambridge University Press, 1912). Bernard identifies the baptismal references clearly, though dating the hymns to the second half of the second century. See also J.H. Charlesworth, *The Odes of Solomon* (Texts and Translations, 13; Pseudepigrapha Series, 7; Missoula: Scholars Press, 1976). D.E. Aune, 'The Odes of Solomon and Early Christian Prophecy', *NTS* 28 (1981–82), pp. 435-60, concludes: 'One centrally important feature of the Odes, and one with parallels in the hymns of the Johannine Apocalypse, is the imaginative presentation of events and conditions of the future as if they were features of present experience'. But Aune tends to confine realized eschatology to the context of early Christian liturgical settings, as in *The Cultic Setting of Realized Eschatology* (Leiden: Brill, 1972).

33. See P.H. Menoud, 'La Mort d'Ananias et de Sapphira (Acts 5.1-11)', in *Aux*

F.V. Filson, reviewing Hurd's work, asked rhetorically, 'Did Paul first preach at Corinth so early in his ministry that it had not yet occurred to him that some Christians would die before the end of the age?',[34] Paul does seem to have held a tenacious belief for a surprisingly long time that deaths among early Christians demanded special explanation, and that eternal life now in the sense of present immortality remained the norm for believers.

It is scarcely surprising that only a few traces of this earliest belief are found in the New Testament. It would have been an embarrassment to all second-generation Christians to recall a mistaken assumption of the first generation. But enough traces of this belief do survive to make this hypothesis a reasonable one. The overcoming of death, Paul is telling the Corinthian Christians, does not after all belong to that part of eschatology so extensively inaugurated as to be already realized on earth. Paul is therefore modifying the views of the first-generation converts, in order to correct their over-enthusiasm and the over-realized eschatology that went with it.[35]

The first stage of Paul's eschatological teaching, prior to his extant letters, can be recovered by reaching behind 1 Corinthians as well as behind the Thessalonian epistles.[36] John Hurd's method helps to achieve this, but his reconstruction needs to take account of the current hypothesis that the Corinthians believed that they were already living the

Sources de la Tradition Chrétienne (ed. O. Cullmann and P.H. Menoud: Neuchâtel–Paris: Delachaux et Niestlé, 1950), pp. 145ff.

34. *JBL* 84 (1965), p. 452.

35. Mistaken beliefs of the Corinthians about suffering and death are linked with their neglect of the suffering and death of Jesus. As R.M. Grant says: 'From what Paul says about the crucifixion of the Messiah in his opening chapters it seems likely that they laid little emphasis on this fact, just as they could not understand the sufferings of the apostles, 1 Cor. 4.9-13', in *A Historical Introduction to the New Testament* (London: Collins, 1963), p. 205. Paul had to rebuke the Corinthians for pneumatic over-enthusiasm in 1 Cor. 12.7ff.; and he still had to rebuke them when he wrote 2 Corinthians. For in 2 Corinthians over-enthusiasm at Corinth helps to explain Paul's references to the arrogance (11.10) of the 'super-apostles' (11.4-5, 12.11) who were itinerant Jewish (11.22) miracle-workers (12.12) bearing letters of recommendation (3.1) listing their accomplishments, and preaching a theology of present glory (4.17) rather than of the cross. D. Georgi first established this identification in his *Die Gegner des Paulus im 2. Korintherbrief: Studien zur religiösen Propaganda in der Spätantike* (WMANT, 2; Neukirchen–Vluyn: Neukirchener Verlag, 1964).

36. See Mearns, 'Early Eschatological Development', pp. 142-45.

resurrection life of Christ through having shared in the drama of conversion and baptism. Hurd's summary of their belief as, 'The End is *at hand*. We shall enter the Kingdom *soon*', is not compatible with their predominantly realized eschatology of baptismal resurrection, perceived as experienced now. Similarly Hurd's statement of their eucharistic theology as 'The body and blood of the Lord will preserve us *until the day*' needs reformulation; is more likely that they saw the eucharist rather as a present sharing in the realized eschatological banquet. Further, Hurd's supposition that the Corinthians denied a bodily fleshly resurrection as gross and unspiritual needs altering, since the Corinthians were not under the influence of Hellenistic 'spiritualizing' of the resurrection-body, but were enthusiasts claiming to experience resurrection life already in their present baptismally raised bodies.

What lay in the future for the Corinthians—as also at first for Paul— was only the universal climactic judgment. But this was then elaborated by an apocalyptic programme of future end-events. In place of baptismal resurrection Paul emphasized future final and general resurrection. In place of the virtually complete presence now of the glorified Christ with his people, Paul gave the 'parousia' a new meaning, applying it to the glorious return of Christ. In place of a process of judgment now, which was soon to climax in a heavenly public epiphany, Paul stressed the last judgment to come; and death was only to be abolished at the end of the sequence.

Paul's theology had undergone a new development, away from realized eschatology, and towards future apocalyptic at the time of his writing 1 and 2 Thessalonians and the 'previous letter' to the Corinthians. Paul realized he was in fact vulnerable to the charge of inconsistency which could also imply lack of integrity, and he shows that he is very sensitive about it. His occasional asperity, evasiveness and stridency could arise from his awareness that he had in fact modified certain aspects of his teaching.

The reasons for Paul's emphasizing futurist apocalyptic eschatology to the neglect of realized eschatology may be identified as four pressures which began to be felt in the late 40s and early 50s AD: 1. His desire to include growing numbers of deceased first-generation Christians in the hope. 2. His desire for an 'eschatological reservation' in order to counter the arrogance of over enthusiasm. 3. His adjustment to increasingly perceived present bodily weakness, infirmities, and sufferings, on his own part and on others'. 4. The necessity to strengthen Christians against a possible impending crisis of persecution, by deploying the apocalyptic promises of God to encourage the faithful to endure to the end.

If Paul's own earliest Christian eschatology was predominantly realized, then his presentation of future apocalyptic teaching in 1 and 2 Thessalonians, in the 'previous letter' to the Corinthians, and in 1 Corinthians, marks a radical re-direction in his thinking and teaching. A revised profile of the development of Paul's eschatology is called for.

JSNT 19 (1983), pp. 73-83

APOCALYPTIC VISIONS AND THE EXALTATION OF CHRIST
IN THE LETTER TO THE COLOSSIANS

Christopher Rowland

Recent studies of the false teaching at Colossae have not neglected to
emphasize the significant Jewish component within the position[1]

1.   See the collection of studies in F.O. Francis and W.A. Meeks, *Conflict at
Colossae* (Missoula: Scholars Press, 1972). Of particular importance is Francis's
essay, 'Humility and Angel Worship in Col. 2.18' (reprinted from *ST* 16 [1963],
pp. 109-34; all references are to the version in *Studia Theologica*). See also W.
Foerster, 'Die Irrlehrer des Kolosserbriefes', in *Studia Biblica et Semitica*
(Festschrift T.C. Vriezen; Wageningen: Veeuman, 1966), pp. 71-80 (he notes the
links with apocalyptic passages like *1 En.* 14; see p. 79); N. Kehl, 'Erniedrigung und
Erhöhung in Qumran und Kolossä', *ZKT* 91 (1969), pp. 364-94; M. Smith,
'Observations on Hekaloth Rabbati', in A. Altmann (ed.), *Biblical and Other Studies*
(Cambridge, MA: Harvard University Press, 1963), pp. 142ff.; J. Lähnemann, *Der
Kolosserbrief* (Gütersloh: Gerd Mohn, 1971), pp. 30ff.; E. Schweizer, *Der Brief an
die Kolosser* (Neukirchen: Neukirchener Verlag, 1976), pp. 121-22 (now translated
into English by Andrew Chester, *The Letter to the Colossians* [London: SPCK,
1982], pp. 125-26 and 161-62. References will be to the English translation); A.T.
Lincoln, *Paradise Now and Not Yet* (Cambridge: Cambridge University Press, 1982);
A.J. Bandstra, 'Did the Colossian Errorists need a Mediator?', in R.N. Longenecker
and M.C. Tenney (eds.), *New Dimensions in New Testament Study* (Grand Rapids:
Zondervan, 1978), pp. 329-43 (Bandstra's argument that there exists a polemic
against mediatorial activities in some Jewish works may well apply to *4 Ezra* and
Syriac Baruch; cf. Michael Stone, 'Paradise in 4 Ezra', *JJS* 17 [1966], pp. 85ff., who
notes the moves against speculative activity in *4 Ezra*, but Bandstra fails to take
account of the nature of the angelophany in the *Apocalypse of Abraham* which seems
to point against his thesis; see C. Rowland, *The Open Heaven* [London: SPCK,
1982], pp. 94ff.); and C.A. Evans, 'The Colossian Mystics', *Bib* 63 (1982), pp. 188-
205. There is a collection of Jewish material relevant to a discussion of the Colossian
false teaching in J.J. Gunther, *St Paul's Opponents and their Background* (Leiden:
Brill, 1973), especially pp. 271ff. For earlier discussion of the problem, see E. Percy,

opposed by Paul.[2] The presence of words like new moon and sabbath in Col. 2.16 appears to point to a Jewish influence on the ideas of Paul's opponents. Though Paul never mentions the false teaching in detail, most commentators expect to be able to find various hints from the letter itself concerning the point of view opposed by the apostle. Indeed, this seems to be particularly true of 2.2-19, where a number of allusions help us to piece together the character of the teaching opposed by Paul.[3] The consensus of scholarly opinion argues that the Colossian Christians had been led to believe that their acceptance of Christ as the key to salvation was not necessarily sufficient and that other rites, like circumcision (2.11), the observance of Jewish festivals (2.16), beliefs concerning the angels in heaven and possibly visions of them (2.18) were needed for the complete religious experience. In response to this Paul stressed the Colossians' release from rites and practices which were appropriate to the old aeon (2.14 and 17) and Christ as the locus of the divine character and wisdom (2.3; 2.9 and 19).[4]

Inevitably the question arises whether the religious climate of the area around Colossae in the middle of the first century AD was influenced by Jewish apocalyptic and mystical ideas.[5] An answer to this question

Die Probleme der Kolosser- und Epheserbriefe (Lund: Gleerup, 1946), pp. 140ff.

2. The case for non-Pauline authorship is set out by E. Lohse, *Colossians and Philemon* (Hermeneia; Philadelphia: Fortress Press, 1971), pp. 84-91 and 175-83, and by E.P. Sanders, 'Literary Dependence in Colossians', *JBL* 85 (1966), pp. 28-45 Pauline authorship is assumed in this essay.

3. 2.18 in particular makes it difficult to agree with M.D. Hooker's doubts about the existence of a false teaching at Colossae reflected in her essay, 'Were there False Teachers at Colossae?', in B. Lindars and S. Smalley (ed.), *Christ and Spirit* (Cambridge: Cambridge University Press, 1973), pp. 315-31. On the importance of the early part of ch. 2 for our understanding of the false teaching, see Bandstra, 'Colossian Errorists', pp. 339-40.

4. There was probably no explicit threat to the supremacy of Christ despite Col. 1.15-20; see Evans, 'Colossian Mystics', p. 203, and F. Francis, 'The Christological Argument of Colossians', in J. Jervell and W. Meeks (eds.), *God's Christ and his People* (Oslo: Universitetsforlaget, 1977), p. 193.

5. My approach to apocalyptic and mysticism is entirely that taken in my book (see above, n. 1). When I use the word 'mystical' I use it in the sense of the apprehension of truths which are beyond human reason. If there is any distinction to be made between apocalyptic and mysticism (and I remain to be convinced that there is a substantial difference), it is that the latter may well involve interest in the higher wisdom for its own sake rather than the improvement of the religious and moral life which such knowledge may bring. It is this last feature which is typical of much

would be much facilitated by knowledge of the type of Judaism prevalent in the area. Unfortunately evidence about Judaism in Colossae is
rather sparse, although it is known that there was a thriving Jewish
community in the area.[6] Such evidence as we do possess about the type
of Judaism to be found in this part of Asia Minor points in the direction
either of a form of syncretism[7] or, if Revelation is typical of the religious
outlook of Jews in this area, of a religion in which apocalyptic and
related mystical ideas were an important component. It is the hypothesis
that the latter was the dominant feature of the Colossian false teaching,
and by implication a significant feature of the Jewish spirituality of the
area, that we intend to test here.

The end of the second chapter contains the most explicit references to
the false teaching (vv. 16ff.). In 2.16 we can discern the ethical rigour of
the teaching, with its emphasis on dietary restrictions (cf. vv. 22f.) and
the observance of certain festivals.[8] Such dietary restrictions fit well into
a situation where an interest in visions of the heavenly world was being
encouraged. We know from certain Jewish apocalypses that strict dietary
preparations were often the prerequisite for the receipt of visions (e.g.
Dan. 10.2-3).[9] But even if it be admitted that such rigorous regulations
with regard to food and drink were intimately bound up with apocalyptic spirituality, the question remains whether Colossians does offer evidence that the false teachers at Colossae were claiming visions of heaven
such as we find in certain apocalypses. The answer to this question will
depend much on the way in which we interpret the difficult verse 2.18.

(though not all) of the apocalyptic literature.

6.   For information about Judaism in Asia Minor, see A.T. Kraabel, *Judaism in
Asia Minor in the Imperial Period* (Diss. Harvard, 1968), pp. 125ff., and
S. Johnson, 'Asia Minor and Early Christianity', in J. Neusner (ed.), *Christianity,
Judaism and Other Greco-Roman Cults* (Leiden: Brill, 1975), II, pp. 74ff. On early
Christianity in the area, see U. Müller, *Zur frühchristlichen Theologiegeschichte:
Judenchristentum und Paulinismus in Kleinasien an der Wende vom ersten zum
zweiten Jahrhundert n. Christ* (Gütersloh: Gerd Mohn, 1976).

7.   This is the explanation favoured by Kraabel, *Judaism*, p. 148. The evidence of
Revelation makes it likely that apocalyptic was a significant component of Anatolian
Judaism.

8.   See Lohse, *Colossians*, p. 123.

9.   See Francis, 'Humility', pp. 114ff., and on the later mystical tradition, see
G. Scholem, *Jewish Gnosticism, Merkabah Mysticism and Talmudic Tradition* (New
York: Jewish Theological Seminary of America, 2nd edn, 1965), pp. 103ff. and
Rowland, *Open Heaven*, pp. 228ff.

A translation is offered which will be supported in the following exegetical notes:[10]

> Let no one disqualify you, taking delight in the humility and worship of angels, which he saw on entering (heaven), being puffed up without reason by his carnal mind.

Paul here seems to be warning the Colossians about those who would attempt to distinguish between believers, accepting some and disqualifying others.[11] The basis for disqualification is their delight[12] 'in humility and worship of angels'. Much attention has centred on the meaning of the words *tapeinophrosynē* and *thrēskeia tōn angelōn*, translated by the RSV 'self-abasement' and 'worship of angels'. Some would translate *tapeinophrosynē* 'fasting', following Hermas, Vis. 3.10.6.[13] Thus the questions of food and drink mentioned in Col. 2.16 and the regulations spelt out in 2.21-22 are all part of the *tapeinophrosynē* practised by the false teachers. Such an interpretation seems very attractive in view of the evidence of the context, but there are problems with this interpretation which can only be fully appreciated by reference to the verse as a whole.

F.O. Francis in an important article has rightly pointed out that the preposition *en* in 2.18 is not repeated before the phrase *thrēskeia tōn angelōn*.[14] This may indicate that the genitive *tōn angelōn* stands in the same relationship to *tapeinophrosynē* as it does to *thrēskeia*. The question is whether one should follow most commentators on the passage and take the genitive only with *thrēskeia*, and, what is more, maintain that the genitive is objective rather than subjective. There seem to be no pressing reasons why the genitive should not explain both *tapeinophrosynē* and *thrēskeia*. What Paul would then be referring to would be the activities of the angels in heaven, their humility and their worship. Thus the references to the false teaching would not be fasting by human

10. For a survey of interpretations, see Francis, 'Humility', pp. 109ff.; Lohse, *Colossians*, pp. 117ff.; and Percy, *Probleme*, pp. 137ff. On the entry into heaven in this verse see also Evans, 'Colossian Mystics', p. 196.

11. Following the translation of *katabrabeuetō* adopted by Francis, 'Humility', p. 110.

12. Francis, 'Humility', p. 113; Percy, *Probleme*, p. 146; and Lohse, *Colossians*, p. 118.

13. See Percy, *Probleme*, p. 148; Francis, 'Humility', p. 114; and W. Carr, 'Two Notes on Colossians', *JTS* 24 (1973), pp. 492-500.

14. 'Humility', p. 130.

beings followed by devotion to exalted angelic beings but entirely concerned with the angels in heaven.

The phrase 'humility and worship of angels' does not appear to make much sense until we recognize that there was considerable interest in the apocalyptic literature in the worship of the heavenly court. Indeed, according to *ARN* 23a the angels in heaven practised humility to an excessive degree.[15] The devotions of the heavenly attendants in the divine court are mentioned on several occasions in Revelation, for example, 4.9-10. Thus in talking about the humility and worship of angels Paul was referring to a regular experience of the apocalyptic visionary. What is more, this was something in which the visionary could himself participate.[16] While it may not be correct to say that the worship of angels by men is unknown in Judaism, as some have supposed,[17] there does not seem to be any strong reason for supposing that Paul was dealing with this particular problem in Colossae.

If we take *tōn angelōn* as a subjective genitive explaining both *tapeinophrosynē* and *thrēskeia*, it is easier to make sense of the following relative clause *ha heoraken embateuōn*.[18] There has been considerable debate about the meaning of this sentence, and several commentators have resorted to emendation of the text in order to make sense of it.[19] This course of action seems rather unnecessary, however, as it is not impossible to make sense of the text as it stands.

The problems emerge when we examine the syntax of the relative

15. See H.L. Strack and P. Billerbeck, *Kommentar zum Neuen Testament aus Talmud und Midrasch* (Munich: Beck, 1922), III, p. 629. There are related ideas in *3 En.* 18; 35.1 and 39; *Apoc. Abr.* 17; 4Q Serek Sirot. There is possibly a hint of angelic humility also in Jude 9.

16. See Francis in *Conflict*, pp. 170ff.; Kehl, 'Erniedrigung', pp. 364ff.; Bandstra, 'Colossian Errorists, pp. 331-32; H.W. Kuhn, *Enderwartung und gegenwärtiges Heil* (Göttingen: Vandenhoeck & Ruprecht, 1966); Lincoln, *Paradise*; and Evans, 'Colossian Mystics', p. 196.

17. E.g. Percy, *Probleme*, pp. 149ff. and L. Williams, 'The Cult of Angels at Colossae', *JTS os* 10 (1908–1909), pp. 413-38. The prohibition of address to angels in the Talmud and the command not to worship angels in Rev. 19.10 and 22.8-9 as well as in *Asc. Isa.* 7.21, may indicate that this was a much more widespread problem than is often supposed. See e.g. W. Lueken, *Michael* (Göttingen: Vandenhoeck & Ruprecht, 1898), pp. 4ff., and P. Schäfer, *Rivalität zwischen Engeln und Menschen* (Berlin: de Gruyter, 1975), pp. 67ff.

18. See Francis, *Conflict*, pp. 179-80; Carr, 'Two Notes', p. 500; and Evans, 'Colossian Mystics', p. 197.

19. See Lohse, *Colossians*, p. 119.

clause. First of all, it is by no means clear what the antecedent of the neuter plural relative is. Secondly, the participle *embateuōn* is normally intransitive, and as a result it is difficult to see how the clause *ha heoraken* can be dependent on that verb, as is presupposed, for example, by the RSV translation. We would have expected a preposition before the relative clause if it were governed by the participle. Thus it seems preferable to suppose that the antecedent of the relative must be the phrase *tapeinophrosynē kai thrēskeia tōn angelōn*.

Parallels have been offered where the verb *embateuein* is used in connection with entry into the shrine after initiation into the mysteries.[20] The problem with this is that it does not appear to make sense of other allusions in Colossians, which give little or no indication of being concerned with the mystery-rites. Accordingly, one has to ask whether F.O. Francis's suggestion, namely, that we have here a reference to the entry of the visionary into the heavenly world for his visions, does not make better sense.[21] While it cannot be demonstrated that *embateuein* is used as a technical term for describing a heavenly ascent, there are occasional examples of the apocalyptic visionary describing his ascent into heaven as an 'entry' into the world above. In *1 En.* 14.9 Enoch speaks of entering heaven after he has been borne thither by the winds of heaven.[22]

There have been two main objections to an interpretation of 2.18 which sees it as a reference to a heavenly ascent and a vision of the humility and worshipful attitudes of the angels in heaven. First, it has to be recognized that in supposing that the nouns *tapeinophrosynē* and *thrēskeia tōn angelōn* are the antecedents of the relative, we have to assume that in this case the relative has been placed in the neuter despite the fact that the antecedents would have led us to expect a feminine plural. This is not an insuperable difficulty, however. A neuter relative following feminine nouns is to be found also in 2.16, though it has to be

20. E.g. M. Dibelius, 'Die Isisweihe bei Apuleius und verwandte Initiations-Riten', in *Botschaft und Geschichte* (Tübingen: Mohr [Siebeck], 1956), pp. 55ff.; and S. Lyonnet, 'L'Epître aux Colossiens (Col. ii.18) et les mystères d'Apollon Clarien', *Bib* 43 (1962), pp. 417-35; but see the criticism of Francis, 'Humility', pp. 120-21 and Percy, *Probleme*, pp. 170ff.

21. Lohse, *Colossians*, p. 118 n. 33, criticizes Francis; but see further support for Francis's approach in Evans, 'Colossian Mystics', p. 198, Schweitzer, *Colossians*, p. 161, and Francis, *Conflict*, pp. 197ff.

22. Other evidence in Francis, 'Humility', pp. 122-23, Evans, 'Colossian Mystics', p. 198 n. 45, and Schweizer, *Colossians*, p. 124.

said that the list does include one neuter noun. A closer parallel is to be found in Col. 3.6, where the neuter plural relative follows a string of feminine nouns.[23] The use of the neuter relative plural would thus refer to the totality of the actions performed by the angels, which the visionary saw during his ascent to heaven.[24]

The second criticism of this solution is more serious. When taken in isolation from its surrounding context, there is every reason to suppose that *tōn angelōn* should be taken as a subjective genitive. The problem comes when we turn to 2.23 and find there the words *en ethelothrēskeia kai tapeinophrosynē kai apheidia sōmatos*. Clearly the words are being used of the activities of men and women and not angels; what is more, they seem to be used in a negative sense.[25] It might appear, therefore, in the light of 2.23 that it would be more natural to interpret the similar terms in 2.18 as referring to devotions performed by human beings and not angels. A difference in the personnel referred to in 2.18 and 23 need not be a difficulty, if we assume that there may have been a tendency for the Colossian teachers to have imitated the behaviour of the angels which they had seen in their visions. Evidence from the Qumran scrolls suggests that there was a close link between the activities of the community and the angels. Just as the angels in heaven had their allotted place in the heavenly liturgy (4Q Serek Sirot ha-Sabbat; cf. *2 En.* 20.3-4), so also the community is given a position corresponding to God's everlasting purposes (1QS 2.22-23; 6.8ff. and 5.23ff.).[26]

23. See further C.F.D. Moule, *An Idiom Book of New Testament Greek* (Cambridge: Cambridge University Press, 2nd edn, 1959), p. 130.

24. The interpretation adopted here has the advantage of maintaining a similar setting for both the humble acts and the worship of the angels in heaven. It is difficult to see how the humility could be part of the things seen when entering heaven unless it was an action performed by angels. Francis's comment, 'Humility', p. 130 ('Instruction in humility for the purpose of obtaining visions is itself the subject of visions'), is not really consistent with the apocalyptic material he examines. It makes better sense of the section to regard the humility not as a reference to the ritual preparation for visions performed by men (e.g. fasting) but as part of what was seen by the visionary. See also Evans, 'Colossian Mystics', pp. 195-96.

25. Those who note the problem posed by 2.23 include Lohse, *Colossians*, p. 119 n. 38, Schweitzer, *Colossians*, pp. 124-25, and R.P. Martin, *Colossians: The Church's Lord and the Christian's Liberty* (Exeter: Paternoster Press, 1972), p. 92. See further on this Francis, *Conflict*, pp. 181-82, and Lincoln, *Paradise*.

26. On the Qumran material, see J. Strugnell, 'An Angelic Liturgy at Qumran', *VTSup* 7 (1960), pp. 318ff., Kehl, 'Erniedrigung', pp. 371ff., H.W. Kuhn, 'Enderwartung', and D.E. Aune, *The Cultic Setting of Realized Eschatology in Early*

Because the Qumran community's life was itself an extension of the life of heaven, we may expect that the practice of heaven would have impinged on their common life. Likewise Paul's opponents in Colossae may have considered that the activities of the angels were not merely of interest to the visionary but important as an example for the righteous to imitate.[27] Thus the use of the same words in vv. 18 and 23 to speak of the activities of the angels in heaven and the behaviour of certain members of the Colossian church is entirely understandable, if we appreciate that the communion with the angels which the false teachers enjoyed had persuaded them to copy the servile attitudes of the angels in their lives as a true reflection on earth of the will of God.

The Colossian false teaching has two major components: the detailed preparations, which were necessary to receive visions (2.16), and the visions themselves (2.18), which offered the recipients a pattern of existence which could be extended to everyday life (2.23). The problem with the teaching is its insistence on further rites and experiences in order to embrace the fulness of religion. It is this aspect which Paul finds so unhealthy; he is not opposed to visions in any way, as 2 Cor. 12.2ff. makes plain. What appears to have worried him was that the Colossians were not interested in Christ as the centre of their religious experience, but in the activities of the angels as a pattern for living which might detract from the example of Christ. It is in this sense only that there was a threat to the position of Christ; there was probably no specifically heterodox christology at Colossae (cf. Heb. 1–3).[28]

In Paul's view the new life in Christ already qualified believers to share the glory of heaven, where Christ was seated in glory (2.11 and 3.1). In Col. 1.12 Paul stresses that already the church has the privilege of sharing 'in the inheritance of the saints in light', surely a reference to communion with the angels (cf. 1QS 11.7-8).[29] The point is made most clearly in 3.1, which stresses that the aim of the believers, the direct consequence of his baptism, is the place where Christ is now seated. This means that it is the Christian's responsibility to seek that which is above, the place where the hope for the future has its origin (1.5). The heavenly

Christianity (NovTSup, 28; Leiden: Brill, 1972). Participation by human beings in the heavenly worship can be found at *Apoc. Abr.* 17; *3 En.* 1.12; *T. Job* 48-49; *Asc. Isa.* 7.37 and 9.31ff.

27. See Kehl, 'Erniedrigung', pp. 348ff. and Schweizer, *Colossians*, pp. 159ff.
28. See Francis, 'Christological Argument', p. 193.
29. So also Lohse, *Colossians*, p. 36.

world is open to the believer by virtue of his baptism (2.12).[30] The consequence of Christ's exaltation is the fact that the Christian has the right
to set his mind on that which is above, without any need to resort to
additional practices or beliefs to enable him to have access to that
realm.[31] Additional practices and revelations obviously had the effect of
separating between the brethren (2.18: *mēdeis hymas katabrabeuetō*).
For Paul such a division was totally unacceptable, not only because all
the mysteries of heaven were to be found in Christ,[32] but also because
baptism had enabled *all* believers to participate in the light of the world
above.[33] It was illegitimate, therefore, for the believer to look outside his
relationship with Christ for knowledge of the world above (2.19),[34] as
the very essence of divinity was to be found in his person (2.9).[35]

---

30. Lohse, *Colossians*, pp. 132-33, and see also E. Grässer, 'Kol iii.1-4 als
Beispiel einer Interpretation *secundum homines recipientes*', *ZTK* 64 (1967),
pp. 139-68. Although he is right to point to the significance of the heavenly ascent for
the understanding of this passage (pp. 161-62), this is more likely to have been
derived from Jewish apocalyptic (see Strack–Billerbeck, *Kommentar*, I, pp. 325 and
277, and A.F. Segal, 'Heavenly Ascent in Hellenistic Judaism, Early Christianity and
their Environments', in W. Haase [ed.], *ANRW* II.23.2 [Berlin: de Gruyter, 1980].

31. The promise of resurrection-life as a consequence of baptism in 3.1 and 2.11
is an advance on the view expressed in Rom. 6.5. See further Lohse, *Colossians*,
pp. 103ff. and R.C. Tannehill, *Dying and Rising with Christ* (Berlin: Töpelmann,
1967), especially pp. 47ff.

32. On this verse see Bandstra, 'Colossian Errorists', pp. 339ff. He outlines the
parallels with Jewish apocalyptic literature (e.g. *2 Bar.* 54.13; 44.14 and 48.24) and
argues that this implies that the Colossian teachers did not seek the revelation of
God's mystery in Christ alone. So also Evans, 'Colossian Mystics', p. 203.

33. Lohse, *Colossians*, p. 36.

34. On this verse, see Evans, 'Colossian Mystics', pp. 198-99.

35. There has been much debate over the meaning of 2.9. In the light of recent
trends in the study of Colossians the possibility should not be ruled out that this verse
too may well be best understood in the light of apocalyptic and mystical ideas.

    The phrase *to sōma tēs sarkos* occurs only in Colossians in the whole of the
New Testament. It is used in connection with the reconciliation wrought by God in
Christ in 1.22. In 2.11 it is found after the word *apekdysis* to explicate the meaning of
the circumcision not made with hands, which in turn is linked with the circumcision of
Christ. Paul means by this the fate he (Christ) endured at his death: the stripping off
of the body of flesh. This implies that at this moment he left one realm of being (the
body of flesh) for another (the body of glory) (cf. Phil. 3.21 and see further the
comments of G. Scholem, *Von der mystischen Gestalt der Gottheit* [Zürich: Benziger,
1962], p. 276; and on the anthropomorphic theology of early Judaism see
A. Marmorstein, *The Old Rabbinic Doctrine of God* [London: Jews' College

Publications, 1927], II, pp. 48ff.). The possibility ought to be explored whether Col. 2.9 may presuppose Jewish ideas about the corporeal aspect of God and the identification of this manifestation of the divinity with the risen and glorified Christ (cf. Justin, *Dialogue with Trypho* 114, and A.F. Segal, *Two Powers in Heaven* [Leiden: Brill, 1973]). From this point of view the significance of the presence of the adverb *sōmatikōs* in 2.9 should not be missed. Commentators consider the significance of the adverb either to be a reference to the incarnation (e.g. E. Schweitzer, *sōma*, *TDNT*, VII, p. 1075) or the reality of the divine indwelling (Lohse, *Colossians*, p. 100). It should be noted, however, that in both the other New Testament uses of the adverb (Lk. 3.22 and 1 Tim. 4.8) the physical aspect is to the fore; the word is not used in a transferred sense. We should, therefore, be open to the possibility that this is true of Col. 2.9 also (on this verse see N. Kehl, *Der Christushymnus im Kolosserbrief* [Stuttgart: Kohlhammer, 1967]). One of the main objections to taking the word here as a reference to the incarnation is the present tense *katoikei* (cf. 1.19). But it is the Platonic background which has always been stressed (see e.g. J. Jervell, *Imago Dei* [Göttingen: Vandenhoeck & Ruprecht, 1960], pp. 223-24, and Lohse, *Colossians*, p. 100 n. 48; but note the criticisms of M. Smith, 'The Shape of God and the Humanity of the Gentiles', in J. Neusner [ed.], *Religions in Antiquity* [Supplements to *Numen*, 14; Leiden: Brill, 1968], pp. 315ff. The presence of the fulness of divinity in bodily form may be illustrated from Jewish sources. We know that exalted angels like Jaoel and Metatron had positions of prominence in the heavenly hierarchy because they had God's name dwelling in them (*Apoc. Abr.* 10-11 and *b. Sanh.* 38b). In addition, the Jaoel tradition is part of a much more complicated theophany tradition in which the appearance of God in human form plays a part (see Rowland, *Open Heaven*, pp. 94ff.). The pre-eminence of Christ could easily be stressed by identifying him with the divine *kābōd* appearing in human form (see also S. Kim, *The Origin of Paul's Gospel* (Tübingen: Mohr [Siebeck], 1981). Recent study has suggested that an important strand of Paul's christology may have owed much to this tradition (Kim, *Origin*, pp. 239ff.). By regarding Christ as the human manifestation of God, known in biblical theophanies and angelophanies, the very embodiment of divine fulness, Paul could point away from the bewildering variety of the apocalyptic visions of the heavenly world to a single-minded devotion to the deity embodied in the Risen Christ. Thus he can be said to speak the language of the Colossian apocalyptists but turns their attention away from the paraphernalia of heaven to the central goal of the mystics, the person of the deity enthroned in glory whom Paul identified with Christ (cf. Evans, 'Colossian Mystics, pp. 203ff.).

PAULINE LETTER-FORM AND RHETORIC

JSNT 37 (1989), pp. 87-101

HELLENISTIC LETTER-FORMS
AND THE STRUCTURE OF PHILIPPIANS

Loveday Alexander

It has become axiomatic in recent years that the critical study of the
Pauline letters must take its starting-point from analysis of the formal
epistolary structures of the Hellenistic world. Deissmann's cheerful belief
that Paul writes 'mostly without any careful arrangement, uncon-
strainedly passing from one thing to the other, indeed often jumping',[1] is
now out of fashion. William Doty insisted in 1973 that

> the contemporary emphasis on the formal nature of Paul's letters is an
> important corrective to...older viewpoints [like Deissmann's]...We have
> begun to appreciate the fact that Paul did have a clear sense of the form of
> what he wanted to write.[2]

Moreover, Doty claims,

> The advantages of having such a sense of Pauline forms are manifold: it
> aids in our reconstruction of letters (such as the Corinthian or Philippian
> correspondence) which have been broken up and rearranged in transmis-
> sion; it gives us a means of differentiating authentic from inauthentic
> letters; it gives us important insights into the structure of any particular
> letter, and hence enables interpretation of any part to be related to the
> whole; and it helps us to understand how Paul conceived of his writing
> letters in contrast to other literary modes (p. 29).

The more formal approach described by Doty has come to dominate
Pauline studies over the last twenty years. At first sight, however, it
seems to have little to offer the student of Philippians. True, Hellenistic

---

1.   A. Deissmann, *Paul: A Study in Social and Religious History* (trans.
W.E. Wilson; London: Hodder and Stoughton, 2nd edn, 1927), p. 14.
2.   W. Doty, *Letters in Primitive Christianity* (Philadelphia: Fortress Press,
1973), pp. 27-28.

letter-formulae are easily recognized in the opening and closing sections of the letter. Commentators are agreed that 1.1-2 constitutes a formal opening (sender; addressee; greeting), and that 4.21-23 contains the closing elements of greetings and benediction. Similarly, there is no real dispute that 1.3-11 provides a classic example of a 'Thanksgiving' section and that 1.12, with its 'disclosure-formula ('I want you to know...') marks the transition to the 'body' of the letter. But the 'body' itself—that is, the real business section of the letter, where the apostle takes in hand whatever subjects have caused him to write in the first place—seems not so far to have felt the full benefits of formal analysis based on the structures and formulae of Hellenistic letter-writing. Doty, in the passage already quoted, finds that formal criteria help only towards the dismemberment of the letter, not towards an understanding of the text as it stands. Even the section which most commentators regard as a unity (1.12–3.1a) is severely curtailed in his analysis:[3]

1.12-18	=	formal opening
2.14-18	=	eschatological conclusion
2.19-24	=	travelogue

Craddock[4] tries harder to account for the whole letter in formal terms, but his divisions and headings owe more to topical analysis than to formal parallels with secular letters:

1.12-26	=	autobiographical disclosure
1.27–2.16	=	exhortation for the meanwhile
2.17–3.1a	=	autobiographical disclosure (travel plans)
3.1b–4.9	=	exhortations for the meantime
4.10-20	=	thanksgiving

Roetzel's useful table of Pauline letter-structures[5] simply describes the whole of 1.12–4.19 as 'The body of the letter'.

There are two problems here. On the one hand, formal analysis, if based on external criteria, might be expected to produce something closer to an agreed result. More importantly, formal analysis needs to be seen to be illuminating if it is to make good its claim to be an essential tool in the reading of Paul's letters. In the case of Philippians, it is tempting to conclude that analysis based on secular letter-forms can

---

3.   Doty, *Letters*, p. 43.

4.   F.B. Craddock, *Philippians* (Interpretation; Atlanta: John Knox, 1985).

5.   C.J. Roetzel, *The Letters of Paul* (Atlanta: John Knox, 2nd edn, 1982; London: SCM Press, 2nd edn, 1983), p. 40.

safely be ignored. Perhaps its claims have been overstated. Why not go back to the perfectly adequate (and more consistent) analyses of Philippians found in the more traditional commentaries, which pay little or no attention to secular letter-formulae and simply follow through the topics covered in the letter in order to unlock its internal logical structure?

Thus, it may be argued, there is broad agreement among commentators[6] that in the opening section Paul talks about himself and his circumstances (1.12-26), that he then turns to the situation of the Philippians (1.27–2.18), followed by a section making plans for the travels of himself and his companions (2.19-30). So far, allowing the apostle to follow his own unstructured bent, as Deissmann would have it, presents no problems: the sequence of thought is clear and logical, if not necessarily predictable. As is well known, the crux in the analysis of Philippians comes at 3.1, where Paul, after apparently winding down towards the close, takes off again into a polemical passage combining exhortation with an impassioned warning about false teachings. This is followed by a return to the personal tone of the first section of the letter (4.2ff.), with personal messages and exhortations and thanks for a gift received: the latter appears to be the immediate occasion for the letter. We did not need formal epistolary analysis to tell us that there is a problem here. Concern about the break in thought at 3.1 goes back to the seventeenth century.[7] Many commentators feel that this section cannot be explained even on the Deissmannian principle of Pauline 'jumping': fragments of three earlier letters, it is suggested, have been combined by an inexpert editor to make this illogical hodge-podge. Conversely, more recent studies which argue in favour of the unity of the letter[8] build on

6.   E.g. F.W. Beare, *A Commentary on the Epistle to the Philippians* (BNTC; London: A. & C. Black, 1959); J.-F. Collange, *L'Epître de S. Paul aux Philippiens* (Neuchâtel: Delachaux & Niestlé, 1973; ET A.W. Heathcote; London: Epworth Press, 1979).

7.   J. Gnilka, *Der Philipperbrief* (Freiburg: Herder, 1968), p. 6; cf. M.R. Vincent, *The Epistles to the Philippians and to Philemon* (ICC; Edinburgh: T. & T. Clark, 1979). For summaries of the critical attack on the unity of Philippians, see R.P. Martin, *Philippians* (NCB; London: Marshall, Morgan & Scott, 1976), pp. 10-22, and D.E. Garland, 'The Composition and Unity of Philippians: Some Neglected Literary Factors', *NovT* 27 (1985), p. 141-73.

8.   E.g. Garland, 'Composition'; W.S. Kurz, 'Kenotic Imitation of Paul and of Christ in Philippians 2 and 3', in F.F. Segovia (ed.), *Discipleship in the New Testament* (Philadelphia: Fortress Press, 1975), pp. 103-26.

the observation of structural and thematic links between ch. 2 and ch. 3, not on the *formalia* of ancient letters. On every hand, it seems, traditional exegesis is both able and willing to deal with the structural problems of Philippians without any assistance from the study of secular Hellenistic epistolography.

Two points of interest emerge from this brief survey. First, traditional analysis following topics rather than form seems to cope perfectly well with the first section of the letter (1.12–2.30). Does a *formal* analysis have anything further to offer here? And secondly, it is widely agreed that the text presents us with two structural problems: the illogical 'finally' and change of subject at 3.1, and the late appearance of the thanks at 4.10-20. Traditional analysis responds here by dismembering the text. Can formal analysis contribute anything of value to the debate at these points?

It is the thesis of this paper that the apparent failure of formal analysis here is due to insufficient use of Hellenistic parallels, not to their overuse. A knowledge of Hellenistic letter-forms can fruitfully be brought to bear on the structural problems of Philippians. Properly handled, such an analysis will work in conjunction with logical and thematic study of the text to illuminate the run of thought and the literary links between one section and another. Certain ground rules must be followed, however, if the enterprise is to be convincing.

1. Formal analysis must be based on careful, pragmatic observation of real letters, not too quick to tie itself down to theoretical structures.

2. Formal analysis must take into account the fact that students of ancient letters are constantly revising their findings in the light of fresh data, or fresher and more subtle analysis.

3. It must be recognized that the 'body' of the Hellenistic letter cannot be subject to such rigorous formal analysis as the opening and closing sections of the letter. The 'body' is fluid, flexible, and adaptable to a wide variety of situations and subjects. There are very few rules in this game; but there are patterns to be observed.[9]

---

9. See especially Doty, *Letters*, pp. 34-37; J.L. White, 'Introductory Formulae in the Body of the Pauline Letter', *JBL* 90 (1971), pp. 1-97; *idem, Light from Ancient Letters* (Philadelphia: Fortress Press, 1986), pp. 202-13.

The particular pattern which I believe will help us here is found in a group of 'family letters' most conveniently published in White, *Light from Ancient Letters*, nos. 102-105.[10] Despite the small numbers involved, the group contains sufficient structural parallelism to make it interesting for our purpose. We are not trying to argue that all family letters follow this pattern, simply that the pattern exists. Note that 104A and 104B, written from the same recruit to his mother on the same day, are in different hands, which must mean that at least one letter and probably both were written by professional letter-writers.[11] The employment of letter-writers even for such ephemeral and personal letters clearly increases the likelihood that a semi-formal pattern would be in use. Koskenniemi (pp. 113-14) remarks on the 'formulaic and monotonous' impression conveyed by the family letters of the papyri: originality and individuality are not sought by these writers, and few of the letters take advantage of the occasion to give any kind of travelogue or impression of the places they are visiting.

The simplest way to convey the formal characteristics of these letters is to set out a translation of one of them, the second of Apolinaris's letters to his mother:[12]

A   Apolinaris to Taesis his mother and lady, many greetings.

B   Before everything, I pray that you are in health, and I myself am in health and I am making your obeisance (προσκύνημα) before the gods here.

C   I want you to know, mother (γεινώσκειν σε θέλω, μήτηρ), that I got to Rome all right on the 25th of the month.
     Pachon and I have been assigned to Misenum, but I do not yet know my century, for I had not set off for Misenum when I wrote you this letter.

D   So I beg you, mother, look after yourself. Don't worry about me, for I have come to a good place. You will do well if you

---

10. On 'Family Letters', see White, *Light*, pp. 196-97; H. Koskenniemi, *Studien zur Idee und Phraseologie des griechischen Briefes bis 400 n. Chr.* (Ann. Acad. Sci. Fennicae Ser. B, 102.2; Helsinki: Akateeminen Kirjakauppa, 1956), pp. 104-14. On the soldiers' letters in particular, see J.G. Winter, 'In the Service of Rome: Letters from the Michigan Papyri', *Classical Philology* 22 (1927), pp. 237-56.

11. Winter, 'Service', p. 239.

12. White, *Light*, n. 104B = P.Mich. VIII 491 (my trans.). Date: second century AD.

write me a letter about your welfare (σωτηρία) and that of my brothers and of all your people.

E As for me, if I find anyone I'll write to you. I definitely won't hesitate to write to you.

F Many greetings to (ἀσπάζομαι) my brothers and Apolinaris and his children and Karalas and his children.
Greetings to Ptolemy and Ptolemais and her children and Heraclous [?] and her children. I greet everyone who loves you by name.

G I pray for your well-being.

A: The *address and greeting* follow the normal pattern 'A to B χαίρειν'. Family letters are particularly likely to expand the bare greeting-formula by the addition of a 'familial modifier' (mother, father, brother, sister) and by increasing the fervency of the greeting (πολλὰ χαίρειν, πλεῖστα χαίρειν).[13]

B: *Prayer for the recipients.* The first reaction of this recruit on arrival in Italy is to pay a visit to the appropriate shrine to offer up a prayer for the family at home (cf. 103B:5-6); others record that they are praying to 'all the gods' (104A:4-5); Apion (103A:6-8), in the same position in the letter, records his own thanks to Sarapis 'because he saved me straightaway when I was in danger at sea'. On the combination of the προσκύνημα-formula with the older prayer for health, see Koskenniemi (pp. 130-45).

C: *Reassurance about the sender.* These letters appear to function like the postcard home from the school trip, conveying the minimum of information beyond the essential 'I'm all right, Mum. Arrived safely.' In 102, 103A, 104A, and 104B this is the first topic mentioned, in 103B and 105 it is reversed with topic D.[14] This section can include the conveying of practical information, such as the writer's Roman name (103A:22) or his army posting (103A:24; 104A:22-23; 105:48), but does not necessarily do so: Apolinaris here and in 104A:11-12 spends quite a

13. F.X.J. Exler, *The Form of the Ancient Greek Letter of the Epistolary Papyri* (Chicago: Ares, 1976 [1923]), pp. 62-63; White, *Light*, p. 196.
14. In 103B the writer's health is also mentioned at the close of the προσκύνημα-formula: 'Before all else I pray that you are well, and I myself am well' (103B:3-4).

bit of time telling his mother that he does not yet know whether he will be assigned to. Much more central to the writers' interest is a general reassurance about their own 'welfare' (σωτηρία). This can take quite a general form, as in 104A:5-7 ('I felt it necessary to inform you about my σωτηρία'), or a more specific account of a journey safely accomplished as in 103A:6-10 ('I thank the Lord Sarapis because, when I was in danger at sea, he saved me straightaway. When I got to Misenum I got a *viaticum* from Caesar of three gold pieces and things are fine'). Apolinar here adds the request to his mother 'not to worry'; this is the major theme of letter 102, where Theonas is at pains to disabuse his mother of the idea that a long failure to write must mean that he is seriously ill.

> C1. Here and in 102:2 the use of the '*disclosure-formula*' (I want you to know') marks off this section as the information-bearing focus of the letter. For the use of the disclosure-formula to introduce the main reason for writing at the beginning of the letter-body, see White, *Light*, p. 207 n. 85; this pattern had by the Roman period displaced the Ptolemaic convention of explaining the reason for the letter *after* the body had been written.

D: *Request for reassurance about the recipients*. In return for his news about himself, the writer requests news from home: 'I want to hear good news about you'. Here again the information content is minimal: what the writer wants is reassurance about the welfare (σωτηρία) of a wide circle of family and friends: 'do not hesitate to write about your welfare and my brothers' (104A:12-14); 'I ask you, my lord father, to write me a note first about your health, secondly about that of my brother and sister...' (103A:11-14). In 105 a repeated request for long-delayed news takes precedence over the writer's news about himself (4-11).

E: *Information about the movements of intermediaries*. Ancillary to this exchange of news is a certain amount of information about the movements of potential letter-carriers, and sometimes parcel-carriers: cf. 104A:5-6 'when I found someone who was going in your direction from Cyrene, I felt it necessary to inform you...'; 104A:14-16 'if you do not find anyone coming in my direction, write to Socrates and he'll send it on to me' (further 102:8-9; 103A:21-22; 103B:7-9; 105:5-8, 12-17, 35-37). Functionally speaking, it often seems to be the case that the very writing of the letter depends on the movements of these intermediaries; it is not so much that intermediaries travel in order to carry letters as the reverse. The carrier has his or her own business reasons for travelling (cf. 105:35-37), and the letter is written in order to take advantage of these movements.

F: *Exchange of greetings with third parties.* A sizeable proportion of these short letters is taken up with the exchange of greetings between various third parties at the writer's or the recipient's place of residence: cf. 104A:16-19; 103A:18-20, 25ff.; 103B:14-21; 105:40-46.

G. *Closing wish for health* following a standard formula.

For our purposes, the most significant structural feature of this letter and others like it is the lack of a clear 'body', if by that we mean a business section framed by, and clearly separable from, the exchange of family greetings and news. Put another way, the whole point of these letters—their real 'business'—*is* this exchange of news between the sender and his family. As White says,

> Almost everything which is discussed in the body of family letters is an extension of the correspondents' interest in each others' welfare...There is no isolable message or body apart from the correspondents' interest in each others' welfare (*Light*, p. 197).

Koskenniemi (p. 107) calls these 'Verbindungsbriefe':

> Of greater interest are the letters which do not in the proper sense contain matters concerned with practical life, or in which such matters do not provide the principal reason for writing the letter. There is a considerable crowd of family letters written without any clearly recognizable external motive other than the concern for communication (*die Pflege der Verbindung*) between the members of the family group (Koskenniemi, p. 106; my trans.).

These letters are found most frequently in the third century AD, but traces of the *motif* can be found in the Ptolemaic period, and a number are known from the first and second centuries AD (Koskenniemi, pp. 106-109).

Analysing Philippians along the lines of the pattern found in Apolinaris's letter yields the following schema:

A: Address and greeting: Phil. 1.1-2
B: Prayer for the recipients: Phil. 1.3-11
C: Reassurance about the sender: Phil. 1.12-26
    C1: This is marked by the disclosure-formula ('I want you to know' v. 12) as the main information-bearing focus of the letter.

D: Request for reassurance about the recipients: Phil. 1.27–2.18
E: Information about the movements of intermediaries: Phil. 2.19-30
F: Exchange of greetings with third parties: Phil. 4.21-22
G: Closing wish for health: Phil. 4.23

We have already seen that commentators find a certain difficulty in defining what is the real 'business' of Philippians. Paul's opening reassurances about himself (1.12-26), and his concern for the recipients (1.27 'you...') are naturally taken as preliminaries to the main point. But what is the main point? The 'hymn to Christ' of 2.6-11 is embedded in (and ancillary to) a number of hortatory points being made in parenetic address to the church (1.27–2.18). The dramatic warning of 3.2ff. appears to be an afterthought ('For the rest, my brethren...', 3.1). Practical sections on the movements of church personnel (2.19-30) and thanks for the gift sent to Paul (4.10-20) are interspersed with further disjointed pieces of parenetic advice to the church (4.1-9). What in all this is the real focus of Paul's letter-writing activity? We may be in a better position to understand what is going on here if we accept that Philippians, like the family letters described by White and Koskenniemi, is a 'Verbindungsbrief', adapted and expanded by Paul and employed with the primary purpose of strengthening the 'family' links between the apostle and the Christian congregation in Philippi. To put it another way, in Philippians as in Apolinaris's letter home, the exchange of news and reassurance which takes up the early sections of the letter *is*, initially at least, the letter's real business.

Thus, as in the family letters, Paul's first subject after the thanksgiving section (1.3-11) is himself and his own welfare (σωτηρία, 1.19). As topical analysis has already noticed, the best heading for 1.12-26 is *'About me'*: Paul's first concern is to reassure the Philippians about his present position. It seems clear that the letter is not written to inform the church that Paul is in prison (they know that already) but to reassure them that the situation is 'all right' in three ways: *first*, because 'what has happened to me has really served to advance the Gospel' (1.12-18); *secondly*, because death, if it should come, is not to be feared (1.19-23); and *thirdly*, and slightly contradictorily, because Paul will probably soon be released anyway (1.24-26).

As in the family letters, again, the centrality of this 'reassurance' message is reinforced by the use of the disclosure-formula in 1.12. For the use of this formula in the Pauline letters, see White ('Introductory

Formulae', pp. 93-94). Sanders had earlier shown how, in the longer letters, Paul introduces a succession of major points with this formula: cf. 1 Cor. 10.1; 11.3; 15.1.[15] Philippians only uses this formula once, so it is a fair initial presumption that the point introduced in v. 12 should be taken as part of the central 'business' of the letter, not merely as a conventional framework to some other 'business'. Moreover, as White observes (*Light*, p. 207), by the Roman period the formal opening of the body of the letter, marked by the disclosure-formula, had become the standard position for 'the explicit explanation of the reason for writing'. Formal analysis thus supports Martin's contention that this apparently casual reassurance is really the clue to the functional centre of Paul's thought in Philippians.[16]

After reassuring his converts about his own position, Paul expresses his own need for reassurance about their welfare. The exhortation of ch. 2 actually begins at 1.27 with an implied request for news: 'so that I may hear of you that you stand firm...' This is Paul's equivalent of the requests for family news found in the soldiers' personal letters: the fact that Paul's concern is for spiritual rather than physical welfare does not detract from the former parallel, and is aided rather than the contrary by the fact that the one word σωτηρία (1.28; 2.12) does duty for both.

Paul's attention to the movements of Timothy and Epaphroditus (2.19-30) also fits well into the pattern. These two are his intermediaries for maintaining contact with the church. Timothy at some future date (v. 19) and Epaphroditus immediately (v. 25), since Epaphroditus's illness has necessitated his immediate return. It seems reasonable to suggest, in fact, that it is precisely this practical feature in the situation which provides the clue to the immediate occasion of the letter: since Epaphroditus is on his way to Philippi, Paul, like other correspondents of

15. J.T. Sanders, 'The Transition from Opening Epistolary Thanksgiving to Body in the Letters of the Pauline Corpus', *JBL* 81 (1962), pp. 348-62, esp. pp. 350-51. Cf. White, 'Introductory Formulae', p. 92 and n. 5. White's refinement of Sanders's classification of the formulae so used does not undermine the fundamental correctness of Sanders's observation.

16. Martin (*Philippians*, pp. 28-43) argues, I think correctly, that the 'root error' Paul is seeking to combat in the letter is 'a presentation of the believer's life in terms of triumphalism and present glory', Paul's present humiliating position 'in chains' is therefore at the centre of the debate, and in stating so firmly at the outset of the letter that this position 'has turned out for the advantage of the Gospel' Paul is in effect setting the agenda not only for 1.12-26 but for chs. 2 and 3 as well. See further below.

his time, seizes the opportunity to renew his contact with the church in writing.[17]

So far, then, Apolinaris's letter can be seen to provide a useful framework for understanding the formal structures of Philippians. But we have not yet attempted to tackle the most serious structural problems, which all occur in the second half of the letter. Up to this point, indeed, the use of formal parallels from secular letters has done little more than to confirm the critical view that the original letter consisted of 1.1–3.1a, closed by the greetings section of 4.21-23. It now remains to examine the *cruces* of chs. 3 and 4 to see what light (if any) can be shed on them from the study of Hellenistic letter-forms.

1. 3.1 τὸ λοιπόν. Translated 'finally' in RSV, this phrase appears to suggest that Paul's mind is moving towards the close of the letter at this point. The long exhortation of ch. 3 must then be either an afterthought (on the principle of Pauline 'jumping') or an interpolation placed here by a later redactor. Despite the fact that a similar phrase occurs in 1 Thessalonians two chapters before the end (1 Thess. 4.1), commentators generally assume that the phrase must belong to the closing formulae of the letter. But observation of family letters suggests otherwise. One of the soldiers' letters cited by Winter ('Service', p. 245), contains the phrase λοιπὸν οὖν βλέπε μὴ πίσθῃς: a firm admonition from a father to his errant son, occurring at line 8 of at least 18 (the end of the letter is mutilated).[18] Winter translates as 'in the future, therefore, see to it that you are not persuaded...' We may also compare a letter cited by Deissmann,[19] the ill-spelled 'letter from a prodigal son'. λοιπόν occurs at line 10 of at least 24 (the end of the papyrus is missing) and is translated by Deissmann, 'furthermore'. Negatively, then, parallels from the papyri suggest that the appearance of the phrase at Phil. 3.1 does not necessarily mark the end of the letter.

2. 3.1 χαίρετε. The word could mean either 'rejoice' or 'farewell', and the latter possibility is often felt to strengthen the belief that 3.1 was originally the ending of the letter and that 3.2ff. was added later (cf. e.g.

---

17. I am grateful to students in my University of Sheffield Philippians class for this suggestion.

18. P.Mich. Inventory no. 191, dating from the early second century AD.

19. B.G.U. III 846, cited by Deissmann, *Light from the Ancient East* (ET of 4th German edn, 1922; repr. Grand Rapids: Baker, 1978), p. 176.

Martin, *Philippians*, p. 17). But although χαίρετε in conversation could well mean 'farewell', I know of no case where it is so used *in a letter*. Letters normally use the infinitive χαίρειν rather than the imperative: out of the hundreds of letters analysed in Exler's study, Exler cites 'about thirty' cases (largely from the second and third centuries AD) where the infinitive is replaced by the optative χαίροις or the singular imperative χαῖρε (Exler, *Form*, pp. 35-36, 67-68). No example of χαίρετε is cited. And, more importantly, the place for this verb is not the end of a letter but the beginning where it means 'Greetings'. Exler knows no instances of χαίρειν as a closing salutation (pp. 69-77). Almost certainly, then, Paul is not saying 'farewell' but repeating the exhortation to 'rejoice' which is so much a feature of this letter.

3. The *positioning* of Paul's thanks for the Philippians' gift at 4.10-20 has also been taken to indicate redactional activity. If the conveying of thanks for the gift delivered by Epaphroditus was part of the purpose of the letter, why does it occur so late? One of the soldiers' letters actually provides a useful parallel here. The recalcitrant letter-writer Theonas also has to thank his mother for a present received. This is somewhat grudgingly expressed: the young soldier seems embarrassed at receiving parcels from home and begs his mother 'not to trouble herself' to send more, once in the letter and again in the margin. This letter is incomplete, but the thanks certainly do not come at the beginning, and, when they come, are less than fulsome: 'Don't bother yourself to send me anything, I received the parcels [unknown word] from Heracleides. Dionytas my brother brought me the parcel and I got your letter' (102.7-9). Paul of course had his own ideological reasons for unease at being in receipt of financial support from one of his churches, when he had refused such help from other churches (1 Cor. 9.3-18; 1 Thess. 2.9). Presumably Theonas also had his own reasons for not wanting his mother to send him any more parcels (we shall probably never know what was in them). But the *formal* point is that in neither letter does the 'thanks' section come at the beginning, and that neither Paul nor Theonas formally thanks the donor at all. Formally, therefore, there is no need to suspect this section of Philippians of being misplaced or mutilated. In fact the critical unease with Paul's apparent lack of courtesy here may well have arisen not from the study of ancient letter-forms but from unconscious adaptation to the conventional epistolary courtesy of our own day, where 'Thank you...' is a common formula for the beginning of a letter-body.

4. The 'Joy Expression' of 4.10 has been thought to belong more properly to the opening of a letter-body: as White says:

> Since expressions of joy usually introduce the body of the letter, the presence of such a formula in Phil. 4.10 supports Robert Funk's proposal that 'this may...be an independent letter, now truncated' (White, 'Introductory Formulae', p. 95).

For more detailed discussion of this type of expression, see Koskenniemi (pp. 75-77); Koskenniemi does not actually say anything here about the normal position of these expressions. In 1986, however, White announced that his views on this had changed:

> More recently, Nils Dahl convinced me that such phrases...tend to maintain contact between correspondents, which is more characteristic of the opening and closing of the letter (White, *Light*, p. 201).

It may be simpler just to stay with Koskenniemi's observation that an expression of joy is the normal accompaniment to the receipt of a letter, while the direct expression of thanks was not the normal custom (p. 77). Its position, then, would depend on the point in the letter at which the receipt of a letter (or gift) is mentioned. In any case, we no longer need to accept that the use of this formula at 4.10 indicates that this verse originally stood at the head of a separate letter.

Negatively, then, the *formalia* of Hellenistic letters give us no warrant for the dismembering of Philippians. We are left with the thematic argument that there is a major break in subject-matter and tone at 3.1b, and to deal with that we have to look further afield. Recent studies have demonstrated that this 'break' is by no means so clear and incontrovertible as earlier commentators believed. Both Kurz (n. 8 above) and Garland (n. 7 above) have pointed out the strong thematic links between ch. 2 and ch. 3. The centrality of humiliation and suffering in the Christ-hymn of ch. 2 is the key to the downward and upward movement of ch. 3, where Paul's own inward and outward *agon* mirrors the pattern exhibited by the hymn. As Martin's analysis shows (n. 16 above), this double pattern also provides the essential key to understanding the reassurances of ch. 1: at the deepest level, the reason why it is 'all right' that Paul is in prison is that this apparently humiliating (not to say dangerous) position brings him into closer identification with the sufferings of Christ. Paul's call to the Philippians to imitate his own example in 3.17 is thus not essentially different from the call of 1 Cor. 1.1: 'Be imitators of me, as I am of Christ' (*pace* Martin, *ad loc.*). Paul's converts are called to follow the pattern of voluntary humiliation exhibited in the Christ-hymn not only in encountering persecution (1.27-30) but also, and perhaps more immediately, in their relationships with one another (2.1-5; 4.2-3).

It is immediately clear that the formal pattern of the familiar letters, moving from reassurance about the safety of the author to a request for good news about the welfare of the recipients, cannot serve as more than a launching-pad for this deeper level of exhortation. With the heightened, sermonic tone of ch. 3 Paul breaks out beyond the constraints of secular letter-forms: a predictable 'family' letter develops into a 'sermon-at-a-distance', a sample perhaps of the sermon Paul would have liked to preach to the Philippians if he were present with them (2.12) (though 2 Cor. 10.10-11 hints that Paul was perhaps better at doing this sort of thing on paper than face-to-face). Nevertheless I believe that we have no better guide to the formal patterns which underlie Philippians than the unpretentious structures of the family letters. The apostle's use of such a structure is itself of some social significance in view of the well-documented propensity of the early Christian groups to regard themselves as 'families' or households, and of the liberal usage of fictive kinship terms like 'brother'. If the primary function of such letters in secular society was the reinforcement of family ties, the same may well be true of at least some Christian letters. Moreover, if this is the letter's primary function, it relieves us of the need to posit some major heresy or conflict within the church as the main reason for writing; the admonition and warnings can assume a more subordinate role in the letter plan. But Philippians also vividly illustrates how, in Paul's hands, a 'family' letter could transform itself into a homily (ch. 3), and back again (ch. 4).

What, in conclusion, of the rival claims of formal analysis, based on secular parallels, versus thematic analysis based on the internal logic of Paul's thought? It has been our intention to suggest a reading of the letter which does justice to both. Formal analysis provides an indispensable framework for understanding the progression of thought in chs. 1 and 2, and in clarifying the status of disputed passages in chs. 3 and 4. The study of Hellenistic letter-formulae signals the centrality of 1.12 to the main message of the letter, marked by the disclosure-formula. But that simple message of reassurance, prompted perhaps by the practical need to take advantage of Epaphroditus's return, is developed by Paul at successively deeper levels, not as a logical argument but following a natural train of thought suggested, at least in part, by the normal conventionalities of the family letter. The centrality of 1.12 thus ties in with observations of a deep unity of thought between ch. 2 and ch. 3 which in turn confirms that the decision to dismember Philippians has been premature.

JSNT 31 (1987), pp. 73-93

MIRROR-READING A POLEMICAL LETTER:
GALATIANS AS A TEST CASE

John M.G. Barclay

1. *Introduction*

I recently heard Professor Christopher Evans describe the New
Testament as 'a bad-tempered book'. He was alluding to the fact that an
extraordinarily high percentage of the documents in the New Testament
are steeped in polemics, arguing with opponents (real or imagined) who
were perceived to be an external or internal threat to the writer's
Christian community. One has only to think of Matthean attacks on the
Pharisees, Johannine polemic against 'the Jews' or the schismatics, and
Petrine abuse of 'the dogs who turn back to their own vomit' to realize
the extent of the New Testament's 'bad temper'; and that is without
considering Paul, who is, perhaps, the most belligerent of them all.

If we are to understand such polemics, we must make every effort to
clarify the origin and nature of the relevant dispute; and an indispensable
ingredient of that effort will be the attempt to reconstruct the attitudes
and arguments of the other side in the debate. However much we may
be predisposed to *agree* with the New Testament authors' arguments,
we will not *understand* their real import until we have critically
reconstructed the main issues in the dispute and allowed ourselves to
enter into the debate from *both* sides. But here we run up against a
formidable obstacle. In most cases we have no independent witness to
the arguments of those under attack in the New Testament; our only
access to their thoughts and identities is via the very documents which
oppose them. Hence the necessity for one of the most difficult and
delicate of all New Testament critical methods: we must use the text
which answers the opponents as a *mirror* in which we can see reflected
the people and the arguments under attack. Like most New Testament

methods, such mirror-reading is both essential and extremely problematic, and it is to some of the problems and possible solutions that I want to address myself in this article.

In what follows I will discuss mirror-reading almost entirely in relation to Galatians. One could apply the same questions and observations to any polemical part of the New Testament, but I choose Galatians partly because it has been the focus of my study for a few years and partly because it provides an excellent test case for my present exercise. Here is Paul at his most polemical, thoroughly involved in extensive argument against opponents. And Galatians itself is our only reliable source of evidence for what the opponents were saying and doing in Galatia. (Acts may, or may not, help us when it comes to Jerusalem, but it says nothing about Paul's disputes in Galatia.) We must therefore address ourselves to the general problems involved in mirror-reading Galatians and the specific pitfalls which await scholars, and then work our way towards a methodology which will help us mirror-read the text with care and accuracy.

2. *The Problems*

Let us consider first some of the general problems which we face in mirror-reading a letter like Galatians. Using different, but equally appropriate, imagery, Morna Hooker has described our problems in deducing the nature of the 'false teaching' under attack in Colossians as 'an extremely difficult task, as prone to misinterpretation as the incidental overhearing of one end of a telephone conversation'.[1] We are all familiar with the problems here: it is so easy to jump to conclusions about what the conversation is about and, once we have an idea fixed in our minds, we misinterpret all the rest of the conversation. But there are three features of the conversation in Galatians which add even more to our difficulties.

1. In the first place, Paul is not directly addressing the opponents in Galatians, but he is talking to the Galatians about the opponents. This means that it is not just a question of trying to piece together what is being said at the other end of the telephone, but of listening in to one side of a dialogue (between Paul and the Galatians) about a third party

---

1.   M.D. Hooker, 'Were There False Teachers in Colossae?', in *Christ and Spirit in the New Testament: Essays in Honour of C.F.D. Moule* (ed. B. Lindars and S.S. Smalley; Cambridge: Cambridge University Press, 1973), p. 315.

(the opponents). Since Paul considers that the Galatians are being 'bewitched' by the persuasion of his opponents (3.1), and since the Galatians are turning all too quickly to the 'other gospel' (1.6), it may be fair to conclude that, generally speaking, in answering the Galatians Paul is in fact countering the opponents themselves and their message. But there are also points in the letter when Paul is manifestly attempting to prise the Galatians away from the opponents, so that what he says to the Galatians could not be read as a direct response to the opponents. For instance, in 5.3, Paul warns the Galatians that everyone who gets himself circumcised will be obliged to keep the whole law. Walther Schmithals leaps on this verse (together with 6.13) to argue that *the opponents* were unaware of the connection between circumcision and Torah-observance;[2] but Paul is instructing the Galatians, not the opponents! Robert Jewett and others consider that, although the opponents knew very well that circumcision involved keeping the whole law, the fact that Paul has to tell the Galatians this fact in 5.3 indicates that the opponents had craftily refrained from passing on this information.[3] But again this is a shaky assumption; the opponents may have made very clear the duties arising out of circumcision, but Paul may nevertheless feel it necessary to hammer home their full unpalatable implications. In other words, the Galatians may be not so much *ignorant as naive*. We must remember that Paul is not directly responding to the opponents' message, but responding to its effects on the confused Christians in Galatia.

2. The second point to remember is that this is no calm and radical conversation that we are overhearing, but a fierce piece of polemic in which Paul feels his whole identity and mission are threatened and there-fore responds with all the rhetorical and theological powers at his command. We hear him not just 'talking' but 'shouting', letting fly with abusive remarks about the Galatians (as credulous fools, 3.1-3) and the opponents (as cowards, fit only for castration, 6.12; 5.12). Jost Eckert and Franz Mussner have done well to highlight this aspect of the letter and to point out how much more difficult this makes it to reconstruct

---

2.   W. Schmithals, *Paul and the Gnostics* (ET Nashville: Abingdon Press, 1972), pp. 32-33; the argument is repeated and expanded in 'Judaisten in Galatien?', *ZNW* 74 (1983), pp. 51-57.

3.   R. Jewett, 'The Agitators and the Galatian Congregation', *NTS* 17 (1970–71), pp. 200-202; cf. E.P. Sanders, *Paul, The Law, and the Jewish People* (Philadelphia: Fortress Press, 1983), p. 29.

what the opponents were really like.[4] We should never underestimate the distorting effects of polemic, particularly in a case like this, where Paul is going out of his way to show up his opponents in the worst possible light, with the hope of weaning the Galatians away from them. We must take into account, then, that Paul is likely to caricature his opponents, especially in describing their motivation: were they really *compelling* the Galatians to be circumcised? And was it really *only* in order to avoid persecution for the cross of Christ (6.12)? I suspect that Jewett has taken these charges too seriously when he proposes that the opponents are acting under the pressure of Judean Zealots;[5] and I am pretty sure that Schmithals has been far too gullible in taking at face value Paul's accusation in 6.13 that the opponents (or those who get circumcised) do not themselves keep the law.[6] This is not to say that Paul could have *wholly* misrepresented his opponents and their message. If he was attempting to persuade the Galatians to abandon the 'other gospel', what he says about it must have been both recognizable and plausible in their ears. Thus the letter is likely to reflect fairly accurately what Paul saw to be the main points at issue; but his statements about the character and motivation of his opponents should be taken with a very large pinch of salt.

It is worth mentioning in this connection another possibility which has been raised by some scholars, namely that Paul may have seriously misunderstood his opponents. This is an essential assumption for Schmithal's case that Paul was actually entertaining Gnostics unawares,[7] and Willi Marxsen made it a central point in his interpretation of the letter.[8] One cannot, of course, discount this possibility altogether, but one must also face its implications. If Galatians is our only evidence for

4.   J. Eckert, *Die urchristliche Verkündigung im Streit zwischen Paulus und seinen Gegnern nach dem Galaterbrief* (Regensburg: Pustet, 1971), pp. 22-26 and 234-36; F. Mussner, *Der Galaterbrief* (HTKNT, 9; Freiburg: Herder, 1974), pp. 27-28.

5.   'The Agitators and the Galatian Congregation', pp. 203-206.

6.   *Paul and the Gnostics*, pp. 33-34 and n. 51 (wrongly claiming support from Schlier and Lightfoot).

7.   See *Paul and the Gnostics*, pp. 18, 47 n. 98, 52 n. 110 and 54 n. 125; P. Vielhauer sharply criticizes Schmithals on this point (*Geschichte der urchristlichen Literatur: Einleitung in das Neue Testament, die Apokryphen und die Apostolischen Väter* [Berlin: de Gruyter, 1975], p. 121).

8.   *Introduction to the New Testament* (ET Oxford: Basil Blackwell, 1968), pp. 50-58.

what the opponents believed, and if, in writing Galatians, Paul laboured under a major misapprehension about them, our search for the real opponents must be abortive. It is one thing to say that Paul has caricatured his opponents: handled cautiously, the text could still yield useful information about them. It is quite another thing to say that despite the whole of Gal. 2.15–5.12 the opponents had no interest in the Torah;[9] that totally destroys our confidence in the only evidence we have. Of course we do not know anything about Paul's sources of information, and we cannot be sure how much he knew about events in Galatia or their true rationale. But we do know he had been there at least once (4.13), and the confidence with which he speaks about their 'change of course' probably indicates a reasonable amount of information.

3. A third complicating factor lies in the linguistic problem of knowing only one partner in a particular conversation. Since the meaning of all statements is, to a large extent, conditioned by their accepted associations within a particular language community, it is especially hard to interpret statements in isolation from their historical and linguistic contexts. In the case of Galatians, while we know a little about one partner in the dialogue, Paul, and can compare the meanings he attaches to similar statements in other contexts, his ultimate conversation partners, the opponents, are unknown to us. The very statements which most directly relate to them (and which we would like to use in order to gain information about them) are also the ones whose precise meaning is determined by the particular interchange between them and Paul. Thus a verse such as 1.10 ('am I now pleasing men or God?') remains obscure until we can hypothesize the other end of the dialogue, and yet it is also among the very verses we need to use in order to reconstruct that dialogue. Such circularity is as inevitable as it is frustrating and highlights the hermeneutical problems inherent in this mirror-reading exercise.[10]

Before we go into detail about the specific pitfalls which lie in wait for the unwary scholar, it may be helpful to offer a comparison which illustrates the difficulties of mirror-reading polemical documents like Galatians. At his enthronement as Bishop of Durham in September 1984, David Jenkins delivered a famous sermon which concluded with a

9. This is the weakest part of Schmithals's thesis, renounced even by those who follow his interpretation in other respects.

10. I owe the general point here to my colleague, John Riches: see the article by A. Millar and J.K. Riches, 'Interpretation: A Theoretical Perspective and Some Applications', *Numen* 28 (1981), pp. 29-53.

number of pointed remarks about the British miners' strike. At that point both sides in the dispute seemed to be intransigent—the miners under Arthur Scargill refusing to allow that more than the totally exhausted pits be closed, and the Coal Board, led by its American-born and tough-minded Chairman Ian MacGregor, insisting on large-scale pit closures. The Government were giving tacit support to the Coal Board, not least in providing massive resources of police to prevent miners' pickets travelling around the country. Jenkins's sermon instantly hit the headlines because he criticized the Government and referred to Ian MacGregor as an 'elderly imported American'. A few days later, the Secretary of State for Energy, Peter Walker, wrote a reply to Jenkins which was published in *The Times*.[11] It occurred to me to wonder how accurately Walker had answered Jenkins's arguments and, with the present methodological question in mind, how well we would do in reconstructing Jenkins's sermon on the basis of Walker's reply alone. Having obtained the full text of Jenkins's sermon I was able to run the experiment, with the following results. Taking Walker's letter, we would know that Jenkins had said that the miners should not be defeated, had implied that the Government wanted to defeat them, had pointed out the problems of a pit-community if the pit closes down, and had made some derogatory remarks about Mr MacGregor (although, interestingly, we would not know about his specific reference to the 'elderly imported American' or his suggestion that MacGregor should resign). Since Walker gives a lengthy exposition of the Government's concern for the coal industry, we might suppose that Jenkins had cited some detailed statistics to show the Government's neglect of miners. How does this compare with what Jenkins actually said in his sermon? The most strik-ing feature of the comparison is that Jenkins's comments on the miners' strike take up less than a quarter of his sermon, so that from Walker's reply alone, one would be totally ignorant of three-quarters of the Bishop's total message. Moreover, although we were right in deducing some of the content of Jenkins's remarks, Walker's reply gave us no hint that Jenkins had also said there should be no victory for the miners on their present terms, that Arthur Scargill should climb down from his absolute demands, and that criticisms could be made of the Government's use of police and the complacent attitude of society as a

11. Jenkins's enthronement sermon was delivered at Durham Cathedral on September 21, 1984. Peter Walker's letter was printed in *The Times* on September 25, 1984.

whole. While Jenkins made specific suggestions about Mr MacGregor which Walker did not pick up, he did not make detailed allegations about the Government's economic record as we might have supposed from Walker's letter. Thus this polemical reply turns out to be a response to a very limited range of issues. It takes particular care to rebut allegations which bear on the personal responsibility of the writer (as Secretary of State for Energy); and it tends to polarize the issues, playing down points on which the two antagonists actually agree. And all this in a setting where the respondent had full access to the facts of the case (he had clearly read Jenkins's sermon) and was obliged to conduct his argument with reason and restraint in an effort to win over sceptical readers of *The Times* like me!

If this situation is at all analogous to Galatians, it may be instructive. I realize there are important points of difference, which mostly induce one to have less confidence in the value of Paul's letter as accurate evidence about his opponents than one can attribute to Walker's letter. It does suggest, however, that there are many aspects of the opponents' message that we can know nothing about because Paul chose not to reply to them. There may also have been many points on which Paul and his opponents agreed but which are submerged by the polarizing effect of his polemic. Moreover, on the analogy of Walker's detailed personal defence, we must acknowledge the possibility that Paul's lengthy self-defence in Galatians 1–2 may not be a reply to a number of specific allegations (as is usually assumed), but may simply pick up almost incidental remarks about his personal credentials.

For all these reasons, the mirror we are trying to use may not be as smooth and clear as we would like. We have to reckon with the possibility that its image is distorted and hazy. Now we see 'through a glass darkly'; and unfortunately we can entertain no hopes of meeting Paul's opponents face to face!

3. *The Pitfalls*

Thus far we have considered some of the major problems which plague any attempt to mirror-read a polemical letter like Galatians. We can now turn to look in more detail at some of the recent attempts to mirror-read Galatians which exemplify the dangerous pitfalls in such an enterprise. Four dangers are particularly noticeable in this regard:

1. The first we may call the danger of *undue selectivity*. In attempting

to discern the opponents' message from the text of Galatians we have got to make some decisions as to which of Paul's statements are particularly revealing for our purpose. Tyson, who addresses himself to the methodological issues more fully than most, confines his search in Galatians to Paul's defensive statements, where Paul answers the opponents' accusations.[12] But this is surely unduly restricting, since much, perhaps most, of the opponents' message may have been entirely free of accusation against Paul; it is interesting that Tyson can make little of the arguments about Abraham and Scripture in Galatians 3–4, although here, if anywhere, Paul seems to be replying to his opponents' arguments.[13] Mussner follows a slightly different tack, isolating possible slogans and objections emanating from the opponents and now reflected in Galatians.[14] Again, while this may be of some help, we have surely got to end up with a reconstruction which can explain the whole letter as, in some sense, a response to the crisis brought about by the opponents. The problem of undue selectivity is highlighted even further by those scholars who read the letter entirely differently. Schmithals dismisses all of Galatians 3–4 as current 'topoi' in Paul's debate with Jews, while the real character of the opponents is revealed in Galatians 5–6, where it can be seen that Paul is responding to pneumatic and libertine Gnostics.[15] We clearly need some criteria by which we can judge which are the most revealing of Paul's statements, while also taking seriously the need to provide an explanation for the entire letter.

2. The second pitfall is the danger of *over-interpretation*. In a polemical letter like this we are inclined to imagine that every statement by Paul is a rebuttal of an equally vigorous counter-statement by his opponents. But a moment's reflection will reveal that this need not be the case at all. In 5.11 Paul raises a forceful question: 'But if I, brethren, still preach circumcision, why am I still persecuted?' We are inclined to

12. J.B. Tyson, 'Paul's Opponents in Galatia', *NovT* 10 (1968), pp. 241-54.

13. This has been plausibly argued by C.K. Barrett, 'The Allegory of Abraham, Sarah and Hagar in the Argument of Galatians', in *Rechtfertigung* (Festschrift E. Käsemann; ed. W. Pöhlmann, J. Friedrich and P. Stuhlmacher; Tübingen: Mohr [Siebeck], 1976), pp. 1-16. See also J.L. Martyn, 'A Law-Observant Mission to Gentiles: The Background of Galatians', *SJT* 38 (1985), pp. 317-23.

14. *Der Galaterbrief*, p. 13, listing 'Schlagworte' and 'Einwände'.

15. *Paul and the Gnostics*, pp. 41-43, 46-55; because Paul's exhortation is directed against 'ecstatic licentiousness', 'it is sufficiently clear that people in Galatia were preaching circumcision but for the rest were thinking and living in libertine rather than legalistic fashion' (p. 52).

mirror-read this as a reflection of a criticism by Paul's opponents, who *accused him* of still preaching circumcision.[16] But it could also be no more than a simple contrast between Paul and his opponents, reminding the Galatians that he, Paul, is in a totally different category from them; in this case *no explicit accusation* need be posited. Or we could even read this verse, as Peder Borgen has suggested, as Paul's reply to a claim made by the intruders in Galatia who *saw themselves as Paul's allies* and were pleased to show how much they were in accord by implying that he, like them, circumcised his converts.[17] Indeed, although I will call them 'opponents' all the way through this article, we must bear in mind the possibility that they did not see themselves in opposition to Paul. It is quite possible for Paul (or anyone else) to count as his foes those who thought they were supporting him!

The same dangers of over-interpretation bedevil the use of other parts of the letter. Because Paul claims he was not dependent on the Jerusalem authorities or any other men in Galatians 1–2, Schmithals jumps to the conclusion that he was being explicitly *accused* of such dependence, and that the only people who would voice such far-reaching accusations would be Gnostics.[18] But again, there are a number of other possible explanations for Paul's line of argument in Galatians 1–2 which do not require one to posit any such Gnostic accusations.[19] Or take Paul's argument about being children of Abraham in Galatians 3; Ropes made a quite unnecessary assumption when he took this to be directed against Gentiles who denied the value of Abraham and the

16. See e.g. F.F. Bruce, *The Epistle to the Galatians: A Commentary on the Greek Text* (Exeter: Paternoster Press, 1982), pp. 236-37; compare the more cautious approach by H.D. Betz, *Galatians: A Commentary on Paul's Letter to the Churches in Galatia* (Hermeneia; Philadelphia: Fortress Press, 1979), pp. 268-69.

17. P. Borgen's interesting thesis is set out in two articles: 'Observations on the theme "Paul and Philo": Paul's Preaching of Circumcision in Galatia (Gal. 5.11)', in *Die Paulinische Literatur und Theologie* (ed. S. Pedersen; Arhus: Aros, 1980), pp. 85-102; and 'Paul Preaches Circumcision and Pleases Men', in *Paul and Paulinism: Essays in honour of C.K. Barrett* (ed. M.D. Hooker and S.G. Wilson; London: SPCK, 1982), pp. 37-46. A similar argument is put forth by G. Howard in *Paul: Crisis in Galatia. A Study in Early Christian Theology* (Cambridge: Cambridge University Press, 1979), pp. 7-11.

18. *Paul and the Gnostics*, pp. 13-32.

19. See the discussion of this passage by J.D.G. Dunn, 'The Relationship between Paul and Jerusalem according to Galatians 1 and 2', *NTS* 28 (1982), pp. 461-78.

Jewish tradition.[20] And how should we interpret Paul's commands in the ethical section 5.13–6.10? If Paul warns the Galatians about immorality and drunkenness in his list of 'the works of the flesh', need we assume, with Lütgert and Schmithals, that there were at least some Galatians Christians who indulged in such libertine excesses in a wild pneumatic license?[21] Or if he encourages those who live by the Spirit to walk in the Spirit, need we take this, with Jewett, as an indication that the Galatians consciously denied the significance of any earthly behaviour?[22] In all these cases the scholars concerned would have done well to reflect on the ambiguities of mirror-reading and to take into account a range of other less extreme possibilities.

3. A third pitfall awaits those who are guilty of *mishandling polemics*. I have already mentioned the inevitable distorting effects of polemical debate and cautioned against taking some of Paul's descriptions of his opponents too seriously. Although we can be fairly sure that they wanted the Galatians to be circumcised, we should be a lot less confident that this had anything to do with 'making a good showing in the flesh' or 'avoiding persecution for the cross of Christ' (6.12). Because Paul constantly pits the cross against the law and circumcision (3.1, 13; 5.11; 6.12, 14-15), many scholars have concluded that the opponents, who taught the law and circumcision, must have *played down* the message of the cross.[23] But can we be so sure about this? They may have been entirely happy to talk about the cross, even emphasize its saving significance, only failing, *in Paul's view*, to see its message as excluding obedience to the law. We can be fairly certain that they would have described any disagreements with Paul in rather different terms, and that some of the issues on which Paul polarizes the two camps, they would have regarded as insignificant or even irrelevant.

Another way in which Paul's interpreters have mishandled his polemics is in unduly taking sides in the debate. Those who are inclined to admire Paul tend to portray his opponents as malicious, confused and theologically bankrupt; those who prefer to 'put Paul in his place' paint a picture of men who were sincere Christians, with admirable intentions

20. J.H. Ropes, *The Singular Problem of the Epistle to the Galatians* (Cambridge, MA: Harvard University Press, 1929), pp. 4-11.
21. W. Lütgert, *Gesetz und Geist: Eine Untersuchung zur Vorgeschichte des Galaterbriefes* (Gütersloh: Bertelsmann, 1919).
22. 'The Agitators and the Galatian Congregation', pp. 209-12.
23. See e.g. Mussner, *Der Galaterbrief*, p. 412.

and a strong theological case to argue. There is a particular danger in the temptation to dress up Paul's opponents with the clothes of one's own theological foes. I suspect this is why, in Protestant circles, Paul's opponents have so often been described as legalistic and mean-minded Jewish Christians, with a streak of fundamentalist biblicism: in exegeting and supporting Paul one can thereby hit out at Jews, Catholics and fundamentalists all at once![24] One of the most patent examples of a scholar falling into this sort of temptation is found in an essay by Helmut Koester.[25] Latching onto Paul's reference to the observance of festivals and the στοιχεῖα τοῦ κόσμου in 4.9-10, Koester concludes that the Judaizers must have emphasized the 'cosmic dimensions' of the law within a context of 'a mythologizing of Old Testament covenant theology'. Paul then turns out to be a theological hero pitting the 'history' of the cross against the covenant 'myth' of the opponents; and the opponents' basic heresy is their failure to 'demythologize'![26] All this, of course, has a lot to do with Bultmann and virtually nothing to do with Paul's opponents; one is tempted to say that it is Koester who is really responsible for concocting myths!

4. The fourth pitfall is that of *latching onto particular words and phrases* as direct echoes of the opponents' vocabulary and then hanging a whole thesis on those flimsy pegs. In one sense this is a further example of 'undue selectivity' but it has the added ingredient of regarding certain words as the very vocabulary of the opponents. A few examples will suffice. In 6.1, Paul addresses 'you who are spiritual (πνευματικοί)'. Lütgert seized on this word, and, with the Corinthian correspondence in mind, took it to be the self-designation of a party of Galatian libertine pneumatics (the second of the two fronts against which Paul had to write his letter).[27] Schmithals and Jewett followed suit, with some modifications, and even Kingsley Barrett uses this phrase to posit the existence of a group who called themselves 'spiritual' and exulted in

24. See E.P. Sanders's devastating critique of the familiar Protestant caricatures of Judaism (and Catholicism), *Paul and Palestinian Judaism* (London: SCM Press, 1977), pp. 33-59.

25. H. Koester, 'ΓΝΩΜΑΙ ΔΙΑΦΟΡΟΙ: The Origin and Nature of Diversification in the History of Early Christianity', *HTR* 58 (1965), pp. 279-318.

26. '...the historicity of the event of the revelation becomes the decisive criterion for the understanding of traditional theologies and mythologies. The failure to apply this criterion, i.e. the failure to demythologize, is identical with the "heresy" of the opponents' (Koester, 'ΓΝΩΜΑΙ', p. 309).

27. *Gesetz und Geist*, pp. 9-21.

their spiritual gifts.[28] In the next verse Paul refers to 'the law of Christ', and recently several scholars have argued that this unusual phrase must derive from the opponents, who saw Christ as a law-giver.[29] Or again, back in ch. 4, Paul uses a rather obscure phrase, τὰ στοιχεῖα τοῦ κόσμου, which means 'the elementary something of the world' and occurs elsewhere in the Pauline corpus only in Colossians (2.8, 20). A chorus of scholars has confidently declared that Paul must here be using his opponents' vocabulary, and that this is an unmistakable sign of their syncretistic tendencies, merging the Torah with astrological specula-tion.[30] To give one more example, since in 3.3 Paul talks of 'beginning in the Spirit and completing in the flesh', a number of exegetes have concluded that the opponents also talked of 'beginning' (with Paul's gospel) and 'completing' or 'perfecting' (with their instructions).[31]

Although none of these suggestions is entirely impossible, I regard all of these attempts to mirror-read single words or phrases with some sus-picion. One needs to spell out exactly what assumptions are involved here. Such an exercise depends on: (a) Paul's knowledge of the exact vocabulary used by his opponents; (b) Paul's willingness to re-use this vocabulary either ironically or in some attempt to redefine it; (c) our ability to discern where Paul is echoing his opponents' language; and (d) our ability to reconstruct the meaning that they originally gave to it. Such is our uncertainty surrounding each of these assumptions that I regard the results of any such exercise as of very limited value. They should certainly not be used as the cornerstone of any theory, as has all too often been done in recent scholarship on Galatians.

At this point I would like to make a few comments on a recent book by Bernard Brinsmead, which is the latest detailed attempt to

28. C.K. Barrett, *Freedom and Obligation: A Study of the Epistle to the Galatians* (London: SPCK, 1985), pp. 78-79. The adjective could be a perfectly innocent description of those who walk in the Spirit (5.16, 25).

29. This suggestion was apparently first made by D. Georgi (see Betz, *Galatians*, p. 300; but I can find no indication of authorship in the text he cites in his n. 71). Betz supports it.

30. See e.g. H. Schlier, *Der Brief an die Galater* (MeyerK, 7; Göttingen: Vandenhoeck & Ruprecht, 1971), pp. 202-207; K. Wegenast, *Das Verständnis der Tradition bei Paulus und in den Deuteropaulinen* (Neukirchen: Neukirchener Verlag, 1962), pp. 36-40.

31. See e.g. Jewett, 'The Agitators and the Galatian Congregation', pp. 206-207; A. Oepke, *Der Brief des Paulus an die Galater* (THKNT, 9; ed. J. Rohde, Berlin: Evangelische Verlagsanstalt, 5th edn, 1984), p. 101.

reconstruct the character and propaganda of Paul's opponents in Galatia.[32] Despite his good intentions and his awareness of the methodological problems involved, Brinsmead manages to fall into all four pitfalls I have mentioned, and a good few more beside. To pick up an example we have just discussed, Brinsmead takes Paul's reference to beginning and completing in 3.3 as an echo of his opponents' vocabulary and then goes on to specify exactly how they used that vocabulary: ἐνάρχεσθαι, he tells us, 'often has the meaning of an act of initiation', while ἐπιτελεῖν 'commonly means a performance of ritual or ceremony which brings to completion or perfection'.[33] This indicates that these terms 'may comprise a technical formula for progress in a religious mystery from a lower to higher stage'.[34] On this, very shaky, foundation Brinsmead swiftly builds the opponents' theological position: their message had 'mystical connotations' and offered circumcision as a sacramental rite of perfection! Within the space of a few pages a 'suggestion' has become a 'certainty' and a whole hypothesis has been built out of a tissue of wild guesses.

What makes Brinsmead's book so disappointing is that he thinks he has found a way of solving the problems of mirror-reading. In a genre-analysis of the text, largely dependent on Betz, he takes the epistle to follow the rules of a law-court defence-speech and to be a continual dialogue with the opponents. But this new methodology solves none of our problems and, in Brinsmead's hands, sometimes creates even more. In distinction from Betz, Brinsmead treats 5.1–6.10 as a 'refutatio' (he never explains why), the part of the speech which is supposed to answer the opponents' arguments.[35] Having imposed this alien rhetorical description on what is a perfectly innocent piece of ethical exhortation, Brinsmead ransacks the material to find what Paul is answering here and concludes that where Paul uses *traditional* forms (catalogues of vices and virtues or words of the Lord), these must represent *the opponents' ethical traditions*. As if this totally unfounded assumption is not enough, Brinsmead then compares these catalogues with those in 1QS 3-4 and, noting the similarities, jumps to the conclusion that the opponents advo-

32. B.H. Brinsmead, *Galatians—Dialogical Response to Opponents* (Chico CA: Scholars Press, 1982).

33. *Galatians*, p. 79.

34. *Galatians*, p. 79.

35. *Galatians*, pp. 44, 53-54, 163-81.

cated an Essene theology and ethics![36] So far from unravelling the complexities involved in interpreting a dialogue, Brinsmead leaps from one incredible assumption to another. His book well deserves David Aune's wry comment that it is 'justified only by faith'![37]

4. *A Possible Methodology*

From what I have said so far one might be tempted to conclude that I consider mirror-reading a polemical text to be an impossible undertaking; in fact, George Lyons has recently written it off as an unworkable technique.[38] Actually I think it is a good deal more difficult than is usually acknowledged, but not wholly impossible. What is needed is a carefully controlled method of working which uses logical criteria and proceeds with suitable caution. The following are what I consider to be the seven most appropriate criteria for this exercise:

1. *Type of utterance.* a. If Paul makes an *assertion*, we may assume that, *at least*, those to whom he writes may be in danger of overlooking what he asserts, and *at most*, someone has explicitly denied it; in between those two extremes there is a range of feasible suggestions, including the possibility that his audience have forgotten what he now reminds them about. b. If Paul makes a *denial*, we may assume that, *at least*, those whom he addresses may be prone to regard what he denies as true, and *at most*, someone has explicitly asserted it; again, between these two extremes there is a range of other possibilities.[39] c. If Paul issues a *command*, *at least*, those who receive it may be in danger of

36. *Galatians*, pp. 164-78.

37. See D.E. Aune's Review in *CBQ* 46 (1984), p. 147.

38. G. Lyons, *Pauline Autobiography: Toward a New Understanding* (Atlanta: Scholars Press, 1985), ch. 2; see e.g. p. 96: 'The "mirror reading" approach to the interpretation of Galatians may be challenged on several bases. It may be shown that the methodological presuppositions on which it rests are arbitrary, inconsistently applied, and unworkable.' He is particularly, and rightly, critical of those who assume that every Pauline denial is a response to an explicit criticism from his opponents (pp. 105-12). But the paragraphs below may go some way to meeting his objection that the whole method is impossibly speculative and unscientific.

39. Betz rightly notes that 'not everything that Paul denies is necessarily an accusation by his opposition' (*Galatians*, p. 6). Lyons, however, fails to explore the range of other possibilities when he concludes that, since Paul's denials need not be directed against specific charges, they 'are often, if not always, examples of pleonastic tautology used in the interest of clarity' (*Pauline Autobiography*, p. 110).

neglecting what he commands, and *at most* they are deliberately flouting it; again their condition could also be anywhere between these two poles. d. If Paul makes a prohibition, there must be *at least* some perceived chance that what is prohibited may be done, and *at most*, someone has already flagrantly disobeyed him; but perhaps it is a case of action being performed in naive ignorance (or a host of other possibilities).[40] Thus each type of statement is open to a range of mirror-images, and one must beware of rash over-interpretation. One can only decide where in this range of possibilities the truth lies when some of the other criteria are brought into play.

2. *Tone*. If Paul issues a statement with emphasis and urgency (he has a variety of ways of doing so), we may conclude that he perceives this to be an important and perhaps central issue. Conversely, the casual mention of an issue probably indicates that it is not, in his view, crucial to the debate.

3. *Frequency*. If Paul repeatedly returns to the same theme it is clearly important for him; conversely, an occasional remark probably signals what he considers to be only a side-issue.

4. *Clarity*. We can only mirror-read with any confidence statements whose meaning is reasonably clear. Where interpretation hinges on an ambiguous word or phrase (or on a contested textual problem), or where we have good grounds for suspecting that Paul's 'description' of his opponents is polemically distorted, we cannot employ that evidence for any important role in our hypothesis.

5. *Unfamiliarity*. While taking into account our limited knowledge of Paul's theology, we may be entitled to consider the presence of an unfamiliar motif in Paul's letter as a reflection of a particular feature in the situation he is responding to.

Most of these criteria are framed in terms of 'mays' and 'mights', which indicates that they need cautious handling, with all due sensitivity to the particular document under consideration. Taken together they should enable one to form some sort of hypothesis which can then be further tested by the last two criteria:

6. *Consistency*. Unless we have strong evidence to suggest that Paul is responding to more than one type of opponent or argument, we should

---

40. Hooker, 'Were There False Teachers in Colossae?', p. 317: 'Exhortation to avoid a certain course of action certainly does not necessarily indicate that those addressed have already fallen prey to the temptation, as every preacher and congregation must be aware'.

assume that a single object is in view. Thus the results of the previous criteria may be tested to see if they amount to a consistent picture of Paul's opponents.

7. *Historical plausibility*. At this point we can bring into play what other evidence we have for contemporary men and movements which could conceivably be the object of Paul's attacks. If our results are anachronistic or historically implausible for some other reason, we will be obliged to start again.

The conscientious application of these criteria may mean that there is only a limited number of facts which we could determine with anything like certainty. But this does not mean that they are excessively negative. New Testament scholars need to learn to be more candid in admitting the real value of their theories, and there is a good case for establishing a sliding scale of hypotheses ranging between 'certain' and 'incredible'. J. Louis Martyn suggests that we need to employ both 'scientific control' and 'poetic fantasy' in this matter.[41] I am not sure that 'poetic fantasy' will help us much, but I agree that one should be able to discuss hypotheses which are not proven beyond doubt, so long as one recognizes their proper status. Ed Sanders does a useful job in this regard, constructing a range of categories into which we may assign hypotheses (in his case, about the historical Jesus). His range runs from 'Certain or Virtually Certain', through 'Highly Probable', 'Probable', 'Possible' and 'Conceivable' to 'Incredible'.[42] Although one could quibble with the semantics, I think these would be useful categories into which one could place one's findings after mirror-reading a letter like Galatians.

5. *Results*

The main purpose of this discussion is to outline some of the methodological issues involved in mirror-reading Galatians. Given the limitations of space it is not possible to attempt a full-scale reconstruction of the opponents' message and identity, but it may help to clarify the application of the seven criteria just mentioned if I conclude with a brief statement of plausible results.[43]

41. Martyn, 'A Law-Observant Mission to Gentiles', p. 313.
42. E.P. Sanders, *Jesus and Judaism* (London: SCM Press, 1985), pp. 326-27.
43. I have set out detailed argumentation for most of the following statements in *Obeying the Truth: A Study of Paul's Ethics in Galatians* (Edinburgh: T. & T. Clark, 1988).

On the basis of Paul's reference to 'another gospel' (1.6-9) it seems clear that the opponents were Christians. Whether they were Jewish or Gentile Christians is slightly less certain because of the ambiguity in the phrase οἱ περιτεμνόμενοι in 6.13 (and the associated textual uncertainty). But in view of verses like 4.30 (apparently meant to apply to the opponents) it is highly probable that they were Jewish. Certainly it would be precarious to build an important thesis about their Gentile origin on 6.13 alone (as did Munck; see criterion 4). Paul associates their message with circumcision, both explicitly (6.12-13) and implicitly (5.2-4, 11-12), and the emphasis and frequency with which he discusses this subject make it clear that he regards this as a central issue (criteria 2 and 3; cf. 2.3-5). It is doubtful that they could or would actually *compel* the Galatians to get circumcised (6.12; cf. 2.14) but they clearly presented their argument with some persuasion (3.1) and won the esteem of many Galatians (4.17). What is more difficult to assess is why they advocated circumcision, since Paul's verdict in 6.12 is partial and probably misleading.

This issue is closely bound up with another: to what extent were they serious in advocating the observance of the Torah? 4.10 indicates that the Galatians had begun to observe some of the Jewish calendrical requirements, and it is unlikely that that was as far as the opponents wanted them to go. In fact Paul's concern about 'works of the law' (3.1-10) and his extended arguments to prove the temporary validity of the law (3.6–4.11), taken together with remarks like 4.21, make it highly probable that the opponents wanted the Galatians to observe the law as circumcised proselytes (criteria 2 and 3). 5.3 is open to a range of interpretations (criterion 1a), although those offered by Schmithals and Jewett find no support in any of the rest of the letter or from any other of our criteria; certainly 6.13a looks very like an exaggerated polemic point. Taking the argument of the letter as a whole, there is sufficient evidence that the Galatians were informed of (and responded warmly to) the requirements of Torah-observance as the hallmark of the people of God.

This may indeed be confirmed by the evidence of the 'paraenetic' section (5.13–6.10). The use of these verses to provide evidence for a libertine group or gnostic/libertine tendencies should be questioned in the light of criterion 1 (c and d) which emphasizes the range of possible reasons for a command or prohibition. There is no evidence in this section, or elsewhere in the letter, which would support taking these verses as a reply to Gnostics or libertines (see again criteria 2 and 3). In some instances Paul is explicitly *reminding* the Galatians of their duties (5.19-21) and in others the abuses he attacks are not specifically libertine (5.15, 26). (In any case all two-front or Gnostic theories run aground on criteria 6 and 7.) In giving his exhortation Paul appears intent on demonstrating that walking in the Spirit is a sufficient alternative to living under the law (5.14, 18, 23; 6.2). If the opponents wanted the Galatians to observe the law they probably argued that only the law could properly regulate their daily life.

It is very probable that another of the opponents' lines of argument, which we may again see reflected in Paul's reply, was an appeal to Scripture, and in particular the Abraham narratives. Paul's repeated references to Abraham (3.6-29; 4.21-31) support this suggestion (criterion 3), while his convoluted use of certain texts may indicate that he is countering their persuasive biblical exegesis (criteria 1 [a and b] and 5).

Paul's extended self-defence in Galatians 1–2 makes it virtually certain that the validity of his gospel and his apostleship was under attack. Unfortunately it is difficult to be more precise about any particular 'charges' since, as we saw above, even quite detailed self-defence can be triggered off by a very few damaging innuendos. However, in the light of 1.1, 10-12 and Paul's repeated attempts to specify his relationship to the Jerusalem apostles, it is probable that the opponents considered Paul to be an unreliable delegate of the Jerusalem church (criteria 1a and b, taken together with criteria 2 and 3).[44] 5.11 may also reflect an accusation that Paul sometimes circumcised his converts, but as an implicit denial it is open to the range of interpretations suggested by criterion 1b and is not elucidated by any other criteria (see Section 3 above).

The questions of the opponents' origin and motivation are even harder to answer. The prominence of Jerusalem in this letter (as well as Galatians 1–2, see 4.25-26) probably indicates that they had some links with the Jerusalem church; but they could have come from Antioch or

---

44. I would maintain this even in the face of Lyons's vigorous argument that no apologetic motif is present here (*Pauline Autobiography*, chs. 2–3). I fail to see how Paul's detailed description of his movements in 1.17-24 can fit Lyons's conclusion that the only purpose of Paul's autobiography is 'as a paradigm of the gospel of Christian freedom which he seeks to persuade his readers to reaffirm in the face of the threat presented by the troublemakers' (p. 171; cf. pp. 158-61). Lyons has not taken sufficient account of Paul's repeated emphases in these chapters, or the fact that the troublemakers must have considered Paul's work in Galatia insufficient.

almost any other church which included Jewish Christians. It would certainly be going beyond the evidence to identify them with the 'false brethren' at Jerusalem (Gal. 2.4; cf. Acts 15.1-5) or the circumcision party at Antioch (2.12). Given Paul's ironic but not wholly negative attitude to 'those in repute' at Jerusalem, it is inconceivable that 'the pillars' had actually commissioned Paul's opponents. It is not impossible that the opponents were acting under Zealot pressure in Palestine (so Jewett), but such a thesis hangs rather precariously from the single thread of Paul's comment in 6.12.

It is conceivable that at some points Paul echoes the exact vocabulary of his opponents: they may possibly have referred to the στοιχεῖα τοῦ κόσμου and the law of Christ and described their purpose as completing Paul's work, but at least in the first two cases we are still in the dark about what they meant by such phrases.

We may then tabulate these results as follows:

Certain or Virtually Certain

1. Paul's opponents were Christians.
2. They wanted the Galatians to be circumcised and to observe at least some of the rest of the law, including its calendrical requirements.
3. They brought into question the adequacy of Paul's gospel and his credentials as an apostle.
4. Their arguments were attractive and persuasive for many Galatians Christians.

Highly Probable

1. They were *Jewish* Christians.
2. They argued from Scripture using, in particular, the Abraham narratives.
3. They expected the Galatians to become circumcised proselytes and to observe the law, as the hallmark of the people of God.

Probable

1. They had some links with the Jerusalem church and thought that Paul was an unreliable delegate of that church.
2. Their scriptural arguments made reference to Genesis 17 and the Sarah-Hagar narratives.

Possible

> They told the Galatians that Paul circumcised his converts in some circumstances.

Conceivable

> They talked of 'completing' Paul's work, made reference to the law of Christ and used the word στοιχεῖα.

Incredible

1. They were Gnostics or gnosticizing to an appreciable degree.
2. They were libertines or played on the Galatians' 'Hellenistic libertine aspirations'.
3. They were syncretists with cosmic or mystical notions about circumcision, the law or keeping festivals.
4. They were directly commissioned by the Jerusalem apostles.
5. Paul was fighting against two distinct groups.

I am well aware that this is not a complete list of those things that we can know about the opponents; but I hope it illustrates the role of the criteria outlined above and the value of collating material on a graduated scale of certainty. Having drawn up this list one could go on to compile a much longer one of all the things that we do *not* know about the opponents, either because we cannot see them clearly enough in Paul's mirror or because he chose not to reflect them at all. I will not indulge in such a tedious exercise, although it should perhaps be a requirement of all serious historical work.[45]

One could also draw up an interesting list of points on which Paul and his opponents would have agreed. This would include at least the following points:

1. Scripture, God's word, is now reaching its fulfilment through Christ.
2. Salvation is now available to Gentiles, in fulfilment of the promises to Abraham.

---

45. I recall the late Sir Moses Finley starting his Cambridge lectures on ancient Sparta with the sobering (if somewhat exaggerated) statement, 'We know nothing about ancient Sparta'!

3. The Spirit has been given to the people of God who believe in the Messiah.
4. God's people should abstain from idolatry and the passions of the flesh.

Such a list would show how much Paul and his opponents had in common and thus help to correct the impression of complete disagreement which the letter to the Galatians conveys.

I am aware that the results tabulated above are not particularly surprising or innovative. It is probably true that a critical methodology like this will tend to be most effective in questioning fashionable but flimsy attempts to build some new reconstruction of the opponents and their message. That is not to say, however, that interesting new things cannot be said on the basis of these results. However, my primary aim has been to discuss the methodological issues involved in mirror-reading a polemical letter. If these cautionary notes and positive suggestions are of any value, they could equally well be applied to Colossians, 2 Corinthians 10–13, the Johannine letters or indeed any other of the many polemical parts of the New Testament.

JSNT 45 (1992), pp. 105-20

THE PASTORAL EPISTLES AND THE ETHICS OF READING

Frances Young

The enquiry undertaken in this paper was stimulated by George Steiner's book, *Real Presences*, subtitled, *Is there anything* in *what we say?*[1] The context of his essay is the present intellectual scene in the humanities: the breakdown of that romantic/historical approach to literature and the arts which may be summed up in the phrase 'thinking the author's thoughts after him'; the advent of the New Criticism, then of structuralism; the development of deconstruction and theories of reader reception. The resultant fascination with critical theory means that it is not just the intention of the author, or even the possibility of 'dialogue' with the author, that has been lost, but the very possibility of meaning and communication.

Yet, says Steiner, 'no serious writer, composer, painter has ever doubted...that his work bears on good and evil... A message is being sent: to a purpose.' 'But the problem I wish to clarify', he continues, 'is a more particular one, often unobserved. It is not so much the morality or amorality of the work of meaning and of art. It is that of *the ethics of its reception.*' The presence of the 'other' impinging upon us requires our respect and attention or, as Steiner puts it, a certain tact, welcome, civility, courtesy. The etiquette of courtesy 'organizes' our meetings with the 'other'. So, he suggests, an initial act of trust underlies all language, aesthetics, history, politics... Our response is a moral act for which we are responsible. In the case of great works of art, 'it is on our capacities for welcome or refusal, for response or imperception, that their own necessities of echo and of presence largely depend'.[2]

So my basic question is: How are we to receive or read in an ethically

---

1. London: Faber & Faber, 1989.
2. Steiner, *Real Presences*, pp. 145-48.

responsible way texts we have learned to believe are pseudonymous? Has the scholarly consensus and what has been called the hermeneutic of suspicion destroyed the possibility of welcoming the Pastorals with courtesy, of beginning without distrust? I will eventually turn to the specific case, but first let us explore this ethics of reception a little further.

Steiner's approach was anticipated in the work of the American literary scholar, Wayne Booth. His important book, *The Company we Keep*,[3] was twenty years in formation. To begin with doubt is to destroy the datum, he suggests,[4] and he contrasts 'analyzing texts' with 'reading stories', reclaiming the traditional notion that actually we read for the sake of personal improvement—we expect to be changed by what we read, as people have been since classical times. In every age until recently literary theory encouraged us to believe that we should keep a critical distance. Booth treats friendship as the principal metaphor of reading. The burden of his book is a rehabilitation of ethical criticism.

Among theologians, the writer who has tackled the ethics of reading is Werner Jeanrond.[5] After exploring the hermeneutics of Hans Gadamer and Paul Ricoeur, and the reading theories of Wolfgang Iser and Stanley Fish, he states, 'No reading is ethically neutral, since every reading represents an answer to a textual claim, an answer which may be responsible or irresponsible'.[6] He sees the reading of a text as 'a dynamic process which remains in principle open-ended', for the reader does more than decipher signs printed on paper: reading always involves the projection of a new image of reality to which both the text and the reader contribute.[7] 'The reader enables the text to influence his/her situation', yet not uncritically. Criticism, or assessment, is what allows the text to speak in the best possible manner and 'for this purpose, to orient the individual reader and the reading community in relation to self-criticism and criticism of content'.[8]

The point that responsible reading involves criticism, not just in the

---

3. Berkeley: University of California Press, 1988.

4. Booth, *The Company we Keep*, p. 32.

5. *Text and Interpretation as Categories of Theological Thinking* (trans. T.J. Wilson; Dublin: Gill and Macmillan, 1988).

6. *Text and Interpretation*, p. 128.

7. *Text and Interpretation*, p. 104.

8. *Text and Interpretation*, p. 113.

sense of articulating and analysing response so as to increase reading competence, but also in the sense of judgment/assessment, Wayne Booth emphasizes too. We discriminate between our friends, after all. Respect for the 'other' involves the articulation of difference. 'Courtesy' towards the text does not require capitulation. Indeed, readers have responsibilities not only to the text (or—Booth does not hesitate to suggest—the author), but also to themselves:

> I serve myself best, as reader, when I both honor an author's offering for what it is, in its full 'otherness' from me, and take an active critical stance against what seem to me its errors or excesses.[9]

(Perhaps we should note that throughout his discussion of the ethics of reading, Booth has difficult questions such as pornography and censorship in the back of his mind: he is not just concerned with classics.)

It seems that respect for the 'other' and respect for the 'self' are involved in responsible reading, and this means the articulation of 'difference'. It is time we turned to the Pastoral Epistles with these perspectives informing our reading, and it would seem that the articulation of differences might be a good place to start.

As soon as we begin to read, we note that the stated reader is Timothy or Titus. 'I' or 'we' are apparently not implied by the text. So to put the question in the simplest and most direct way possible: can we read responsibly a text which belongs to another's private correspondence? Further reading of these texts soon legitimates our involvement, however. The content of these letters is clearly not meant to be private. The subject matter concerns the proper public ordering of a community, and therefore these documents were from the beginning public documents and meant to be so.

So, to identify the implied readership, as distinct from the stated readership, is to envisage a Christian community somewhere, sometime (the texts might offer clues, but they are not explicit) in the first (or possibly second) century. 'We', the present readers, are not part of that community. Can we responsibly read texts if we are not the implied readership? Clearly we can and do, but the distinction between the implied reader and the actual reader should enable us to grasp the importance of what Jeanrond has called 'reading genres'.[10] In the case of a modern novel,

---

9. *Text and Interpretation*, p. 135.
10. *Text and Interpretation*, p. 117.

the implied reader is likely to be much closer to the actual reader than in the case before us—although identity will never be exact: for example, the implied reader might be one who can spot the allusions to Shakespeare or the Beatles, and the actual reader might lack the knowledge or experience to be capable of doing so. The closeness of identity, however, usually ensures that the implied function of reading the novel is approximately the same for text and reader, and so there is but one 'reading mode' implied. For a biblical text, however, Jeanrond can point to several 'reading genres' that relate to the function of reading such a text, or the use to which the text is being put:

> When, for example, a letter of St Paul is sent by post to a community, it is in the first place the function of communication which stands in the foreground. If, on the other hand, one reads out the same text at a liturgical service, what stands in the foreground is the religious teaching character. The same text can again be studied as a document of its time, its documentary function is accentuated in this case.[11]

On this analysis, then, it would seem that, until recently, biblical criticism had become wedded to the 'documentary' reading mode: hence, in reaction, the welcome given to the new 'literary' methods.

But when Jowett in *Essays and Reviews*[12] controversially argued that the Bible should be read like any other literature, he did not envisage such a narrowing historical or documentary outcome. Espousing the kind of philological and historical reading then current in standard classical education—the Bible was to be read like Sophocles and Plato—did not rule out appropriation by the reader, since the 'romantic' view that one could and should 'think an author's thoughts after him' was firmly entrenched. So, to learn the language of the author and enter into the author's mind was the route to grasping meaning. For Jowett this was the answer to the false multiplication of senses and to spurious and divisive doctrinal readings, and he was confident that this historical principle would validate the sublimity of Scripture and release its transcendent quality, recognizing that there are depths which to the author may be 'but half revealed'.[13]

One hundred and thirty or so years later we have become disillusioned, not just because of the breakdown of the romantic reading, but

11. *Text and Interpretation*, p. 117.
12. B. Jowett, 'On the Interpretation of Scripture', in *Essays and Reviews* (London: Longman, Green, Longmans and Roberts), pp. 330-433.
13. Jowett, 'On the Interpretation of Scripture', p. 380.

also because there has been no agreement about the 'original meaning', any more than there was about the proper doctrinal reading. Furthermore, the practice of historical reading has both highlighted the problems of identifying the 'original author' of many biblical texts and caused scholars to adopt the documentary reading mode, increasingly attempting to reconstruct the original situation and context rather than reading the text as addressed to readers who were expected to respond.

To return to the Pastorals, what is the appropriate 'reading mode' for 'us', readers here and now who are not identical to the implied readers in the texts?

Clearly, reading them as historical documents is an important possibility, and recent attempts at sociological study of the Pauline communities and their institutionalization do exactly that, as have earlier studies concerned with the church order, setting, authorship, the identity of the implied opposition and so forth. But such reading tends to analyse and exploit texts rather than read and assimilate them: the dynamic balance of an ethical reading as outlined earlier is missing.

Another of Jeanrond's possibilities presents itself, namely to read them as liturgical/canonical texts within a reading community claiming a certain continuity with the original reading community. This possibility, while undoubtedly legitimate, falls, I suggest, into a somewhat special category, and inspection of the current lectionary of the joint liturgical group proves that such reading is successful largely because it is selective of passages which are acceptable to the current reading community—in other words such reading is rarely capable of a responsible reading of whole texts. To explore a canonical reading would take another paper, but I will return to the liturgical reading now and again as we proceed.

The third possibility is to respond to the text imaginatively as it asks to be read. That is, to read it as a communication to implied readers, taking seriously what the implied author wishes to communicate, so being open to the courteous and sympathetic reception of the 'other', while being free to retain a certain critical distance. In this way there is a dialectic between the response of the implied readers and our actual response, and both critical assessment and responsible appropriation become genuine possibilities.

It is this third possibility which seems to me to constitute an 'ethical reading', since it respects what Wayne Booth calls the ethos of the text,

while allowing readers to recognize their 'double' identity and their consequent responsibilities to themselves as well as to the author/text. It is
not exactly any of Jeanrond's reading genres, but, so far from reading
genres constituting a hierarchy, as he suggests,[14] I think in practice I
shall show that an ethical reading of this kind requires an appropriate
interaction between the different reading genres he isolates.

So far then we have been focusing on the first area of 'difference'
which needs to be articulated and clarified, namely the implied and
actual readership. There is a sense in which the reading strategy proposed by attending to this necessitates something similar to Ricoeur's
method of 'entering the world of the text', and that introduces the
second major area of 'difference' that needs to be articulated. The text
implies a whole 'world' of assumptions and cultural norms which
present readers share only partially or not at all. (That, of course, is
common to all acts of reading in the sense that the implied author of a
text inhabits or creates a 'metaphoric' or 'symbolic world' of meaning
which is likely not to have the same identical boundaries as the reader's
symbolic world.)

   In the case of the Pastorals, that 'other world' is not exactly like the
world of fictional narrative. An extreme example of such an imaginative
world would be *Watership Down*, which invites the reader to accom-
pany the implied author into a very strange, and largely self-contained,
world of the imagination in which remarkably realistic rabbits behave
remarkably like human beings in human societies. To enter the 'world'
of the Pastorals is not like that. Yet it is to enter a fictional world in two
senses: the sense in which all our 'worlds' are sociolinguistic interpretative constructs, and in the sense that the responsible reader has to reconstruct in the imagination a situation that is not existent. To do so
responsibly requires the interaction of the text-content, which evokes its
world, with other accumulated data from the historical world from
which the text comes. The success of the operation will depend to a
considerable extent on the knowledge and imaginative capacity of the
interpreter, a competence which can be constantly improved by learning
and practice. Thus, reading as historical document is part of reading
responsibly (as I said, the reading modes need to inform one another!).

14. *Text and Interpretation*, p. 117.

Four areas of 'difference' between the world of the Pastorals and our world can be usefully articulated, although to do justice to any of them lies outside the scope of this paper. Yet the articulation of these 'differences' may be precisely what creates the potential for sympathetic engagement, imaginative identity and sensitive criticism, so it must be attempted, however sketchily.

The first area I wish to highlight is the difference in the reading process. For most people today reading is a private activity, but it seems that in the ancient world, even though one might read privately in a study, that process was usually rehearsal for public recitation. Reading was a performance of dramatic quality; writing was only a way of recording the voice, the spoken word. Even a letter was treated as a way of making an absent person present.

All texts from the ancient world were meant to be persuasive documents, and authors were concerned about getting the best reception—they were audience-oriented. So, texts were rhetorical pieces addressed to an audience, intended to move that audience and effect a result. An ethical reading that respects the 'otherness' of these texts requires that we listen to what they have to say, allow ourselves to identify with the implied audience and be open to persuasion rather than be critically distanced. So, here the reading mode comes close to what Jeanrond calls the liturgical reading genre. Yet audiences in most contexts reserve the right to disagree—even heckle—and insofar as we are not actually the implied readership, we may need to oscillate between sympathy and distance. So, the character of the reading-process to which these texts belonged reinforces two points already made: these texts are public documents, and an ethical reading requires both criticism and respect.

Secondly, these texts both imply and seek to foster certain kinds of social relationships within the 'hearing' community, and between that community and the outside world. Unless we take seriously the historical enterprise to uncover that context, we cannot enter into an informed relationship with the text. Recent work highlights the nature of the Graeco-Roman household and the analogy between the organization of the early church and such a household. This is reflected clearly in the duty-codes of these texts, essentially household-codes adapted to church use, with a strong emphasis on a good church overseer having to have the same qualities as the head of a household. We can understand the concern of a marginalized group to avoid contention and disruption of the basic social unit, and the need to be accepted as respectable by the neighbours. There may be both defensive and missionary motives at work in the attempt to order the community as the household of God. All these points have been discussed in the scholarly literature and would repay closer investigation if there were space here.[15]

What has been overlooked in these discussions is, I suggest, the influence of synagogues, which were also often adapted households. It is a common observation that new religious movements ape older styles of organization: the New Age movement has produced bishops! The history of the synagogue is itself somewhat problematic, but it must have pre-dated the arrival of the church, and in some sense provided a model. It is perhaps no surprise to find that women have acceptable, although well-defined, roles in a society conceived as a household (however patriarchally structured from our perspective), whereas synagogue influence might encourage the view that the praying quorum consists only of adult males, each of whom is a *bar mitzvah*. And the vexed question of the relationship between the often (but, I suggest, erroneously) identified ἐπίσκοπος in the singular, and the plural πρεσβύτεροι may well be illuminated by analogy with the *chazan ha-knesset* who organized the meeting for prayer and the senior members of the community who represented the Jewish community in the civic life of the locality and generally exercised leadership.

However, leaving further pursuit of these questions to other occasions, the point of raising them here is simply to signal the impossibility of too straightforward an application to the actual readers here and now of the advice given in these texts to their implied readership. The implied readers belonged to a different social world.

The third area of difference relates to this, in that the sociology of knowledge has alerted us to the social dimension of all understanding and belief. However, it is important to specify the unarticulated or implied beliefs and assumptions 'incarnated' in the sociolinguistic community to which both implied author and implied readers belonged.

15. Recent relevant studies include: R.E. Brown, *The Churches the Apostles Left Behind* (New York: Paulist Press, 1984); M.Y. MacDonald, *The Pauline Churches: A Socio-Historical Study of Institutionalisation in the Pauline and Deutero-Pauline Writings* (SNTSMS, 60; Cambridge: Cambridge University Press, 1988); P.A. Towner, *The Goal of our Instruction: The Structure of Theology and Ethics in the Pastoral Epistles* (JSNTSup, 34; Sheffield: JSOT Press, 1989); D.C. Verner, *The Household of God: The Social World of the Pastoral Epistles* (SBLDS, 71; Chico, CA: Scholars Press, 1983).

Some of these, like belief in God, some of us may share. The reading community may claim to have a certain continuity with the original community that received these texts. Yet there may well be subtle differences in the resonances even of those ideas or beliefs we think we share, and there will be some hard, if not impossible, texts for present readers (e.g. 1 Tim. 2.11-15).

This leads us into the fourth distinguishable area of difference, namely the articulated beliefs, ideas, norms, standards, advice, warnings and the like, which constitute the content of the text, and which an ethical reading requires us to hear sympathetically, but perhaps not adopt uncritically.

The further we get into this process of articulating differences in order to enter the world of the text, the more we have to recognize that just as important as the reading genre is the text genre. Taking the text-type of the documents under discussion at face value, we have letters. The stated author of these letters is Paul, who addresses the stated reader, Timothy or Titus. The different, implied readership has already been noted: these are in some sense public community documents, not private letters. What about the implied author?

The mere fact of these texts being letters implies Paul's absence, and the written text becomes a way of evoking his presence. How long or how distant has Paul's absence been? Timothy and Titus are recognized as those who bear his mantle and his authority, and they in turn give authority to the ἐπίσκοπος, the deacons and the presbyters, whose functions and character form a principal concern in the body of the letters. The letters would appear to be indirectly addressed to communities in order to confirm the authoritative position of their leaders as inheritors of the tradition and authority of Paul. So, the text-type slips from the surface genre of personal letter, to the implied genre of manual of instruction. Furthermore, the need for this manual seems to relate to an implied, specific crisis, a situation in which that tradition is under threat from teachers of 'gnosis falsely so-called'. The manual aims at establishing an enduring order for the preservation of this authoritative tradition in the face of such threats.

Thus, an ethical reading requires the placing of these texts in a plausible narrative, the implied narrative of events that caused these texts to be authored. Only as the reader is drawn into such an implied narrative can a truly sympathetic reading occur.

What I have indicated so far strongly suggests that such an implied narrative involves the absence of the stated author, and a crisis in a community which looks to the stated author as probably founder, certainly hero, undoubtedly authority. The texts are rooted in a social situation. An ethical reading demands that that situation be taken with the utmost seriousness. But does it demand Pauline authorship? Could it not be that here too is an important area of 'difference' to be articulated?

In the modern world, pseudonymity easily gets associated with deception (although we accept quite willingly the notion of a 'pen name'). But suppose the fear of admitting that Paul was not the actual author of these texts is a modern 'culture-specific', linked with our excessive individualism and worship of creative originality.

The ancient world was far more interested in tradition than novelty, which was one of the problems faced by the promulgators of this 'new superstition', Christianity. Ancient wisdom was valued rather than creative genius, and the great work of art was far greater than its often anonymous creator. There are enough analogies from that culture to make it entirely plausible that an anonymous disciple or anonymous disciples took on the persona of Paul in order to preserve what they believed to be the genuine Pauline tradition in a situation in which it was under threat. In fact we have several examples of exactly that among the apocryphal literature: for example, the third epistle to the Corinthians in the *Acts of Paul*, and the *Epistle to the Laodiceans*. The implied narrative and the implied readership seem to demand an implied author other than the stated author, and a truly ethical reading, which takes seriously the ethos of the text, requires us to recognize that, if we are to respect the text's true 'otherness'.

The problem for us is the consequent loss of respect for these texts in the eyes of modern readers, who are immediately made suspicious if the possibility of pseudonymity is proposed. So, quite apart from the fundamentalist reaction, in much modern scholarship the Pastorals have become a sad fall-away from the great theology of Paul, and merely provide examples of the loss of a charismatic dynamic in the process of institutionalization, rather than seeming texts worth reading for their inspirational qualities. An ethical reading should perhaps redress that insult.

Let us then agree that an ethical reading, which respects the claim of these texts, requires us to recognize that they fit into an implied narrative in which (1) the surface text-type is not its implied text-type, the letter-form having become 'classic' for early Christian communication, doubly convenient in this case because it makes a figure of the past still accessible; (2) the readership implied is not the stated recipients; and (3) the implied author is not the stated author. What then is the rhetoric of these texts? How are we, the present readers, to respond to them?

The rhetorical dynamic of texts is based in the interaction between speaker, hearer and subject matter, and each of these poles was subject to analysis in the ancient rhetorical textbooks which were used in schools to train effective public speakers. Methods of argument related to each pole. The so-called 'logical' arguments related to the subject matter (*logos*) and were intended to convince of its truth and rightness. The so-called 'ethical' arguments were designed to create an atmosphere of trust in the speaker, to substantiate a claim to be listened to on the basis of the speaker's *ethos*, his character, habits and so forth.[16] The so-called 'pathetic' arguments were intended to move the hearer, to stimulate *pathos*, such as sympathy with a defendant in court so as to acquit, or enthusiasm for taking a corporate decision like declaring war. The response of the hearer was an essential part of the intention: rhetoric was called the art of persuasion, and assent to the speaker's viewpoint was its aim.

To analyse the rhetorical dynamics of the Pastorals presupposes, therefore, the whole of our previous discussion, and can conveniently be set out in a diagram in which each pole has three possible 'levels', roughly similar to Jeanrond's three reading genres, all of which may interact with one another, while some oscillation between levels one and two is apparent in the text itself.

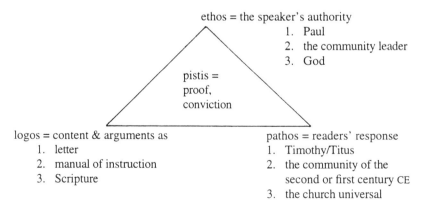

ethos = the speaker's authority
1. Paul
2. the community leader
3. God

pistis = proof, conviction

logos = content & arguments as
1. letter
2. manual of instruction
3. Scripture

pathos = readers' response
1. Timothy/Titus
2. the community of the second or first century CE
3. the church universal

16. Here the term 'ethical' is being used in a technical sense within rhetorical convention, not as previously in discussing 'ethical reading', where normal English usage suggests the sense.

The time has come to do some reading, in other words to consider some passages in the light of all this.

Titus 3.4-8a

The 'saying you can trust' formula seems to alert the implied readers to reliable bits of tradition, and what we have here is itself somewhat formulaic—a summary of the essential gospel. It is a popular expression of Paul's doctrine of grace, although not expressed in his characteristic language. It is linked with the 'bath of re-birth', an un-Pauline phrase, somewhat like the language of contemporary mystery religions but clearly referring to baptism and having entirely Christian associations if you consider other streams of New Testament tradition (e.g. the dialogue with Nicodemus in John 3).

The rhetoric works at levels 2 and 3; it is a bit artificial at level 1, but is clearly the way the complicated Paul was simplified for general consumption. That should command respect. A Christian reader easily identifies with the text and, in a mission situation, others might be persuadable.

1 Timothy 6.11-16

This reads as direct address to a church leader, which can work rhetorically at all three levels. Christ is the example put before the leader by the one who gives the charge. It is easy to imagine Paul saying this to Timothy, with the same words applying also at levels 2 and 3, although, as women take leadership positions in churches, the third level becomes increasingly problematic unless broadened to include women alongside the 'man of God'.

Yet the idea of Christ's testimony before Pilate is closer to martyr exhortations in the wider church than anything we find in authentic Pauline literature; and the final doxology clearly comes from liturgical traditions used in the implied community and is not characteristically Pauline.

What should be noted, however, is that an ethical reading of the text demands that we allow ourselves to imagine what it would mean for a church leader to be persuaded by this rhetoric and to live that way, rather than focusing solely on the difficulties of Pauline authorship.

What is noticeable is that most of the passages actually used in the current lectionaries fall into these categories: they work at levels 2 and 3, while fitting more or less easily into the 'fictional' surface text-type, with its stated author and reader.

But let us now consider passages which exploit the character of the 'speaker' or stated author, therefore challenging the suggestion that the surface-presentation of the text has fictional elements. These are the 'ethical' arguments in the rhetorical sense of the term, establishing the character and authority of the persuader.

1 Timothy 1.12-17

Here is a Paul we recognize, testifying to his call to apostleship and hinting that his converts should imitate him—or is it? There is a subtle and interesting shift. Paul has become the typical Gentile 'sinner', his sin exemplified in his past persecution of the Church, a theme deeply important to the narrator of Acts but not to the authentic Paul of the Epistles. Paul is set before us as the converted sinner, exemplifying the sure tradition ('the saying you may trust') that Christ Jesus came into the world to save sinners. Yes, the theme of God's grace and patience is Pauline, but here is the great theme of Paul's theology couched in popular slogan, not Pauline argument, simply to be accepted and not fought for with passion.

So how are we to account for the first person testimony? In the apocryphal work known as the *Acts of Peter*, Peter is presented as preacher, and in first person testimony he sets himself forth similarly as the great sinner who denied Christ and was forgiven. As time passes, both Peter and Paul become idealized model Christians, who embody the gospel (cf. v. 16, 'that I might be typical'), and whose personal testimony is imaginatively set before the Church as a pattern, in a way that would subsequently become typical of evangelical preaching.

Large sections of 2 Timothy seem to be of this character, but one further example must suffice.

Titus 3.3

Here Paul is depicted as identifying himself with the situation of the implied readers who have been converted in ways he has not. He was a Pharisee of the Pharisees, blameless according to the law (Phil. 3.5-6), not one lost in folly and disobedience, a slave to passions and pleasures and so on.

What we find in the Pastorals, then, is the portrait of a model figure, who is clearly the authoritative leader with the charisma to persuade the implied readers. It is not an entirely false picture, but it is idealized, and its rhetorical function is to authorize the authors, together with the network of church leaders who inherit Paul's mantle.

But not just to authorize: rather, to persuade others to follow the hard path of suffering and persecution Paul once took for the sake of the gospel. Much of the text is implicitly about change, conversion, transformation, a new way of life into which the implied readers have been taken up, and which they are to preserve by following the advice given in the letters. The rhetoric of these texts requires us to attend to their persuasive voice, not just to exploit them as historical documents, and that is what an ethical reading would seek to do.

The rhetoric of these epistles may enable us, then, to respond positively to their persuasive message and to respect their claim to attention. However, if we turn to passages that do not appear in the lectionaries, the 'otherness' of their differences might well demand a process of ethical or ideological criticism in the 'judgment' sense, rather than whole-hearted response. Surely the perspective of those household codes turned church codes enjoins culture-specific duties on church members and church leaders. They are, after all, illuminated by other ancient texts characterizing, for example, the good general. Surely they belong to level 2 only. Let us consider an example.

1 Timothy 3.2-7

In such a passage the content will certainly appear differently depending upon reading mode. Managing a household is a different thing in the case of the modern nuclear family from the kind of social unit the implied author and readers knew, an extended kinship network, with servants and slaves, tenants and workers, and clients—a large sub-set of the city or state. Nor is it likely that a recent convert would get rapid preferment in our post-Christian world.

And yet, do we not in fact have here an important set of qualities, many of which are not simply culture-bound? The ways in which a bishop may develop an upright and inoffensive character or lifestyle may in practice be somewhat different in different communities at different points in history, yet the language is 'translatable', even if it loses some dimensions in a 'foreign' sociolinguistic setting.

Furthermore, the interaction of conventional and specifically Christian standards, which may be observed by an informed reading at level 2, may provide interesting analogies for the development of analogous codes of practice in the Christianity of a different social world, thus enabling a creative reading at level 3 which may go beyond the text, but remain within its spirit.

In conclusion, I suggest that an ethical reading of the Pastoral Epistles is possible, even if we accept their pseudonymity. Such a reading will involve both respect for texts that have in fact mediated the Pauline tradition to the later church, and responsible assessment of their content from the present readers' perspective, as distinct from that of the implied readers. So this ethical reading will attend to the following questions:

1. To what extent is the claim of these texts that they pass on the authoritative tradition of Paul valid? In what ways is that tradition appropriately developed further for a new situation?
2. In what ways do these texts confirm or challenge communities/churches which now claim to be in the same tradition? What is acceptable straightforwardly as advice? What needs rethinking in a different sociocultural milieu? How is the ethos of these texts to affect the ethos of these communities? What inspires to radical reform?

In other words, a responsible reading must involve attention both to past meaning and future potential. And maybe then the suspicion or neglect with which these little letters have been treated will be superseded by a recognition of their power to transform, to communicate Paul's gospel in simple summary slogans, to motivate mission, to confirm Christian identity and even, with some critical adaptation, to structure positively relationships within the Church.

INDEXES

INDEX OF REFERENCES

OLD TESTAMENT

NEW TESTAMENT

4.2	143
1 Peter	
1.12	143
1.14	143
2.11	143
4.2	143
4.3	143
4.16	47
2 Peter	
1.4	143
2.10	143
2.18	143
3.3	143
3.15-17	61

1 John	
2.1	32
2.12	32
2.16	143
2.18	32
3.7	32
3.14	216
3.18	32
4.4	32
5	213
5.21	32, 133
2 John	
1	32
4	32
13	32

3 John	
4	32
Jude	
5	127
9	224
16	143
18	143
Revelation	
1.10	211
4.9-10	224
9.6	143
18.14	143
19.10	224
21.14	32
22.8-9	224

PSEUDEPIGRAPHA

Apoc. Abr.	
10–11	229
17	224, 227
23	142
24	142
24.10	145
Apoc. Mos.	
19.3	142, 145
19.25	142
Asc. Isa.	
7.21	224
7.37	227
9.31	227
Ass. Mos.	
5.5-6	39
2 Baruch	
44.14	228
48.24	228
54.13	228
3 Baruch	
4.16	199
1 Enoch	
14.9	225

2 Enoch	
20.3-4	226
3 Enoch	
1.12	227
18	224
35.1	224
39	224
4 Ezra	
8.30	198
8.31-36	190
8.39	198
8.51	198
4 Maccabees	
1.3	143
1.33-35	145
2.1	143
2.5	143
2.6	143, 145
3.2	143
3.22	143
17.21-22	186
18.8	142
Pss. Sol.	
1.1	43
1.2	43

1.3	43
1.4	43
1.5	43
1.6	43
1.7	43
1.8	43, 48
2.3	48
2.12	48
3	44, 46, 47, 51
3.1-2	42
3.1	42
3.2	42
3.3-4	42, 51
3.3	42, 44, 51
3.4	42
3.5-8	42
3.5-6	47
3.5	42, 43
3.6	42
3.7	42
3.8	42, 44, 45, 52
3.9-12	42
3.9	42, 43
3.10	42
3.11	42
3.12	42, 49

QUMRAN

JEWISH AUTHORS

CHRISTIAN AUTHORS

INDEX OF AUTHORS